Nonsexist Research Methods

Nonsexist Research Methods

A Practical Guide

MARGRIT EICHLER

Ontario Institute for Studies in Education

Boston
ALLEN & UNWIN
London   Sydney   Wellington

Allen & Unwin, Inc.
8 Winchester Place, Winchester, MA 01890, USA.

The U.S. Company of
Unwin Hyman Ltd,

P.O. Box 18, Park Lane, Hemel Hempstead, Herts HP2 4TE, UK
40 Museum Street, London WC1A 1LU, UK
37/39 Queen Elizabeth Street, London SE1 2QB, UK

Allen & Unwin Australia Pty Ltd,
8 Napier Street, North Sydney, NSW 2060, Australia

Allen & Unwin (New Zealand) Ltd, in association with the Port Nicholson Press Ltd
60 Cambridge Terrace, Wellington, New Zealand

Library of Congress Cataloging-in-Publication Data

Eichler, Margrit.
  Nonsexist research methods.
  Bibliography: p.
  Includes index.
  1. Social sciences — Research. 2. Sexism. I. Title.
H62.E453 1987   300'.72   87-11477
ISBN 0-04-497044-7
ISBN 0-04-497045-5 (pbk.)

British Library Cataloguing in Publication Data

Eichler, Margrit
  Nonsexist research methods: a practical guide.
1. Sexism in social science research
I. Title
300'.72   H62
ISBN 0-04-497044-7
ISBN 0-04-497045-5 Pbk

Set in 10 on 12 point Zapf Light by Oxford Print Associates Ltd
and printed in Great Britain by
Billing and Son Ltd, Worcester

Contents

Acknowledgments   *page* ix

1   Sexism in Research   1

The Four Primary Problems

2   Androcentricity   19

3   Overgeneralization   48

4   Gender Insensitivity   65

5   Double Standards   85

The Three Derived Problems

6   Sex Appropriateness, Familism, and Sexual Dichotomism   106

7   Guidelines for Nonsexist Research   129

Epilogue   166

Appendix: Nonsexist Research Checklist   170

Index   177

About the Author   183

Acknowledgments

This book is the result of several years of study in the area of sexism in scholarship and nonsexist alternatives. It has thus profited immensely from the various debates and publications on this topic. Many but not all of the authors who have contributed to this debate are cited in the text. I have also profited over the years from discussions with students. In particular, however, I am grateful to Paula Caplan, Marjorie Cohen, Jill Vickers, Marylee Stephenson, and Wendy McKeen for reading and commenting on the entire manuscript, and to Robert Brym and Rhonda Lenton for reading and commenting on portions of the manuscript. The comments of the readers also resulted in several important changes in the final version. Finally, my greatest debt goes to Linda Williams, who provided invaluable research assistance at various points during the writing of the book.

I would also like to thank the following people for providing me with specific references: Paula Caplan, Ursula Franklin, Ester Greenglass, Thelma McCormack, Paul Olson, Ruth Pierson, Monica Townson, and Paul Wiesenthal.

The guidelines contained in the book have gone through many revisions and applications. Part of them were developed within the framework of a federal committee, the Canadian Women's Studies

Advisory Committee of the Secretary of State's Women's Programme. This committee was established to advise the federal government on where to locate five chairs on women's studies endowed by the Canadian government for the five geographic regions of Canada. Having received a broad rather than narrow mandate, the committee added the development of a set of guidelines for nonsexist research to its agenda. The entire committee, consisting of June Gow (chair), Donna Greschner, Gilberte Leblanc, Donna Mergler, Beth Percival, Charlotte Thibault, Jennifer Stoddart, and myself screened and discussed two earlier versions of the guidelines contained in this book. In particular, Donna Mergler contributed to the present shape of the guidelines.

Finally, I wish to acknowledge gratefully the excellent copy-editing done by Patricia Miller. Lisa Freeman-Miller of Allen & Unwin was a dream come true in what you hope for in an editor.

Chapter 1
Sexism in Research

1.1 Introduction
1.2 Sexism in research
1.3 The seven sexist problems
    1.3.1 Androcentricity
    1.3.2 Overgeneralization/Overspecificity
    1.3.3 Gender insensitivity
    1.3.4 Double standards
    1.3.5 Sex appropriateness
    1.3.6 Familism
    1.3.7 Sexual dichotomism
1.4 Organization and history of this book
1.5 Sexism and scientific objectivity
1.6 Solving the problem of sexism in research

1.1 Introduction

Over a century ago, a schoolmaster named Edwin A. Abbott wrote an amusing "Romance of Many Dimensions," entitled *Flatland*,[1] in which he described the adventures of the Square, a being from a two-dimensional universe (Flatland), who explores a one-dimensional universe (Lineland) and a three-dimensional universe (Spaceland).

The Square describes the inability of the King of Lineland, a one-dimensional being, to grasp the essence of a two-dimensional universe, and then describes his own incapacity to believe in the existence of a three-dimensional universe. It is only when he is physically lifted out of his own universe and sees it from above (a dimension that is nonexistent in his own Flatland) that he becomes capable of intellectually grasping the existence of three-dimensional space.

When the Square returns to his own country, he eagerly tries to spread the Gospel of Three Dimensions, but is predictably put into prison as a dangerous lunatic, where he languishes at the end of the novel, "absolutely destitute of converts."

The following is an excerpt in which our hero, the Square, tries to convince the King of Lineland that there are, in fact, two dimensions. He argues that, in addition to Lineland's motions of Northward and Southward, which are the only directions in which lines can move in Lineland, there is another motion, which he calls from right to left:

KING: *Exhibit to me, if you please, this motion from left to right.*
I: *Nay, that I cannot do, unless you could step out of your Line altogether.*
KING: *Out of my Line? Do you mean out of the world? Out of Space?*
I: *Well, yes. Out of your Space. For your Space is not the true Space. True Space is a Plane; but your Space is only a Line.*
KING: *If you cannot indicate this motion from left to right by yourself moving in it, then I beg you to describe it to me in words.*
I: *If I cannot tell your right side from your left, I fear that no words of mine can make my meaning clear to you. But surely you cannot be ignorant of so simple a distinction.*
KING: *I do not in the least understand you.* (Abbott, 1952:62)

Like the King of Lineland, we have been brought up in an intellectually limited universe. Our dilemma is that all our major concepts, our way of seeing reality, our willingness to accept proof, have been shaped by one dimension – one sex – rather than by two. For as long as we remain within this intellectual universe, we are incapable of comprehending its limitations, believing it to be the only world that exists. In order to truly understand our universe, we must create a vantage point that allows us to observe it both for what it is and for what it is not. Not an easy task, as the Square found out when he tried to explain the existence of left and right to a person who had never experienced them.

Similarly, none of us has ever lived in a nonsexist society: moving toward nonsexist scholarship is comparable to trying to comprehend a dimension that we have not materially experienced. We can describe it in theoretical terms, but we cannot fully appreciate its nature until we are able to lift ourselves out of our current confining parameters. This involves becoming aware of sexism in research and starting to eliminate it.

Sexism in research was first recognized as a major problem around the mid-1970s. While books and articles that pointed out the problem existed before that time,[2] it is only since the mid-1970s that critiques have appeared with some regularity and in more mainstream outlets.

In the early 1970s and continuing into the 1980s, various organizations, publishers, and publication outlets began adopting rules about the use of nonsexist language,[3] and recently, about nonsexist content.[4] Nevertheless, sexism in research is still badly understood. Even less well understood is how to conduct research in a nonsexist manner.

This book has two major objectives: (1) to present an analysis of sexism in research that enlarges our understanding of this problem and sensitizes students and researchers to sexism in its various manifestations; and (2) to provide guidelines for solving the problem that offer clear and concise means of creating nonsexist alternatives.

1.2 Sexism in Research

Most analyses of sexism in research focus either on one discipline or subject area or else on one type of sexism.[5] Indeed, we do not tend to speak of "types of sexism," but of "sexism," pure and simple.[6] The term "sexism" suggests that we are dealing with *one* problem that may manifest itself in different areas differently, but which nevertheless is a single basic problem – what one might call the "big blob" theory of sexism.

This book takes a different approach. Sexism is here broken down into seven different types. Of these seven types, four are primary and three are derived. *Primary problems* are those that cannot be reduced one to the other, although they coexist and often overlap. *Derived problems* are problems that are not logically distinct from the primary problems but which appear so frequently that they warrant being identified by a special label. The primary problems are: (1) *androcentricity*, (2) *overgeneralization*, (3) *gender insensitivity*, and (4) *double standards*. Derived problems are: (5) *sex appropriateness*, (6) *familism*, and (7) *sexual dichotomism*. There is a certain arbitrariness about identifying seven, rather than, say, six or five or eight sexist problems in research.[7] There is also a certain arbitrariness in the manner in which the boundaries have been drawn. The seven problems presented here have emerged through many attempts to order the otherwise diverse materials concerning critiques of sexism. The success of the approach presented here does not depend on acceptance of this categorization as the best possible or on correctly pigeonholing empirical problems under their appropriate theoretical labels, however. Instead, what is important is recognizing that sexism is multidimensional rather than unidimensional, identifying a sexist problem as such, and rectifying it. In other words, the seven problems are intended to serve as tools to facilitate the recognition and correction of sexism in research, rather than as an ultimate system of categorization.

It is helpful to think of the four primary problems as a set of movable circles. They all have a different core, and sometimes they overlap very heavily, sometimes only at the periphery, sometimes not at all. Occasionally, all four circles may overlap. Thus there may be more than one correct classification of a problem. The three derived problems, in contrast, can be thought of as constituting inner rings that are strongly defined within two of those larger circles.

The following preliminary definitions of all seven problems will be expanded in Chapters 2–6, where more extensive illustrations are provided. Chapter 7, organized by components of the research process, offers a set of guidelines for detecting and eliminating sexism in research.

1.3 The Seven Sexist Problems

1.3.1 Androcentricity

Androcentricity is essentially a view of the world from a male perspective. It manifests itself when ego is constructed as male rather than female, such as when "intergroup warfare" is defined as a "means of gaining women and slaves." In this case, the "group" is defined as consisting only of males, since the women are what is "gained." From an androcentric perspective, women are seen as passive objects rather than subjects in history, as acted upon rather than actors; androcentricity prevents us from understanding that both males and females are always acted upon as well as acting, although often in very different ways. Two extreme forms of androcentricity are *gynopia* (female invisibility) and *misogyny* (hatred of women).

This definition raises a difficulty that must be acknowledged. Theoretically speaking, problems of perspective could come in two versions: one female, one male. The female version would be gynocentricity, or a view of the world from a female perspective. I have labeled this problem androcentricity rather than, for instance, andro-gynocentricity for two reasons. First, the problem is so overwhelmingly biased in the male direction that to accord a female version of the problem equal status would be inappropriate. I have, however, included the few examples of incipient gynocentricity that I found in my search of the literature. Second, it is not really possible to find a form of gynocentricity that is in any way comparable to androcentricity, for the simple reason that we live in an androcentric social, political, and intellectual environment. Thus even when we attempt to take a *consciously* female perspective, this attempt occurs within an overall intellectual environment in which both our vehicle for thought (language) and the content of thought (concepts) are colored by thousands of years of overwhelmingly androcentric thinking. It is therefore both misleading and inaccurate to treat possible gynocentricity as comparable to actual androcentricity. However, it is important to acknowledge that sexism can theoretically come in two forms, and to remind ourselves that neither is acceptable in scholarship.

1.3.2 *Overgeneralization/Overspecificity*

Overgeneralization occurs when a study deals with only one sex but presents itself as if it were applicable to both sexes. Its flip side is overspecificity, which occurs when a study is reported in such a manner that it is impossible to determine whether or not it applies to one or both sexes. Using a sample of male workers and calling it a study of social class is an instance of overgeneralization; the same problem arises when one uses the term "parents" to refer exclusively to mothers (ignoring fathers). Overspecificity occurs when single-sex terms are used when members of both sexes are involved (e.g., "the doctor . . . he, or "man is a mammal"). Many (but not all) of the problems involving sexist language belong in this category.

There is considerable overlap between overgeneralization/overspecificity and androcentricity. Nevertheless, one cannot be equated to the other. A study may be androcentric without being overgeneral, such as when male violence against women is dismissed as trivial or unimportant (thus maintaining male over female interests) although the actors are correctly identified by their sex. A study may also be overgeneral or overspecific without being necessarily androcentric, such as when a study uses all male subjects (e.g., male students) or all female subjects (e.g., mothers) but presents the findings in general terms ("students" respond well to ability grouping, or "parents" tend to teach their children concepts through ostensive definitions).

1.3.3 *Gender Insensitivity*

Gender insensitivity is a simple problem: it consists of ignoring sex as a socially important variable. It sometimes overlaps with overgeneralization/overspecificity, but the two are not identical: In the case of general insensitivity, sex is ignored to such a degree that the presence of overgeneralization or androcentricity cannot even be identified. If a study simply fails to report the sex of its respondents, or if a policy study completely ignores the different effects of, let us say, a particular unemployment insurance policy on the two sexes, then we cannot identify whether male or female subjects were included or whether males or females would differentially profit from or be hurt by a particular policy. In a completely gender-insensitive study, it would be impossible to identify other problems because information necessary to do so is missing.

1.3.4 Double Standards

The use of double standards involves evaluating, treating, or measuring identical behaviors, traits, or situations by different means. A double standard is by no means easy to identify, although it may sound easy: it involves recognizing behaviors, traits, or situations as identical when they bear different labels or are described in different terms. For instance, some psychological disorders occur only in one sex. To find out whether or not a given example is an instance of the application of a double standard, one must (1) identify a larger category for the disorder; (2) determine whether there is a complementary disorder for the other sex; (3) identify whether the two are equivalent; and (4) determine whether they are evaluated in different ways. Only when all these preconditions obtain are we dealing with a double standard. If the disorder appears in only one sex, no double standard is involved.

Identification is not made easier by the fact that a researcher may have used different instruments to measure identical attributes of the sexes. For example, social status is currently derived by using different measures for the sexes (for further discussion of this specific problem, see Chapter 5). However, this different measurement coincides with an actual difference in social standing between the sexes, a difference that we are incapable of measuring adequately because we have no sex-free instrument at our disposal. Identification of a double standard thus involves distancing oneself to some degree from the social context as it is presented – not a simple thing to do, and never perfectly achieved.

A double standard is likely to be inspired by, or lead to, androcentricity, but it need not necessarily do so. Using female-derived categories of social status for women and male-derived categories for men is an instance of a double standard in the use of instruments, but it is neither gender insensitive nor androcentric nor overgeneral/overspecific.

1.3.5 Sex Appropriateness

Sex appropriateness, our first "derived" category, is nothing but a particular instance of a double standard, one that is so accepted within the relevant literature that it is proudly acknowledged with special terms: for example, "appropriate sex roles," or "appropriate gender identity." The absence of appropriate gender identity is called *dysphoria,* and it is classed as a psychological disorder. Sex appropriateness becomes a problem when *human* traits or attributes are assigned only to one sex or the other and are treated as more important for the sex to which they have been assigned. It is *not* a problem when we are dealing with a truly sex-specific attribute, such as the capacity to ejaculate or to give birth to children. It *is* a problem when it is applied to such human capacities as child rearing (as opposed to child bearing).

This particular example of a double standard has been singled out from the overall discussion of double standards because sex appropriateness is still widely accepted within the social science literature as a legitimate concept.

1.3.6 Familism

Familism is a particular instance of gender insensitivity. It consists of treating the family as the smallest unit of analysis in instances in which it is, in fact, individuals within families (or households) who engage in certain actions, have certain experiences, and so on. It is *not* a problem of sexism when no such attribution occurs. Another manifestation of familism occurs when the family is assumed to be uniformly affected (positively or negatively) in instances in which the same event may have different effects on various family members.

This problem has been singled out from the general discussion of gender insensitivity for the same reason that sex appropriateness has been singled out from the discussion of double standards: It is a very well-accepted practice within the social sciences to engage in familism, and is, at present, still considered to be entirely legitimate.

1.3.7 Sexual Dichotomism

Sexual dichotomism is another subaspect of the use of double standards. It involves the treatment of the sexes as two entirely discrete social, as well as biological, groups, rather than as two groups with overlapping characteristics. It leads to an exaggeration of sex differences of all types at the expense of recognizing *both* the differences *and* the similarities between the sexes. It is particularly important to recognize sexual dichotomism as a form of sexism because it is sometimes used as a "cure" for gender insensitivity. When this occurs, it is simply a case of substituting one form of sexism for another; and it is doubly misleading because it creates the illusion of having achieved a solution.

1.4 Organization and History of this Book

This book is organized around two major axes: type of sexist problem, and component of the research process in which particular types of problems may appear. Chapters 2 through 5 each deal with one primary problem, Chapter 6 deals with the three derived problems, and Chapter 7 and the checklist (see Appendix) are organized around the various components of the research process. This structure evolved after a period of trial and error in which I tried to organize the book only around the type of problem, or only around the research components. Being dissatisfied with both, I eventually settled on a compromise structure that combines both organizing principles.

The problem-oriented chapters include examples drawn from actual research. The majority are taken from recent issues of journals, mostly from 1985. Occasionally, other publications are used (books, reports of committees), and occasionally I also draw on other researchers' critiques of sexism. However, the ease with which examples can be drawn from academic journals demonstrates the pervasiveness of sexism: It exists in every social science discipline[8] and in virtually any nonfeminist publication, no matter how respectable or how current. Moreover, the problems are similar regardless of discipline or publication outlet.[9]

My method was simple: I went into a library and picked up whatever recent issue of journals from different disciplines was lying on top in the journal pigeon holes. I assumed that it would make little difference which journal or issue I picked, and that I would find at least one example of sexism in every single one.[10] Sadly, this turned out to be correct.

This method of finding many of my examples also points to a major limitation in this book that must be made clear: There is a large element of chance involved in who and what gets cited. Depending on which journal issue I picked up first, the example may have been taken from psychology when I could just as well have taken it from anthropology or sociology. The same applies to authors. The examples presented here are, therefore, just that: examples, no more, no less. They are not indicative of the degree or type of sexism prevalent in any particular author, field of investigation, or discipline.

It is possible, indeed likely, that particular problems are more prevalent in certain disciplines or subject areas than in others (or indeed, that a particular problem does *not* occur in some disciplines). However, to demonstrate this is not a task undertaken in this book. It is clearly a second step. Nor is there any intent to pronounce on the relative frequency or importance of each of the problems. That, too, is clearly a second step. The intention here is simply to demonstrate the existence of distinct types of sexism that occur in the social sciences, to offer means for their identification, and to provide suggestions for their solution.

Chapter 7 presents a systematic discussion of potential sexist problems following the various components of the research process. Because the analysis is meant to be generally applicable to various disciplines and methodological approaches, not all components are applicable to all studies. For instance, many studies do not have a policy component. Other studies do not ask direct questions of respondents. All studies, on the other hand, presumably use major concepts, have a title, and ask a research question, even if only implicitly. In addition, please note that although the guidelines have gone through a process of considerable testing and revision, I make no claim that all the problems of sexism in research are included in them. We are constantly becoming aware of new problems.

The guidelines set forth in Chapter 7 are meant to assist in the identification and eventual resolution of sexist problems. They do not, of course, solve other research problems: a study may be entirely nonsexist and still be trivial or otherwise bad research. However, a study cannot be sexist and constitute good research. The guidelines therefore spell out a set of necessary but not sufficient criteria for good research.

1.5 Sexism and Scientific Objectivity

One spinoff from the various critiques of sexism in research has been a renewed doubt about the possibility of objectivity in the social sciences. While academicians have traditionally assumed that objectivity is a hallmark of their work, feminist scholars have challenged this assumption. Some feminist researchers even maintain that objectivity is, in principle, impossible to achieve, and that the most we can do is to admit to an unabashed subjectivity, our own as well as everybody else's.[11] However, the logical consequence of such a principled stance is that research, including the implied cumulative knowledge it generates, is impossible.

This seems rather like throwing out the baby with the bathwater. Instead, it is more useful to identify the various components commonly included under the heading of objectivity and look at them separately, in order to eliminate the problematic aspects of objectivity while maintaining the useful ones. One scholar who engages in such a process of separating useful from harmful components of objectivity is Elizabeth Fee.[12] She suggests that the following "aspects of scientific objectivity ... should be preserved and defended":

> The concept of creating knowledge through a constant process of practical interaction with nature, the willingness to consider all assumptions and methods as open to question and the expectation that ideas will be subjected to the most unfettered critical evaluation. ...[13]

Fee also rejects certain aspects of "objectivity" in research. For example, she rejects as not helpful the notion that objectivity requires a distancing of the researcher from the subject matter, and of the production of knowledge from its uses. Likewise, she rejects as unnecessary the divorce between scientific rationality and emotional or social commitment; she also rejects the assumption that knowledge must flow only from the expert to the nonexpert and thus that a dialogue is not possible. She deplores the prevailing split between subject and object, in which the knowing mind is active and the object of knowledge entirely passive. Such a structure of knowledge results in a depersonalized voice of abstract authority that legitimizes domination. Finally, she rejects as impossible the complete freedom of research from its sociopolitical environment.

Though she focuses on the concept of the "scientific process" and not on "objectivity" per se, Karen Messing argues that "the ideology and the background of the researcher" can influence the research process at eleven different stages:[14]

- the selection of the scientists,
- their access to facilities for scientific work,
- the choice of research topic,
- the wording of the hypothesis,
- the choice of experimental subjects,
- the choice of appropriate controls,
- the method of observation,
- data analysis,
- interpretation of data,
- the publication of results,
- and the popularization of results.[15]

Jill McCalla Vickers list as one of her methodological rebellions "the rebellion against objectivity,"[16] which she sees as (a) "treating those you study as objects and objectifying their pains in words which hide the identity of their oppressors," or (b) "being detached from that which is studied."[17] She accepts objectivity as "the rules which are designed to facilitate intersubjective transmissibility, testing, replication, etc."[18]

Finally, Evelyn Fox Keller has beautifully demonstrated that objectivity has been largely equated with masculinity.[19] She discusses particularly the misconception that objectivity requires detachment of the knower, both in emotional as well as in intellectual terms. Moreover, she argues that

> the disengagement of our thinking about science from our notions of what is masculine could lead to a freeing of both from some of the rigidities to which they have been bound, with profound ramifications for both. Not only, for example, might science become more accessible to women, but, far more importantly, our very conception of "objective" could be freed from inappropriate constraints. As we begin to understand the ways in which science itself has been influenced by its unconscious mythology, we can begin to perceive the possibilities for a science not bound by such mythology.[20]

It seems, then, that it is possible to be critical of the way in which objectivity has been defined without having to abandon the concept and sink into the morass of complete cultural subjectivism. We need to separate clearly objectivity from detachment and from the myth that research is value-free. Neither of the latter two conditions is, in principle, possible for any researcher (or anybody else). Our values will always intrude in a number of ways into the research process, beginning with the choice of the research question; and we will necessarily always be informed by a particular perspective. Nor is there any need to detach ourselves emotionally from the research process – in fact, this is impossible, and what appears as scholarly detachment is in reality only a matter of careful disguise.

Objectivity remains a useful and important goal for research in the following ways:

(1) a commitment to look at contrary evidence;

(2) a determination to aim at maximum replicability of any study (which implies accurate reporting of all processes employed and separation between simple reporting and interpretation, to the degree that these are possible);

(3) a commitment to "truth-finding" (what Kenneth Boulding has called veracity);[21] and

(4) a clarification and classification of values underlying the research: nonsexist research, for instance, is, based on the value judgment that the sexes are of equal worth, while androcentric research grows out of the belief that men are of higher worth (and therefore more important) than women.

I find it useful to think of objectivity as an asymptotically approachable but unreachable goal, with the elimination of sexism in research as a station along the way.

1.6 Solving the Problem of Sexism in Research

When we regard a problem as simple, a single solution often seems appropriate. Once we begin to differentiate among different and distinct components of a problem, however, different and distinct solutions become a necessity. When we fail to make the proper distinctions, we may – unwittingly and despite the very best intentions – replace one problem of sexism with another.

The analysis of sexism in language provides a case in point. Early and incisive studies of sexism in language convinced a number of organizations and individuals that sexist language was unacceptable in scholarly research (or elsewhere, for that matter!).[22] Typically, these analyses pointed out the use of so-called generic male terms as sexist, and often they included reference to such demeaning terms as "girls" for "women," or nonparallel terms (Mrs. John Smith but not Mr. Anne Smith, or the use of Mrs. or Miss, which indicate marital status, versus Mr., which does not).

As a consequence of these critiques, guides were published that replaced so-called generic male terms with truly generic terms: policeman became police officer; fireman, fire fighter; postman, mail carrier; workman, worker; chairman, chairperson; mankind, humanity; and so on. In effect, occupational and other terms were "desexed." The generic "he" was replaced with "he or she," or "s/he," or "they," or "one," or "people," and so on. Guides of this type continue to be important and useful, but unless care is taken as to how and when and in what context these gender-neutral terms are used, another form of sexism may inadvertently enter the picture.

The use of male (or sex-specific) terms for generic situations is one form of overgeneralization, one of our sexist problems. However, there is another aspect to the same problem: the use of generic terms for sex-specific situations, which is just as problematic as is the first manifestation. For example, if researchers talk about workers in general while only having studied male workers (constantly and cautiously using "they," "people," "the individual," "the person," and so on, with nary a female in sight), they simply replace one sexist problem with another in the manner in which language is used.[23] Language that employs "nonsexist" generic terms for sex-specific situations creates the same problem in reverse and constitutes at one and the same time an example of both overgeneralization and gender insensitivity.[24] In other words, when the content is sex specific, the language used should also be sex specific.

Sexism takes more than one form, and therefore ways to combat it may also take more than one form. The trick is to develop criteria that help us determine which solution is appropriate when. This is the major purpose of this book.

Notes

1 Edwin A. Abbott, *Flatland: A Romance of Many Dimensions* (New York: Dover, 1952).

2 See, for instance, Ruth Hershberger, *Adam's Rib* (New York: Harper & Row, 1970), first published in 1948; or the special issue on sexism in family studies of the *Journal of Marriage and the Family* 33: 3, 4 (1971).

3 An early example are the guidelines by Scott, Foresman and Co., "Guidelines for improving the image of women in textbooks" (Glenview, IL, 1972); see also "Guidelines for equal treatment of the sexes in McGraw-Hill Book Company publications" (n.d.); "Guidelines for nonsexist use of language," prepared by the American Psychological Association Task Force on Issues of Sexual Bias in Graduate Education, *American Psychologist* (June 1975): 682–684; "Guidelines for nonsexist use of language in National Council of Teachers of English publications" (March 1976).

4 For example, the Canadian Psychological Association approved a set of nonsexist

guidelines in 1983; see Cannie Stark-Adamec and Meredith Kimball, "Science free of sexism: A psychologist's guide to the conduct of nonsexist research," *Canadian Psychology* 25: 1 (1984): 23–34. The Canadian Sociology and Anthropology Association passed a motion at its general annual meeting in 1984 that all official publications must be nonsexist in language and content; see Margrit Eichler, "And the work never ends: Feminist contributions," *Canadian Review of Sociology and Anthropology* 22, 5 (1985): 619–644, esp. p. 633; "AERA guidelines for eliminating race and sex bias in educational research and evaluation," *Educational Researcher* 14, 6 (1985). The American Sociological Association published a set of guidelines in one of its publications; see "Sexist biases in sociological research: Problems and issues," *ASA Footnotes* (January 1980): 8–9, but its major journal, the *American Sociological Review*, does not require that articles be nonsexist in language and content. The Social Sciences and Humanities Research Council in Canada published a booklet suggesting that sexist research is bad research; see Margrit Eichler and Jeanne Lapointe, "On the treatment of the sexes in research" (Ottawa: Social Sciences and Humanities Research Council of Canada, Minister of Supply and Services, 1985); however, the assessment forms for projects do not include a criterion that the research be nonsexist. For an overview of strategies adopted by Canadian professional social science organizations and scholarly journals, see Linda Christiansen-Ruffman et al., "Sex bias in research: Current awareness and strategies to eliminate bias within Canadian social science" (Report of the Task Force on the Elimination of Sexist Bias in Research to the Social Science Federation of Canada, 1986).

5 See, for instance, Shulamit Reinharz, Marti Bombyk, and Janet Wright, "Methodological issues in feminist research: A bibliography of literature in women's studies, sociology and psychology," *Women's Studies International Forum* 6, 4 (1983): 437–454; and Margrit Eichler with the assistance of Rhonda Lenton, Somer Brodribb, Jane Haddad, and Becki Ross, "A selected annotated bibliography on sexism in research" (Ottawa: Social Sciences and Humanities Research Council of Canada, 1985).

6 This is not always true. Sexism is occasionally broken down into different ways in which it manifests itself, but such different manifestations are usually *not* seen as logically distinct. As an example, see Kathryn B. Ward and Linda Grant, "The feminist critique and a decade of published research in sociology journals," *Sociological Quarterly* 26, 2 (1985): 139–157.

7 Indeed, my first attempt to identify a set of superordinate sexist problems involved six, rather than seven problems; see Margrit Eichler, "Les six péchés capitaux sexistes," in Huguette Dagenais (ed.) *Approches et methodes de la recherche féministe*. Actes du colloque organisé par le Groupe de recherche multidisciplinaire féministe, Mai 1985. (Université Laval:Maquettiste, 1968):17–29.

8 I do not mean to imply that the problem does not exist in the natural sciences as well. Indeed, we know that it does, as recent analyses have eloquently demonstrated; see, for example, Ruth Hubbard, Mary Sue Henifin, and Barbara Fried (eds.), *Women Look at Biology Looking at Women: A Collection of Feminist Critiques* (Cambridge, MA: Schenkman, 1979); Ruth Bleier, *Science and Gender: A Critique of Biology and Its Theories on Women* (New York: Pergamon Press, 1984); Marian Lowe and Ruth Hubbard (eds.), *Woman's Nature: Rationalizations of Inequality* (New York: Pergamon, 1983); Sandra Harding and Merrill B. Hintikka

(eds.), *Discovering Reality: Feminist Perspectives on Epistemology, Metaphysics, Methodology, and Philosophy of Science* (Dordrecht: D. Reidel, 1983). This book restricts itself to the social sciences for the simple reason that I am not competent to write about the natural sciences.

9 Feminist writings may be sexist as well. However, since the likelihood is much smaller than with nonfeminist writings, my search would have been much more arduous, and it simply is not the major problem, I did not include feminist journals in my search.

10 However, it should be noted that I did apply a criterion in selecting journals from within the same discipline: In cases where there were several journals from the same discipline, I favored the ones with the longest run, as indicated by volume number (the higher the number, the longer the run) on the assumption that the older the journal, the more established it could be assumed to be. In addition, the selection is heavily biased toward U.S. and Canadian journals.

11 This is, for instance, the position taken by Liz Stanley and Sue Wise in *Breaking Out: Feminist Consciousness and Feminist Research* (London: Routledge & Kegan Paul, 1983). They argue

> We don't believe that "science" exists in the way that many people still claim it does. We don't see it as the single-minded objective pursuit of truth. "Truth" is a social construct, in the same way that "objectivity" is; and both are constructed out of experiences which are, for all practical purposes, the same as "lies" and "subjectivity." And so we sell all research as "fiction" in the sense that it views and so constructs "reality" through the eyes of one person. (p. 174)

12 Elizabeth Fee, "Women's nature and scientific objectivity," in Marian Lowe and Ruth Hubbard (eds.), *Women's Nature: Rationalizations of Inequality* (New York: Pergamon, 1983): 9–27.

13 Ibid., p. 16.

14 Karen Messing, "The scientific mystique: Can a white lab coat guarantee purity in the search for knowledge about the nature of women?" in Marian Lowe and Ruth Hubbard (eds.), *Women's Nature: Rationalizations of Inequality* (New York: Pergamon, 1983):75–88.

15 Ibid., p. 76.

16 Jill McCalla Vickers, "Memoirs of an ontological exile: The methodological rebellions of feminist research," in Angela Miles and Geraldine Finn (eds.), *Feminism in Canada: From Pressure to Politics* (Montreal: Black Rose, 1982): 27–46.

17 Ibid., p. 40.

18 Ibid. In a more recent article, Vickers pushes toward a new epistemology; see Jill Vickers, "So then what? Issues in feminist epistemology." Unpublished paper presented at the 4th annual meeting of the Canadian Women's Studies Association, Winnipeg, 1986.

19 Evelyn Fox Keller, *Reflections on Gender and Science* (New Haven: Yale University Press, 1985).

20 Ibid., pp. 92–93.

21 Kenneth E. Boulding, "Learning by simplifying complexity: How to turn data into

knowledge," in *The Science and Praxis of Complexity*, contributions to the symposium held at Montpellier, France, 1984 (Tokyo: United Nations University, 1985): 31. I would like to thank Ursula Franklin for drawing my attention to this quote.

22 Some of the early studies include Virginia Kidd, "A study of images produced through the use of a male pronoun as the generic," *Movements: Contemporary Rhetoric and Communication* (Fall 1971): 25–30; Joseph W. Schneider and Sally L. Hacker, "Sex role imagery and the use of generic man in introductory texts," *American Sociologist* 8 (1973): 12–18; some of the later studies include Jeannette Silveira, "Generic masculine words and thinking," *Women's Studies International Quarterly* 3, 2/3 (1980): 165–178; Janice Moulton, George M. Robinson, and Cherin Elias, "Sex bias in language use: "Neutral" pronouns that aren't," *American Psychologist* 33, 11 (1978): 1032–1036; Mary Vetterling-Braggin (ed.), *Sexist Language: A Modern Philosophical Analysis* (Totowa, NJ: Littlefield, Adams, 1981); John Briere and Cheryl Lanktree, "Sex-role related effects of sex bias in language," *Sex Roles* 9, 5 (1983): 625–632.

23 There is one exception to this general rule. When a communication is intended to solicit the representation of both sexes, even though only one is represented at a given point in time, it may be appropriate to use nonsexist language, as in announcements advertising jobs so far held only by men (for example, fire fighters, police officers, or chairpersons).

24 Another instance in which an attempt to avoid sexism may inadvertently lead to another type of sexism occurs when researchers trying to avoid gender insensitivity fall into the error of sexual dichotomism by treating sex as a categorical variable for all sorts of social phenomena.

Chapter 2
Androcentricity

2.1 Introduction
2.2 Types of androcentricity
    2.2.1 Male viewpoint or frame of reference
    2.2.2 Construction of the actor as male
    2.2.3 Gynopia or female invisibility
    2.2.4 The maintenance of male over female interests
    2.2.5 Misogyny and blaming women
    2.2.6 Defending female subjugation or male dominance
2.3 Manifestations of androcentricity in the research process
    2.3.1 Androcentricity in language
    2.3.2 Androcentric (and gynocentric) concepts
    2.3.3 Androcentricity in the research design
    2.3.4 Validation of research instrument
    2.3.5 Formulation of questions and questionnaires
2.4 Conclusion

2.1 Introduction

Androcentricity is, in its most basic expression, a vision of the world in male terms, a reconstruction of the social universe from a male perspective. Specifically, it expresses itself in a construction of ego as male rather than female, with a concomitant view of females as objects rather than subjects, as acted upon rather than as actors. The male is the reference point; the female, the "other," is located in relation to him, as Simone de Beauvoir has so eloquently argued.[1]

Androcentricity results in the maintenance of male over female interests. This may take the form of trivializing problems experienced by women, where males are the originators of these problems, or it can take the form of an argument for maintaining a situation that favors males over females. Further, it can lead to a failure of vision, what Shulamit Reinharz has called *gynopia*: "the inability to perceive the very existence of women as fully human actors."[2] The extreme form of androcentricity is outright misogyny: hatred of women.

Theoretically, sexism in research could take the form of either androcentricity or gynocentricity (in which the world is perceived in female terms, the social universe is reconstructed from a female perspective, and so on). Realistically speaking, however, the problem is not gynocentricity but androcentricity, quite simply because men constitute the dominant sex, not women. Occasionally we find examples of incipient gynocentricity, but they are rare indeed. Finally, androcentricity may be practiced by both male and female authors. Being born female does not make one automatically capable of transcending androcentricity. Likewise, being born male does not prevent one from conducting nonsexist research and writing in a nonsexist manner.

In this chapter, we will first consider various ways in which androcentricity manifests itself. This is followed by a discussion of the stages of the research process in which it may appear.

2.2 Types of Androcentricity

2.2.1 Male Viewpoint or Frame of Reference

A male viewpoint or frame of reference results in the construction of the actor as male rather than as either male or female or both female and male, while at the same time asserting general applicability. It leads to female invisibility, helps to maintain male over female interests, and may lead to blaming women. It is thus a shorthand expression for a conglomerate of aspects of androcentricity that will be dealt with in the following sections. In addition, however, it indicates a commitment to an androcentric theory, framework, model of reality, or way of proceeding, even when the sexism has become obvious. We will consider just one example of this here.

In a passage on social ascription and social theory, the author discusses racial-ethnic and gender ascription in the human capital and structural functionalist literatures. He notes that

> while it is difficult to summarize and analyse them briefly and neatly, they all orbit around some conception of efficiency, both narrowly economic and otherwise. Thus, when the economic returns to human capital are found to be less for some racial-ethnic groups than for others, or less for women than for men, it is often assumed (rather than shown) that this occurs because of some unmeasured sources of racial-ethnic or gender differences in productivity. . . . The reason for this is most likely that, according to the principles of marginal productivity theory, the distribution of marginal products *is* identical with the distribu[t]ion of earned income. ... And one naturally hesitates to remove one of the cornerstones from the edifice of modern microeconomics on grounds of a few tenants who apparently cannot be accommodated.[3]

After a fair criticism of sexism in microeconomics, the author suggests that one "naturally hesitates to remove one of the cornerstones ... on grounds of a few tenants who apparently cannot be accommodated." Aside from the fact that the "few tenants" actually constitute the majority of people (namely all women plus some men from particular racial-ethnic groups), imagine the reverse situation: a general theory of social ascription that regrettably does not apply to men. I doubt that many social scientists would hesitate to remove it as a cornerstone of theory even though its nonapplicability to "a few" male tenants was its only drawback. We cannot point to an example of this reverse case because a general theory that did not apply to men would never gain the status of a general theory; hence there is no need to dislodge it.

A less obvious form of using a male frame of reference occurs when events are evaluated by their effects on males only. For instance, the Rennaissance is commonly regarded as a progressive era in Western civilization. It was, however, a time during which women lost many of the privileges they had enjoyed during the period of chivalry.[4] This era appears "progressive" only when one considers its effects on men but not on women.

2.2.2 Construction of the Actor as Male

This aspect of androcentricity constructs the actor as male only. When females are considered at all in such a context, they appear as objects, as acted upon, rather than as coactors.

Looking at a recent article on sociobiology in the *Canadian Review of Sociology and Anthropology*, we find the following statement:

> Do ritualized aggression and lethal conflict serve similar functions among humans? Alcock ... concludes that most threatening or violent disputes are employed to resolve contested ownership over scarce or potentially limiting resources. ... Sociologist Van den Berghe ... interprets intergroup warfare as a rational means of gaining livestock, women and slaves, gaining or keeping territory, or gaining, controlling and exploiting new territory.[5]

In this statement, "intergroup warfare" is defined as warfare among males of different groups, while women are among the resources to be gained or controlled (after livestock and before slaves). In other words, women are not conceptualized as group members; if they were, their presumed nonparticipation in warfare would need some comment and consideration. If, upon investigation, it turned out that women did not in fact actively participate in "intergroup warfare," then clearly the term is a misnomer. A more appropriate label might be "warfare among males of different groups" or simply "male intergroup warfare," which would at least make clear the fact that only one sex is engaging in this practice. Such identification also raises the question of what the relationships among the women of different groups might have been like – and if, why, and how they were different from those of males. Presumably, at this point, a scholar would then propose a *general* theory, as opposed to a sex-specific theory, of "intergroup warfare."

Such an analysis of the meaning of concepts is not mere

quibbling over words, as becomes obvious when one pursues this issue further. Sticking for the moment with the same topic and author, we find in a different article in the same journal issue statements about the "proximate causes and seeds of warfare."[6] In trying to explain warfare, the author examines group cohesiveness and argues:

> In our work, the axiom of inclusive fitness provides a raison d'etre for group membership since individuals have a genetic interest in kin fitness. Groups serve as organizational vehicles in which individuals can monitor, and if necessary protect, the fitness of related members, having subsequent bearing on their own inclusive fitness. The more cohesive the group, the more members can effectively assess their inclusive fitness. In this respect, inclusive fitness would predispose genetically related individuals to band together beyond, say, the extended family.[7]

In addition to a genetic interest, the author also hypothesizes that environmental factors are important. His speculation runs as follows:

> In early hominid evolution, membership in an expanded group would likely have increased each individual's access to scarce resources and ability to manage others. Hunting in numbers, for example, would have enabled primitive man to overcome large game. Numbers would also have reduced susceptibility of individuals to attack by predators. To facilitate hunting and prevent attack, groups would almost certainly have served as information centres for defining and locating resources and predators. The more these features of group membership enhanced inclusive fitness (the rate of reproduction, quality of offspring, survival), the more group members would have been deterred from splintering off. In short, the social behavior of early humans probably was structured largely by both defense against large predators and competition with them. . . .[8]

At first glance, these two passages, seem perfectly nonsexist, except for one lapse in language, the reference to "primitive man." If the passage were meant to apply to both sexes, the term would be overspecific. As it turns out, however, the term is quite literally correct, because the passages talk only about primitive man and not primitive woman.

On a previous page of the article, the existence of an incest taboo was implicitly accepted.[9] Presumably this means that women, who, after all, are needed to improve the inclusive fitness of a group, typically are not from the same group as the males with whom they mate. In other words, the various groups presumably practiced some form of exogamy. In the first cited article, we found that women might be obtained through intergroup warfare of males.

This means that the concept of "group cohesion" applies only to males and not to females, since typically the females would join, for mating purposes, a group other than the one into which they were born. In such a case, approximately half of the group members were not banding together beyond the extended family in order to increase their inclusive fitness. Where does this leave the entire theory?

Turning to the second paragraph quoted, the prevailing assumption is that large game hunting was an exclusively male activity. Therefore, the statement that "groups served as information centres" about predators is obviously again about male groups and not mixed-sex groups. At best, then, the statements can be half true – applicable to one half of the population only. In that case, it is surely inappropriate to make the statements in as general and imperative a form as the one in which they presently appear.

Other concepts in general use in anthropology are also sometimes constructed with ego defined as male. To provide one more example from this same article, the author suggests that early human history can be divided into three periods of sociality, all of which involve (variously small or large) "polygynous, probably multi-male bands."[10] Polygyny (having many wives) is a concept in which ego is constructed as male. A female version would be "husband sharing," "joint husbands," or the like. However, it is the combination of the term "polygynous" with "multi-male" that establishes the male reference in a particularly clear manner, and which relegates women to the status of nonactors. If the males are polygynous, the groups are not only multi-male, but also multi-female. However, by having defined women only as wives, and not as actors or group members in their own right, they become completely invisible, as is evidenced in the following passage:

one of the first evolutionary steps taken as weapons developed was to severely restrict individuals from changing groups. From the resident's point of view, the admission of an extragroup conspecific would lead to now dangerous rank-order confrontations. The closing of hominid groups would have resulted in two beneficial effects from the standpoint of inclusive fitness. First, because males increasingly tended to remain in their natal group the genetic interrelatedness among the adult males, and in the group as a whole, would increase. This would have increased solidarity among group members and thus cohesion of the group per se.[11]

Once more, it is obvious that the group is conceptualized as consisting of males who have assorted wives who have no effect whatsoever on group cohesion and solidarity. The "individual" and the "resident" are *male* individuals and residents, not females, since women *did* change groups. The possibility of rank-order confrontations among women, and their possible consequences, is not even considered relevant, since in effect women have been defined as unimportant in the context of the group.

So far, our examples of androcentricity have been taken from one author and from one particular approach to the social sciences. As with all other types of sexism, constructing the actor as male is a practice that is found in a wide variety of approaches, authors, and disciplines. For example, to stay for a moment with the concept of polygyny, we find a definition of it, in quite a different context, as a description of concubinage in Anglo-Saxon England:

A man might have a plurality of sexual partners, specifically where one of these is a legal spouse and the other a concubine with customary privileges but without legal recognition. Alternatively, we are concerned with cases in which a man has no legal sexual partner but a publicly recognized consort. These circumstances are more accurately defined by the term concubinage than polygyny, which actually refers to a situation in which a man is permitted to have more than one wife at a time on a fully legal basis, though it is rare for the several wives to share equal social status.[12]

This definition is not wrong, but it is clearly one-sided and created from the perspective of one sex despite the fact that polygyny concerns both sexes equally. What would the definition look like from the perspective of women? Clearly, it would read quite differently: it would also be more complicated, because we would need to distinguish between the wives and the concubines as well as take into consideration wives with monogamous husbands (those who do not avail themselves of the opportunity of having multiple sexual partners even though this would be socially acceptable).

It is often the entire concept of society that is conceptualized in androcentric terms. One such instance of an androcentric vision appears again in the stratification literature. In discussing functionalist approaches to stratification, this author asks rhetorically:

> Is stratification, then, necessary for placement and motivation? It is not logically necessary, of course, or this aspect of the theory would be true by definition, rather than empirically testable and potentially falsifiable. It is possible that people of talent might undertake the training required for functionally important positions and fulfill their duties without differentials in extrinsic rewards, perhaps moved to do so by "alternative motivational schemes." ... Individuals could be socialized to think of it as their self-rewarding duty, for example, to take on important tasks and to do them well, as in the notion of noblesse oblige. ... Unfortunately, however, we seem to lack convincing contemporary or historical examples of societies with such alternative motivational schemes.[13]

The statement that we lack examples of such "alternative motivational schemes" ignores one of the most important functional tasks of all times, peoples, and strata: care of the young. For centuries women have fulfilled this vital task (and how many other tasks can truly be called vital?) due not to extrinsic rewards but to an "alternative motivational scheme." Ignoring what women have done thus leads to a misinterpretation on a grand scale.

To give one final example, the concept of the suburb as a "bedroom community" conceptualizes the entire population of the suburbs in terms of those people who leave in the morning to go to their paid work. At the time at which this concept emerged, it meant primarily employed males. Most women, practically all children, and some men would remain in the suburbs. For them, therefore, the suburbs did not serve as a bedroom community.[14]

In the above examples we can see that constructing ego as male

not only leads easily to the portrayal of women as passive, a
acted upon, but it also sometimes results in their co
invisibility. On the other hand, it is important not to commit the
error of assuming agency or activity on the part of women in cases
in which it is inappropriate. This problem is discussed in sections
2.2.5 and 2.2.6.

2.2.3 Gynopia or Female Invisibility

To illustrate gynopia, or female invisibility, we move to economics,
to an article on "The Demand for Unobservable and Other
Nonpositional Goods."[15] The author defines positional goods as

> those things whose value depends relatively strongly on how they
> compare with things owned by others. Goods that depend relatively
> less strongly on such comparisons will be called nonpositional
> goods. As noted, the nonpositional category includes, but is not
> limited to, goods that are not readily observed by outsiders.[16]

This article rests on the premise that useful insights into people's
economic behavior can be gained by the view that the utility
function (or what psychologists would call the structure of
motivation) is shaped by the forces of natural selection. In order to
clarify his point, the author presents an example of an individual, A,
who is concerned about his children. He discusses his choice of
work environment, his feelings, his ranking in the income hierarchy,
his level of ability, his work for his true marginal product, his ability
to devote more of his resources to the purchase of "x," and so on.
The following quotation gives a taste of the completely male
connotations:

> If people are certain of their rank in the positional goods hierarchy,
> the model as it is expressed above does not produce a stable
> outcome. The lowest-ranking member of the hierarchy could initially
> move past the second-lowest ranking member by increasing his
> consumption of positional goods; and the second lowest-ranking
> member could then restore the original ordering by carrying out a
> similar shift of his own. But then the lowest-ranking member could

reduce his consumption of positional goods without adversely affecting his ranking, which would already be as low as it could get. In turn, the second lowest-ranking member could then reduce *his* consumption of nonpositional goods without penalty, and in like fashion the high-ranking members would one-by-one have an incentive to follow suit.[17]

There are two ways in which this passage can be interpreted. One could assume that it simply employs sexist language by using the male term as a generic term, in which case we are dealing with an instance of overgeneralization at the level of language. Alternatively, the reference is truly exclusively male and is not meant to be applicable to women. In the example given above, we seem to be dealing with the latter case, as is evidenced by the author's statement that "the average length of job tenure is much higher for union than for nonunion members"[18] and his supporting footnote:

> Jacob Mincer . . . finds, for example, that quit rates in the union sector are about one-half as large as in the nonunion sector for young men and about one-third as large for men over 30.[19]

Similarly, he backs up his statement that "we also know that union members earn significantly higher wages than do nonunion workers with comparable job skills"[20] with the footnote:

> Mincer . . . for example, finds ability-adjusted union wage premiums of 6–14 percent for men under 30, and 4–12 percent for older men.[21]

The fact that the author's evidence is strictly applicable to males does not lead him to reflect on whether his generalizations are equally applicable to women, nor does it lead him to indicate in the title of his article that he is really only discussing the demand for unobservable and nonpositional goods for males.

Similar criticisms have been made of the discipline of history and the work of specific historians. For example, as Ruth Pierson and Alison Prentice point out:

The eminent socialist historian Eric Hobsbawm failed to include women in his 1971 theoretical plea for a social history so all-encompassing that it would become a history of all society.[22] In 1978, he admitted the justness of the criticism "that male historians in the past, including marxists, have grossly neglected the female half of the human race," and included himself among the culprits. ... Another example of bias is Philippe Aries' path-breaking study of the history of childhood, which deals almost exclusively with male children.[23]

2.2.4 *The Maintenance of Male over Female Interests*

Maintaining male over female interests may take various forms. One of them is a trivializing of problems experienced by women at the hands of men. An example of this can be found in a recent publication of Statistics Canada, *Divorce: Law and the Family in Canada*.[24] For instance, when discussing grounds for divorce, the authors start out by noting that

> it would appear that the bases of divorce vary with the sex of the players. In Table 6 it is apparent that women petitioners select grounds different from those habitually chosen by men.[25]

Just considering, for a moment, the grammar of this sentence, it would seem reasonable to assume that men petition for divorce more often than women, or at least that men and women petition for divorce with approximately the same frequency, since women are compared with men rather than the other way around. However, looking at the table this sentence refers to, we find that the authors are discussing 330,740 wives who have petitioned for divorce as opposed to only 173,890 husbands who petitioned for divorce.

The paragraph cited above then continues:

> The principal category for both sexes is noncohabitation. However, it is more popular with men since they rely on it half the time while women petitioners rely on it just over a third (37%) of the time. Men also use adultery considerably more often than women: 36.6% as compared to 27.5%. However, in both cases, adultery is the second most often pleaded ground.

As we have already noted, men rarely (5.4%) plead grounds of mental and/or physical cruelty. Rather mental and/or physical cruelty are "female" grounds invoked by women petitioners far more frequently (19.0%) than men....

Generally, men use adultery or noncohabitation (85.5%) and although women use these grounds as well, they make much more use of the remaining possibilities. These differences may be due to fundamental differences between men and women or they may simply reflect that more grounds are easily used by women than men. We have already discussed this likelihood with reference to mental and physical cruelty. It also seems plausible that such grounds as imprisonment, rape, and alcohol or narcotics addiction are much more easily used by women even though in general, these grounds are not heavily relied on. Essentially adultery and noncohabitation seem the only two particularly effective choices available to men. In addition, these two grounds are the easiest to prove.[26]

Contrast this discussion with the fact that 66 percent of all divorce petitions are made by women, not men, as the table that is being discussed shows. It seems that the only important grounds for divorce are those cited by men, and that women "choose" other grounds because they "use them more easily" than men. There is no recognition that perhaps the differential grounds for divorce may reflect differential behavior of women and men during marriage. Such reflection would, of course, be less than flattering to men, since it suggests that men are much more likely to abuse their wives mentally or physically – as indeed other studies confirm[27] – than women are to abuse their husbands.

Nor is the incidence of cruelty so low. When we combine the cases in which wives petition for divorce in which cruelty is cited as either the sole reason or as one factor among others, we find that 29.9 percent of all female petitions, or 98,892 cases, in the years under consideration cited cruelty as a ground for divorce, compared to 173,890 men who petitioned for divorce for *any* reason whatsoever. It is hardly adequate, under these circumstances, to conclude:

Although there are 15 individual grounds for divorce, most divorcing Canadians rely on only three: cruelty, adultery or separation for not less than three years.... The first two are fault-oriented and together account for 44.9% of all cases, while the latter (noncohabitation) places an emphasis on marriage failure, accounting for 41.0% of all cases.

These grounds are differentially invoked by men and women – men rely on noncohabitation and tend to ignore cruelty, while women use cruelty more often although their most often chosen category of grounds is also noncohabitation (separation).[28]

"Men tend to ignore cruelty" while "women use cruelty more often" is comparable to arguing that some crime victims choose to press charges for stealing, while others prefer to press charges for assault. Descriptions of this type trivialize a very substantial problem that women experience at the hands of men. They thus constitute euphemistic descriptions of male behavior. By failing to identify a social problem as such, they implicitly serve male over female interests.

Another example of the same type of problem can be found in an anthropological study of *Yanomamo: The Fierce People*.[29] The author, Napoleon Chagnon, provides innumerable examples of male violence among the Yanomamo. Wife abuse predominates in their everyday existence. Warfare is often conducted as a means of abducting women in order for the men of a particular clan to acquire more wives. Rape is part of this abduction, and men are considered to be perfectly within their rights to beat their wives for the slightest provocation, such as when the wife is slow in preparing a meal. Chagnon discusses and illustrates wife abuse throughout his text, yet there is only one paragraph describing how the women perceive this abuse, and this is based on an overheard conversation.

Women expect this kind of treatment and many of them measure their husband's concern in terms of the frequency of the minor beatings they sustain. I overheard two young women discussing their scalp scars. One of them commented that the other's husband must really care for her since he had beaten her on the head so frequently.[30]

Chagnon bases his interpretation of the women's general attitude on only one overheard conversation. He never directly asks any of the women how they felt. Furthermore, by inserting the term "minor beatings" into his analysis, he makes a judgment that may be quite inappropriate, given that the woman received scalp scars as a result. There are many other examples of sexism in this book, but trivializing male abuse of females is one clear instance of placing male interests above female interests.

Another form of maintaining male over female interests can be found in a recent report of the Economic Council of Canada.[31] In this annual review, the Council included, for the first time ever, a special chapter on Women and Work. It therefore warrants some attention.

The Council documents, in two separate tables, the rather gross earnings differentials between women and men in the twenty highest and twenty lowest paid occupations for 1970 and 1981. The Council then comments on these tables as follows:

> Within both the highest- and the lowest-paid activities there has been some progress in narrowing the female/male earnings gap. When adjusted for hours worked per year, the gaps narrow; and it seems likely that they would narrow still further if they were adjusted for education and experience. Nevertheless, the gaps remain very wide. This suggests that the principle of equal pay for equal or equivalent work must continue to be enforced vigorously. Yet, if there is to be further substantial improvement in the relative earnings of women, the issue goes beyond that to more basic questions of training related to market needs, the balancing of family and career aspirations, and greater occupational diversification. Progress is being made, but slowly, and mostly by the young. Among older women who lack the specialized training needed for many of today's better-paid jobs, the route has been more difficult.[32]

These comments are truly ironic, for two reasons. The report identifies the following as the "more basic questions": training related to market needs, the balancing of family and career aspirations, and greater occupational diversification. But the comparisons made are *within* occupations, where appropriate training presumably exists; this sample thus represents women who *have* contributed to female diversification (since they *are* in the highest-paid jobs); and the report fails to mention that the wage differentials are significantly higher (both in an absolute as well as in a relative sense) in the highest- not the lowest-paid occupations.

The summary further neglects to alert us to the fact that in some of these jobs women actually lost ground in a relative sense vis-á-vis men: for 16 percent of the women in the highest-paid occupations (namely for directors general, optometrists, veterinarians, university teachers, members of legislative bodies, administrators – teaching, and air transport foremen), the wage differential *increased* between 1970 and 1980. For women in the lowest-paid occupations, the gap increased by 11 percent: Women working as babysitters; workers on farms; in horticulture and animal husbandry; in occupations in fishing, hunting, and trapping; and as barbers and hairdressers lost ground to men. Taking all occupations considered into account, it remains true that for the majority of women in both the highest- and lowest-paid occupations, the wage gap decreased somewhat.

However, another table informs us that if we control hourly earnings by education level, men with less education consistently make more than do women with more education.[33] Thus a man with secondary schooling or less makes more than a woman with a nonuniversity diploma or certificate or some university training, while a man with similar educational qualifications makes more than does a woman with a bachelor's degree or certificate; in turn, a man with a bachelor's degree makes more than does a woman with a postgraduate degree. These figures suggest forcefully that the problem is *not* primarily one of training, for with the same amount of training, women make substantially lower hourly wages. (This means that the overall wage difference cannot be explained by the fact that women may potentially work fewer hours than men because the comparison is based on *hourly*, not weekly or monthly, earnings).

In its conclusions, the report recommends adequacy in terms of alternative forms of child care, pension rights for women, and encouragement for women and girls, "along with young men, to acquire nontraditional skills that will facilitate wider occupational choice in subsequent years" (p. 107). While there is nothing wrong with these recommendations and the previously cited recommendations, they nevertheless do not address the fact that women and men *within the same occupations* experience wide income gaps. What is conspicuous by its absence is a recommendation to pursue

vigorously a program of equal pay for work of equal value, which is
referred to in the text passage cited above as a principle that "must
continue to be enforced vigorously."

All else remaining equal, given that women with the same
educational level have significantly lower hourly earnings than
men, educational programs alone will *not* eliminate the wage gap,
although they may have other beneficial effects. By focusing on
educational achievements rather than on systemic wage differentials,
however, this analysis diverts attention from a significant structural
problem. Instead, it assesses the chief difficulty as an individual
problem: get a better education and reconsider your family
commitments, if you are a woman (apparently this is not necessary
if you are a man), and your problems will disappear. The only
drawback to this advice is that, as the report documents, heeding it
will not make the problems disappear.

2.2.5 Misogyny and Blaming Women

Maintaining male over female interests may take the extreme form
of outright misogyny (that is, hatred of women) and blaming
women. These two phenomena are so closely related that they can
be treated as one and the same, since very often blaming women
takes the form of blaming them for the fact that they (or their
children) are victimized. This is especially true when the discussion
concerns sexual violence: from a misogynistic perspective, sexual
violence against women (and children) is implicitly justified (that is,
the victims deserve to be victimized); thus the woman is "blamed"
for her victimization and becomes not the victim but the accused.
Such bias may be blatant (as in the above example) or subtle, but in
any case, it constitutes the adoption of a male perspective and thus
is an instance of androcentricity.

Our first example comes from the journal *Child Development*.[34]
The article deals with "seductive mother-toddler relationships."
One must first of all ask oneself to whom the described behaviors
are seductive? To the infant? To the mother? Or to the adult (male
or female) observer who applies the standards of an adult male?

Seductive behavior is described as follows:

At times this took the form of certain kinds of physical contact (squeezing the buttocks, stroking the stomach, and even grabbing the genital area). At other times it involved sensual teasing, a plaintive voice, or promises of affection if the child would comply. In all cases these behaviours were viewed as seductive, not because they were intended to lead to frank sexual contact, but because "in addition to being insensitive and unresponsive to the needs of the child, they [drew] the child into patterns of interaction that are overly stimulating and role inappropriate." ... The behaviour involved either physical contact motivated by the mother's needs, rather than by the child's, or manipulating the child using sensuality. In no case was it responsive to bids by the toddler.[35]

It is important to note that in *no* case were the behaviors intended to lead to frank sexual contact. Their classification as "seductive" therefore does *not* derive from the actual context but from extrapolation of what these behaviors would mean were they addressed to an adult male. A better term might be "manipulative sensuality" or simply "excessive control and manipulation."

The language in this study vacillates between being specific and being overgeneral. A good example is provided in the following section, where we find that "parent-child relationships" in fact refer to mother-child relationships, and even more specifically, often (but not always) to mother-son relationships:

We are interested in understanding parent-child relationship systems, including the relation between one parent-child relationship and the relationship between that parent and another child. If particular qualities of parent-child relationships can be defined, we may explore whether distinct but predictable qualities likely characterize the relationships of that parent with other children in the family. Where the mother is seductive with her son, what is the nature of her relationship with her daughter? Were one not investigating a sample of largely single mothers, such as ours, spouse and father-child relations also could be included.[36]

It is in the context of this "sample of largely single mothers" that the inappropriateness of the term "seductive maternal behavior" becomes particularly clear. In view of the mounting evidence that many males do indeed engage in "frank sexual contact" with their children, it seems highly ironic to identify behavior that does *not* lead to such contact with a term that indicates that it does.

This lopsidedness becomes upsettingly clear when one reads through the entire article. The authors state that

> we believe that seductive behaviour towards a child, and dissolution of generational boundaries more generally, is a reflection of the parent's relationship history and ongoing needs. A parent behaves seductively toward a child because their own needs for nurturance have been unmet and because they learned in childhood that parents may attempt to meet their own emotional needs through their children.[37]

Presumably, all the parents that are being discussed here are in fact mothers. Talking about parents rather than mothers in this context is singularly inappropriate (underspecific) when sex is such a crucial variable. We learn later, quite a bit later than the passage just cited, that

> interview data concerning incest history were compared for 19 mothers having "high generational boundary" dissolution scores ... with the other 170 mothers in the sample. While only 8% of the larger sample reported a history of being sexually abused in the family, 42% of the target mothers reported such experiences.[38]

Forty-two percent of the "target mothers" suffered from incest, but they do *not* themselves engage in incest. Instead, the "seductive" behavior, inappropriate though it may be, seems relatively harmless when compared with incest.

The scale for measuring the dissolution of generational boundaries in this study

> was designed to capture an age-related transformation of the seductive patterns that was more far-reaching [than nonresponsive intimacy]. The broader issue of generational boundary dissolution may be manifest other than in strictly physical terms. Mother and child may behave as peers, mother may defer to the child for

direction (role reversal), or mother may be charmed and amused by
the child at the expense of providing the direction he needs. For
example, the child deliberately misplaces a shape. Mother clucks her
tongue and laughingly says, "What are you doing now, you devil,
you?" Then they both put their head on the table and giggle.[39]

It is this type of "dissolution of generational boundaries" that
constitutes a "more far-reaching" transformation of the seductive
pattern, but both this and incest (of the adult male with the female
child) are termed "boundary dissolution." Clearly the term trivializes
the male assault and problematizes comparatively harmless female
behavior.

The general androcentric bias of this study is blatantly obvious in
other concepts employed. For instance, the authors state:

> One might predict that mothers would be concordant for seductive
> behaviour with male siblings (a style of relating to boys) but not
> opposite-sex siblings, where there would be no relation.[40]

Here we encounter the curious constructions of "male siblings" and
"opposite-sex siblings." Siblings to whom? Clearly to the male child.
Everybody else is – most of the time but not always – described in
relation to this male child, rather than in terms reciprocal to one
another. Moreover, "target dyads" are described as "mother-sister
dyads,"[41] as compared to "target other-male dyads" and "target
mother-sister dyads."[42] Who is the implied referent in this set of
concepts? Not the mother, because if so, the dyads would have been
identified as mother-son and mother-daughter dyads (mother-son is,
in fact, sometimes used).

The authors note toward the end of their article that

> the results distinguish the construct we are defining from a
> generalized seductiveness concept. There was not concordance in
> seductive behavior across siblings. While it certainly may be the case
> that some mothers are seductive with more than one son, not one
> such case emerged in our data, and the other findings of this study
> suggest that mothers are unlikely to be seductive with sons and
> daughters alike.[43]

Note the continuing androcentricity: Whose siblings? One might suspect that siblings are seductive among themselves if it were not for the overall context of the article. In addition the substantive statement contained in this passage underlines the inappropriateness of the term "seductive behavior," which in effect equates incest with a wide range of possibly inappropriate but less serious behaviors. In no case did a mother engage in truly sexual behavior, and in no case was more than one child involved, while men often *do* sexually abuse their children and grandchildren and often abuse more than one child.

The entire area of sexual abuse is one in which sexist theories predominate. Judith Herman, in an overview of various theories on sexual abuse of children, has noted that

> the doctor, the man of letters, and the pornographer, each in his accustomed language, render similar judgements of the incestuous father's mate. By and large, they suggest, she drove him to it. The indictment of the mother includes three counts: first, she failed to perform her marital duties; second, she, not the father, forced the daughter to take her rightful place; and third, she knew about, tolerated, or in some cases actively enjoyed the incest.[44]

Diana E. H. Russell comments on this passage:

> It has been easier to blame mothers than to face the fact that daughters are vulnerable to sexual abuse when they do not have strong mothers to protect them from their own fathers and other male relatives. But mothers should not have to protect their children from their children's fathers! And a mother's "failure" to protect her child should not be seen as a causative factor in child sexual abuse.[45]

What we see, then, is the tendency to accuse women of inappropriate or negligent – sometimes even criminal – sexual behavior with their children, when it is men who, statistically, are the real abusers. Women suddenly emerge as active rather than passive, just at the moment when blame is being assigned for the sexual mistreatment of children.

2.2.6 Defending Female Subjugation or
Male Dominance

Mary Daly, in her book *Gyn/Ecology*,[46] provides a detailed analysis of several forms of female subjugation, mutilation, and degradation in different cultures and at different times, including the Indian rite of *suttee* (widow-burning), the Chinese custom of footbinding, and African customs of genital mutilation. She also shows clearly that many scholars implicitly or explicitly have defended such rites, which result in horrible suffering or death for women. There is no need to repeat this analysis here, but let us consider one example from Daly's work:

> If the general situation of widowhood in India was not a sufficient inducement for the woman of higher caste to throw herself gratefully and ceremoniously into the fire, she was often pushed and poked in with long stakes after having been bathed, ritually attired, and drugged out of her mind. In case these facts should interfere with our clear misunderstanding of the situation, Webster's invites us to re-*cover* women's history with the following definition of *suttee*: "the act or custom of a Hindu woman *willingly* cremating herself or being cremated on the funeral pyre of her husband as an indication of her *devotion* to him [emphases by Daly]." It is thought-provoking to consider the reality behind the term *devotion*, for indeed a wife must have shown signs of extraordinarily slavish devotion during her husband's lifetime, since her very life depended upon her husband's state of health.[47]

My later edition of Webster's[48] defines suttee as "a Hindu widow who immolates herself on the funeral pile of her husband; the voluntary self-immolation by fire of a Hindu widow."

2.3   Manifestations of Androcentricity in the Research Process

2.3.1   Androcentricity in Language

Most forms of sexism in language fall under the general rubric of overgeneralization/overspecificity and are therefore considered in the following chapter. However, one aspect of this problem is properly identified as falling into the area of androcentricity: the sequencing of the sexes. It is impossible to avoid mentioning one sex first when both are considered; this is not an issue at all if there is some reasonable alternation as to which sex gets mentioned first. However, if one sex is consistently mentioned first (for example, by combinations of "men and women" or "he and she" or "Mr. and Mrs. Smith"), and such combinations are elevated to the level of grammatical rules, a mild form of androcentricity results. Conversely, if the mention of females consistently precedes that of males, a mild form of gynocentricity results. (I did not encounter any examples of the latter form of bias, and therefore the problem is identified solely as one of androcentricity).

2.3.2   Androcentric (and Gynocentric) Concepts

One important way in which concepts can be sexist occurs when the concept includes a hidden one-sex referent. For example, the concept of the suburb as a "bedroom community" has as a referent the working adult male who leaves the suburb in the morning to return in the evening. For women who are housewives or who work in the neighborhood as waitresses, in beauty salons, as bank tellers, or as teachers (and for children who attend a neighborhood school, go to a day care center, or stay at home), the suburb is definitely *not* a bedroom community.

Two other examples of androcentric concepts are those of "group cohesion," which, as defined in sociobiology, focuses exclusively on the males within a group; and "intergroup warfare," which in fact refers to males of different groups who battle against each other.

Likewise, the concept of polygyny (many wives) refers to the male who has multiple wives, rather than to the female who shares her husband. An equivalent female term might be "husband sharing." An anthropological study about "husband sharing" would certainly be organized quite differently than one about "polygyny." Of course, the concept of polyandry (many husbands) has a female referent; here the corresponding male term might be "wife sharing."

Another way in which androcentricity appears in concepts is the inclusion of a demeaning attribute with a sex indicator, as in the concept of the "masochistic woman." Paula Caplan offers this analysis:

> What ... is the behavior that in women has led to their being called masochistic? Much of it is in fact *learned* behavior, the very essence of femininity in Western culture. Girls and women are supposed to be nurturant, selfless (even self-denying), and endlessly patient. What often goes hand in hand with these traits is low self-esteem. Since no one with decent self-respect would be endlessly nurturant and consider it unnatural to want something for herself, society must train women to believe that without their nurturant behavior, without what they can give to another person, they are nothing. . . .
>
> Once females have been trained in this way, and act nurturant, charitable, and compassionate, this behavior is then labeled masochistic.[49]

The reverse form of this bias would be the use of misandrist concepts (that is, terms that include a demeaning attribute with a male sex indicator). I did not find any examples of this within the literature that I examined, nor could I or friends and colleagues whom I asked recall any. This fact in and of itself says something about the state of the literature. Nevertheless, it does not rule out the possibility that misandrist concepts may exist.

2.3.3 *Androcentricity in the Research Design*

A very pervasive way in which research can be androcentric is through an androcentric perspective that shapes an entire study. The previously discussed example from sociobiology concerning warfare in "primitive man" provides one such example. The problems are defined from a male perspective, and the variables examined are those that affect men, while those affecting women are ignored. There is no discussion, for example, of whether group cohesion was generated in women through joint nursing of children. In this specific case, both the overall research question and specific questions addressed to the data are so intertwined that they cannot be meaningfully separated from each other. In other instances, only specific questions addressed to respondents can be identified as androcentric.

A broader issue emerges when we consider the cumulative effect of androcentricity in many studies within an area (as opposed to the androcentric bias of one particular study). Scholarly research is supposed to be embedded within its appropriate literature. If an entire area has been shaped by androcentric research (as is likely to often be the case), it is necessary to consider the area carefully as a whole and ask oneself whether, for instance, the variables considered important include those that are particularly important for women. Many feminist critiques of traditional ways of "doing history" center on this issue.

The reverse problem occurs when researchers identify as female an activity in which both women and men participate. One noted family researcher found it necessary to emphasize that "clearly, the terms *family* and *mother-child interaction* are not the same."[50] He continues, "Gradually, in studies of family behavior, fathers are being admitted as participants, but most investigators have not begun to treat families as empirical entities."[51]

An androcentric focus may also be a problem even when a researcher plans to include both males and females in a study. If the area of research is one from which women traditionally have been excluded from consideration,[52] it may be necessary to plan an exploratory pilot study (prior to the main study) to assess the adequacy of the variables normally used in this type of research.

2.3.4 *Validation of Research Instrument*

If a research instrument is developed and validated for one sex only and is then used for the other sex, it cannot be considered validated. For example, if a research instrument is developed and validated on males but used on both sexes, it introduces an androcentric bias. Such was the case with Kohlberg's famous model of the development of moral judgment, which he derived from an empirical study of eighty-four boys whose development he followed for a period of over twenty years.[53] Another well-known example of this source of bias is the widely used distinction between "instrumental" and "expressive" leaders, which was developed by observing the behavior of male undergraduate students,[54] and was subsequently used to describe the proper roles for husbands (instrumental leaders) and wives (expressive leaders).[55] Similarly, if an instrument were developed and validated using females only and were then applied to both females and males, it would introduce a gynocentric bias.

2.3.5 Formulation of Questions and Questionnaires

We have already noted that research questions may be biased in a number of ways. Here we are concerned with the actual questions posed to respondents, such as in survey research, qualitative interviews, or opinion polls, where a single question may be posed to respondents. An androcentric bias may appear in the manner in which questions are formulated.

For instance, where the intent of a question is to compare attitudes about males and females with respect to some capacity, questions are sometimes formulated so that one sex or the other serves as the norm against which the other is measured (thus eliminating the possibility for surpassing the normative sex). Take, for example, the following statements (respondents were asked to agree or disagree with them):

- It is generally better to have a man at the head of a department composed of both men and women employees.

- It is acceptable for women to hold important political offices in state and national government.[56]

In these cases female heads of departments or female incumbents of important political offices are measured against the norm established by male incumbents. The wording of the statements makes it impossible for the respondent to indicate that he or she might see female department heads or office holders as *preferable*. Thus only half of the possible spectrum of responses is allowed for.

The items could, of course, be rephrased to allow for the full range of possible responses:

- What do you think is generally better: To have a woman or a man at the head of a department that is composed of both men and women employees?

- . . . to have women or men hold important elected political offices in state and national government?

Permissible responses to such items could then be:

- It is much better to have a man.
- It is somewhat better to have a man.
- It makes no difference.
- It is somewhat better to have a woman.
- It is much better to have a woman.

2.4 *Conclusion*

Androcentricity takes many forms, including a male viewpoint or frame of reference, the construction of an actor as male, female invisibility, misogyny and blaming women, and the defense of cultural practices that directly subjugate or harm women. These various manifestations are, of course, not independent of one another. We can think of them as different facets of the same phenomenon.

Androcentricity may manifest itself in all components of the research process, but the two most important manifestations are in concepts and in the overall research design. It is thus not easy to eliminate. We need to step out of the accepted mode of thinking to ask ourselves: Does this concept or research design address the concerns and viewpoints of women and men equally? If not, a new approach is called for.

Such a new approach can be called a "dual perspective," as opposed to a single (male) perspective. In the absence of a female perspective that is developed as well as a male perspective, applying a dual perspective necessarily involves reinvestigating issues about which we thought we already knew enough.

We need to create baseline data sets that are comparable for women and men. This will mean, for quite a while, putting special emphasis on studying women rather than men, in order to start redressing the current imbalance. It also implies looking at both men and women from a female rather than a male perspective. Both sexes must be understood as gendered people. In the process, we will learn new things not only about women, but about men as well.

Notes

1 Simone de Beauvoir, *The Second Sex* (New York: Bantam, 1972). See also Jean Bethke Elshtain, "Women as mirror and other: Toward a theory of women, war, and feminism," *Humanities in Society* 5, 1/2 (1982): 29–44.

2 Shulamit Reinharz, "Feminist distrust: Problems of context and content in sociological work," in David N. Berg and Kenwyn K. Smith (eds.), *Exploring Clinical Methods for Social Research* (Beverly Hills, CA: Sage, 1985): 153–172, quote on p. 170.

3 Alfred A. Hunter, *Class Tells: On Social Inequality in Canada*, 2nd ed. (Toronto: Butterworths, 1986): 185. It should be noted that in spite of the formulation of this paragraph, this author is one of the sharpest critics of the human capital approach, precisely because of its sexism; see Margaret A. Denton and Alfred A. Hunter, *Equality in the Workplace: Economic Sectors and Gender Discrimination in Canada: A Critique and Test of Block and Walker . . . and Some New Evidence*. Women's Bureau, Ser. A, No. 6 (Ottawa:Labour Canada, 1984).

4 Edward B. Fiske, "Scholars face a challenge by feminists," *New York Times* (Nov. 23, 1981): 1.

5 R. Paul Shaw, "Humanity's propensity for warfare: A sociobiological perspective," *Canadian Review of Sociology and Anthropology* 22, 2 (1985): 158–183, quote on p. 166.

6 R. Paul Shaw, "Merging ultimate and proximate causes in sociobiology and studies of warfare," *Canadian Review of Sociology and Anthropology* 22, 2 (1985): 192–201.

7 Ibid., p. 196.

8   Ibid.

9   Ibid., p. 195.

10 Ibid., p. 197.

11 Ibid., pp. 197–198.

12 Margaret Clunies Ross, "Concubinage in Anglo-Saxon England," *Past and Present* 108 (1985): 3–34, quote on p. 6.

13 Hunter, *Class Tells*, p. 33.

14 Lyn H. Lofland, "The 'thereness' of women": A selective review of urban sociology," in Marcia Millman and Rosabeth Moss Kanter (eds.), *Another Voice* (Garden City, NY: Anchor, 1975): 144–170.

15 Robert H. Frank, "The demand for unobservable and other nonpositional goods," *American Economic Review* 75, 1 (1985): 101–116.

16 Ibid., p. 101.

17 Ibid., p. 106.

18 Ibid., p. 111.

19 Ibid., p. 111, fn. 15.

20 Ibid., p. 111.

21 Ibid., p. 111, fn. 18.

22 E. J. Hobsbawm, "From social history to the history of society," in Felix Gilbert and Stephen R. Graubard (eds.), *Historical Studies Today* (New York: Norton, 1971): 1–26.

23 Ruth Pierson and Alison Prentice, "Feminism and the writing and teaching of history," in Angela Miles and Geraldine Finn (eds.), *Feminism in Canada: From Pressure to Politics* (Montreal: Black Rose, 1982): 103–118, quote on p. 109.

24 D. C. McKie, B. Prentice, and P. Reed. *Divorce: Law and the Family in Canada.* Statistics Canada Cat. #89–502E (Ottawa: Minister of Supply and Services, 1983).

25 Ibid., p. 140.

26 Ibid.

27 See, for instance, the overview discussions in Diana E. H. Russell, *Sexual Exploitation: Rape, Child Sexual Abuse, and Workplace Harassment* (Beverly Hills, CA: Sage, 1984); and Julia R. and Herman Schwendiger, *Rape and Inequality* (Beverly Hills, CA: Sage, 1983). For wife battering in Canada, see Linda MacLeod, *Wife Battering in Canada: The Vicious Circle.* Canadian Advisory Council on the Status of Women (Ottawa: Minister of Supply and Services Canada, 1980).

28 McKie et al., *Divorce*, pp. 148–149.

29 Napoleon Chagnon, *Yanomamo: The Fierce People* (New York: Holt, Rinehart and Winston, 1977). This section is based on a paper written by Joanne Beaudoin, entitled "Yanomamo: The Fierce People – A Critical Analysis of Sexist Content" The paper was written for a seminar taught by M. Eichler at the Ontario Institute for Studies in Education. The student chose to criticize Chagnon's work because it was presented in another course as a good example of a case study in cultural anthropology.

30 Chagnon, *Yanomamo*, p. 83.

31 Economic Council of Canada, *On the Mend: Twentieth Annual Review* (Ottawa: Minister of Supply and Services, 1983).

32 Ibid., p. 89.

33 Ibid., Table A13, p. 118.

34 L. Alan Sroufe, Deborah Jacobvitz, Sarah Mangelsdorf, Edward DeAngelo, and

Mary Jo Ward, "Generational boundary dissolution between mothers and their preschool children: A relationship systems approach," *Child Development* 56, 2 (1985):317–325.

35 Ibid., p. 317.

36 Ibid., p. 318.

37 Ibid.

38 Ibid., p. 322.

39 Ibid., p. 320.

40 Ibid., p. 318.

41 Ibid., p. 319.

42 Ibid., p. 322.

43 Ibid., p. 323.

44 Judith Herman, *Father-Daughter Incest* (Cambridge, MA: Harvard University Press, 1981):42, as quoted in Russell, *Sexual Exploitation*, p. 264.

45 Russell, *Sexual Exploitation*, p. 264.

46 Mary Daly, *Gyn/Ecology: The Metaethics of Radical Feminism* (Boston: Beacon, 1978).

47 Daly, *Gyn/Ecology*, p. 116. In this passage, Daly cites P. Thomas, *Indian Women through the Ages* (New York: Asia Publishing, 1964): 263; this author describes the situation in Muslim India of widows who tried to escape cremation, writing that "to prevent her escape she was usually surrounded by men armed with sticks who goaded her on to her destination by physical force."

48 *Webster's* does not provide a date of publication. But I presume that I have a later edition as Daly's book appeared in 1978, and my edition lists Carter as U.S. president.

49 Paula J. Caplan, *The Myth of Women's Masochism* (New York: E. P. Dutton, 1985): 35–36.

50 Frank F. Furstenberg, Jr., "Sociological ventures in child development," *Child Development* 56, 2 (1985): 281–288, quote on p. 284.

51 Ibid.

52 For some of the reasons that researchers give to justify the exclusion of women from their research design, as well as consequences of such a practice, see Suzanne Prescott, "Why researchers don't study women: The responses of 62 researchers," *Sex Roles* 4, 6 (1978): 899–905.

53 Carol Gilligan, *In a Different Voice: Psychological Theory and Women's Development* (Cambridge, MA: Harvard University Press, 1982), p. 18. There has been considerable debate about Gilligan's own work, which, at times, exhibits the problem of sexual dichotomism.

54 Robert F. Bales and Philip E. Slater, "Role differentiation in small decision-making groups," in Talcott Parsons and Robert F. Bales (eds.), *Family, Socialization and Interaction Process* (Glencoe, IL: Free Press, 1955): 259–306.

55 For a more far-reaching critique, see Margrit Eichler, *The Double Standard* (London:Croom Helm, 1980):39–48.

56 These are items from the Brogan and Kutner inventory; see D. Brogan and N. G. Kutner, "Measuring sex-role orientation: A normative approach," *Journal of Marriage and the Family* 37 (1975): 391–399, but are here quoted from Kenrick S. Thompson, "Sex role orientation: A primer of scale construction," *International Journal of Sociology of the Family* 14, 1 (1984).

Chapter 3
Overgeneralization

3.1 Introduction
3.2 Sexist language
   3.2.1 Use of sex-specific terms for generic purposes
   3.2.2 Use of generic terms for sex-specific purposes
3.3 Overgeneral titles
3.4 Overgeneral concepts
3.5 Overgeneral methods
   3.5.1 Inappropriate wording of questions
   3.5.2 Overspecificity in reporting on the methods employed
3.6 Overgeneral data interpretation
3.7 Conclusion

3.1 Introduction

Overgeneralization may occur in the identification of a research project, in the language employed, in the concepts used, in the methods used, and in the interpretations made. It takes place each time a study deals with one sex only but presents itself as if it were of general (rather than sex-specific) applicability. This error is typically committed for both sexes, although in a sharply divergent manner: men's experience tends to be seen as an appropriate basis for making general statements about practically anything but the family; women's experience tends to be seen as an appropriate basis for overgeneralization only about some aspects of family life or reproduction. The flip side of overgeneralization is overspecificity: a description of research that masks the true nature of the study.

3.2 Sexist Language

Sexist language tends to be defined as language that uses male terms for generic purposes, and indeed, this is the most frequent form of overgeneralization at the level of simple language. However, this definition is insufficient. Language is sexist whenever it uses (a) sex-specific terms for generic purposes (overgeneralization); or (b) generic terms for sex-specific purposes (overspecificity). In addition, language is sexist when it uses nonparallel terms for parallel situations, but this is a form of sexism that falls under the rubric of double standards and will be considered in more detail in Chapter 5.

3.2.1 Use of Sex-Specific Terms for Generic Purposes

The journals that were examined for sexism contained numerous instances of male terms used in a supposedly generic manner, but I did not find any female terms used in a supposedly generic manner.[1] (I *did* find the use of generic terms to refer to females only. See section 3.2.2.) We are here dealing with the time-honored practice of using "he," "man," or "mankind" as supposedly generic terms, and although some journals and some authors attempt to avoid this form of sexism, evidence of this practice can still be found.

So, for instance, institutions continue to be "manned" rather than staffed,[2] and "mankind" continues to be equated with humanity.[3] In other sources, we find that "man is a small group animal,"[4] and that the individual who joins an interest group is identified as "he," as is the individual who has some idea of what present and potential benefits are worth, or the person who is wooed by environmental lobbies.[5] In another article, the journalistic community is identified as the "journalistic fraternity," which, given the number of female journalists, is clearly inappropriate,[6] and the next door neighbor is also a "he":

> Imagine a friendly backyard conversation in which a governing member sets out to explain to his next-door neighbor why it is in everybody's interest to use part of the citizen's taxes to prevent him from receiving some kind of information about his world.[7]

Likewise, a sophisticated voter is presented as "he" in an article that analyzes Gallup Poll data that presumably are derived from female as well as male respondents.[8] Similarly, the "marginal individual, the one whose consumer surplus from entering the market is lowest" is also a "he."[9]

The examples cited above are not trivial. In a recent and highly acclaimed book on constructing questionnaires for survey research, the opening paragraph reads as follows:

> The central thesis of this book is that question wording is a crucial element in maximizing the validity of survey data obtained by a question-asking process. . . .
>
> The importance of the exact wording of the questions seems obvious and hardly worth dwelling on. The fact that seemingly small changes in wording can cause large differences in responses has been well known to survey practitioners since the early days of surveys.[10]

The authors then discuss how the word "you" can be either singular or plural and therefore tends to be a source of confusion. They suggest the use of "you, yourself," "you or any member of this household," or "you and all other members of this household" to ensure correct understanding of the meaning of a question.[11]

All of this is excellent advice, but the authors seem unaware that a similar confusion exists when dealing with supposedly generic words that are used for two purposes, that is, sometimes to indicate only males, and sometimes to mean both males and females. That this is not a simple oversight but is in fact not perceived by the authors becomes evident when one considers some of the sample questions that they supply. Although the book is otherwise most helpful, questions that use sexist language elicit no comment from the authors as being unspecific, inappropriate, ambiguous, or confusing. For instance, when providing a set of questions designed to measure attitudes toward freedom of speech, they provide the following examples without commenting on the language:

> There are always some people whose ideas are considered bad or dangerous by other people. For instance, somebody who is against all churches and religion . . .
>
> > A. If such a person wanted to make a speech in your city . . . against churches and religion, should he be allowed to speak, or not? . . .
>
> Or consider a person who believes that blacks are genetically inferior.
>
> > A. If such a person wanted to make a speech in your community claiming that blacks are inferior, should he be allowed to speak, or not? . . .
> >
> > C. If some people in your community suggested that a book he wrote which said blacks are inferior should be taken out of your public library, would you favor removing this book, or not?
>
> Now, I should like to ask you some questions about a man who admits he is a Communist.
>
> Consider a person who advocated doing away with elections and letting the military run the country.
>
> > A. If such a person wanted to make a speech in your community, should he be allowed to speak, or not?[12]

These questions engender two different sets of problems, depending on how the responses are interpreted by the researcher. If the responses are taken to signify attitudes toward freedom of speech for all people, females as well as males, then clearly they are inappropriately phrased. It is quite possible that attitudes toward female, as opposed to male, homosexuals (another category of people identified later in this set of questions) would be quite different with respect to their right to speak, teach in a college or university, or have their book in a public library. The same might be true about attitudes toward male or female communists, promilitary people, racists, and so on. Extending results of this study to women without reformulation of the questions would be a serious overgeneralization.

On the other hand, if the questions were intended to identify people's attitudes toward freedom of speech for males only, this should have been made explicitly clear. For instance, the researcher might ask about a person and then specify "if a man . . . " and "if a woman . . . " were to do the following, should this be allowed or not? In this way, the referent would be absolutely clear.

3.2.2 *Use of Generic Terms for Sex-Specific Purposes*

This source of bias is caused by the use of generic terms to describe all-female or all-male groups. While I did not encounter a single example of a female term used for generic purposes (which does not mean that such terms do not exist), I did find a number of terms that sounded generic but which identified, in fact, only female or only male respondents. In the case of exclusively female referents, all of the examples I found dealt with some aspect of family or reproduction, while the use of generic terms as male referents covered a large range of areas.

We begin with an example of overgeneralization of female respondents. One frequently encountered generic term that is often employed to identify females only is "single parents." For instance, in a recent article entitled "Single Parents, Extended Households, and the Control of Adolescents," we find the following gross overgeneralization:

> Most of our analyses in this paper compare mother-only families with families containing both the biological father and the biological mother. . . . Families containing step-parents are not included in our basic analyses. . . . We also omit the few single-parent families headed by a father, thus providing a more homogeneous set of families for our comparisons. Essentially, family structure in this paper refers to

families in which the biological mother is always present and the biological father is either present or absent and not replaced by a step-father.[13]

Clearly, to identify this research as a study of single parents, given that only single mothers are considered (and that single fathers have deliberately been excluded), is highly inappropriate.

It is, however, not only the term "single parent" that is identified with mothers; the more general term "parent" is also often utilized inappropriately. For example, a study entitled "How Parents Label Objects for Young Children: The Role of Input in the Acquisition of Category Hierarchies" is, in fact, a study about how *mothers* teach concepts to their 2- to 4-year-old children, *not* about how mothers *and* fathers teach them.[14]

In the first few pages of this article, we read constantly about parents: "Parents use basic level terms much more than terms at other levels in their speech to children. ... Parents may discuss categories at different levels in ways to help children understand hierarchical organization. ... Parents often introduce basic level terms through ostensive definition. ... " and so on.[15] This use of the term "parents" continues until we come to a passage that reads:

A parent is not likely to point to an object and say, "This is a vehicle." She is much more likely to anchor at the basic level, saying, "This is a jeep; a jeep is a kind of vehicle."[16]

It is unclear whether the combination of "parent" and "she" means that the other studies cited also refer only to mothers. Since we know from other research that there are significant differences between male and female speech patterns, this would be a very important fact to establish.

When we come to the description of the author's own study, we learn that

in the two studies reported here, parents were asked to teach concepts at different levels to their 2- to 4-year-old children. In the first study, parents taught basic and superordinate concepts to their children. In the second study, another set of parents taught basic and subordinate concepts. The parents' teaching strategies were analyzed in terms of their potential usefulness for children who are attempting to learn about principles of hierarchical classification. ....[17]

It is only when we come to the description of the methods used in these two studies that we learn that the subjects in the first study were fourteen mother-child pairs, and in the second study, sixteen mother-child pairs.[18] We also learned in a footnote that

> although all requests for subjects were addressed to "parents", virtually all of the respondents were mothers. One father did volunteer, but his son refused to cooperate, and thus could not be included in the study.[19]

A similar problem is encountered with the use of the terms "fertility" or "childlessness." For example, a recent article entitled "Childlessness in Canada 1971: A Further Analysis" examines correlates of childlessness in younger and older cohorts of ever-married (that is, married, widowed, divorced, or separated) women.[20] The article overgeneralizes in that it ignores mothers who have never been married (an overgeneralization, but not a sexist one) and male fertility altogether (a sexist overgeneralization). Although this is common practice among demographers, it is sexist nonetheless to equate childlessness with female childlessness. It leaves us ignorant about male childlessness and, in this case, ignorant of half of the phenomenon purportedly under study: Husbands of wives who are childless may not be childless themselves; conversely, husbands of wives with children may never have had a biological child themselves.

Examples of the use of generic terms for male-sex-specific studies or behaviors abound. Rather than belabor the point about overgeneral language, I will provide examples of the use of generic terms for males only in later sections as we consider identification of projects, research methods, and data interpretation. It is important to note, however, the overlap between overgeneral language and an androcentric perspective that is found in the use of generic terms for male-specific studies or behaviors. One reinforces the other.

3.3 Overgeneral Titles

In the previous section, we encountered several overgeneral titles (for example, childlessness in Canada turned out to be female childlessness; parents who label objects for young children turned out to be mothers; and single parents who control adolescents [or fail to] turned out to be exclusively mothers). All of the articles to be considered in the following sections also have overgeneral titles. For instance, an article entitled "The Elderly Sick Role: An Experimental Analysis" deals with the male sick role only.[21] Similarly, an article entitled "Ability Grouping and Contextual Determinants of Educational Expectations in Israel" deals with male students only.[22] Likewise, an article entitled "Number of Siblings and Educational Mobility" deals with male mobility only.[23]

The latter article is interesting in that the context of the article itself is *not* overgeneral. The article examines the impact of the father's education on his son's schooling and finds that this influence is conditional on "sibsize" (the number of sisters and brothers). The article does identify itself as a study of male mobility, not social mobility in general, and, indeed, we remain ignorant of the influence of sibsize or mother's education on women's educational mobility. Had the article been entitled "Number of Siblings and Educational Mobility from Father to Son," overgeneralization would not be a problem here.

The formulation of accurate titles (and other means of identifying research, such as key words, abstracts, and the like) is an important step in reducing sexism in research. If all the male-oriented studies were to state explicitly in their titles that they apply to males only, a significant amount of existing social science research would be properly identified, and the problem of imbalance of knowledge concerning males and females would become visible. Likewise, if the titles of female-specific studies relating to family and reproductive issues were not overgeneralized, a similar imbalance would also become visible. Making imbalances visible is not a solution to the overriding problem of selective attention, but it is certainly an important first step. "Truth in labeling" could result not only in less overgeneralization in interpretation and method, but also, one would hope, ultimately in more inclusive research.

3.4 Overgeneral Concepts

Just as language and titles can be overgeneral, so too can a concept itself be overgeneral, beyond the level of simple language. In order to recognize whether a concept overgeneralizes, we need to identify (a) the purported referent and (b) the empirical referent within the concept. When the purported referent is general while the empirical concept is sex-specific, we are dealing with an instance of overgeneralization. For example, in the concept of "universal suffrage" as applied to the French Revolution, the purported referent is all people, since the concept uses the term "universal." In fact, the empirical referents were male only, since women did not win the vote at that time.[24] The purported referents and the empirical referents do not match; hence we are dealing with an instance of overgeneralization. Similarly, the concepts of "child-lessness" or "fertility," when they are used to cover female childlessness and fertility only, are examples of the same problem.

An example of overspecificity in a concept can be found in the title of a recent article on "Nativity, Intermarriage, and Mother-Tongue Shift."[25] The term "mother-tongue" is overspecific since it refers not necessarily to the mother's tongue, but to the language a child first learns at home: it may be his or her mother's tongue, father's tongue, or a third language altogether. Although the author states that children are "probably more likely to speak their mother's first language ... than their father's first language,"[26] the concept remains inexact and could be replaced by mother's tongue, father's tongue, or parental tongue (when the same language is shared by both parents).[27]

3.5 Overgeneral Methods

Overgeneralization in methods can occur through inappropriate wording of questions (if questions are asked of respondents) and through underspecificity in reporting on the methods employed.

3.5.1 Inappropriate Wording of Questions

In the section on the use of sex-specific terms for generic purposes
(3.2.1), we looked at one example of the wording of questions
intended to measure freedom of speech. (These questions were
taken from NORC General Social Surveys). A recent article on
urbanism and tolerance[28] used a data set based on these questions
"because they provide the most recent data using identical
wordings for items tapping tolerance."[29] These questions ask about
attitudes toward "people whose ideas are considered bad or
dangerous by other people," such as "somebody who is against all
churches and religions," "a person who believes that blacks are
genetically inferior," "a man who admits he is a Communist," "a
person who advocates doing away with elections and letting the
military run the country," and "a man who admits that he is
homosexual."

The author identifies this set of questions as "items [that] tap
respondents' willingness to allow expression of various ideas rather
than support for the ideas or the persons holding them."[30] Fair
enough, but since the context of the questions makes it clear that
"the persons holding such ideas" are males, an important dimension
of the concept of tolerance is lost. Either this loss must be
acknowledged, in which case the title as well as the discussion
must specify that this is an article examining tolerance toward
males who hold certain ideas, or women need to be included in the
wording of the questions. This could be done by identifying the
"person" as "he or she"; or by asking questions about women and
men; or by creating two questionnaires, one that referred to women
and one that referred to men, and using a split sample. The latter
two techniques would allow for an analysis of whether respondents
are more tolerant toward women or men who express various ideas,
or whether there is no such difference.

3.5.2 Overspecificity in Reporting
on the Methods Employed

Another problem one encounters from time to time is overspecificity
in the reporting on methods employed. Other related methodological
problems will be considered in the chapter on gender insensitivity.

In a recent article that employs secondary data analysis on citizen contacting in seven countries,[31] the authors use a data set from a seven-nation study by Verba, Nie, and Kim. Examples of citizen contactors are described as follows:

> unemployed workers looking for jobs, veterans with questions about military benefits, social security recipients in search of lost checks, builders seeking government contracts, and property owners angling for tax abatements are obvious instances. In developing nations, the list of contactors would also include peasants looking for access to markets, new city dwellers trying to adjust to their new living environment, and parents trying to keep their sons out of the army or looking for recommendations to help their children into universities.[32]

This list of examples might well include women. Women may be unemployed and looking for jobs, they may be social security recipients in search of lost checks, and so on. However, as one reads further, the description becomes unclear. The authors state that

> the approaches drawing on social and economic variables take no account of whether the person considering contacting believes it likely that he will succeed in affecting the political influential or whether the potential contactor has personal incentives or political obligations to help others.[33]

We then find a hypothesis that states that

> the greater the number and strength of political ties and obligations that a person has, the more likely he is to approach a government official to help himself or others. . . .[34]

and we learn that

> the variables are derived from answers to survey questions about whether or not the respondent has contacted local or extralocal

government officials or other powerful persons for help in addressing the needs of respondent, his family, friends, neighborhood, workmates, community or other social group, during the preceding two years. Particularized contacting combines local and extralocal efforts to help the contactor and his family.[35]

At this point, confusion reigns. Are female respondents included or are they not? The language suggests that they are excluded, but we cannot be sure.

On the same page, however, we stumble across a statement that suggests that indeed women were included, for we learn that individuals were ranked "by a combined measure of income and education that distinguishes sex levels on a cross-culturally equivalent scale."[36] Surely, this must mean that male and female contactors were included in the sample – possibly even some of the contactees were female? This impression is shattered by the last sentences of the article:

> The party and campaign activist is the focal point for the contacting efforts of the people around him. Because he has the political connections and the political obligations, they turn to him for political assistance. This connection becomes the structural basis of the political ties that account for much of the social contacting that exists throughout the world.[37]

If, then, women were included, the language is highly inappropriate, and the reporting on the methods employed is overspecific. Given that there are significant differences in male and female political participation, it would furthermore have been theoretically important to do an analysis by sex and to test the various variables while taking sex into account. For instance, do education and political activism have the same effect on women's likelihood of contacting as they do on men's? This is a problem of gender insensitivity and will be discussed in Chapter 4. Finally, the way in which women are ranked in terms of income and education introduces an androcentric bias as discussed in Chapter 2.

3.6 Overgeneral Data Interpretation

When language and methods are overgeneral, it is almost inevitable that data interpretation will also overgeneralize. We will here consider only two recent examples of this problem.

First, a recent article on the elderly sick role[38] reports on a small experiment in which 126 undergraduate students responded to a vignette that was experimentally manipulated. It read as follows (manipulated variables in brackets);

> Mr. A. is [forty-eight years old, seventy-eight years old]. He is a widower, and has a daughter who lives about a mile from his home. He is a veteran, and now [works as a tailor, is retired]. Recently he has complained of back trouble which he says is painful and which interferes with his normal activities.[39]

Respondents were then asked "if this man or a member of his family should ask you for advice on some of the following matters, how would you respond?"

The design is clearly oriented toward one sex: a man who is supposed to represent "the elderly." Notwithstanding this clear sex identification, the title, the discussion, the data interpretation, and the conclusions are all couched in general terms. This is evident in the following excerpts from the results and discussion sections:

> The failure to achieve any significant effects by age for the expectations of role exemption and physician utilization argues against the existence of an ascribed elderly sick role along these dimensions of the Parsonian model. ... Not depending on others or expressing need is a basic element of the socialization experience of our respondents. ... There is some evidence that younger people, both lay and professional, may be hesitant to put the aged in dependent roles ... the tendency for respondents not to expect the elderly to recover can be viewed as having a basis in reality. ... However, from a sociological point of view the ascription of a terminal sick role to the elderly is a result of stereotyping.[40]

It is particularly ironic that in a study of the sick role of the elderly the referent is male, given that there are more elderly females than males and that the sick roles of females and males are defined quite differently. To make this article nonsexist, then, either the sex of the referent individual would also have to be manipulated and the data analyzed accordingly, or the identification of the study, its data interpretation, and its conclusions would have to be restricted to the *male* elderly sick role.

Our second example comes from the education literature. The title of the article, "Ability Grouping and Contextual Determinants of Educational Expectations in Israel,"[41] suggests that this is a general article on educational expectations in Israel. In fact, this is a study of "all male Jewish students who attended eighth grade in the national Religious and National school systems during 1968/69. The sample consists of 21,289 students, who attended 957 schools."[42] Footnote 1 informs us that "since that study [the Judas Matras's Life History Study of Jewish Men] concerns men only, data were not retrieved for females or non-Jewish students. Recently, a similar Life History study of women was completed. However, the Seker files for women are not yet available."[43]

Neither the introduction to the study, nor its discussion, nor its conclusion make us aware of the fact that this is a one-sex study. The introduction states:

> This paper concerns the determinants of educational expectations among Israeli primary school students. We focus on the effects of school contexts on expectations and on the way these are conditioned by ability *grouping*. Previous research reveals small contextual effects on educational outcomes and tends to dismiss their importance in the educational attainment process.
>
> In the present study, we compare the magnitude of contextual effects on expectations in a population of contextually heterogeneous schools, some of which practice ability grouping and some of which do not. The essence of our argument is that among dissimilar schools contextual effects can be large. However, where students are grouped, contextual school effects on expectations are eliminated and are replaced, in part, by group effects.[44]

The article continues in this vein. The conclusions are also grossly overgeneral, given that only the male half of the Israeli student population was considered. Nor do we learn whether the schools were coeducational or had only male students. Since one of the crucial variables is homegeneity versus heterogeneity, this might be of special significance when discussing ability grouping. Since girls were seen as heterogeneous enough to be excluded from the study, their participation or lack of it in ability groups might at least have been mentioned.

The discussion of the results begins as follows:

> To summarize, we have shown that where schools are highly variable in student-body composition they can exert strong contextual effects on grades and educational expectations. In ungrouped Israeli schools the effects of contextual aptitude and socioeconomic status on grades are negative and serve to attenuate inequality between ethnic and socioeconomic groups. Contextual effects on educational expectations are also large, but they operate in opposite directions and offset one another.[45]

The interpretation of the data, therefore, suffers from severe overgeneralization due to the fact that girls are not considered and that this fact is not taken into account in the body of the text. It is also, one suspects, a reflection of an androcentric bias, since if this article were based on girls only, one could expect it to be entitled "Ability Grouping and Contextual Determinants of Educational Expectations for Girls in Israel."

3.7 Conclusion

Unlike identifying androcentricity in research, identifying – and rectifying – overgeneralizations or instances of overspecificity is a relatively straightforward and comparatively simple matter. While appropriate identification in language, concepts, methods, and data interpretation would not rectify all aspects of sexism in research (e.g., a lopsided attention to certain issues), it would make such phenomena more visible, thus facilitating their eventual correction.

Notes

1 The one term that might be considered an exception is "mother tongue," but since this term is used to deal with cases of "mother tongue," "father tongue," and "parent tongue," the problem is one of overspecificity rather than overgeneralization. See section 3.4.

2 R. Paul Shaw, "Humanity's propensity for warfare: A Sociobiological perspective," *Canadian Revue of Sociology and Anthropology* 22, 2 (1985): 227–232, quote p. 173.

3 Ibid., p. 176.

4 Roger Krohn, "Is sociobiology a political or research program?" *Canadian Review of Sociology and Anthropology* 22, 2 (1985): 227–232, quote p. 229.

5 John Mark Hansen, "The political economy of group membership," *American Political Science Review* 79, 1 (1985): 79–96, quoted on pp. 80 and 81.

6 Philip E. Converse, "Power and the monopoly of information," APSA Presidential Address, 1984, *American Political Science Review* 79, 1 (1985): 1–9, quote p. 2.

7 Ibid.

8 Henry W. Chappell, Jr., and William R. Keech, "A new view of political accountability for economic performance," *American Political Science Review* 79, 1 (1985): 10–27; see, e.g., pp. 13 and 15.

9 Joseph E. Stiglitz, "Information and economic analysis: A perspective," *Supplement to the Economic Journal* 95 (1985): 25.

10 Seymour Sudman and Norman M. Bradburn, *Asking Questions: A Practical Guide to Questionnaire Design* (San Francisco:Jossey-Bass,1982):1.

11 Ibid., p. 40.

12 Ibid., pp. 129–131.

13 Sanford M. Dornbush et al., "Single parents, extended households, and the control of adolescents," *Child Development* 56, 2 (1985): 326–341, quote p. 328.

14 Maureen A. Callanan, "How parents label objects for young children: The role of input in the acquisition of category hierarchies," *Child Development* 56, 2 (1985): 508–523.

15 Ibid., pp. 508–509.

16 Ibid., p. 510.

17 Ibid.

18 Ibid., pp. 510, 516.

19 Ibid., p. 510, fn. 1.

20 Nigel Tomes, "Childlessness in Canada 1971: A further analysis," *Canadian Journal of Sociology* 10, 1 (1985): pp. 37–68.

21 William Fisher, Arnold Arluke, and Jack Levin, "The elderly sick role: An experimental analysis," *International Journal of Aging and Human Development* 20,3(1984–85):161–164.

22 Yossi Shavit and Richard A. Williams, "Ability grouping and contextual determinants of educational expectations in Israel," *American Sociological Review* 50, 1 (1985): 62–73.

23 Judith Blake, "Number of siblings and educational mobility," *American Sociological Review* 50, 1 (1985): 84–95.

24 In fact, the term did not refer even to all males as class and race were hidden distinctions as well.

25 Gillian Stevens, "Nativity, intermarriage, and mother-tongue shift," *American Sociological Review* 50, 1 (1985): 74–83.

26 Ibid., p. 77.

27 This particular study dealt with children, about 10 percent of whom were "children of linguistically heterogamous marriages";ibid., p. 78, fn. 3.

28 Thomas C. Wilson, "Urbanism and tolerance: A test of some hypotheses drawn from Wirth and Stouffer," *American Sociological Review* 50, 1 (1985): 117–123.

29 Ibid., p. 119, fn. 1.

30 Ibid.

31 Alan S. Zuckerman and Darrell M. West, "The political bases of citizen contacting: A cross-national analysis," *American Political Science Review* 79, 1 (1985): 117–131.

32 Ibid., p. 117.

33 Ibid., p. 119.

34 Ibid.

35 Ibid., p. 122.

36 Ibid.

37 Ibid., p. 131.

38 Fisher, Arluke, and Levin, "The elderly sick role," pp. 161–165.

39 Ibid., p. 163.

40 Ibid., p. 164.

41 Shavit and Williams, "Ability Grouping," pp. 62–73.

42 Ibid., p. 64–65.

43 Ibid.

44 Ibid., p. 62.

45 Ibid., p. 70.

Chapter 4
Gender Insensitivity

4.1 Introduction
4.2 Ignoring sex as a socially significant variable
4.3 Failing to analyze sex-differentiated data by sex
4.4 Treating other-sex opinions as fact
4.5 Failing to consider the sex of all participants in the research process
4.6 Decontextualization
4.7 Sex-blind policy evaluations and proposals
4.8 Conclusion

4.1 Introduction

Gender insensitivity, our third primary sexist problem, is in many ways the simplest one. It appears in only one form, rather than in multiple forms, as we found with androcentricity and overgeneralization. It quite simply consists of ignoring sex as an important social variable.

Such gender insensitivity may or may not be an outgrowth of an androcentric bias. In most cases, it will be difficult or impossible to tell, because typically in a piece of work that is gender insensitive, the reader is not given sufficient information to determine, for instance, the sex of participants in the research process; it is simply regarded as too unimportant to mention.

4.2 Ignoring Sex as a Socially Significant Variable

While sifting through the various journals that provide the bulk of examples for this book, I found an entire issue of the *American Journal of Psychology* in which every single article is blind to sex as an important social variable. Of the seven substantive articles in that issue, one might potentially argue that for one of the articles,[1] sex is not an important variable (the article attempts to quantify beauty in an abstract sense). On the other hand, confirmation of any hypothesis about beauty depends on experiments in which subjects rate the beauty of various figures; one can therefore legitimately ask whether sex plays a role in determining aesthetic pleasure. The literature that is reported is not discussed in terms of a sex effect. This may either mean that the studies reported are also gender insensitive, or it may mean that these particular authors have ignored any reference to gender in their use of previously published material.

All of the other articles in this issue involve experimental subjects. One article[2] examines subjects' ability to recall prose passages read to them. The subjects are described as "104 college students who participated in the experiment as part of a course requirement. Half were enrolled in educational psychology courses at the University of Illinois, and half were enrolled in psychology courses at Millkin University."[3] No mention of the sex of the respondents is made. Given that there are observed differences in verbal ability between the sexes, one wonders why it is more important to identify the students' university affiliations than their sex. Presumably they were both female and male – but who knows?

The next article[4] examines learning of a perceptually isolated or prelearned item in a continuous series. Three experiments are reported. Subjects of the first experiment are identified as "96 student volunteers from sections of the introductory psychology course at Western Washington University. Participation was en-

couraged as part of a course requirement." Subjects in the second
experiment were presumably the same, since "Experiment 2 was in
keeping with the design of Experiment 1 except that prelearning
one of the trigrams was substituted for perceptual isolation. . . . All
other methodological features matched those described for
Experiment 1."[5] The write-up suggests that the subjects in
Experiment 3 were probably the same students as well.[6] At no point
is there any discussion of the respondents' sex.

The next article[7] investigates the relative preferences of rhesus
monkeys for reward probability versus amount. Subjects are
identified as "8 rhesus monkeys . . . with test experience. There
were 4 males and 4 females, between 4 and 6 years of age."
Experimental groups were structured to have equal female and
male participation, but the results are not analyzed (or discussed)
in terms of the sex of the subjects. While the research design is not
gender insensitive, the data interpretation is.

Another article[8] examines how stimulus probability affects
encoding. Two experiments are described. Subjects of the first
experiment are identified as "24 right-handed members of the
University of Michigan paid-subject pool."[9] Participants in the
second experiment are described as "36 right-handed members of
the University of Michigan paid-subject pool."[10] Since the sex of the
subjects is not identified, it is clear that no analysis by sex was
made.

A subsequent article[11] describes three experiments investigating
the differences between two types of spatial location memory:
memory for the location of individual items in an array, and
memory for occupied, as opposed to unoccupied, locations in an
array. Experiment 1 examined the memory of elderly adults and
young college students. Participants are described as follows:

> Participating in Experiment 1 were 52 persons, 24 community-
> dwelling elderly individuals (mean age = 69.4 years, range = 60–80
> years) and 28 undergraduate psychology students at the University of
> North Carolina at Charlotte (UNCC) (mean age = 21.2 years, range =
> 17–30 years). College students were given course credit for participating.
> The older group was made up of volunteers recruited from the
> "Charlotte Senior Scholars" organization and from UNCC's summer
> "Elderhostel" program.[12]

Experiment 2 was undertaken to replicate the findings of Experiment 1 and to compare item location memory and occupied location memory for objects and matched words. Subjects are described as follows:

> Participating in Experiment 2 were 96 persons: 48 community-dwelling elderly individuals (mean age = 68.2 years, range = 59–80 years) and 48 students from the University of North Carolina at Charlotte (mean age = 19.0 years, range = 17–25 years). Elderly individuals were obtained in response to a newspaper story indicating the need for participants. All subjects were paid for their participation.[13]

Experiment 3 examined memory for occupied locations independent of item location and location memory. Participants in this last experiment were described as follows:

> Because the analyses of Experiments 1 and 2 evinced no interactions of age and memory for occupied locations, only college students were tested in Experiment 3. Participants were 48 undergraduates (mean age = 20.4 years, range 17–24 years) from the University of North Carolina at Charlotte. Subjects were either paid or given course credit for participation.

The study concludes that

> spatial memory is not a simple, global process. Different components of spatial memory may be affected differently by variations in stimulus characteristics or experimental design, and these components may or may not interact with each other depending upon the demands of specific tasks."[14]

It seems reasonable to ask whether the sex of the person remembering has any effect on the memory, particularly given the fact that differences in spatial–visual abilities are one of the few consistently documented sex differences.[15] Since the data are not analyzed by sex (assuming that both sexes participated, as seems likely), the question remains unanswered. The final article[16] exhibits the same pattern as the preceding ones. Six experiments are described, and in each case, the identification of subjects is sketchy and inconsistent, but always gender insensitive.

Looking at these articles as a group, and knowing full well that such articles are usually written in isolation from one another (but are nevertheless indicative of the editorial policy of the journal), we can see that the subjects are described generally in an extremely poor, nonstandardized manner, ranging from simple numbers ("46 observers") to identification of *how* they were chosen, whether or not they were paid, which university or organization they belonged to, their age, whether they were right-handed or not, whether they had participated in a previous experiment or not, and so on. In the case of the article on the rhesus monkeys, the sex of the subjects was identified, but in the six articles dealing with humans, not a single one specified the sex of its subjects. One is thus inclined to assume that sex may be of some importance when studying monkeys (but not enough to warrant an analysis), while for the study of humans, sex is not important (in fact, it is considered so irrelevant that it is not even mentioned).

One should not suppose that only psychology can be gender insensitive; in fact, such insensitivity can be found in all of the social sciences. Linda Christiansen-Ruffman has reported in a study of articles on participation in voluntary organizations that in

all volumes (1972–1983) of the *Journal of Voluntary Action Research* ... the vast majority of articles have ignored gender almost totally. In 232 of the 260 articles or 89%, sex or gender was neither a prime nor secondary analytic focus.[17]

In spite of the relative ease in collecting data on sex or gender, only 11% included this variable as part of analysis, and the variable received only very minimal attention in a number of the 17 cases in which gender was treated as one of the secondary foci. This lack of attention is not unique to this particular journal. In examining the participation literature contained in the Abstracts of the Association for Voluntary Action Scholars for the first three issues and for the most recent issue, the percentages were even lower than the Journal in terms of a focus on women.[18]

After examining all of the articles that focus on sex and/or gender (whether this was mentioned in the title or not) and all articles devoted to women, the author concludes:

> Thus women are not only relatively invisible, but theories of participation are not applicable in some of the few times when research is reported. ... The confusion and ambiguity in language (does "he" refer to a male person or to any person) reflects and is symptomatic of an analytic confusion.[19]

As a final example of the confusion and inaccuracy of gender-insensitive research, we shall consider a study of out-migration and subsequent return migration from and to Newfoundland.[20] This study reports on a survey of Newfoundland returnees (55 percent male, 47 percent female) and on additional data collected in the Bay of Islands in 1981 and 1982. At some point it is noted that "66 persons" were interviewed,[21] so presumably this constitutes the sample mentioned later.[22] We learn that, according to another survey, "63 percent of males and 55 percent of females had emigrated. In turn, 62 percent of migrant males and 48 percent of females returned."[23] This is a significant difference in return rates. It would have been most interesting to learn how many of the 66 "persons" were males and females, but we are not given this information. Instead, we find some tables that identify the occupational status of returned migrants (a table that does not include the category "housewife"), as well as another table that lists reasons for leaving Newfoundland. In this table, "family matters" are listed as reasons in only 5.5 percent of the cases, which suggests that perhaps all the "persons" were men? In any case, there is no breakdown by sex in the tables and none that can be reconstructed from the text. For example, we learn that the savings migrants brought with them "tend to be modest."[24] Given earning differentials between women and men, one would assume that there would be a significant difference in amounts saved by men and by women, but there is no way to determine this.

There is also a table on motivation for return migration, which lists as reasons "household head unemployed" and "household head didn't like job."[25] It remains unclear who is a household head.

The unemployed male? The female if she is not married? The employed female? A passage preceding this particular table only compounds the confusion:

> Half of surveyed household heads reported unemployment at some time of each year since returning, and nearly 30 percent were unemployed at the time of the 1979 survey. (An equivalent percentage of respondents' spouses were also unemployed at this time.)[26]

Although we do not know the sex composition of the sample, we can be reasonably sure that it includes men (or consists entirely of men); if it included only women, the sample would have been characterized as female. At least some – possibly all – household heads were married (they had spouses according to the preceding quotation); one can assume that they were male, since the usual practice is to define the male as the head of household and the wife as the spouse, rather than the other way around. However, this distinction remains unclear, and the information that can be gleaned from this article is thus, like the migrants' savings, very modest.

4.3　Failing to Analyze Sex-Differentiated Data by Sex

Sometimes, data are collected on both sexes but the analysis fails to take sex into account. One example is a study that examines the relationship among coping resources, life changes, and negative changes in health among the elderly.[27] The sample on which this study is based consisted of 132 males and 167 females. Coping resources examined were: self-efficacy, religiosity, social resources, marital status, occupational status, and income. The results are described as follows:

> The results of the present study suggest that of the several variables often cited in the literature as coping resources, only one of them,

income, seems to serve this function for the elderly. Social resources, religiosity, marriage, and the presence of a confidant were not significantly related to illness, either as a main effect or in interaction with life change. And, although feelings of self-efficacy and occupational status both showed significant salutory main effects, during times of high life change they appear to be coping inhibitors. For the elderly, it seems that possessing these characteristics serves to impede rather than facilitate an effective coping response.[28]

In speculating on the meaning of these findings, the authors offer several hypotheses, such as the following, to explain the failure of high occupational status to function as a coping resource:

One might speculate that the latter finding is a function of the fact that high status persons suffer greater loss of ego in the face of the unavoidable and potentially humiliating life events that accompany old age (e.g., retirement, physical impairment, moving to a care facility). The life changes in old age are, in a sense, powerful status levellers. . . . Any such status leveling or shifting to new status criteria would involve more loss for individuals of high occupational status than for those of low occupational status.[29]

Had the data been analyzed separately by sex of respondent, it is conceivable that the pattern found would have been different, since men tend to have higher-status occupations (and thus presumably will experience greater leveling) than women. Until the data are analyzed by sex, we cannot place much confidence in these conclusions. Similarly, the fact that marital status had no effect as a coping resource could mean that it truly is not a coping resource for either women or men; it could also mean that it has a negative effect on one sex and a positive effect on the other, effects that cancel each other out when the analysis is done on both sexes together. This latter hypothesis is suggested by the fairly consistent findings that marriage tends to place greater demands on women than on men. In addition, given that men tend to marry women who are younger than themselves, and that women live, on average, longer than men, it is reasonable to assume that many of the married women had to care for their husbands (who were older than they were), while few of the men would have had to care in the same manner for their wives.

Neglect of sex as an analytic variable, like other sexist research practices, can be found in all areas of the social sciences. In political science, we find a similar example: Sidney Verba and Norman Nie's study of political participation in America.[30] In this study, Verba and Nie developed six measures of participation in order to score a variety of groups for "over-" or "under-" representation in political participation. The total extent of Verba and Nie's discussion of female–male differences in participation is the conclusion that "men are somewhat over-represented in the most activist political groups but not to a very great degree."[31] However, as Judith Hicks Stiehm notes in her critique of Verba and Nie's work, the authors do find differences in the participation of blacks and whites "to be both important and interesting."

A full chapter is devoted to their analysis. But what did the data show? What did the table look like which produced these conclusions? Black-white differences on the six measures varied from 4–27%. There was a 15% average difference. Female-male differences ranged from 11 to 28% with a 19% average difference. Female-male differences were clearly greater than black-white yet the female-male data were essentially disregarded while the black-white data were carefully discussed.[32]

Stiehm also notes that this volume won an American Political Science Association Award as the best new book in its field, and that it was especially commended for its methodology.[33] Gender insensitivity indeed!

Failing to analyze data by sex when they have been collected on both sexes may thus severely limit the utility of any findings and may, in fact, hide some of the most important aspects of a phenomenon. This would be true for all cases in which there is a significant social difference between the sexes. Because gender only rarely does *not* serve as a differentiating variable, the only safe course to take is to routinely analyze data by sex; if and only when it is shown empirically to be insignificant, collapse the data.[34]

Failing to do so can have not only serious theoretical consequences, but even more serious policy consequences as well. Constantina Safilios-Rothschild has documented this point in an overview article on women's invisibility in agriculture.[35] She notes that census statistics indicate that in most sub-Saharan countries, from two-fifths to over half of those economically active in agriculture are women, yet women's role in agriculture is nonetheless minimized.[36] Turning to Sierra Leone as a case study, she notes that

> the available statistics indicate that 45% of persons economically active in agriculture in 1970–71 were women, and research undertaken in different districts and chiefdoms suggests that most of these women were not unpaid family workers. Despite the very active role that women play in agriculture in Sierra Leone, international development agencies still view them primarily as unpaid farm labor responsible only for time-consuming and unskilled tasks such as weeding. Women farmers and women's active involvement in agriculture usually remain invisible because data on farmers are not disaggregated by sex in agricultural mission reports and feasibility studies.[37]

She then discusses an evaluation study that underlined the fact that women farmers are not only auxiliary farm workers but independent farmers in their own right, involved in the cultivation of cash crops – and not only in subsistence agriculture. Despite this fact, ongoing agricultural development programs are overwhelmingly directed to male farmers.

Here we are dealing not only with a problem of gender insensitivity, but also with androcentric bias, because the criteria used to determine eligibility for participation in the project are geared toward male and not female farmers. The problem is compounded by methodological bias: "The project did not keep information on the gender of the registered (or participating) farmers, and for this reason it was possible to believe that the project was reaching all farmers regardless of sex."[38] Being gender sensitive is certainly no guarantee of nonsexist policies, but it is a necessary precondition for assessing the degree of sexism in a given policy or project.

4.4 Treating Other-Sex Opinions as Fact

So far, we have looked at examples of gender insensitivity that are characterized primarily by failing to take sex into account. There is another, less obvious, form of gender insensitivity, in which a researcher asks members of one sex questions about both sexes and treats the answers as facts rather than opinions. While it is not wrong to ask males about their opinions of females and vice versa, it is wrong to treat answers about the other sex as if they were facts rather than opinions.

For example, in Chapter 2 (Androcentricity) we looked briefly at an ethnographic account of the Yanomamo, the "fierce people." We found that the study was conducted from a male viewpoint. The author, Chagnon, used two main informants to aid him in gathering his data. Not surprisingly, both were men. Given that the Yanomamo have a patriarchal, misogynist culture, there is a distinct possibility that Chagnon would not have been able to use women as informants had he wanted to do so. Likewise, a hypothetical female coresearcher might have been denied access to the village altogether. Practical problems in contacting women directly therefore surely existed. Nevertheless, the author should acknowledge the inevitable bias that derives from using male informants only. This acknowledgment is missing.

Instead, when discussing the subject of spousal infidelity, Chagnon describes his chief informant's marriage as follows: "She [the wife] and Kaobawa have a very tranquil household. He only beats her once in a while and never very hard. She never has affairs with other men."[39] Obviously (or so one would think), in an investigation of female infidelity in marriage, the husband is probably the least authoritative source. The only logical person to ask is the woman herself, especially when the penalty for female infidelity may be severe abuse and disfigurement. In this case, the wife might not have described their household as "very tranquil," since the family violence is directed at her. The source of information is also an important issue in historical research. All efforts should be made to gather information from a variety of sources. In those cases in which data are available from only one sex, this fact should be acknowledged and its implications explored.

Looking at another article already cited in Chapter 3 (Over-generalization), the study of single parents and the control of adolescents, we find that the interviewers asked the adolescent and one of the parents to answer independently four questions on decision making. The answers of the adolescent and the parent were then combined, as were answers that referred to the separate influence of the mother and the father, so that the parents are treated as a unit.[40]

This latter practice – conflating the mother's and father's opinions into a single "parental" attitude – is an example of familism, which will be discussed in Chapter 6. However, the practice of asking one spouse about the other seems to be sometimes acceptable within certain areas of investigation. For example, in family decision-making research, the woman will sometimes be asked who makes the decisions in her family: her husband, herself, or both of them.[41] This practice continues although we know that the responses of wives and husbands often differ considerably.[42] Compare this to asking respondents not only about their own voting behavior, but also about that of other household members. How much trust would we put in the accuracy of data generated in such a manner, beyond regarding them as perceptions that may or may not be in accord with reality?

4.5 Failing to Consider the Sex of All Participants in the Research Process

The two examples we have just looked at are really specialized instances of a more generalized problem: a failure to consider the sex of all the participants in the research process. These referred to informants in an ethnographic study and respondents in a social-psychological study. Depending on the type of study, there may be the following participants:

- the research subjects or respondents
- the researcher or research team
- the experimenter(s)

- experimenter(s)' confederate(s) in experimental research

- interviewers

- informants

- authors of statements (e.g., in historical research)

- sexually identified stimuli (e.g., cue cards that depict females and/or males in various situations, girl or boy dolls, animals identified as female or male, and so on)

We have already discussed the need to take the sex of research subjects, respondents, and informants into account. The sex of the researcher or of the members of the research team may also be important, depending on whether there is any direct interaction between the researcher and the subjects of the study. It is probably not important in statistical analyses, for example, assuming that other potential sources of sexism have been eliminated from the research process.

On the other hand, where researchers interact directly in some form with their respondents, the sex of the researchers may be important, depending on the subject under investigation. The same applies to interviewers. In some areas of investigation, it has been shown that the information obtained by male and female interviewers is comparable; in areas that are differentially sensitive for members of the two sexes (such as incest, abuse, battering, prostitution, sexual behaviors, infertility, male–female relations in general, and feminism), responses may vary with the sex of the interviewer. In all cases in which participant observation methods are employed, the sex of the researcher will be significant. While it will not always be possible to control for the sex of interviewers and researchers due to practical constraints, at a minimum the sex of the researcher-interviewer should be explicitly mentioned and possible effects should be considered.

Parallel comments apply to the role of experimenters or experimenters' confederates. It is a very well documented fact that subjects may respond differently according to the sex of experimenters and other participants in the research process.[43] In addition, there is evidence to show that experimenters behave differently toward subjects on the basis of their sex.

> Because experimenters behave differently to male and female
> subjects even while administering the same formally approved
> procedures, male and female subjects may, psychologically, simply
> not be in the same experiment at all. In order to assess the extent to
> which obtained sex differences have been due to differential behavior
> toward male and female subjects, it would be necessary to compare
> sex differences obtained in those studies that depended for their data
> on a personal interaction with the subject and those that did not.[44]

Finally, the argument for identifying and controlling for sexually
identified cues or stimuli in experiments is parallel to that for being
sensitive to the gender of participants in the research process: it is
simply a matter of accuracy and clarity to control for the sex of all
visual, material, and other cues.

4.6 Decontextualization

So long as the social positions of males and females are significantly
different, it will be necessary to recognize that a given situation may
have very different meanings and implications for the members of
each sex. For instance, marriage has very different implications and
consequences for women than it does for men.[45] Likewise, divorce
tends to be a very different experience for the female and the male
involved in it.[46] Similar arguments have been made about political
participation,[47] participation in education,[48] and the experience of
particular residential locations.[49] Failing to ask whether a situation
has different implications for females and males affected by it is
another common form of gender insensitivity.

Let us consider the example of an alternative model to explain the
emergence and development of nineteenth-century industrialization.[50] Among other things, the authors note that

> the central and defining experience of each new generation was
> automatic and collective induction into local industry. Young people
> in these regions seemed to absorb the knowledge required in
> production incidentally, as a natural part of growing up.

At the same time youngsters in these districts learned about products and production methods, they learned the rules of competition and whom they could trust to abide by them. ... This was as important for those who spent their working lives inside large firms as for those who went into business for themselves. For instance, at the same time as the "cellar lad" starting out in Sheffield steelworks imbibed knowledge about metallurgical materials and methods, he learned to appraise the character of his workmates and superiors.[51]

In the nineteenth century, there were also many girls and women working in various local industries. While at its beginning the quoted passage seems applicable to all workers, toward the end it takes on a distinctly male character: the "cellar lad ... he learned." However, the article continues to speak in general terms:

In a world where youngsters were often trained to study character as a condition of economic survival it was important to maintain a character that would bear scrutiny. ...

Thus the process of socialization created a community across and within generations that protected the economy as a whole against the consequences of short-term calculations of advantage. ...

But this experience of community went hand in hand with the expectation that exceptional talent and drive would be rewarded.[52]

It is likely that females could *not* expect that their exceptional talent and drive would be rewarded in the same manner in which males could. The authors thus ignore one entire dimension of the issue they are discussing by failing to ask about the situation of females versus that of males involved in industry in the nineteenth century. By ignoring this context, the authors fail to see that, although both males and females participated in industry, their experiences were likely to be sharply divergent.

In another example we find an example of gender insensitivity that overlaps with androcentricity. The question at issue is what causes observed male/female income disparity. The authors posit what they call the "marriage asymmetry hypothesis" against the "employer discrimination hypothesis." The former maintains that

marriage enhances male and reduces female incomes, because of
unequal child and house care responsibilities, and because the
marriage partners act as a team, in effect raising total incomes, which
are misleadingly assigned to the husband alone by our statisticians.[53]

This argument hinges on a comparison of the average annual
earnings of full-time male and female married and unmarried
workers. The authors find that the wage differential between
unmarried male and female workers is much smaller than that
between married male and female workers.

There are at least two problems with this analysis. First of all, the
vast majority of women and men marry at some point. Since the
analysis contrasts only never-married workers against all others
(including those who have married but are then divorced or
widowed), the authors have ruled out well over 90 percent of the
relevant population as irrelevant, hardly a useful approach. More
important, the men and the women who never marry during their
entire lifetime constitute very different groups, as Jessie Bernard
has pointed out:

> By and large, both men and women tend to marry mates with the
> same general class and cultural background; there is "homogamy."
> But within that common background, men tend to marry women
> slightly below them in such measurable items as age, education, and
> occupation, and, presumably, in other as yet unmeasurable items as
> well. The result is that there is no one for the men at the bottom to
> marry, no one to look up to them. Conversely, there is no one for the
> women at the top to look up to; there are no men who are superior to
> them.[54]

Thus she characterizes the never-married women as the "cream-of-
the-crop" and the never-married men as the "bottom-of-the-barrel."

By ignoring the context of being unmarried, the study's conclusions
about the effect of sex on wages are highly misleading. In addition,
the researchers' findings in favor of the "marriage assymetry
hypothesis" in effect deny that there is wage discrimination on the
basis of sex, thereby protecting male interests. The study thus
suffers from androcentric bias as well.

4.7 Sex-Blind Policy Evaluations and Proposals

A particularly important subform of contextual gender insensitivity emerges in studies that either concern policy directly or have policy implications. One example is provided by the recent report of the Royal Commission on the Economic Union and Development Prospects for Canada.[55] The Commission recommends, among other things, free trade between the United States and Canada. This would cause, among other things, the loss of jobs in the manufacturing and service sectors.[56] These losses would occur primarily in sectors that have high concentrations of female workers: textiles, clothing, small electrical products, sporting goods, toys and games, and leather products. Two-thirds of the workers in these six industries are women. Benefits from free trade are expected for urban transit and forestry products, sectors dominated by men.

The Commission does recommend substantial temporary adjustment policies to retrain and relocate displaced workers who are suitably adaptable. However, this requires that workers indicate a "willingness to undertake adaptive behaviour"; this usually translates into a readiness to relocate. For married women this is often a virtual impossibility, since most families live where employment is available to males simply because the males are better paid.

This report thus proposes a policy that promises to have disproportionately disadvantageous consequences for women, and it offers a remedy for these consequences that would be available only on a very restricted basis. A nonsexist approach would have recognized the differential effect and either not recommended this particular policy or else suggested compensatory policies that would be tailored to the needs of the sex most disadvantaged.

4.8 Conclusion

Gender insensitivity appears essentially in one form: ignoring sex as a socially important variable. This silence about sex often makes it impossible to determine whether other sexist problems (e.g., androcentricity or overgeneralization) are present as well. Because of this, overcoming gender insensitivity is an important precondition for identifying and correcting other forms of sexism in research. One derivative form of gender insensitivity, familism, is so important that it will be discussed in greater detail in Chapter 6.

Notes

1 Frank Boselie and Emanuel Leeuwenber, "Birkhoff revisited: Beauty as a function of effect and means," *American Journal of Psychology* 98, 1 (1985): 1–40.

2 Stephen G. Whilhite, "Differential effects of high-level and low-level postpassage questions," *American Journal of Psychology* 98, 1 (1985): 41–58.

3 Ibid., p. 43.

4 Louis G. Lipman, "Serial isolation and response production," *American Journal of Psychology* 98, 1 (1985): 59–76.

5 Ibid., p. 66.

6 Ibid., p. 71.

7 Charles W. Hill and Arthur J. Riopelle, "Probability-reward preferences of rhesus monkeys," *American Journal of Psychology* 98, 1 (1985): 77–84.

8 David E. Irwin and Robert G. Pachella, "Effects of stimulus probability and visual similarity on stimulus encoding," *American Journal of Psychology* 98, 1 (1985): 84–100.

9 Ibid., p. 87.

10 Ibid., p. 92.

11 Thomas J. Puglisi, Denise Cortis Park, Anderson D. Smith, and Gregory W. Hill, "Memory for two types of spatial location: Effects of instruments, age and format," *American Journal of Psychology* 98, 1 (1985): 101–118.

12 Ibid., p. 104.

13 Ibid., p. 108.

14 Ibid., p. 115.

15 This belief may be ill-founded, however. New research has questioned whether sex-related differences in spatial abilities actually do exist; see Paula J. Caplan, Gael M. Macpherson, and Patricia Tobin, "Do sex-related differences in spatial abilities exist? A multilevel critique with new data," *American Psychologist* 40, 7 (1985): 786–799.

16 Jose Aparecida Da Silva, "Scales for perceived egocentric distance in a large open field: Comparison of three psychophysical methods," *American Journal of Psychology* 98, 1 (1985): 119–144.

17 Linda Christiansen-Ruffman, "Participation theory and the methodological construction of invisible women: Feminism's call for appropriate methodology," *Journal of Voluntary Action Research* 14, 2–3 (1985): 96.

18 Ibid., fn. 6, p. 107.

19 Ibid., p. 96–97.

20 Barnett Richling, "'You'd never starve here': Return migration to rural Newfound-land," *Canadian Review of Sociology and Anthropology* 22, 2 (1985): 236–249.

21 Ibid., p. 238.

22 Ibid., p. 243.

23 Ibid., p. 237.

24 Ibid., p. 245.

25 Ibid., p. 244.

26 Ibid., p. 237.

27 Ronald L. Simons and Gale E. West, "Life changes, coping resources, and health among the elderly," *International Journal of Aging and Human Development* 20, 3 (1984–85): 173–189.

28 Ibid., p. 183.

29 Ibid.

30 Sidney Verba and Norman Nie, *Participation in America* (New York: Harper & Row, 1972). This is not as recent an example as the others cited but is included because of the important place this study occupies in American political science.

31 Verba and Nie, *Participation*, pp. 98–101.

32 Judith Hicks Stiehm, "The unit of political analysis: Our Aristotelian hangover," in Sandra Harding and Merrill B. Hintikka (eds.), *Discovering Reality: Feminist Perspectives on Epistemology, Metaphysics, Methodology, and Philosophy of Science* (Dordrecht: D. Reidel, 1983): 31–44; quote from p. 33.

33 Ibid., p. 32.

34 It should be noted that a finding of sex similarity often is significant in its own right.

35 Constantina Safilios-Rothschild, "The persistence of women's invisibility in agriculture: Theoretical and policy lessons from Lesotho and Sierra Leone," *Economic Development and Cultural Change* 33, 2 (1985): 299–317.

36 Ibid., p. 300.

37 Ibid., p. 307.

38 Ibid., p. 308.

39 Napoleon Chagnon, *Yanomamo: The Fierce People* (New York: Holt, Rinehart and Winston, 1977): 15. This section is based on Beaudoin's paper (see Chapter 2, note 33).

40 Sanford M. Dornbusch et al., "Single parents, extended households, and the control of adolescents," *Child Development* 56, 2 (1985): 326–341.

41 For example, see Joyce E. Elliott and William Moskoff, "Decision-making power in Romanian families," *Journal of Comparative Family Studies* 14, 1 (1983): 39–50.

42 See Craig M. Allen and Murray A. Straus, "'Final say' measures of marital power: Theoretical critique and empirical findings from five studies in the United States and India," *Journal of Comparative Family Studies* 15, 3 (1984): 329–344.

43 Robert Rosenthal, *Experimenter Effects in Behavioral Research* (New York: Irvington, 1976): 42–56. For the degree to which this is ignored, see Irwin Silverman, "The experimenter: A (still) neglected stimulus object," *Canadian Psychologist* 15, 3 (1974): 258–270.

44 Rosenthal, *Experimenter Effects*, p. 56.

45 See Jessie Bernard, *The Future of Marriage* (New York: Bantam, 1972); Lillian Rubin, *Worlds of Pain: Life in the Working-Class Family* (New York: Basic Books, 1976).

46 Lenore Weitzman, *The Divorce Revolution: The Unexpected Social and Economic Consequences for Women and Children in America* (New York: Free Press, 1985).

47 For example, Thelma McCormack, "Toward a nonsexist perspective on social and political change," in Marcia Millman and Rosabeth Moss Kanter (eds.), *Another Voice* (Garden City, NY: Doubleday, 1975): 1–32; also "Good theory or just theory? Toward a feminist philosophy of social science," *Women's Studies International Quarterly* 4, 1 (1981): 1–12. For empirical evidence see Joni Lovenduski and Jill Hills (eds.), *The Politics of the Second Electorate: Women and Public Participation* (London: Routledge and Kegan Paul, 1981).

48 For example, Jane S. Gaskell, "The reproduction of family life: Perspectives of male and female adolescents," *British Journal of Sociology of Education* 4, 1 (1983): 19–38.

49 Anne B. Shlay and Denise A. DiGregorio, "Same city, different worlds: Examining gender and work based differences in perceptions of neighborhood desirability," Cornell University, unpublished paper, n.d.

50 Charles Sabel and Jonathan Zeitlin, "Historical alternatives to mass production: Politics, markets and technology in nineteenth-century industrialization," *Past and Present* 108 (1985): 133–176.

51 Ibid., pp. 152–153.

52 Ibid., pp. 153–154.

53 Walter Block and Michael A. Walker, *On Employment Equity: A Critique of the Abella Royal Commission Report*. Focus No. 17 (Vancouver: The Fraser Institute, 1985), n. 37, p. 103.

54 Jessie Bernard, *The Future of Marriage* (New York: Bantam Books, 1972): 36.

55 Royal Commission on the Economic Union and Development Prospects for Canada, *Report* (Ottawa: Minister of Supply and Services, 1985), 3 vols.

56 This section follows the analysis by Marjorie Cohen, "The MacDonald Report and its implications for women," National Action Committee on the Status of Women, 1985. Reprinted as "Weakest to the wall," *Policy Options* 6, 10 (Dec. 1985).

Chapter 5
Double Standards

5.1 Introduction
5.2 Double standards in language
    5.2.1 Use of nonparallel terms for females and males
    5.2.2 Use of different grammatical modes for the sexes
5.3 Double standards in concepts
    5.3.1 Concepts premised on unequal treatment of equal attributes in the two sexes
    5.3.2 Asymmetrical concepts
    5.3.3 Value-laden concepts
5.4 Double standards in methods
    5.4.1 Asking different questions of the sexes
    5.4.2 Using different research instruments for the sexes
    5.4.3 Coding procedures
5.5 Double standards in data interpretation
5.6 Double standards in policy evaluations and recommendations
    5.6.1 Simple double standards in policy evaluations and recommendations
    5.6.2 Complex double standards in policy evaluations and recommendations
5.7 Conclusion

5.1 Introduction

A double standard is used when identical behaviors or situations are evaluated, treated, or measured by different criteria. Double standards can be found in language, concepts, methods, interpretation of data, and policy conclusions. The use of a double standard is often difficult to recognize because it is not necessarily introduced along overtly sexual lines, but rather in an indirect manner. Analyzing materials for the existence of a double standard therefore often involves two steps: first, determining whether any sex-based elements are present (whether overtly or indirectly), and second, establishing whether or not the situations discussed are, in fact, comparable.

5.2 Double Standards in Language

5.2.1 Use of Nonparallel Terms for Females and Males

One form of a double standard in language consists of the use of nonparallel terms for males and females in parallel situations. The expression "man and wife" is one example. The phrase should either be "husband and wife" (thus designating both spouses by their marital status) or "man and woman" (thus identifying both by their sex). The custom of referring to females by their first names, while referring to males by their last names is another. For example,

> Olive Schreiner and Havelock Ellis came to know one another during the first half of 1884. Their relationship opened formally, with an admiring but critical letter from Ellis about *African Farm*, and a grateful, rather coy response from Olive. . . . Ellis was born four years after Olive.[1]

One nonsexist way of avoiding this double standard would be to use first and last names for both female and male actors.

5.2.2 Use of Different Grammatical Modes
for the Sexes

This is a very important problem that goes far beyond the choice of language, but which can be identified easily through language. It is essentially an issue of data interpretation and may be a manifestation of either a double standard (this is certainly the case in straight grammatical terms) or androcentricity. Conceivably, a double standard might also reflect gynocentricity, but again I did not find any examples of this in the literature I reviewed.

To illustrate the problem, let us examine an anthropological description of sex roles and social sanctions in primitive societies:

> Most of the restrictions imposed by primitive societies upon a woman's freedom stem from one or another aspect of her reproductive role. Restrictions connected with pregnancy have been noted, as well as those imposed during the period after childbirth and during lactation. Among many people, limitations are placed upon the activities of women during their menstrual periods as well. Societies vary markedly, however, in the degree to which they curtail a menstruating woman's participation in social life. In a few societies, the only restriction placed upon her activities is that she may not engage in sexual intercourse. In a few other societies, menstruation involves strict seclusion and isolation. The majority of primitive peoples surround the woman with specific restrictions, leaving her free to move about with certain exceptions. Always she is forbidden sexual intercourse, frequently she may not go into the gardens, and may not participate in religious ceremonies.[2]

In this passage, women are consistently described in the passive mode. It is unclear who constitutes "society" (the active agents who place restrictions on women's activities), but according to the text, the women are the passive recipients of these restrictions. It is the grammar of the text that makes us aware that we are dealing with a particular view of the role of women that may or may not be appropriate. This becomes very obvious when we rewrite this passage and identify women as active agents rather than as passive objects to be acted upon. The rewritten passage might read as follows:

Most of the female taboos in primitive societies are directly related to one or another aspect of woman's reproductive role. Pregnancy taboos have been noted as well as post-partum taboos and taboos concerning lactation. Among many peoples, women refrain from certain activities during their menstrual periods as well. Societies vary markedly, however, in the degree to which a woman refuses to participate in social life during menstruation. In a few societies, the only activity she refuses to engage in is sexual intercourse. In a few other societies, menstruation may lead women to completely separate themselves, both physically and socially, from men. In the majority of primitive peoples, women engage only in specific withdrawals and maintain their usual social relations in all other cases. Always, however, the woman refuses to engage in sexual intercourse; frequently, she will not enter the gardens or refuses to cook for men. Her power may be such that, if she touches the man's hunting or fishing gear, calamity may befall him. She will only do so, therefore, if she wishes him ill. Finally, she may refuse to participate in certain religious ceremonies.[3]

The image that emerges from this description is substantially different from the one conveyed in the original passage. Unfortunately, we do not have sufficient information to decide which version is closer to the truth. In such a case, it would be appropriate to write up the information in a neutral manner that does not prejudge who acts and who is acted upon. A version rewritten in this manner might read as follows:

Most of the taboos concerning women in primitive societies are related to one or another aspect of woman's reproductive role. Pregnancy taboos have been noted as well as post-partum taboos and taboos concerning lactation. Among many peoples there are menstrual taboos, as well. Societies vary markedly, however, in the type of menstrual taboos that are prevalent. In a few societies, the only female taboo is one on sexual intercourse. In a few other societies, menstruation involves strict seclusion and isolation. The majority of primitive peoples have specific taboos for women, leaving them free to move about with certain exceptions. Always, there is a sexual intercourse taboo; frequently, there is a gardening taboo, a cooking taboo or a taboo against touching the male's hunting and fishing gear, and a taboo on participation in religious ceremonies.[4]

This version leaves open the question of who acts and who is being acted upon.

It is therefore important to look at the grammatical structure of scholarly writing in order to recognize implicitly sex-related statements that are being made through the language. Writers should write in the active mode about both sexes, rather than treating one sex in the active voice and the other in the passive. Such shifts will certainly require new forms of data collection as well as new interpretations of data already collected. For instance, when dealing with victims, it emphatically does not mean that one may imply – through use of language – that victims cooperate in their victimization. Instead, it means examining the situation from the victim's perspective in order to express the victim's resistance, helplessness, fear, rage, or mute acceptance of the situation. Writing about both sexes in the active voice reinforces the need to examine a given a situation from each sex's perspective.

5.3 Double Standards in Concepts

5.3.1 Concepts Premised on Unequal Treatment of Equal Attributes in the Two Sexes

The most basic form of a double standard in concepts is an unequal treatment of equal attributes for the two sexes. The concept of "head of household" or "family head," often criticized already, provides a good example. This concept continues to be employed by scholars[5] in spite of the various criticisms that have been leveled against it. This concept is often employed without definition (as is the case with the term "family head" in the example cited here), but one assumes it means that only unmarried women living with dependent children and married men are counted as household or family heads, while married women are referred to as "spouses of head" or some such term.

If we reflect for a moment on what we do when we employ such a term, it becomes clear that this is a classic example of a concept based on a double standard. If a woman is married, she becomes the spouse of a head; if a man is married, he becomes the head. If a woman or a man is unmarried, each is a head or "unattached individual" (if no dependents live with them). The same attribute – being married – thus has different consequences for women than it does for men.

This tradition of assigning different labels to men and women stems from a time when men were considered to be the "breadwinners" of their families and wives were considered to be their husbands' dependents. Whether historically the concept was always used appropriately is not a question to be examined here;[6] there is no doubt, however, that it is an inappropriate term for wives who have legal equality with their husbands or independent incomes, whether this be through their earnings or through some other means. On the other hand, for some historical analyses the concept will adequately reflect the social reality of the time.

Identifying all married men as heads of household or family therefore creates not only a double standard for married women; it is also inaccurate when applied to married men who share financial responsibility for their households/families with their wives. A few may even be at home, fulfilling the role traditionally reserved for the "spouse of head." Typically, once such a concept has been introduced and accepted, data analysis is then based on this concept. This means that very different categories may be treated as if they were comparable.

5.3.2 Asymmetrical Concepts

Another form of a double standard at the level of concept formation consists of the coining and use of asymmetrical, one-sided terms. For example, the concept of the "schizophrenogenic mother,"[7] if not coupled with a concept of the "schizophrenogenic father," is asymmetrical, since it directs us to look at the mother for tendencies that may foster schizophrenia and not look at the father. Such asymmetrical concepts can have serious consequences for theory development, as manifested in the pervasive tendency toward mother-blaming in psychological literature. We find two similar instances in the use of, first, the concept of "unwed mother" when it is not coupled with the concept of "unwed father," and second, the term "maternal deprivation" to describe mothers who do not look after their children on a full-time basis, when the equivalent behavior by fathers is not identified as "paternal deprivation."

In order to recognize this type of double standard, we therefore need to ask whether a concept describes a situation, trait, or behavior that could theoretically be found in both sexes. Where the concern is found to be applicable to both sexes but identified with only one, asymmetry exists. The solution is to use a symmetrical pair of concepts (such as schizophrenogenic father and mother, or paternal and maternal deprivation). This implies, of course, that identical research instruments must be used for both sexes.[8]

5.3.3 Value-Laden Concepts

Another form of a double standard in concepts is a differential value judgment of an existing sex difference in a conceptual pair. For example, Dale Spender[9] suggests that the conceptual pair of "field independence" and "field dependence" (that is, ability to be more aware or less aware of a printed number within a particular context) contains a clear value judgment because independence is generally more highly valued than dependence is. This distinction also happens to coincide with a secondary sex difference: men are more likely to be field-independent, while women are more likely to be field-dependent. If we reverse the value judgment, by labeling what is now identified as "field independence" as "context blindness" and changing "field dependence" into "context awareness," the implied value judgment becomes clear.

A similar problem arises with the conceptual pair of "primary earner" and "secondary earner." These terms correspond roughly to employed married men and employed single adults (primary earners) and to employed married women and youths (secondary earners). The value hierarchy is explicitly expressed. In practice this distinction tends to follow sexual lines for married people, although it is sometimes justified by higher income. Since women are unlikely to *choose* to be paid less than men, the categorization thus adds insult to injury. This use of a double standard becomes particularly pernicious when this conceptual pair is utilized to justify the disentitlement of "secondary earners" from certain public programs, such as Unemployment Insurance. At this point we can see how the use of a double standard overlaps with androcentricity, where male interests are maintained at the expense of female interests.

5.4 Double Standards in Methods

5.4.1 Asking Different Questions of the Sexes

In research, we ask questions both in a direct manner and in an indirect manner. If we ask direct questions, we actually address them to a person. More fundamental, however, are the indirect questions underlying such direct questions. These emerge from our research interests and direct our choice of subject matter.

If we find that the sexes are consistently asked different questions even when the circumstances are equivalent, we are dealing with a double standard in the formulation of research questions. For example, children generally have two parents, a mother and a father, but often only the mother's influence on the child's psychosocial development is examined. Such a one-sided approach leads inevitably to one-sided data, which will, inevitably, lead to inappropriate interpretations.

An example of this double standard is found in mother blaming. A recent overview article provides a systematic analysis of psychiatric and psychological journals concerning the etiology of psycho-pathology by examining how mothers and fathers are treated – differently or the same – in the literature explaining psycho-pathology.[10] The authors read and classified a total of 125 journal articles; they found that altogether 37,492 (or 72 percent of the total) words were used to describe the mothers, versus 14,416 (28 percent of the total) words used to describe the fathers. Moreover,

> Specific examples of problems in which the mother or the father was mentioned were noted, and a mother:father ratio was computed. That ratio was 346:73 – or almost 5:1 – in the 125 articles. In other words, when authors wanted to illustrate some problem or other, and when they used only mother or father for this purpose, they chose father only 17% of the time.[11]

If we ask different questions of the two sexes, we will receive different answers about them. In 28% of the articles examined, the mother was the only parent investigated for psychopathology or a contribution to the child's problem. This stands in stark contrast to the total absence of articles in which only the father was investigated in this way.

Related to this is that 82% of articles included information about the mother's psychological functioning. Information was given about the father's psychological functioning in 54%. Problems were said to be found with the mother, with no description given of how these conclusions were reached, in 62% of articles; similar reports with respect to the father were found in only 26%.[12]

In addition to the bias introduced by asking different questions about the sexes, implicit questions – those that are not posed directly to respondents by which implicitly underlie the research – can also introduce a double standard. Such a double standard can be difficult to identify because it reveals itself, not in the questions asked, but in the interpretation of the data. For example, a companion article by the same two authors[13] provides examples of the unequal provision of information about mothers and fathers that is due to implicit, unformulated questions. No systematic comparison between the sexes is made; instead, different bits of information are offered for each sex. This is demonstrated in the following quote:

> For instance, at the beginning of a case history, the following was noted: "The father, a brick layer, was 35 yr old when the patient was born. He is healthy. The mother was 33 yr old when the patient was born; she is 'nervous.'" ...[14] The father is described in terms of his occupation, then his age, and then a positive statement about his (apparently physical) health; the mother is described in terms of her age and a negative comment about her emotional functioning. Later in that article, the authors write that the father hit the child and was very dominating and that the patient cried every time he talked about his father and feared that his father did not love him. One can only speculate why, if the father treated his disturbed son this way, the father is described at the start of the case history in terms of his occupation and his physical health, whereas the mother is described only as "nervous." After three case histories – the most vivid by far being the one just described – the authors reached the following conclusion: "Mothers of patients with Klinefelter's syndrome are often overprotective or anxious. ... The behavior disturbance may start at the age of 4–5 if their mothers do not protect them or take care of them.[15]

> Such a conclusion is particularly intriguing in view of the fact that the mothers in the case histories were described as overprotective and anxious, and the only serious psychopathology noted for any parent was that of the father just described.[16]

Thus it is not the questions themselves, but the assumptions implicit in those questions, that introduces the double standard.

5.4.2 *Using Different Research Instruments for the Sexes*

Whenever a study utilizes different instruments for the two sexes, unless it concerns research about a sexually determined biological factor, we are dealing with an application of a double standard. A very obvious example is the use of two different versions of a questionnaire constructed for male and female respondents. This seems to be less common today than it was in the past. However, one way in which a double standard is still routinely practiced in the construction of research instruments hinges on the question of the socioeconomic status of respondents.

The issue of nonsexist approaches to social stratification is a thorny and hotly debated one.[17] At present, no satisfactory alternatives to the current (sexist) approaches have yet been developed, in spite of considerable efforts to that end.[18] Nevertheless, many social scientists continue to use some measure of socio-economic status or social class that is sexist in some respect. The brief discussion offered here should not be mistaken as an effort to discuss this issue fully.

In the previously discussed article by Dornbush and others on the control of adolescents,

> Each adolescent was assigned to a group in terms of the education of the father or male guardian or, in the absence of a father or male guardian, the education of the mother or female guardian.[19]

In other words, the measurement of education (which is part of the measure of social class used in this article) always carries a value for a male parent or guardian but a zero value for a mother or female guardian when a male counterpart is present. This is particularly problematic when we consider the role of the guardian. Where there is a male guardian, there is no information about whether the child lives with him. Presumably, the child lives with the mother (single fathers were excluded from the study), yet the male guardian is seen as more important in establishing the social class of the adolescent than is the mother with whom the child actually lives.

We learn, further along in the text, that

> when we control for family income, no comparisons are possible within the high-income group because of the limited number of mother-only households with high incomes. ... Repeating this analysis for parental education gives results that are similar to those when family income is the measure of status. Controlling for measures of social class does not affect the consistent relationship between mother-only households and higher rates of adolescent deviance.[20]

It is unclear who or what has been compared with respect to social class: some present fathers versus some absent male guardians versus some present mothers?

As stated, critiques of such practices have been frequent, while solutions to this problem are more difficult to offer. However, in a simple case such as the one offered above, it should be possible to classify both parents in terms of their education, thus avoiding a double standard in measurement through differential treatment of the sexes in the research instrument.

In a specific critique of a similar practice, Judith Hicks Stiehm was able to recompute women's socioeconomic status using an alternative approach.[21] She criticizes Verba and Nie's study of political participation[22] for measuring the socioeconomic status of women and men differently. In the study, women were ranked according to a socioeconomic status index derived from data on (1) education, (2) family income, and (3) occupation of head of household. Stiehm argues:

> The rationale is that SES is not a measure of individual standing but a measure of social access or of offsprings' economic potential. The assumption is that for social activities and economic prediction the family functions as a unit and that the adult male's influence is primary. ... However, most political action is individual action. Only individuals vote or are selected for office. It would seem appropriate, then, that political scientists consider individuals as individuals. After all, a male lawyer, a female lawyer, and the wife of a male lawyer do

not enjoy equal access to political power even if they do enjoy a
similar life-style and even if their children do have similar economic
opportunities.[23]

She proceeds:

The conventional way of assigning SES is designed to yield similar
male-female status distributions. It is the argument of this paper that
if women were assigned SES independent of their male relatives,
male and female status distributions would be found to be dissimilar.
Specifically, women would almost disappear from the highest SES
categories; they would also move out of the lowest categories. Both
facts are relevant to thinking about political participation and social
policy.[24]

She then reclassifies female respondents in three different ways
with respect to their socioeconomic status and finds that in each
case the distribution shifts in very important ways, thus substantiating
her point.

The problem of inadequate ways to measure socioeconomic
status for women and men equally is not really solved by attempts
to construct two different measurement instruments.[25] It is helpful
to have instruments that are developed from and for female
samples only; such instruments – when used in a strictly sex-
specific manner – may be useful. If the result is that incumbents of
the same occupations are grouped differently depending on their
sex, however, we are dealing with another form of a double
standard that prevents us from making comparative statements
about the relative positions of the sexes.

5.4.3 Coding Procedures

A very blatant example of a double standard in methods consists in
coding identical responses differentially by sex. A prominent
example of this procedure is provided by the old Strong Vocational
Interest Blanks (no longer in use), in which different coding sheets
were used to interpret the responses of girls and boys. Boys and
girls with identical responses were consequently steered toward

different occupations, such as doctor or nurse, on the basis of identical responses. Coding methods should be uniform, as is now the case with these tests.

5.5 Double Standards in Data Interpretation

In section 5.4.1 it was observed that asking different questions of the sexes will inevitably result in distorted data interpretation. Returning to the example used in that section on the scapegoating of mothers in psychological journals, the authors observe of their review of 125 journal articles that

> the father's absence or lack of involvement with the family was noted but not said to contribute to the child's problem in 24% of articles, but in only 2% was the mother's absence or uninvolvement noted but not said to be contributory. . . . The child's pathology was attributed at least in part to the mother's activity in 82% of articles, to the mother's inactivity in 43%, to the father's activity in 43%, and to the father's inactivity in 39%.[26]

Other forms of sexism in the design of a study may also lead to a double standard in data interpretation. To return to an example discussed in the chapter on gender insensitivity (the study of Newfoundland migration patterns), we learn that

> male Newfoundlanders residing on the mainland tend to participate more in the work force than do other Canadians or Newfoundlanders remaining at home, while experiencing unemployment rates similar to those of mainlanders. For male returnees to Newfoundland, on the other hand, rates of unemployment are the highest for any provincial group. Moreover, nearly 20 per cent of male returnees eventually drop out of the work force entirely.[27]

While we learn about unemployment among the male emigrants, we do not learn about it among the female emigrants, nor is it clear from the text whether male Newfoundlanders' rates were compared to male mainland rates or to combined male and female mainland rates. This both continues a gender-insensitive analysis and introduces a subtle double standard, insofar as female unemployment is apparently unworthy of attention.

5.6 Double Standards in Policy Evaluations and Recommendations

Policy research in its initial phases can involve all types of sexism. In addition, however, a double standard may enter into the evaluation of existing or proposed policies or recommendations for new policies. It is not always easy to recognize whether a double standard has been applied, since different terms may be used to create the impression that a single standard has been employed. We can thus distinguish between a simple double standard, in which it is obvious that the behavior of the sexes is measured differently, and a complex double standard, in which the same phenomenon occurs but in a less-obvious manner.

5.6.1 Simple Double Standards in Policy Evaluations and Recommendations

Decisions made by judges can be understood as one form of policy interpretation, with the difference that judicial decisions are an application of existing law and have themselves the force of law; the same cannot be said of all policy recommendations. It is all the more important, therefore, to scrutinize judicial decisions for sexism, and in particular, for the existence of a double standard. Several researchers have demonstrated[28] that judges tend to discriminate against mothers involved in custody disputes when they are working for pay. If and when the same activity – in this case, working for pay – is seen in a different light for fathers and for mothers, a simple double standard has been applied.

Another example of a simple double standard in policy recommendations can be found in a recent report on "surrogate" motherhood and other issues submitted by the Ontario Law Reform Commission.[29] Counter to other, similar reports, this report recommends legalizing surrogate motherhood arrangements (in which one woman contracts with a couple to bear a child for them, usually after having been artificially inseminated with the semen of the man, and usually for a fee).

There are many problems with this report, but only one instance of a double standard will be mentioned here. The Commission suggests that the parents involved in such a contractual arrangement be scrutinized by appropriate legal, social, and medical agencies. However, the degrees of scrutiny to be applied to the prospective social parents and to the surrogate mother are so different that they cannot possibly be seen as applying the same standard. For the prospective surrogate mother, recommendation 43 states:

> In assessing the suitability of a prospective surrogate mother, the court should consider, among other factors, her physical and mental health, her marital and domestic circumstances, the opinion of her spouse or partner, if any, and the likely effects of her participation in a surrogate motherhood arrangement upon existing children under her care.[30]

In addition, the parties to the contract "should be required to consider, and to agree upon a resolution" of, among other things, "prenatal restrictions upon the surrogate mother's activities before and after conception, including dietary obligations; and ... conditions under which prenatal screening of the child may be justified or required, for example, by ultrasound, fetoscopy or amniocentesis."[31] This policy represents a massive invasion into the life of the surrogate mother. And the recommendation is unclear about how the prenatal restrictions on the mother would be monitored.

The Commission also recommends that the child be seized from the surrogate mother in case she changes her mind and wishes to keep it. Indeed, the report recommends that "where the court is satisfied that the surrogate mother intends to refuse to surrender the child upon birth, the court, prior to the birth of the child, should be empowered to make an order for transfer of custody upon birth."[32] In a worst-case scenario, such an attitude might lead to virtual imprisonment of the surrogate mother in order to impede her from leaving the country and thus breaking the contractual arrangement.

In comparison to the restrictions on the surrogate mother, the Commission considers a homestudy of the social parents (as is legally required before parents are accepted as prospective adoptive parents) to be too "invasive." Specifically, the report states:

> We believe that the rigorous intervention in the case of adoption by strangers is an inappropriate regulatory model for surrogate mother-hood arrangements. In most cases, we anticipate that such arrange-ments will involve artificial insemination of the surrogate mother by the semen of the male partner of the couple wishing to raise the child. Since he is the natural father of the child, we do not consider it appropriate that he be treated as a stranger, and that he and his partner be subjected to the invasive scrutiny of a homestudy. While there may be occasions where artificial conception technology is employed to achieve a pregnancy where the male is not the natural father, we consider that such cases will be relatively few in number and, therefore, should not affect the view espoused above.[33]

The Commission did eventually recommend that the prospective parents be assessed by the court as to their ability to provide the prospective child with an adequate upbringing,[34] but this "assess-ment" seems in no way comparable to the one that the surrogate mother would have to undergo. When it comes to the rights, obligations, and degree to which scrutiny of her situation seems appropriate to the commission, it seems irrelevant that the surrogate mother is the natural mother of the child in question.[35]

5.6.2 Complex Double Standards in Policy Evaluations and Recommendations

For an example of a complex double standard in policy recommen-dations, we shall consider the policy concequences of using a concept based on the conceptual pair of primary and secondary earner (see section 5.3.3). One of the background papers prepared for the MacDonald Commission considered the issue of income security for Canadian workers.[36] In this study, the author proposes some very useful streamlining of the income security system by abandoning a system of personal tax exemptions in favor of a system of universal demogrants. In addition, he also proposes a complete revamping of the Canadian Unemployment Insurance scheme. This restructuring hinges on the classification of unemployed workers as "unemployed employable" (those who would be certified as such and be effectively guaranteed work or, failing that, unemployment insurance); "those who 'cannot' work (the permanently disabled and severely handicapped); and those whom society deems 'should not' or 'need not' work (the elderly and perhaps single parents with preschool children)."[37]

The article is remarkable for its nonsexist language. With the exception of some footnotes (e.g., footnote 66 and 67) in which "wives" and "males" are identified as unemployment insurance recipients, the article speaks about workers, persons, and families. Sex is not presented as a relevant variable in categorizing someone as an unemployed employable or as a person who society deems should not work. It is only through the distinction of secondary and primary earners that a double standard along sexual lines is introduced: "In the majority of cases, secondary workers in families with another full-time worker would not qualify for special employment."[38] They are the "losers," persons who would be displaced from their current unemployment insurance benefits. This "would mainly affect the non-certified unemployed – persons still drawing substantial UI benefits but not awaiting recall, and unemployed persons in families still with one substantial earner."[39] In other words, "Unemployed married workers with a spouse employed full time at average or higher wages will lose net benefits."[40] As a consequence, "Some secondary workers who have been attracted by the current generous UI treatment of unstable and irregular work would withdraw from the labour market, improving job opportunities and perhaps raising wage rates for lower-wage primary workers."[41]

Who are the primary and the secondary workers? While families will be permitted to designate their primary workers, we know that females earn on average 64 percent of what males earn, and thus in the overwhelming majority of cases, the wife will be designated a secondary worker, and the husband a primary worker. The plan in effect amounts to disentitling most wives from drawing unemployment insurance benefits.[42] The double standard – different treatment of married male and female workers – in this case is not simple, since it is not stated in these terms, but rather complex, since it is achieved via a differential conceptual pair, namely that of primary and secondary earner. Recognizing it as a double standard therefore requires recognizing the sexual dimension in the distinction, the double standard inherent in the conceptual pair itself, and the consequences for women and men in the economy.

5.7 Conclusion

As we have seen, recognizing a double standard may not always be easy. In the case of a simple double standard, no major problem exists: when the same responses are coded differently by sex, we are dealing with a very obvious form of the double standard. When dealing with concepts that are attached to one sex only, however, the issue becomes more complicated. In order to decide whether or not a double standard exists, we need to first determine if the quality referred to in the concept also exists in reference to the other sex; by definition, the available literature (provided there is any) will be classified under a different heading. If this is the case, we need to identify a superordinate concept under which two apparently different concepts can be shown to be the same.

In the case of a complex double standard, there are at least two steps involved: (1) identifying some component of the research process (a conceptual pair, a research question, a policy recommendation) as gender-based even though this may not be immediately visible; and (2) identifying whether or not this component is treated by one standard or by a sexual double standard.[43]

Notes

1 Ruth First and Ann Scott, *Olive Schreiner* (New York: Schocken Books, 1980), pp. 124–125.
2 Clellan S. Ford, "Some primitive societies," in Georgene H. Seward and Robert C. Williamson (eds.), *Sex Roles in Changing Society* (New York: Random House, 1970):

25–43, quotation from pp. 22–23. My analysis of this study appeared earlier in Margrit Eichler, *The Double Standard: A Feminist Critique of Feminist Social Science* (London:Croom Helm,1980):22–28.

3 Eichler, *The Double Standard*, pp. 25–26.

4 Ibid., pp. 23–24.

5 For example, Arthur J. Mann, "Economic development, income distribution, and real income levels: Puerto Rico, 1953–1977," *Economic Development and Cultural Change* 33, 3 (1985): 485–502.

6 "The idea of an individual male wage-earner supporting his family was unfamiliar in the first half of the nineteenth century." See Catherine Hakim, "Census reports as documentary evidence: The census commentaries 1801–1951," *Sociological Review* 28, 3 (new series) (1980): 551–580.

7 See A. M. Brodkin, "Family therapy: The making of a mental health movement," *American Journal of Orthopsychiatry* 50, 1 (1980):4–17.

8 There are, of course, some obvious exceptions to this general rule. It would not be a useful question to ask a man how many children he has given birth to. It is, on the other hand, a highly relevant question to ask a man how many biological children he has.

9 Dale Spender, *Man-Made Language* (London: Routledge and Kegan Paul, 1980): 164–165.

10 Paula J. Caplan and Ian Hall-McCorquodale, "Mother-blaming in major clinical journals," *American Journal of Orthopsychiatry* 55, 3 (1985):345–353.

11 Ibid., p. 347.

12 Ibid., p. 349.

13 Paul J. Caplan and Ian Hall-McCorquodale, "The scapegoating of mothers: A call for change," *American Journal of Orthopsychiatry* 55, 4 (1985): 610–613.

14 J. Nielsen, S. Bjarnason, U. Friedrich, A. Froland, V. H. Hansen, and A. Sorensen, "Klinefelter's syndrome in children," *Journal of Child Psychology and Psychiatry* 11 (1970): 109–119, quote from p. 116.

15 Ibid., p. 117.

16 Caplan and Hall-McCorquordale, "Scapegoating," pp. 610–611.

17 For some of the more recent literature on the issue, see Joan Acker, "Women and stratification: A review of recent literature," *Contemporary Sociology* 9 (1980): 23–39; John H. Goldthorpe, "Women and class analysis: In defense of the conventional view," *Sociology* 19, 4 (1983): 475–488; Michelle Stanworth, "Women and class analysis: A reply to Goldthorpe," *Sociology* 18, 2 (1984): 159–170; Anthony Heath and Nicky Britten, "Women's jobs do make a difference: A reply to Goldthorpe," *Sociology* 18, 4 (1984): 475–490; John H. Goldthorpe, "Women and class analysis: A reply to the replies," *Sociology* 18, 4 (1984): 491–499; Robert Erikson, "Social class of men, women and families," *Sociology* 18, 4 (1984): 491–499; Angela Dale, G. Nigel Gilbert, and Sara Arber, "Integrating women into class theory," *Sociology* 19, 3 (1985):384–409.

18 See Acker, "Women," and Monica Boyd and Hugh A. McRoberts, "Women, men, and socioeconomic indendices: An assessment," in Mary G. Powers (ed.), *Measures of Socioeconomic Status: Current Issues*. AAAS Selected Symposium 81 (Boulder, CO: Westview, 1983): 129–159.

19 Sanford M. Dornbush et al., "Single parents, extended households, and the control of adolescents," *Child Development* 56 (1985): 326–341, quotation from p. 328.

20 Ibid., p. 332.

21 Judith Hicks Stiehm, "The unit of political analysis: Our Aristotelian hangover," in Sandra Harding and Merrill B. Hintikka (eds.), *Discovering Reality: Feminist Perspectives on Epistemology, Metaphysics, Methodology and Philosophy of Science* (Dordrecht: D. Reidel, 1983): 31–44.

22 Sidney Verba and Norman Nie, *Participation in America* (New York: Harper & Row, 1972).

23 Stiehm, "Unit," p. 33.

24 Ibid., p. 34.

25 One such example is contained in Dale, Gilbert, and Arber, "Integrating Women," pp. 384–409.

26 Caplan and Hall-McCorquodale, "Mother-Blaming," p. 349.

27 Barnett Richling, "'You'd never starve here': Return migration to rural Newfoundland," *Canadian Review of Sociology and Anthropology* 22, 2 (1985): 236–249, quote on p. 238.

28 See the literature she cites as well as some of the data in Phyllis Chesler, *Mothers on Trial: The Battle for Children and Custody* (New York: McGraw-Hill, 1986).

29 Ontario Law Reform Commission, *Report on Human Artificial Reproduction and Related Matters* (Toronto: Ministry of the Attorney General, 1985).

30 Ibid., vol. 2, p. 282.

31 Ibid., p. 284.

32 Ibid., p. 252.

33 Ibid., pp. 234–235.

34 Ibid., p. 282.

35 The term "surrogate" mother itself is based on a double standard. It presents the biological mother as a nonmother, while the sperm donor is identified as simply the "father." The heartache that can ensue from such contracts has been vividly played out in the famous case of "Baby M," in which both the contractual mother and the contractual father wanted to have custody of the child. (It was eventually awarded to the father, but the case has been appealed and continues.)

36 Jonathan R. Kesselman, "Comprehensive income security for Canadian workers," in Francois Vaillancourt (ed.), *Income Distribution and Economic Security in Canada*. Collected Research Studies, Royal Commission on the Economic Union and Development Prospects for Canada (Toronto: University of Toronto Press and Minister of Supply and Services, 1985): 283–319. I would like to thank Monica Townson for drawing my attention to this article. My analysis takes off from hers, in Monica Townson, "Women and the Canadian economy," keynote address to the symposium on Women and the Economy, sponsored by the Canadian Advisory Council on the Status of Women, Ottawa, March 1986.

37 Ibid., p. 284.

38 Ibid., p. 295.

39 Ibid., p. 299.

40 Ibid., p. 310.

41 Ibid., p. 311.

42 The same would be true for unemployed youths, but this is seen as a problem deserving of a special exception: "To relieve severe youth unemployment and reduce incentives for families to fragment, it would be desirable to allow

additional family workers such as older dependent children to participate in the employment programs." Ibid., p. 307.
43 There are, of course, double standards that are based on variables other than sex, such as race, age, economic status, and so on. The analysis provided in this chapter should be transferable to such instances, with the appropriate substitutions.

Chapter 6

Sex Appropriateness, Familism, and Sexual Dichotomism

6.1 Introduction
6.2 Sex appropriateness
    6.2.1 Research designs based on sex appropriateness
    6.2.2 Policy recommendations premised on notions of sex appropriateness
    6.2.3 Sex-role transcendence as a form of mental illness
    6.2.4 Sex appropriateness as a sexist problem
6.3 Familism
    6.3.1 Introduction
    6.3.2 Attribution of individual actions, experiences, or properties to the household/family
    6.3.3 Attribution of equal benefit or detriment to the members of a family unit
    6.3.4 Familism as a sexist problem
6.4 Sexual dichotomism
    6.4.1 Introduction
    6.4.2 Sexual dichotomism in concepts
    6.4.3 Sexual dichotomism in the research design
    6.4.4 Sexual dichotomism in methods
    6.4.5 Sexual dichotomism as a form of sexism
6.5 Conclusion

6.1 Introduction

This chapter will deal with the three remaining sexist problems: sex appropriateness, familism, and sexual dichotomism. They have been identified as "derived" not because they are unimportant, but because they can be logically derived from one of the major problems: Sex appropriateness is a subform of a double standard. Familism is an extreme form of gender insensitivity, often in combination with androcentricity. Sexual dichotomism, finally, is an extreme form of a double standard.

They are treated as individual problems here for two reasons: First, these three problems – sex appropriateness, familism, and sexual dichotomism – constitute distinct and well-accepted aspects of contemporary scholarship. It is therefore partially in an attempt to highlight them that they are treated separately rather than as subaspects of the four primary problems. Related to this is the second reason: One of the major aims of this book is to break down sexism in research into manageable components; these components are more easily and clearly identifiable if they have names.

6.2 Sex Appropriateness

Sex appropriateness is a concept based on the assumption that there are behavior patterns or character formations that are more appropriate for one sex than for the other. For example, sex roles are accepted as appropriate (rather than as a manifestation of a double standard). Similarly, it is still widely accepted that sex identity includes a large package of traits that have nothing to do with physical sexual characteristics but everything to do with what is socially constructed as appropriate for the sexes. Indeed, people are seen as deviant or problematic if their conceptions of their proper role or character are broader than what prevailing sex (or gender) roles prescribe. Instead, of course, we should recognize social prescriptions that define certain human traits and behaviors as appropriate for only one sex as the real problem.[1] The assumption of sex appropriateness leads to research approaches and methods that accept existing sex roles as nonproblematic and to the belief that sex-role (gender-role) transcendence is a form of social or psychic disease, rather than a form of mental well-being.

6.2.1 Research Designs Based on Sex Appropriateness

One of the most common ways in which sex appropriateness distorts our understanding of social processes consists in assuming a division of labor in which women are seen as responsible for childcare and home care, while men are simply ignored. For example, a recent article[2] (like many articles before it) examines the impact of maternal employment on children, beginning with the following passage:

> With the increasing number of mothers in the work force, especially among mothers with preschool children, there is a need to understand how this important social change affects children. The present investigation examines one way in which the maternal employment situation may influence the socialization process. More explicitly, why mothers are working outside the home and what employment means to mothers are addressed as possible powerful influences on how mothers think about their children.[3]

I have yet to read a study that begins with the following statement:

> With the high number of fathers in the work force especially among fathers with preschool children, there is a need to understand how this important social phenomenon affects children. The present investigation examines one way in which the paternal employment situation may influence the socialization process. More explicitly, why fathers are working outside the home and what employment means to fathers are addressed as possible powerful influences on how fathers think about their children."[4]

This study could have been very interesting if the author had asked both parents about their work experiences and how these affect their relationship with their children. Instead, we learn that both parents were asked, in interviews,[5] about sources of satisfaction and stress:

> Two of the sources of satisfaction and stress assessed were parents' feelings about their children and, for those mothers working outside the home, their employment. ... Some examples of items dealing with maternal employment are: "How do you feel about working?" "How does this work out so far as you and your child are concerned?" and "Are there things about your job that you particularly like or dislike?"[6]

Apparently fathers and housewives/mothers were asked different questions. We are confronted here with an assumption of sex appropriateness: childcare is seen as a maternal role, and not as a paternal role. This leads to a double standard in methods, in which different questions are asked of the sexes although the situations are comparable (both mothers and fathers had paid jobs). The effect of this approach is that the relationship between employed mothers and children is made problematic, while the relationship between employed fathers and their children, as well as that between housewife-mothers and their children, is implicitly seen as nonproblematic. Ultimately, this leads to a form of mother-blaming in the data interpretation: Mothers employed full-time

> couched their sons' activity in negative terms. Further, they described their sons as being demanding and noncompliant. Such terms seem congruent with the notion that full-time maternal employment may compound the undersocialization of sons. ... This interpretation lends partial support to the hypotheses put forth by Hoffman ... that greater undersocialization may account for the poorer academic performance of sons whose middle-class mothers are employed.[7]

Where in all of this is the father? It appears that he has no implicit duty to socialize his son. The mother is once again guilty.

In this particular study, the interviews were open-ended, so the exact wording of questions (except in the style as cited above) is not available. The same problem may, of course, appear in studies that use a structured interview approach, as in the following example. In this study,[8] which examined the daily lives of women in 538 Toronto families, we find a set of questions that are also premised on some notion of sex appropriateness:

- What do you think is different in your children's day because you have a job? (asked of the mother)
- If your children have to get in touch with you at work, how easy or difficult is it for them to reach you?
- How often do you feel a conflict between being a mother and "working"?[9]

The implication is that a conflict exists as a result of the mother's paid work but not of the father's paid work. These questions could have been asked of both sexes; of course, this would have meant interviewing both sexes, thus doubling the sample, complicating the study, and probably increasing costs. But the result would have been a more informative and reliable study about family/work conflict.[10] It is important also to note here that granting agencies might question the increased costs of broadening the study. It is therefore essential not only for academic researchers themselves to become aware of sexism in research, but also to educate granting agencies on this score in order to encourage funding for nonsexist research.

Another recent article[11] tries to explain wives' labor force participation by examining the relative impact of attitudinal factors and family economic resources. The analysis is based on data from the Edmonton Area Study, consisting of responses to four questions that are identified as "gender-related issues."[12] The four questions are as follows:

(1) Do you approve or disapprove of "a married woman working, if she has pre-school age children and a husband capable of supporting her."

(2) Do you agree or disagree that "housework is more rewarding than having an outside job."

(3) that "a woman is likely to feel unfulfilled unless she becomes a mother."

(4) that "a husband should be entirely responsible for earning the living for a family (under normal circumstances)."[13]

Three of these four questions (1, 3, and 4) are premised on a notion of sex appropriateness. Question 2 is nonsexist, since it is couched in general terms. The other questions all assume a division of labor in which it is considered problematic if the mother has paid employment or the father is not the sole economic provider. These questions could be made nonsexist by coupling them with equivalent questions about the other person. In particular, Question 3 (about the importance of motherhood for a woman) must be coupled with a question about the importance of fatherhood for a man in order to yield meaningful information. *Only* when we know about the reactions of both sexes to being a parent can we draw any inferences whatsoever about parenthood as a gender-related issue. It is quite conceivable that both a male and a female respondent may hold strong notions about parenthood that have nothing whatsoever to do with any assumed sex appropriateness. However, by asking only one-sided questions, such an interpretation is not possible because half the necessary data are missing.

Another recent study[14] demonstrates how asking questions about sex-appropriate behavior in a nonsexist manner can produce quite different results. In this case, blue-collar women and men, white-collar women and men, male and female teachers, and male and female decision makers were asked to agree or disagree with the following statement:

If a married woman has to stay away from home for long periods of time in order to have a career, she had better give up the carer.[15]

Fifty-nine percent of the male and 65 percent of the female blue-collar workers agreed with the statement, as opposed to 34 percent of the male and 13 percent of the female decision makers.[16] It would be reasonable to interpret such a finding to mean that female blue-collar workers have the most conservative notions about their sex roles, with the majority of them perceiving a conflict between career and family for a married woman with children.

These respondents were also asked to agree or disagree with the following statement:

> If a married man has to stay away from home for long periods of time in order to have a career, he had better give up the career.[17]

This time we find that 34 percent of the male and 49 percent of the female blue-collar workers agreed with this statement, as opposed to 25 percent of the male and 13 percent of the female decision makers.

Subsequently, a so-called double standard score was computed to assess how many people would want a married woman to give up her career without wanting a married man to give up his career, and vice versa. This was achieved by cross-tabulating the responses to both questions. The results are fascinating: 25 percent of male and 12 percent of female blue-collar workers, and 9 percent of male and 0 percent of female decision makers exhibited a double standard with respect to their family and career expectations for women and men.

By asking both sides of the question rather than assuming sex appropriateness, we thus arrive at a totally different conclusion. Now the male blue-collar workers appear to be the most conservative group, albeit to a significantly lesser degree than our first interpretation suggested. The female blue-collar workers appear to have responded to the first question in the way they did, not because of adherence to traditional sex roles, but because they place a higher value on family life than on work life for *both* spouses.

6.2.2 Policy Recommendations Premised on Notions of Sex Appropriateness

In an otherwise interesting article[18] on fathers' birth attendance and their involvement with their newborns, the author in effect ends up arguing that traditional sex roles that do not involve the father in direct parenting should be recognized professionally as an acceptable option. He suggests:

Researchers need to realize that paternal support can be represented by a wide range of behaviours, and that families most likely adopt patterns of interaction maximizing the match between roles, skills, and needs. The implication is that in some cases the optimal pattern of paternal support may involve little direct participation in child care. Perhaps investigators would do well to examine broad patterns of paternal involvement (e.g. support of the mother) rather than focussing on specific aspects of fathering behaviour (e.g. number of diapers changed).[19]

This thought is strongly reinforced in the conclusion:

What is required is a balanced approach where fathers, in consultation with their partners, choose at all stages of the parenting process levels of involvement that are consistent with their skills, desires, and perceived roles.

A father's attitudes concerning his sex role, the fathering role, the support he receives from his partner, and other related variables exert considerable impact on paternal involvement. ... Among the most productive goals that we as professionals can have is to facilitate a realistic, positive perception of a wide range of paternal roles in relation to pregnancy, birth, and the transition to parenthood.[20]

Initially children have an absolute need for care that exists independent of their parents' skills, desires, and perceived roles. Since the author makes no statements about the mother's skills, desires, and perceived roles, he presumably wishes to offer choice to fathers, thus potentially reducing choice to mothers – assuming that if fathers choose not to participate in the caring process, mothers will be left with doing it on their own.

6.2.3 *Sex-Role Transcendence as a Form of Mental Illness*

Returning one more time to the previously cited review of 125 journal articles on the etiology of psychopathology,[21] we learn that

moving to reviews of the literature in the articles studied, in 28% a traditional division of labour was explicitly regarded as normal and healthy, and deviation from it was assumed to be pathogenic. Nontraditional division of labour was never regarded as normal and healthy. Traditional sex roles (in terms of behavior) and traditional family structures (two-parent, heterosexual) were regarded as normal and healthy, and any deviation from this as pathogenic in 43% of articles. In no article was the converse true.[22]

In other words, in nearly half of the literature surveyed, the authors found that sex-role transcendence was considered to be deviant.

6.2.4 Sex Appropriateness as a Sexist Problem

It would be interesting to examine how many recent introductory textbooks in sociology and psychology still discuss sex or gender roles and sex or gender identity in terms of "appropriate" behavior and socialization. To the degree that the term "sex appropriate" is seen as an acceptable yardstick against which to measure and judge behavior, we are dealing with a form of sexism. This does not mean that the concepts of sex role or sex identity should be eliminated. They remain useful *descriptive* (but not prescriptive or explanatory) terms. Sex appropriateness appears not only when the labels are present, but also when research designs or data interpretation are guided by the notion that there are sets of behaviors or traits that are appropriate for one sex but not for the other.[23] Instead, behaviors and traits should be judged by criteria other than which sex engages in or displays them.

6.3 Familism

6.3.1 Introduction

Familism is a specific form of gender insensitivity. It consists of taking the family as the smallest unit of analysis in cases in which it is in fact *individuals*, or a collection of individuals, who engage in particular actions.[24] The use of families or households as the smallest unit of analysis is, of course, not always sexist. There is nothing problematic about providing particular definitions of a household or family and assessing, for example, how many households or families in a country fall into these categories, or how many households are affected by particular tax provisions, and so on. A problem does exist, however, when an action or experience is attributed to a family or household when in fact the action is carried out, or the event is potentially differentially experienced, by individuals within the unit; or when the family is credited with properties that are actually the aggregate properties of the individuals within it. A problem also exists when households or families are treated as a unit, the members of which suffer or profit equally from events that in fact have a differential impact on different members.

6.3.2 *Attribution of Individual Actions, Experiences, or Properties to the Household/Family*

We find quite frequently that households are assumed to do things that are in fact performed by individuals within them (and by no means all individuals within them). Economic analyses in particular tend to assume that households make decisions, buy and sell, react or fail to react to constraints and opportunities, and so on.

For example, we read that "households make joint decisions about their portfolios of assets and their labour supply, choosing among the labour contracts offered by the different firms."[25] Or we read about the "buying effort by households."[26] And "the household that buys Y and sells N gets to consume.... thus the household's decision problem ... the household's profit income ... all of which the household takes as given."[27] This approach hides the fact that women and men tend to participate differentially in decisions that affect the household and the family,[28] and that what is presented as something decided by the household or family may, in fact, have been decided against the wishes of, and/or to the detriment of, one or more of its members.

Nor do households or families per se engage in actions. For instance, when scholars write that "families" care for their children and for the aged, in effect they attribute individual actions to the unit as a whole. For example,[29]

When gerontologists do discuss the more concrete tasks and

activities which constitute family involvement with the elderly, they invoke a language which obscures the feminine nature of that care. Nowhere has this been more evident than in studies of the frail and ill elders, where euphemisms abound for care provided by women in families. Brody[30] claims the phrase "alternatives to institutions" should be read "daughter" of the elderly person. Chappell[31] amends that to "daughter or wife." Framed in public language, or that of large scale organizations rather than domestic groups, the private actions of individual women engaged in caring for older members of their family are translated into "family support systems"[32] and "family as a health service organization."[33]

This is not the only way in which familism may manifest itself. In psychology and sociology, we sometimes find the assumption that parents always act as a unit and in concert when in fact this may not be the case. For instance, in one particular study children were asked:

> Do you have any ideas about the sort of job you'd like to do when you leave school? What do you think your parents would like you to do when you leave school?[34]

This question presupposes that both parents have an idea of what they want their child to do after he or she has finished school, and that they agree on this issue. What happens if Dad wants his child to become a nurse while Mom wants her to become a statistician? The simple solution to this problem is, of course, to ask two questions in order to identify whether or not the parents' wishes are identical (what would your mother like you to become? . . . your father?) and to proceed in the analysis from there.

A parallel problem consists in attributing an individual property to the entire unit in cases in which members of the unit do not necessarily equally own or display this property. A simple example of this type of familism occurs when racial or ethnic family membership is determined on the basis of only one of the family members' background, such as when a family in which the husband/father is Pakistani, while the wife/mother is Dutch, is classified as Pakistani rather than as mixed Pakistani/Dutch. If the family were classified as Dutch it would, of course, be exactly the same problem.[35]

This type of sexism also occurs when the incomes of the individual family members are treated as "family income." This would be appropriate if all family members were legally and socially entitled equally to the income of all family members. Since this is generally not the case, however, it is inappropriate unless the data are presented in disaggregated as well as aggregated form. This issue leads us to the next manifestation of familism.

6.3.3 Attribution of Equal Benefit or Detriment to the Members of a Family Unit

We know from several studies that husbands and wives do not, in fact, have equal say over money earned by one of the spouses.[36] In policy studies in particular, it is very important to keep in mind who within a family unit generates income, and who has control over it. We cannot assume that a particular amount of money is necessarily of equal benefit to all members, irrespective of who controls it. To return to the example on unemployment insurance used in Chapter 5, the Commission proposed that "secondary earners" be disentitled from unemployment benefits on the basis of "family income." (The primary earner's income refers in most cases to the husband's income.) By treating the husband's income as family income, this policy would in effect disentitle the secondary earner (i.e., the wife) from her personally earned benefits on the assumption that she shares this income of her husband. Loss of job would thus be compounded by loss of earned unemployment insurance benefits.

The assumption of equal benefits is often expressed by such terms as "joint utility functions" or "optimization." For instance,

> Barro has argued that it may be optimal for households to react to an increased deficit by increasing their saving by an equal amount. Consequently, neither aggregate demand nor interest rates may rise. Households will so react if capital markets are perfect, if they understand the intertemporal budget constraints they face, and if they have operative altruistic intergenerational transfer motives.[37]

What is sexist about this approach? The bold assertion that something is "optimal" for a household when it may in fact have quite different effects on the various household members. One analysis that empirically tested the assumption of joint utility maximizing is Folbre's study of Philippine households.[38]

> Folbre rejects Becker's assertion of an altruistic, but nevertheless joint-utility maximizing unit where individual preferences are consistent with maximizing family welfare. Analysis of the data on family expenditures on various members revealed that women received less than the accepted levels of nutrition and men received more. Girls had much less time spent on them than boys, and after the age of nine more of the family income was allocated to sons.[39]

6.3.4 Familism as a Sexist Problem

Many researchers routinely talk about the family as if the unit as a whole experienced or did things in the same manner, or as if any differences in the impact on, or activities of, individual family members are irrelevant. This is a particularly entrenched form of gender insensitivity that has a pervasive impact on policy formation in particular. A judgment that a particular policy (action, experience, benefit) is good for the entire family unit must in all cases be preceded by a study that examines the effects of such policy on *each* member. Only when it has been demonstrated (not assumed) that the effect is beneficial – or at least not detrimental – to each and every family member can the statement be made that it is "good for the family."

Familism may also distort the attribution of properties to families. In cases in which the experiences (traits, behaviors) of male and female family members are disparate, ignoring such differences will create a picture that is inaccurate for one or both. It is like a couple that wishes to buy one suit that they can both wear. If one of them is four feet tall, and the other six feet tall, their joint height would be five feet. If they, accordingly, buy a "family suit" for a five-foot-tall person, it will fit neither one. Collective attribution of *any* property should therefore be made only after the individuals' attributes have been examined and found to coincide.

6.4 Sexual Dichotomism

6.4.1 Introduction

Sexual dichotomism is an extreme form of a double standard. It consists of treating the sexes as two discrete, rather than overlapping, groups.[40] It is neither a new problem, nor a newly recognized one, but it has become more common. It tends to appear when researchers attempt to avoid another form of sexism: gender insensitivity. Sexual dichotomism is certainly not gender insensitive; on the contrary, sexual dichotomism occurs when gender sensitivity is perverted into a form of scholarly gender apartheid.

Sexual dichotomism may manifest itself in concepts as well as in the overall research design. In general, whenever we postulate categorical social distinctions between the sexes, we are engaging in sexual dichotomism.[41]

6.4.2 Sexual Dichotomism in Concepts

In cases in which human attributes are identified with one sex or the other, a form of sexual dichotomism results. The identification of estrogen and testosterone as "female" and "male" hormones, respectively, is a case in point. Both females and males have estrogen and testosterone in their bodies, albeit in quite different proportions.

This issue becomes more important when dealing with character attributes. There are "generally recognized" character attributes that are seen as masculine or feminine, such as independence or leadership capacity (on the masculine side), or emotionality or sensitivity (on the feminine side). Since both males and females can (and do) display these attributes, albeit in different proportions, the characterization of these traits as masculine or feminine suggests that their display in the other sex is somehow "unnatural."

6.4.3 Sexual Dichotomism in the Research Design

A preeminent example of sexual dichotomism occurs when part or all of a research design is premised on the notion that the sexes are discrete groups. Masculinity–femininity scales are one such example. The most famous of these scales is part of the Minnesota Multiphasic Personality Inventory (MMPI). The "MMPI is the most used psychological test in the world. Its results are analyzed and interpreted thousands of times daily."[42]

> Profiles generated by testee responses to the instrument's items are often given great credibility in diagnosing pathology and categorizing personality traits. It can be assumed that decisions affecting people's lives are often made based, at least in part, on the interpretation of these profiles.[43]

One part of the instrument, the so-called scale five, is a masculinity–femininity scale. Its original objective was to identify "homosexual invert males."[44] Attempts to make the scale serve this purpose, and to use it to distinguish female homosexuals from "normals," were not successful.

The scale was also designed to discriminate between men and women. A recent evaluation of the utility of the scale states categorically:

> Clearly the MMPI Mf scale does not do what it was intended to do. It does not measure homosexuality in any clearcut way nor does it measure characteristics that reliably divide males from females.[45]

Nevertheless, "scores on Scale Five have come to be routinely reported in the MMPI profile."[46]

In fact, researchers are still constructing new scales from the items contained in the MMPI. One recent effort involves the construction of a scale purportedly measuring a "gender dysphoria syndrome" in males, the "Gd" scale.[47] The Gd scale consists of 31 items that represent three factors: identification with stereotypic feminine interests; denial of male interests; and affirmation of excellent physical and mental health.[48]

Leaving aside for a moment the paradox that affirmation of excellent physical and mental health is taken as one indicator of what is perceived as a gender identity disorder, responses that are seen as indicative of this disorder include affirmation of the following items:

- I enjoy reading love stories.
- I would like to be a nurse.
- I like collecting flowers or growing house plants.
- I like to cook.
- If I were a reporter I would very much like to report news of the theater.
- I used to like hopscotch.
- I think I would like the work of a dressmaker.
- I would like to be a private secretary.

Among the responses that indicate the presence of the disorder are negation of the following items:

- I like mechanics magazines.
- I think I would like the work of a building contractor.
- If I were a reporter I would very much like to report sporting news.
- I like or have liked fishing very much.
- I like adventure stories better than romantic stories.

Using these items, males will be judged to suffer from a personality disorder when they admit to liking to cook, being interested in theatre news, liking flowers and houseplants, and so on, while failing to like mechanics magazines, fishing, and being interested in sports news. They must also profess excellent physical and mental health to be judged as having a psychological disorder. "Any individual with a raw score of 17 or above on the Gd scale would be viewed as having a high probability of a diagnosis of gender dysphoria."[49]

This scale represents an extreme form of sexual dichotomism. Certain characteristics (human attributes) found in both males and females are classified as either masculine or feminine on the basis of prevailing stereotypes in a given society at a certain point in time.[50] The fact that some males display these attributes is not taken as an indication of inappropriate labeling. The sexual dichotomy that has been artificially created is accorded more weight than reality itself is. Indeed, the authors suggest that "the greatest usefulness of the scale may lie in its potential for identifying and predicting gender identity conflicts in a *nonascribed* gender dysphoric patient population. ... Once these patients' gender identity conflicts are identified, they can be appropriately assigned for treatment."[51] In other words, those poor men who did not know that they were sick, believing themselves in excellent mental and physical health, and having a range of interests and skills that is greater than that of many other men, could finally be cured of this affliction. Including the concept of androgyny in the construction of Mf scales does not solve the problem of sexual dichotomism, as has been shown elsewhere.[52]

In anthropology, we not infrequently find analytical frameworks that dichotomize the sexes and associate the dichotomy with other – also dichotomized – concepts. Such a scheme might look as follows:[53]

male	:	female
culture	:	nature
public	:	domestic
production	:	reproduction
agent	:	object
articulate	:	inarticulate
superior	:	inferior
active	:	passive
authority	:	influence

The problem is compounded when such frameworks are given the status of universal applicability and significance.[54]

6.4.4 *Sexual Dichotomism in Methods*

Gd scales are not the only way in which sexual dichotomism may manifest itself. Certain methods may also result in sexual dichotomism. To provide just one example: The manner in which tests of significance are sometimes used may result in sexual dichotomism. This is not to say that the use of tests of significance is sexist, but merely that they may be used in a sexist manner.

In a conventional test of significance, there are three basic steps:

> (1) The researcher sets up a null hypothesis ... which he or she is typically interested in rejecting in favour of the research hypothesis. ... (2) A probability model is specified. ... (3) The test statistic is computed, and a decision made about whether or not to reject the null hypothesis.[55]

Since theories cannot, in principle, be proven, researchers utilizing such techniques will concentrate on rejecting false alternatives. "While the null hypothesis does not necessarily have to assume 'no difference' ... the practise is so common that textbooks often define the null hypothesis in this way."[56] Tests of significance group all effects into two classes: present or absent. As applied to gender differences, the inference drawn is that the specific gender difference under investigation either exists or does not exist. Given that the null hypothesis is usually "no difference," rejecting the null hypothesis results in an affirmation of the existence of a difference. In a cumulative sense, this may have a very peculiar effect.

> Findings are defined as significant at some specified level if the null hypothesis is rejected. The inference is drawn that some 'cause' is at work. Alternatively, if it appears that chance alone might have produced the sample results, no other explanation is thought necessary. A non-significant finding is rarely regarded as a refutation of the research hypothesis; instead the usual conclusion is that the study failed to establish that the differences were there. The success of the research as measured in terms of significance tests influences the chances that the report will be published. Therefore, in a cumulative manner, sex differences are exaggerated. Tresemer[57] argues that there is a "great iceberg" of studies, unpublished because

of their inability to reject the hypothesis of no difference, that never come to light or that do not report their results separately by sex.

Finally, significance tests are often misinterpreted as measures of importance or substantive significance.[58]

In this instance, therefore, a particular statistical technique, if applied to gender differences in the described manner, is likely to exaggerate sex differences over similarities. In other words, it will exaggerate the importance of gender as a categorical variable. Wherever techniques have this effect, we are dealing with a case of sexual dichotomism in methods.[59]

6.4.5 Sexual Dichotomism as a Form of Sexism

Just as a complete de-sexing of language may be misperceived as being nonsexist, so sexual dichotomism may be mistaken as a remedy for gender insensitivity. Avoiding one mistake by making another does not make things any better, however. Whenever the sexes are treated as categorically different groups in instances in which *human* attributes are assigned to one or the other sex, sexual dichotomism results.

6.5 Conclusion

Sex appropriateness, familism, and sexual dichotomism are three common problems in research. Sex appropriateness consists of taking a set of historical assumptions about the "proper" behavior and the nature of the sexes and giving them a normative status. Familism consists of attributing individual properties to the family unit or ignoring relevant intrafamilial differentiation. Sexual dichotomism, finally, consists of treating the sexes as two discrete groups, rather than as overlapping groups, by attributing human properties to only one sex and by ignoring intragroup differences. It is thus a modern version of biologism, which treats a biological variable (sex) as if it were a social variable.

The solution to this latter problem is emphatically not, as has been proposed, to stop "seeing two genders."[60] We must be gender sensitive *and* avoid falling into the trap of sexual dichotomism, or, to turn it around, we must avoid sexual dichotomism *and* avoid falling into the trap of gender insensitivity. If we fail, we will only have substituted one sexist problem for another.

Notes

1 For an extensive discussion of the inherent sexism in the use of sex (gender) roles or sex (gender) identity as *explanatory* rather than descriptive variables, see Margrit Eichler, *The Double Standard: A Feminist Critique of Feminist Social Science* (London: Croom Helm, 1980), chaps. 2 and 3.

2 William F. Alvarez, "The meaning of maternal employment for mothers and their perceptions of their three-year-old children," *Child Development* 56, 2 (1985): 350–360.

3 Ibid., p. 350.

4 There is an emergent literature on fathers and an incipient realization that the employment situation of fathers does very much affect the socialization process; however, this particular article does not display such knowledge, nor do many others.

5 Ibid., p. 352.

6 Ibid.

7 Ibid., p. 356.

8 William Michelson, *From Sun to Sun: Daily Obligations and Community Structure in the Lives of Employed Women and Their Families* (Totowa, NJ: Rowman and Allanheld, 1985).

9 Ibid., p. 199.

10 I am using this particular study as an example because it is (a) important, (b) recent, and (c) has the advantage of presenting the complete survey instrument within the book, a practice that is unfortunately not always followed, making the type of criticism engaged in here impossible. Ironically, some of the better studies thus get singled out for criticism rather than more grossly biased ones.

11 Graham S. Lowe and Harvey Krahn, "Where wives work: The relative effects of situational and attitudinal data," *Canadian Journal of Sociology* 10, 1 (1985): 1–22.

12 Ibid., p. 10.

13 Ibid., p. 11, t. 1.

14 Margrit Eichler, *Families in Canada Today: Recent Changes and their Policy Consequences* (Toronto: Gage, 1983).

15 Ibid., p. 67.

16 Ibid., p. 68.

17 Ibid., p. 71.

18 Rob Palkovitz, "Fathers' birth attendance, early contact, and extended contact with their newborns: A critical review," *Child Development* 56, 2 (1985): 392–406.

19 Ibid., p. 398.

20 Ibid., p. 405.

21 Paula J. Caplan and Ian Hall-McCorquodale, "Mother-blaming in major clinical journals," *American Journal of Orthopsychiatry* 55, 3 (1985): 345–353.

22 Ibid., pp. 349–350.

23 There are, of course, many behaviors and traits that are not appropriate for anybody, such as unprovoked violence.

24 I am here treating the use of families or of households as units of analysis as indicative of the same problem, rather than as distinct issues. One might call the problem "householdism" when the term household is used, but this would add nothing but another ugly neologism.

25 Jacques H. Dreze, "(Uncertainty and) the firm in general equilibrium theory," *Supplement to the Economic Journal* 95 (1985):14.

26 Peter Howitt, "Transaction costs in the theory of unemployment," *American Economic Review* 7, 5 (March 1985): 192.

27 Ibid., p. 94.

28 See the vast literature on family decision-making. A few references (from which many other references can be gleaned) include Robert J. Meyer and Robert A. Lewis, "New wine from old wineskins: Marital power research," *Comparative Family Studies* 7, 3 (1976): 397–407; Wayne Hill and John Scanzoni, "An approach for assessing marital decision-making processes," *Journal of Marriage and the Family* 44, 4 (1982): 927–941; Craig M. Allen, "On the validity of relative validity of 'final-say' measures of marital power," *Journal of Marriage and the Family* 46, 3 (1984): 619–629.

29 The following quote is from Emily M. Nett, "Family studies of elders: Gerontological and feminist approaches." Paper presented at the annual meeting of the Canadian Sociology and Anthropology Association, 1982, pp. 10–11.

30 E. Brody, "Innovative programs and services for elderly and the family." Testimony before the Select Committee on Aging, U.S. House of Representatives, 96th Congress, Washington, D.C., 1980.

31 Neena L. Chappell, "The future impact of the changing status of women." Plenary address presented at the research workshop on Canada's Changing Age Structure: Implications for the Future, Burnaby, B.C., 1981.

32 J. Treas, "Family support systems for the aged: Some social and demographic considerations," *Gerontologist* 17 (1977): 486–491.

33 Victor W. Marshall, Carolyn J. Rosenthall, and Jane Synge, "The family as a health service organization for the elderly." Paper presented at the annual meeting of the Society for the Study of Social Problems, Toronto, 1981.

34 Judith A. Cashmore and Jacqueline J. Goodnow, "Agreement between generations: A two-process approach," *Child Development* 56, 2 (1985): 495.

35 Until 1981, the Canadian census reported only the respondent's paternal ancestry. This was changed, starting with the 1981 census. See Canada, *1981 Census Dictionary* (Ottawa: Minister of Supply and Services, 1982): 15.

36 See Meredith Edwards, *Financial Arrangements within Families: A Research Report for the National Women's Advisory Council* (Canberra: 1981). Edwards provides other references to the literature.

37 Paul Evans Alson, "Do large deficits produce high interest rates?" *American Economic Review* 75, 1 (March 1985): 85.

38 N. Folbre, "Household production in the Phillipines: A non-neoclassical approach," *Economic Development and Cultural Change*, Working Paper 26 (1983): 1–31. The discussion in this section follows Margaret A. White, "Breaking the circular hold: Taking on the patriarchal and ideological biases in traditional economic theory." OPSPA Paper 7, Women's Studies Centre, OISE, Toronto, 1984.

39 White, "Breaking the Circular Hold," p. 12.

40 Ruth Hershberger, *Adam's Rib* (New York: Harper & Row, 1970), makes this point in a most amusing manner. See particularly n. 1 on pp. 203–212 on the concept of "normality."

41 We are also falling into a primitive form of biologism, a point made by R. W. Connell in "Theorizing gender," *Sociology* 19, 2 (1985): 260–272. He points toward a curious paradox that ensues when assuming the stance of sexual dichotomism (he does not use this term):

> a social fact or process is coupled with, and implicitly attributed to, a biological fact. The result is not only to collapse together a rather heterogeneous group (do gays suffer from malestream thought, for instance; or boys?). It also, curiously, takes the heat off the open opponents of feminism. The hard-line male chauvinist is now less liable to be thought personally responsible for what he says or does in particular circumstances, since what he says or does is attributable to the general fatality of being male. (p. 266)

42 Martin R. Wong, "MMPI Scale Five: Its meaning, or lack thereof," *Journal of Personality Assessment* 48, 3 (1984): 279–284, quote on p. 282.

43 Ibid., p. 279.

44 Ibid.

45 Ibid., p. 280.

46 Ibid.

47 Stanley A. Althof, Leslie M. Lthstein, Paul Jones, and John Shen, "An MMPI Subscale (Gd): To identify males with gender identity conflicts," *Journal of Personality Assessment* 47, 1 (1983): 42–49.

48 Ibid., p. 47.

49 Ibid., p. 48.

50 It strikes one as particularly ironic that skills like cooking are included in the scale, given the current high degree of divorce in North America and the likely attendent need for men to cook for themselves. In my opinion, cooking should be seen as a necessary survival skill for every human adolescent and adult. I would class its lack as a social and psychological problem for any adult, male or female.

51 Ibid., p. 48.

52 See Margrit Eichler, *The Double Standard* (London: Croom Helm, 1980): 69–71.

53 Joanne C. J. Prindiville, "When is a mother not a mom? Reflections on the contributions of cross-cultural studies to models of sex and gender." Unpublished paper, delivered at the CRIAW Conference, Vancouver, 1983, p. 6.

54 Ibid.

55 Rhonda Lenton, "What statisticians can learn from feminists and feminists from statisticians." Unpublished paper, Dept. of Sociology, McMaster University, 1986.

56 Ibid.

57 David Tresemer, "Assumptions made about gender roles," in Marcia Millman and Rosabeth Moss Kanter (eds.), *Another Voice* (Garden City, NY: Anchor Books, 1975): 308–339.

58 Lenton, "What statisticians can learn."

59 There are, of course, other instances of such usage. For example, box score tallies can be used such that they distort sex differences as well as similarities; see Paula J. Caplan, "Beyond the box score: A boundary condition for sex differences in aggression and achievement striving," *Progress in Experimental Personality Research* 9 (1979): 41–87.

60 Sarah H. Matthews, "Rethinking sociology through a feminist perspective," *The American Sociologist* 17, 1 (1982): 29–35.

Chapter 7
Guidelines for Nonsexist Research

7.1 Introduction
7.2 Limitations of the guidelines
    7.2.1 Limitations in knowledge
    7.2.2 Studies without sexual relevance
    7.2.3 Applicability of the guidelines to individual studies versus fields
        of study
7.3 How to use the guidelines
7.4 Sexism in titles
7.5 Sexism in language
7.6 Sexist concepts
    7.6.1 Androcentric (gynocentric) concepts
        7.6.1.1 Construction of ego as male
        7.6.1.2 Misogynist (misandrist) concepts
    7.6.2 Overgeneral concepts
    7.6.3 Concepts premised on a double standard
        7.6.3.1 Concepts premised on unequal treatment of equal
                attributes in the two sexes
        7.6.3.2 Asymmetrical concepts
        7.6.3.3 Value-laden concepts
        7.6.3.4 Concepts premised on notions of sex appropriateness
    7.6.4 Familistic concepts
    7.6.5 Concepts based on sexual dichotomism
7.7 Sexism in the research design
    7.7.1 Sexism in the choice of research question or frame of reference
        7.7.1.1 Androcentric frame of reference

7.7.1.2 Androcentric or gynocentric formulation of research questions

7.7.1.3 Research questions based on a double standard or sex appropriateness

7.7.2 Choice of research instruments

7.7.2.1 Double standards in choice of research instruments

7.7.2.2 Sexual dichotomism in choice of research instruments

7.7.3 Androcentric choice of variables

7.7.4 Neglecting the sex of participants in the research process

7.7.5 Taking the family as the smallest unit of analysis

7.7.6 Inappropriate comparison groups

7.8 Sexism in methods

7.8.1 Androcentricity in the validation of research instruments

7.8.2 Gender insensitivity in reporting on sample

7.8.3 Sexist bias in the formulation of questions or questionnaires

7.8.4 Sexual dichotomism in methods

7.8.5 Treating other-sex opinions as facts

7.8.6 Double standards in coding procedures

7.9 Sexism in data interpretation

7.9.1 Androcentricity in data interpretation

7.9.2 Overgeneralization in data interpretation

7.9.3 Gender insensitivity in data interpretation

7.9.4 Sex appropriateness in data interpretation

7.10 Sexism in policy evaluations and recommendations

7.10.1 Gender insensitivity in policy evaluations and recommendations

7.10.2 Double standards in policy evaluations and recommendations

7.1 Introduction

So far, we have identified four major and three derived sexist problems. We have looked at concrete examples as they appear in the literature, sometimes in rather gross form, sometimes in more subtle form. The point of identifying sexism in research is, of course, to eliminate it. This chapter will, to that end, provide a framework for conducting nonsexist research. The guidelines proposed here can be applied to an individual piece of research – either one's own or someone else's. They are relevant both when formulating a research project and when evaluating a finished piece of research. And they are applicable to all of the social sciences.

The various types of sexist problems have been sufficiently discussed in the preceding chapters. It is worth reiterating one important point, however: This book is intended not to help you "correctly" identify a type of sexism in a given piece of work but to identify sexism *in some way* and to overcome it without falling into a different mode of sexist thinking.

This chapter and the checklist included in the Appendix are organized by component of the research process. Just as the various sexist problems tend to occur together, so too the various components of the research process overlap. It is nevertheless helpful to break the research process down into components in order to group various questions together.

It is also difficult to identify the various stages of the research process in a manner that is applicable to a wide range of approaches. Although there is some logical progression to the way in which this chapter is organized – I begin with the title (which is usually the first thing one reads) and conclude with policy evaluations and recommendations (which, if they exist, are usually the last part of a study) – we should not think of these stages as exclusively sequential. For example, in order to assess whether or not a title is overgeneral, we must be familiar with the entire content of a study. Similarly, concepts are such a fundamental aspect of research that they are invariably used in the earliest stages of the research process: A research design is not possible without concepts. Concepts are also central to data interpretation, and new concepts may be introduced in the latter stages of a study in order to make sense of the data.

Finally, because different disciplines and different researchers use different approaches, not all aspects of the guidelines will be applicable to all studies. For example, many researchers do not ask direct questions of respondents but instead evaluate existing sources of data: statistics, written documents (such as diaries, newspaper articles, immigration policies, and school records), and so on. In such cases comments that address the formulation of questions to respondents are obviously not applicable.

7.2 *Limitations of the Guidelines*

The guidelines do not always work equally well in all circumstances. In particular, they are limited when (a) relevant knowledge is insufficient; and (b) a study has no sexual relevance.

7.2.1 *Limitations in Knowledge*

Critiques of sexism in research are rarely possible with only superficial knowledge of a particular discipline or subject area. While we must achieve some distance from our work and from the assumptions of our own disciplines in order to detect sexism, we also need an understanding of a field of study before we can make a thorough critique of it. In doing the research for this book, for example, I was occasionally forced to eliminate an article from consideration because I lacked sufficient knowledge to understand the problem under consideration or the methodology being employed to explore it. Similarly, in the chapter on gender insensitivity, I argued that the comparison between ever-unmarried males and ever-unmarried females for the purpose of exploring the causes of female–male salary differentials is invalid because the two groups are different in essential ways: one group consists of the "cream-of-the-crop"; the other of the "bottom-of-the-barrel." My ability to make this critique hinged on my knowledge that such a difference exists and has been demonstrated. Without this knowledge, I would have failed to perceive the sexism inherent in the study. Using the guidelines will not magically make one an expert in all areas, and the more trenchant critiques (and, one hopes, nonsexist alternatives) will have to emerge from within the various disciplinary groups. Finally, we may realize that a study is sexist only after a prolonged period of time, and sometimes even when a conscious effort has been made to eliminate sexism. Using the guidelines should speed up this process, but it will be neither an easy nor a quick route to travel.

7.2.2 Studies Without Sexual Relevance

Only very rarely did I encounter in my search for examples studies that were clearly not sex or gender related. One such example is a study exploring the west-to-east migration of the early Polynesians and their Lapita predecessors in terms of recently acquired data on equatorial westerlies (i.e., winds) and associated ocean current effects.[1] Clearly this type of study is relevant to understanding an important aspect of human behavior – large-scale migration patterns by water – but since the proferred explanations all hinge on wind and current patterns and sailing constraints that result, I found no sexually relevant statements. The author once used the term "fishermen" instead of an appropriate nonsexist term,[2] but this is not a significant concept in the article. In fact, if the word had simply been dropped, nothing would have been substantially changed.[3]

One cannot properly say that the guidelines do not work in this case: they work in demonstrating that the study is not sexist. However, in most instances I would not phrase this conclusion so strongly. Returning again to the use of the ever-unmarried males and females as comparison groups, it is possible to argue in retrospect that sexism existed even though it was not immediately apparent.

7.2.3 Applicability of the Guidelines to Individual Studies versus Fields of Study

The guidelines are meant to be used primarily to assess individual research studies. The guidelines should also be helpful in conducting overview assessments of broader fields of study, although I have not yet tried to use them systematically for this purpose. Moreover, because the accumulated knowledge of different disciplines and fields of study emerges through individual studies, a critical assessment of both our own and other people's (largely unconscious) sexism is ultimately the most effective way in which to overcome sexism in research more generally.

7.3 How to Use the Guidelines

The remainder of this chapter is organized by component of the research process: formulation of the title (section 7.4), use of language (section 7.5), development of concepts (section 7.6), choice of research instrument (section 7.7), methodology (section 7.8), data interpretation (section 7.9), and policy evaluations and recommendations (section 7.10). The various ways in which sexism occurs at each stage of the research process are discussed in each section. Following the general description of the problem, each section includes a series of questions that should be asked in order to determine whether or not a sexist problem exists. The questions are meant to be used sequentially: once you have determined that a particular problem does not exist (or if you have identified a problem and remedied it), go on to the next series of questions. Each section then concludes with suggested solutions for eliminating sexism.

The checklist included in the Appendix to this book is to be used in conjunction with this chapter. It is organized along two axes. The horizontal axis identifies each stage of the research process (formulation of the title, use of language, and so on). The vertical axis is organized by type of sexist problem (overgeneralization, androcentricity, and so on). The checklist is cross-referenced to appropriate sections in the remainder of this chapter (under Text References: Identification/Resolution) and to relevant discussion in earlier chapters (under Text References: Description/Examples).

Suppose, for example, that you want to determine whether or not you have introduced sexism by your use of language. Go first to the section in the checklist labeled "Research Component: Language." Five ways in which the use of language introduces sexism are identified (note that certain types of bias, for example, double standards, can manifest themselves in several ways). In order to evaluate your choice of language, turn to section 7.4 (Sexism in Language) and ask yourself the questions listed there. If you answer "yes" to any of these questions, read through and apply the appropriate solutions. If you are unsure as to whether or not you have introduced a certain problem (or if you do not understand the problem or solutions), turn back to the appropriate section in one of the earlier chapters for a more detailed explanation.

It is worth noting, finally, that the solutions offered here are helpful only in the case of studies still in progress. For studies that have already been completed, the questions can serve to help identify sexism and thus they will alert you to problems that may exist in a relevant literature. It is hoped that this will enable you and others to avoid repeating past errors, which is, after all, what research is all about.

It may well be that there are forms of sexism that have not been discussed here. We may be blind to particular forms of sexism that reveal themselves only after we have made progress in eliminating other, more salient manifestations. I have no doubt, however, that systematically applying these questions to research in the social sciences will take us one large step forward toward a more accurate – and more useful – analysis of social reality.

7.4 Sexism in Titles

Titles are important in identifying research. They are incorporated into computer referencing systems, and are often the primary means of establishing the relevancy of someone's work to your own. They also serve as a screening mechanism that structures access to publications. Making titles appropriately reflect the content of a study will not solve all problems of sexism in research, but it will help make sexism visible. Imagine what might happen if some of the studies discussed earlier were entitled: "A Model of Male Political Participation," "Conceptions of the Male Elderly Sick Role," "Effects of Ability Grouping on Male Israeli Students," "Male Class Tells," "A Study of Male-Dominated Reform Movements in the Nineteenth Century in America," or "Men's Propensity for Warfare: An Androcentric Socio-biological Perspective." A quick computer scan, for instance, would enable the student to conclude that much research needs to be done on women.

QUESTIONS. In order to determine if a title is sexist, ask yourself the following three questions:

- Does this title evoke the image of general applicability? If yes, is it in fact equally applicable to both sexes?

- Does this title contain a sexist concept? (See section 7.6 as to what questions to address to concepts.)

- Does this title contain sexist language? (See section 7.4 as to what questions to address to language.)

SOLUTIONS. If you answered "yes" to any of these questions, either the title or the content needs to be changed.

7.5 Sexism in Language

Language may be sexist through overgeneralizing or overspecifying, through being androcentric, or through using a double standard. Using sexist language is like trying to paint a delicate picture with a large painter's brush: The tool is not sensitive enough for detailed and complicated work that needs a more precise instrument. Just as the use of a brush that is too broad and unwieldy is likely to lead to sloppy pictures, so the use of sexist language is likely to lead to sloppy thinking. While fixing the language will sometimes solve a problem, at other times it simply makes another problem visible, as happens when one makes a title content-specific, thus revealing the narrowness of the study.

Sexism in language may take several forms. The most commented-upon form of sexism in language concerns the use of male terms for generic purposes. This practice once took the form of a grammatical rule and is still regarded in this light by some people, even though it results in nonspecific language. The reverse of this form of sexism occurs when authors use generic terms when, in fact, they are dealing with only one sex, such as when they write about parents but mean only mothers, refer to workers but have only male workers in mind, and so on.

Another form of sexism in language occurs when males and females are referred to by nonparallel terms in parallel situations, such as in the expression "a man and his wife" ("he" is used as the reference point, "she" is defined in relation to him). The legal practice of wives taking their husbands' last names upon marriage is simply the same practice elevated to a legal custom.

A rather minor form of sexism in language, not comparable in importance with the others but nevertheless irritating, occurs when one sex is consistently named before the other, and when such sequencing takes on the characteristics of a grammatical rule.[4]

A fifth and very important sexist language practice concerns the use of different grammatical modes for the sexes. This issue hovers at the border between language and concepts, because it relates to data interpretation rather than simply to different modes of expression. It may not be possible to turn a written passage in which men are dealt with in the active mode (they do, act, and so on) and women in the passive mode (something is being done to them) into nonsexist form by simply changing grammatical structure. Indeed, there are instances in which one mode is clearly inappropriate (as in descriptions of the Indian custom of *suttee*, in which the active mode – widows immolating themselves – is inappropriate).

QUESTIONS. In order to determine whether or not language is sexist, ask yourself the following five questions:

- Are any male (or female) terms used for generic purposes?
- Are any generic terms employed when, in fact, the author(s) is (are) speaking about only one sex?
- Are females and males in parallel situations described by nonparallel terms?
- When both sexes are mentioned together in particular phrases, does one sex consistently precede the other?
- Are the two sexes consistently discussed in different grammatical modes?

SOLUTIONS. If you answered "yes" to any of these questions, you have identified a case of sexism in language. The remedy, if dealing with your own text, is fairly straightforward:

- In the case of the use of *sex-specific terms for generic purposes* or of *generic terms for sex-specific purposes*, use generic terms when making generic statements, and sex-specific terms when discussing one sex only.

- If males and females in *parallel situations* are referred to in nonparallel ways, equalize their treatment; for example, a "man and his wife" become a "couple," a "husband and wife," or a "woman and a man." If a wife has legally taken her husband's name, you must, of course, refer to her by her legal name, but use the same form for both males and females (for example, refer to both by their first and last names). The one exception to this rule applies when research describes a practice from a time in which nonparallel terms were or are in fact employed to refer to women and men. In such instances, you should distinguish between description and interpretation: In the case of description, nonparallel treatments must be faithfully reproduced, but in the case of interpretation, you can and should employ parallel terms.

- In cases in which *one sex is consistently named first*, alternate the sequencing in some manner.

- If the sexes are consistently discussed in *different grammatical modes*, ask yourself what is missing from the overall picture. It seems a safe enough assumption that no human being is restricted only to passively enduring or actively doing. Then, reconstruct and include the missing part. Depending on the circumstances, this may range from a very minor to a very major job.

7.6 Sexist Concepts

When we deal with concepts, we go beyond language to the meaning attached to a word or phrase *within a given context*. The same concept (for example, head of household) may or may not be sexist depending on whether it accurately describes or distorts a given social relationship. Therefore, we cannot evaluate a concept's sexist connotations without taking its context into consideration.

Concepts are a major research tool. It is sometimes difficult to see the tool itself as a potential problem. In order to recognize sexist concepts, at least two steps are necessary. First, identify concepts crucial to the study at hand. Second, subject these concepts to the questions that follow. If you answer "yes" to any of these questions, you have identified a sexist concept. Concepts may be androcentric, overgeneral, or based on a double standard or the notion of sex appropriateness. Each case is addressed separately below.

7.6.1 *Androcentric (Gynocentric) Concepts*

Concepts may be androcentric (or gynocentric) in any of two ways: by having a male (or female) referent, or by being demeaning to women (or men).

7.6.1.1 *Construction of Ego as Male*

In instances in which a concept is used as if it were generally applicable to both sexes, ask yourself who or what the concept refers to in order to determine whether or not the concept has a one-sex referent. For example, to whom does the concept of "the suburb as a bedroom community" refer? It presents itself as general but in fact refers only to a portion of the population. Similarly, the concepts of "group cohesion" and "intergroup warfare" sound inclusive but may be used with all-male referents, in which case they are androcentric.

Sometimes the referent is not hidden but is open, as in the concepts of "polygyny" or "polyandry." These are concepts that indicate a relationship that affects both sexes, but they are defined from the perspective of one sex only.

QUESTIONS. In order to determine whether or not a concept is androcentric (gynocentric), ask yourself the following questions:

- To whom or what does the concept appear to refer (who is the theoretical referent)? To whom or what does the concept *empirically* refer? Does it seem to refer to both sexes but empirically refer to one sex only?

- Does the concept refer to a relational quality expressed from the viewpoint of one sex only?

SOLUTIONS. If your answers to these questions indicate a mismatch between theoretical and empirical referents, the two must be made to match, either by changing the concept and making it sex-specific, or by changing the content and making it applicable to both sexes. Where relational qualities are concerned, they must express the viewpoint of both sexes. This may involve utilizing either a conceptual pair or a superordinate concept, whichever is appropriate.

7.6.1.2 *Misogynist (Misandrist) Concepts*

Some concepts demean one sex or the other, as in the case of the "masochistic woman." (Note that critical concepts that describe a negative reality are not included under this heading.)

QUESTION. In order to determine whether or not a concept is misogynistic (or misandristic), ask yourself the following question;

- Does the concept demean one sex?

SOLUTION. If you answered "yes" to this question, replace the demeaning concept with a nondemeaning one.

7.6.2 *Overgeneral Concepts*

In order to recognize an overgeneral concept, you need to identify both the purported referent and the empirical referent. Examples of overgeneral concepts include the use of the term "universal suffrage" to mean adult male suffrage, or the terms "childlessness" or "fertility" to describe female childlessness or fertility. Similarly, a concept is overspecific if its purported referent is one sex but it in fact applies to both sexes, as in the use of the phrase "mother tongue" to indicate the language spoken in a home in which a child grows up.

QUESTION. In order to determine whether or not a concept is overgeneral/overspecific, ask yourself the following question:

- Does the concept use a sex-specific descriptor in instances in which it is empirically applicable to both sexes?

SOLUTION. If you answered "yes" to this question, the empirical and theoretical referents must be made to match.

7.6.3 Concepts Premised on a Double Standard

There are at least three different ways in which a concept may be informed by a double standard: by being premised on unequal treatment of the sexes, by being asymmetrical, and by being value-laden within a sexual context.

7.6.3.1 Concepts Premised on Unequal Treatment of Equal Attributes in the Two Sexes

In order to recognize this double standard, you must determine whether the concept is based on an attribute that is potentially present in both sexes but is treated differently on the basis of sex. An example of such differential treatment is the use of the terms "head of household" or "head of family" to refer to adult married males, while adult married females are referred to as "spouses." The same attribute (being married) is treated differentially (the husband is designated "head," while the wife is designated "spouse").

QUESTION. In order to determine whether or not a concept is based on unequal treatment of equal attributes, ask yourself the following question:

- Is the concept premised on an attribute that is present in both sexes but is operationally defined in such a manner that it will categorize females and males differently?

SOLUTION. If you answered "yes" to this question, you need to create a concept that categorizes females and males equally if they display equal attributes.

7.6.3.2 *Asymmetrical Concepts*

In order to recognize an asymmetrical concept, you need to determine whether a sex-specific concept describes a situation, trait, or behavior that is theoretically present in both sexes but is linked to one sex only. Examples of asymmetric concepts include the use of the phrase "schizophrenogenic mother" when it is not coupled with the concept of "schizophrenogenic father," "unwed mother" when not linked with "unwed father," and "maternal deprivation" when not linked with "paternal deprivation."

QUESTION. In order to determine whether or not a concept is asymmetrical, ask yourself the following question:

- Does the concept refer, in a sex-linked manner, to a situation, trait, or behavior that exists for both sexes?

SOLUTION. If you answered "yes" to this question, change the concept so that it expresses *human* attributes in sex-nonspecific terms.

7.6.3.3 *Value-Laden Concepts*

A value-laden conceptual pair is one in which a sex-related division is created by assigning different labels that contain value judgments about certain characteristics when no such value judgments are warranted. (There are cases in which such value judgments are warranted, as when dealing with violence or abuse). Examples of value-laden conceptual pairs include "field independence" and "field dependence," "productive work" and "unproductive work," and "primary earner" and "secondary earner."

QUESTIONS: In order to determine whether or not a concept is inappropriately value laden (i.e., sexist), ask yourself the following questions:

- Does the conceptual pair correspond largely to a sexual division?
- If so, is the differential value attached through choice of words to the male- and female-dominated attributes justified?

SOLUTION. If you answered "yes" to the first question and "no" to the second, reformulate the conceptual pair so that equal value is assigned to male- and female-dominated attributes.

7.6.3.4 Concepts Premised on Notions of Sex-Appropriateness

In all known societies, people consider certain behaviors and traits to be more appropriate for one sex than for the other; however, there is great variability in what is considered appropriate (or "normal" or "healthy") for either sex in different societies. Such concepts as "sex roles" and "sex identity" are useful descriptors, but when a given behavior or trait is presented as unproblematically "appropriate," it introduces a double standard.

QUESTION. In order to determine whether or not a concept is based on some notion of sex appropriateness, ask yourself the following question:

- Is the concept premised on the notion that certain *human* behaviors, traits, or attributes are appropriate for one sex only?

SOLUTION. If you answered "yes" to this question, identify socially sex-assigned attributes by descriptive but not prescriptive labels in order to eliminate the assumption of sex *appropriateness*.

7.6.4 Familistic Concepts

Concepts that attribute individual properties, attributes, or behaviors to families or households are gender insensitive. Examples of such gender-insensitive concepts include use of the term "family support systems" when it is generally individual women who render support, or use of the variable "family income" when dealing with earned income of one individual.

QUESTION. In order to determine whether or not a concept is gender insensitive, ask yourself the following question:

- Does the concept attribute individual properties, attributes, or behaviors to families or households?

SOLUTION. If you answered "yes" to this question, identify individual properties, attributes, or behaviors as such.

7.6.5 Concepts Based on Sexual Dichotomism

Sexual dichotomism occurs when concepts are derived from the notion that the sexes are two entirely discrete social as well as biological groups. This happens whenever human traits are defined as masculine or feminine, or human biological phenomena (such as testosterone or progesterone) are labeled "male" or "female."

QUESTION. In order to determine whether or not a concept is based on sexual dichotomism, ask yourself the following question.

- Does the concept define certain human attributes, capacities, traits, or behaviors as either masculine or feminine?

SOLUTION. If you answered "yes" to this question, identify human attributes or capacities as such, rather than as belonging to one sex or the other.

7.7 Sexism in the Research Design

Sexism may enter into the research design in the form of androcentricity, gender insensitivity (including familism), or a double standard (including sexual dichotomism). Different aspects of a research design are applicable to different kinds of studies, but at a minimum, all research designs involve choosing a research question and using some frame of reference.

7.7.1 Sexism in the Choice of Research Question or Frame of Reference

Sexism can enter into the research design in two ways: through the relevant literature and through the design of a particular study. Because so much social science research has, by and large, been sexist, chances are that the way in which a particular topic is customarily addressed in the relevant literature will be sexist as well. It is therefore necessary to assess *critically* the relevant literature with respect to potential sexist elements, in order to avoid making the same mistakes. This applies to all components of previous research, including language used, concepts employed, and so on, but is particularly important for the overall frame of reference. There are three ways in which sexism may enter into the choice of research question or adoption of a framework: The framework adopted may be androcentric, the major research question chosen may be formulated in an androcentric or gyno-centric manner, or the research question may be based on a double standard.

7.7.1.1 Androcentric Frame of Reference

An androcentric frame of reference is created when the major research question is formulated in such a way that only men are seen as actors while women are treated as objects that are acted upon.

This is the case, for example, with the sociobiological explanation of "intergroup warfare" in "primitive man" discussed previously. In such instances, women become largely invisible. Similarly, an androcentric framework is adopted when male behavior is treated as the norm and female behavior is seen only in relation to this norm, as was the case in another article we discussed that explained the "choice" of reasons for divorce by female and male petitioners. Finally, a frame of reference is androcentric when it results in attaching blame to women where it is unjustified (as when blaming victims, rather than the perpetrators, for sexual assaults, or blaming mothers for problems with children without considering the role of fathers or extraneous factors).

QUESTION. In order to determine whether or not a research frame of reference is androcentric, ask the following question:

- Substitute the word "woman," or such nonsexist terms as "person," "individual," "worker," "citizen," "consumer," "patient," or "elderly person," each time the author uses the so-called generic term "man." Does the statement still make sense?

SOLUTION. If these substitutions render the statements nonsensical, you have uncovered an androcentric bias. In order to remedy this problem, recast the study by exploring the females' situation, or revamp the study as one pertaining to one sex only. This latter alternative is not appropriate when the topic deals with relational issues (for example, "group cohesion" where there are both women and men in the group).

QUESTION.

- Are men treated as actors, women as acted upon?

SOLUTION. If you answered "yes," add a second set of questions about women as actors and men as acted upon to the research design.

QUESTION.

- Is male behavior taken as the norm, and female behavior as the deviation that needs to be explained?

SOLUTION. If you answered "yes," either expand the framework by assessing male behavior against female behavior, or establish a genuinely sex-unrelated behavior as the norm. The latter is not feasible if the behavior in question is strongly sex differentiated.

QUESTIONS.

- Are women blamed? If so, is the blame justified?
- Are women victims or perpetrators?
- Are the perpetrators held responsible for their deeds?
- Is the role of male participants in the process adequately considered?
- Are overall structural factors adequately taken into account?

SOLUTION. Where there are victims, perpetrators must be held responsible for their actions. Consider the role of male participants in the process as carefully as that of female participants; take overall structural factors into account.

7.7.1.2 Androcentric or Gynocentric Formulation of Research Questions

An androcentric or embryonically gynocentric[5] formulation of the research question exists when a phenomenon that affects both sexes is studied primarily by focusing on one sex only. This is often the case with social stratification studies, in which women have been largely excluded from consideration, or in family studies, in which men have been largely excluded from consideration in their role as parents.

QUESTIONS. In order to determine whether or not a research question is androcentric (gynocentric), ask yourself the following questions:

• Does the phenomenon under consideration affect both sexes?

• If so, does the literature give adequate attention to the role of both sexes? In particular, in studies concerning families and reproduction, has the role of men been given adequate attention? In all other subject areas, has the role of women been given adequate attention?

SOLUTION. If a phenomenon affects both sexes but has been studied primarily with respect to one sex only, include the excluded sex in your research design. Alternatively, this may be a case in which a one-sex study is appropriate, provided that it focuses on the hitherto excluded sex. When a field of study is so biased toward one sex that the other sex is virtually ignored, the problem may lie with the overall *balance* of the research rather than with any one individual study.

7.7.1.3 Research Questions Based on a Double Standard or Sex Appropriateness

In two-sex studies, respondents are sometimes asked different questions even though the same instrument may be used on both sexes. This is often the case with studies using some measure of socioeconomic status, or when both women and men are asked about a potential work–family conflict for married women, but not for married men.

QUESTION. In order to determine whether or not a research question is based on a double standard or sex appropriateness, ask yourself the following question:

- Are both sexes asked the same questions?

SOLUTION. If not, develop instruments that ask the same questions of both sexes.

7.7.2 Choice of Research Instruments

Sexism may also enter the research design through the choice of research instruments that are based on either a double standard or sexual dichotomism.

7.7.2.1 Double Standards in Choice of
         Research Instruments

Researchers occasionally develop different instruments for male and female subjects. This may even be done in response to an androcentric instrument in order to overcome such bias, as is the case with an instrument especially developed to measure the socioeconomic status of women. However, data generated from such instruments do not allow us to make comparative statements. In a few exceptional cases, different instruments for the two sexes are necessary, as when examining certain physical illnesses and sex-related symptoms. However, even in such cases the questions should be as nearly equivalent as possible.

QUESTIONS. In order to determine whether or not a research

instrument introduces a double standard, ask yourself the following questions:

- Is the same instrument used for both females and males? If not, is the use of a differential instrument justified by physical differences between the sexes?

SOLUTION. If different instruments are used without compelling reasons, develop an instrument that is applicable to both sexes. If different instruments are necessary, justify them in detail.

7.7.2.2 *Sexual Dichotomism in Choice of Research Instruments*

Particular research instruments occasionally divide the sexes into two discrete groups, even though in reality females and males overlap in some of the dichotomized characteristics. This is the case with masculinity–femininity scales. The use of such instruments results in empirical reality being subordinated to stereotypic notions.

QUESTION. In order to determine whether a research instrument introduces sexual dichotomism, ask yourself the following question:

- Does the research instrument divide the sexes into two discrete groups when, in fact, they have overlapping characteristics?

SOLUTION. If you answered "yes," adopt new research instruments that do not dichotomize overlapping distributions of traits.

7.7.3 Androcentric Choice of Variables

In two-sex studies, androcentricity may enter the research design through the designation of "important" variables. For example, in the studies on group cohesion among early hominids, the research emphasizes male-dominated activities without considering female-dominated activities (such as nursing, cooking, and care of children) that may very well contribute to or affect group cohesion.

QUESTIONS. In order to determine whether or not the choice of variables has introduced an androcentric bias, ask yourself the following questions:

- What are the major variables examined in this study? Are these variables equally relevant to women and men? If most of the variables pertain to men, is there an equivalent number of variables pertaining primarily to women?

SOLUTION. If you answered "no," correct the imbalance by including variables that affect women. In areas in which we know little about the major factors that affect women, a pilot study may be required.

7.7.4 Neglecting the Sex of Participants in the Research

Gender insensitivity occurs when the sex of participants in the research process is neglected. In studies in which both sexes participate as subjects but the breakdown by sex is not reported, crucial information necessary to interpret the findings is missing. Likewise, the sex of research personnel who come into direct contact with respondents may affect the respondents' answers. Finally, the authorship of statements is important in understanding possible biases, omissions, and emphases.

QUESTIONS. In order to determine whether gender insensitivity has been introduced by failing to report the sex of participants in the research process, ask yourself the following questions:

- Who are the relevant participants in the research process?
- Is their sex reported?
- Is their sex controlled for? If not, is the potential effect of the sex of the participants explicitly acknowledged and discussed?

SOLUTION. Always report the sex of participants. Control for the sex of participants wherever possible. If this is impossible for practical reasons, acknowledge and discuss the potential effects of the sex of the various participants in the research process.

7.7.5 Taking the Family as the Smallest Unit of Analysis

Taking the family as the smallest unit of analysis is not necessarily sexist. A researcher who wishes to describe the various types of families within a society will properly take the different types of families or households as the smallest unit of analysis. It is sexist practice (familism) only in two instances: (1) if the family is attributed behaviors, experiences, benefits, problems, or detrimental effects that are, in fact, attributes of individuals within the family unit (as is the case when individual income is treated as "family" income, or when the family is treated as a care support system for the elderly when only individuals within the family render such care); and (2) when the family is credited with experiencing something (whether positive or negative) in instances in which the same event may have disparate effects on the various family members (as in the cases of the effects of marriage or divorce, joint utility functions, or the assumption of the optimization of family resources).

QUESTIONS. In order to determine whether or not the family has properly been taken as the smallest unit of analysis, ask yourself the following questions:

- Is the issue under consideration anything that is in fact an attribute, experience, or behavior of an individual within the family unit rather than of the unit as the whole?

- Is it possible that the event under consideration may have different effects on various family members?

SOLUTION. If you answered "yes" to either of these questions, the use of the family as the smallest unit of analysis is inappropriate. Identify the individual actors within the unit as such, and study the potentially different effects of the event under investigation by the sex of family members. This may require a drastic revision of the research design.

7.7.6 Inappropriate Comparison Groups

Much gender-sensitive research requires comparing male and female groups with each other. However, male and female groups are occasionally compared when it is inappropriate for the comparison at hand (although not necessarily for other purposes). For instance, if the incomes of male and female groups are to be compared, it is important to ensure that the groups are otherwise comparable (on variables known to influence income, such as education, type of occupation, and so on). The failure to use appropriate comparison groups may lead either to the false attribution of a phenomenon to sex when it is in fact due to some other variable, or to the false attribution of a phenomenon to some other factor when sex is in fact the important variable.

QUESTIONS. In order to determine whether or not gender insensitivity has been introduced by using inappropriate comparison groups, ask yourself the following questions:

- Are any explicit or implicit comparisons made between the sexes? If so, are the sex groups being compared equivalent on all those variables that are likely to have an influence on the outcome under investigation?

SOLUTION. If you answered "no" to the second question, create comparable groups. If this is impossible for practical reasons (for example, you cannot meaningfully compare social factors leading to breast cancer in women and men), carefully list and discuss the variables that differentiate the two groups.

7.8 Sexism in Methods

Obviously, a short book of this type cannot discuss all of the methods used in the social sciences. Some issues that might have been discussed in this section were discussed in the previous section on research design because the distinction made here between research design and methods is an artificial one. Choice of methods is an integral part of the overall research design as are concepts and language used.

So far, we have not identified any method that could not be used in either a sexist or nonsexist manner. In principle, then, methods per se are neither sexist nor nonsexist; it is the way in which they are used (or misused) that makes them (non)sexist.

Methods may be sexist in several ways: (1) through the use of instruments in a manner based on sexual dichotomism; (2) if they formulate questions in an androcentric manner; (3) if they rely on notions of sex appropriateness as an explanatory variable; (4) if they treat other-sex opinions as statements of fact about the other sex; or (5) if they incorporate a double standard.

7.8.1 Androcentricity in the Validation of Research Instruments

Androcentricity is introduced in methods if a research instrument is developed and validated on males only but is subsequently used on both sexes (if it were developed and validated on females only and were subsequently used on males and females, it would be an instance of gynocentricity).

QUESTIONS. In order to determine whether or not androcentricity (gynocentricity) has been introduced through the validation of research instruments, ask yourself the following questions:

- Has this research instrument been developed and validated on one sex only? If so, is it used on both sexes?

SOLUTION. If you answered "yes" to both questions, restrict the use of the instrument to the sex for which it was developed and validated; alternatively, redevelop and validate the instrument with both sexes.

7.8.2 Gender Insensitivity in Reporting on Sample

Researchers occasionally fail to report the sex composition of their sample, as was the case in a number of articles considered in Chapters 3 and 4. Failure to report the sex composition of the sample makes adequate assessment of the meaning of the data impossible.

QUESTION. In order to determine whether or not gender insensitivity has been introduced in this manner, ask yourself the following question:

- Is the sex composition of the sample adequately reported?

SOLUTION. If you answered "no," report the sex composition of the sample.

7.8.3 Sexist Bias in the Formulation of Questions or Questionnaires

Individual questions or questionnaires may be biased because they use sexist language, are formulated in an androcentric manner, or are based on some notion of sex appropriateness. Questions employ sexist language if they use "man" in its supposedly generic sense (as in the earlier example of a study exploring attitudes toward "a *man* who admits he is a communist" in order to measure tolerance). Questions that do not allow for the total range of possible answers because males are taken as the norm and females are judged accordingly are androcentric (for example, as in asking respondents to agree or disagree with the statement "It is generally better to have a man at the head of a department composed of both men and women employees" and omitting "It is generally better to have a woman . . ."). Finally, questions may be biased by being premised on the notion of sex appropriateness (for instance, by assuming a particular division of labor between the sexes as normative when asking "How often do you feel a conflict between being a mother and working?" without asking an equivalent question about fathers).

QUESTIONS. In order to determine whether or not a questionnaire or an individual question is biased in a sexist manner, ask yourself the following questions:

- Does the question use generic terms for sex-specific purposes or sex-specific terms for generic purposes?

- Does the question take one sex as the norm for the other, thus restricting the range of possible answers?

- Is the question premised on some notion that particular behaviors are appropriate for one sex but not for the other, either explicitly or implicitly, by failing to ask equivalent questions for the other sex?

SOLUTIONS. If sexist language is employed, change it to nonsexist language. If one sex is taken as the norm, reformulate the question to allow for the complete range of theoretically possible responses. If the question assumes that a particular behavior is appropriate for one sex only, reformulate the question to probe the existence of this behavior in both sexes.

7.8.4 Sexual Dichotomism in Methods

Sexual dichotomism is introduced by any method that divides *human* attributes into male and female attributes (as is the case in masculinity–femininity scales) or which treats the sexes as categorically different groups on the basis of *human* attributes.

QUESTION. In order to determine whether or not sexual dichotomism has been introduced in methods, ask yourself the following question:

- Does this particular method categorize males and females into discrete groups on the basis of attributes that can be found in *both* groups?

SOLUTION. Categorize nondiscrete traits in nondiscrete ways.

7.8.5 Treating Other-Sex Opinions as Facts

Researchers sometimes ask members of one sex about the other sex. This may provide very useful information, so long as the researcher keeps in mind that the opinions of one sex about the other must never be confused either with fact or with the opinions of the other sex about itself. Where such confusion occurs, we are dealing with an instance of gender insensitivity.

QUESTIONS. In order to determine whether or not gender insensitivity has been introduced in this manner, ask yourself the following questions:

- Are opinions asked of one sex about the other (including in indirect form, for example, by using historical information)? If so, are they treated as opinions of one sex about the other or as fact?

SOLUTION. If you answered "yes" to these questions, reinterpret other-sex opinions as statements of opinions and no more.

7.8.6 Double Standards in Coding Procedures

If the same responses are interpreted differently by sex (by using different coding instructions, for example) a very blatant double standard is created.

QUESTION. In order to determine whether or not coding procedures are based on a double standard, ask yourself the following question:

- Are identical coding procedures used for females and males?

SOLUTION. If you answered "no," make coding procedures uniform for both sexes.

7.9 Sexism in Data Interpretation

Many of the sexist problems that arise in data interpretation are a consequence of sexism introduced earlier in the research process: in concepts, in the research design, in methods. By eliminating sexism in these components, some of the sexism in data interpretation will also be eliminated. Nevertheless, it is possible for sexism to enter independently at the data interpretation stage through androcentricity, overgeneralization, gender insensitivity, or sex appropriateness.

7.9.1 Androcentricity in Data Interpretation

Data may be interpreted in an androcentric manner by using a male viewpoint or frame of reference, by accepting or justifying female subjugation or male dominance, or by blaming victims.

It is difficult to disentangle the use of a male viewpoint or frame of reference in the research design from that in the data interpretation. Once data are gathered from such a male perspective, it will be difficult or even impossible to avoid carrying this problem over into the data interpretation stage. However, in cases in which there is no way to alter existing data collection processes (for example, in the case of secondary analyses), at a minimum, any existing bias in the research design must be pointed out, and appropriate caution must be exercised in interpreting such data.

The justification of female subjugation or male dominance in the name of some supposedly superior value (for example, cultural tradition or the integrity of ethnic customs) is a direct abrogation of the human rights of females. The defense of bodily mutilation or death or abrogation of basic human rights through data interpretation or otherwise is always inappropriate. Similarly, it is equally inappropriate to blame a clear victim (as in the case of father–daughter incest); interpreting data to blame the victim only adds insult to injury.

QUESTIONS. In order to determine whether or not an androcentric bias has been introduced during data interpretation, ask yourself the following questions:

- Are the implications of findings for both females and males explicitly considered?

- Are biases in the data collection process explicitly acknowledged and their implications discussed?

- Is there any justification of female subjugation or male dominance? Is any form of bodily mutilation, death, or other abrogation of human rights justified in the name of a supposedly higher value?

- Is there a clear victim? If so, is the victim blamed for her (occasionally his) victimization?

SOLUTIONS. If you answered "yes" to the first question, consider the implications of findings for both sexes. If you answered "yes" to the second question, acknowledge any biases that cannot be eliminated, explicitly discuss the importance of such bias, and adjust your conclusions accordingly. If you answered "yes" to the third set of questions, describe and analyze your findings but in no case excuse or justify them. If you answered "yes" to the final set of questions, identify the circumstances (or individuals) that led to victim-blaming and eliminate such blame from your interpretations.

7.9.2 *Overgeneralization in Data Interpretation*

Overgeneralization in data interpretation occurs when researchers use only a one-sex sample or focus their attention on one sex only but phrase their conclusions in general rather than in sex-specific terms.

QUESTIONS. In order to determine whether or not data interpretation is overgeneral, ask yourself the following questions:

- Is only one sex considered? If so, are conclusions drawn in general terms?

SOLUTIONS. If you answered "yes" to both questions, make the conclusions sex-specific, or, alternatively, alter the research design so that both sexes are considered.

7.9.3 *Gender Insensitivity in Data Interpretation*

Gender insensitivity in data interpretation takes two basic forms: ignoring sex as a socially significant variable, and ignoring a relevant sex-differentiated social context. As an example of the first form, researchers occasionally collect data on both sexes but fail to analyze these data by sex. This problem may occur during the research design (for example, by utilizing a computer program that does not allow for analysis by sex), or it may be restricted to the interpretation stage if the researcher simply fails to look at the importance of sex. Such oversight may result in serious distortions in conclusions, particularly in cases in which the distribution of traits is systematically different for the sexes. Results based on such gender-insensitive data interpretation will give an inaccurate picture for both males and females.

Decontextualization is the second way in which data interpretation can be gender insensitive. This occurs when researchers fail to realize that the same event or situation (for example, marriage, divorce, political participation, and so on) may have very different implications for the sexes.

QUESTIONS. In order to determine whether or not data interpretation is gender insensitive, ask yourself the following questions:

- Are data collected on both sexes? If so, are they analyzed by sex? Is the difference or lack thereof between the sexes considered?
- Does the particular situation or event under consideration have potentially different implications for the two sexes? Have these been explicitly considered and discussed?

SOLUTIONS. If you answered "yes/no/no" to the first set of questions, reanalyze the data by sex and discuss the results. If you answered "yes/no" to the second set of questions, explore and discuss the potentially different implications of the impact of such events or situations on both sexes.

7.9.4 Sex Appropriateness in Data Interpretation

A double standard is introduced in data interpretation when data are interpreted as being consistent with some preconceived notion about what is (or is not) appropriate for one sex or the other.

QUESTION. In order to determine whether or not a double standard based on sex appropriateness has been introduced during data interpretation, ask yourself the following question:

- Are sex roles (or sex identities) seen as normatively appropriate?

SOLUTION. If you answered "yes" to this question, acknowledge sex roles (and sex identities) as socially important and historically grown, but make clear the fact that they are not necessary, natural, or normatively desirable.

7.10 Sexism in Policy Evaluations and Recommendations

Policy studies are one particular type of social science study and are singled out here for consideration because of their effect on people's lives: some policy studies actually do lead to policies, or at least influence them to some degree. It is, of course, impossible to make nonsexist policy evaluations or recommendations if the preceding research has been sexist because the requisite knowledge base is not present. On the other hand, it is quite possible to make sexist policy evaluations or recommendations on the basis of nonsexist research; policies are necessarily informed by some value against which they are gauged, whether this is done explicitly or implicitly. Given this, the nature of policy recommendations and evaluations thus depends on whether both the research and the values on which it is based are informed by the notion of sex equality or inequality.

For instance, let us assume a study conducted in a nonsexist manner concludes that a particular economic policy would disproportionately hurt employed wives. If policymakers hold that the right to work under equivalent circumstances should apply equally to women and men, they will recommend rejecting such a policy. If they hold that "male breadwinners" should be favored over "secondary earners," they will evaluate the policy positively. There are several ways in which policy evaluations and recommendations can be sexist.

7.10.1 *Gender Insensitivity in Policy Evaluations and Recommendations*

It is possible that the same policy may have different effects on women and men because of the historically grown differences between the sexes. In order to assess whether or not this will be the case, it is necessary to conduct studies in a gender-sensitive manner, separately assessing the impact of policies on women and men. Particular care must be taken to ensure that the family is not treated as a unit in which individual family members share uniform experiences or benefit (or suffer) equally from particular policies.

QUESTIONS. In order to determine whether or not a policy evaluation or recommendation is gender insensitive, ask yourself the following questions:

- Does this policy affect both sexes?
- If yes, is the position of the sexes comparable with respect to the important factors that inform and are governed by this policy?
- Is the effect of this policy positive for both sexes?

SOLUTIONS. If you answered "yes" to all of these questions, the policy is not gender insensitive, but you should clearly demonstrate, not simply affirm, that this is the case. If you answered "yes" to the first question but "no" to any of the others, the policy is biased, but this does not necessarily mean that it should be abandoned. If the policy is meant to right an old unfair situation, for example, there may be good reason for maintaining it. Or if the policy is disadvantageous for one sex but is nevertheless highly desirable for other reasons, it may be more appropriate to develop compensatory policies. (Such a situation might apply if environmental concerns supported reducing work opportunities within one sector.) In any case, arguments supporting such policies should be made explicit; state the values that underlie such policies and demonstrate how the policy supports them. If there is no such justification for a biased policy, or if compensatory policies cannot be enacted, the policy should be reevaluated in terms of its impact on both sexes.

7.10.2 Double Standards in Policy Evaluations and Recommendations

Analysts occasionally recommend policies that reward or punish people differentially by sex for the same trait. Such is the case when mothers involved in custodial disputes are penalized for having a paying job while fathers are rewarded for it, or when "surrogate" mothers are subjected to highly intrusive investigative measures while even mildly intrusive measures are considered unacceptable for the social fathers and their spouses.

The issue is more complex when such differential treatment is based on some other, ostensibly nonsexual, criterion that corresponds largely to a division by sex. This is the case, for example, when primary earners are treated differently from secondary earners with respect to entitlement to public benefits.

QUESTIONS. In order to determine whether or not policy evaluations or recommendations are based on a double standard, ask yourself the following questions:

- Are the same circumstances evaluated differently on the basis of sex?
- Is there a division that corresponds largely to a division by sex and for which differential treatment is recommended?

SOLUTION. If you answered "yes" to these questions, the policy should be reevaluated so that the sexes are treated in the same manner, regardless of whether such differential treatment is directly or indirectly based on sex.

Notes

1 Ben R. Finney, "Anomalous westerlies, El Nino, and the colonization of Polynesia," *American Anthropologist* 87, 1 (1985): 9–26.

2 Ibid., p. 21.

3 The sentence as a whole reads: "While I doubt if many successful colonies were planted by fishermen or coastal voyagers accidentally blown to some uninhabited island, a scenario that solely stresses systematic voyages of exploration and colonization presumes far too much order and predictability in what must have been a most uneven and hazardous expansion."

4 I once had my usage of "women and men" in a manuscript reversed to "men and women" by a copyeditor. Upon my protest she told me that this was a grammatical rule. I let it go because there were more important issues to fight about, but it is clearly a sexist rule.

5 Gynocentricity is characterized as embryonic because at the present time it is virtually impossible to be truly gynocentric – we are missing all the necessary tools for it, due to the overwhelming androcentric bias.

Epilogue

In this book, we have looked at a number of examples of sexism in existing research and have developed a set of guidelines for recognizing sexism in existing research and avoiding it in current and future research. In the process, we have identified seven different types of sexism. It is important to realize that sexism comes in different forms: little is gained if we eliminate one type of sexism only to replace it with another one.

These guidelines for nonsexist research provide us not with substantive answers but with a new set of questions. This is how true progress in knowledge takes place: not primarily by finding new answers to old questions (although that, of course, is also important) but by posing new questions that will eventually generate new answers. Becoming aware of sexism in research does just that. It provides a perspective that allows us to ask new questions and thus opens up new ways of looking at the world. To illustrate this principle in action, let us return to a few of the examples that were used previously to illustrate certain types of sexism.

The following are questions that might be asked about four of the topics that we discussed in this book: intergroup aggression and conflict, social stratification, fertility and childlessness, and the

166

elderly. Note how the elimination of sexist bias that ignored, distorted, or misinterpreted sex differences enables us to see these problems in a different light; new questions, new research agendas, and eventually new answers and new policies thus emerge almost automatically.

Intergroup Aggression and Conflict

- Did women participate in group conflict? In what manner?

- What effect did the introduction of extra-group women have on group cohesion? Did group cohesion exist between males and females? If not, what form did social cohesion take, and what was the relationship of mothers to their offspring? If yes, how was cohesion affected by the entry and departure of women? What was the nature of female–female relations? How did it compare to female–male relations? To male–male relations?

- What is the meaning of "inclusive fitness" for female members of a group? How does this relate to women's role in warfare?

Social Stratification

- What constitutes "human capital" for a woman? What are the effects of accumulating this capital for women? Does the same asset constitute human capital for men? If so, what are its effects on men? If not, why not? Are there gender-neutral forms of human capital?

- Since women have historically undertaken the care of the young for intrinsic rather than extrinsic rewards, are there also men who undertake comparably demanding and important tasks for intrinsic rewards? If so, who are the men, and what are the tasks? If not, why not? How does this affect our understanding of social stratification in general?

Fertility and Childlessness

- What are the fertility rates of men? How have they changed over time? In what way are they different from female fertility rates?

- What is the age-specific proportion of men who father children with women to whom they are not married? Are they single or married to someone else? Is there a group of men who father such children comparable in size to the group of unmarried women who give birth, or is it only a relatively small group of men who are responsible for a relatively large number of pregnancies?

The Elderly

- Are there gender differences in the way elderly sick women and men are perceived? If so, what are they? Do males and females have the same or different perceptions of elderly men and women? What are the policy implications of any differences that do exist?

- Do elderly women and men use different coping resources? If so, what are they? Are some resources that facilitate coping in one sex neutral or negative in their impact on the other sex? If so, why? How does this affect our understanding of the relationship between coping resources and health effects in general?

This is only a small sampling of questions that emerge from an analysis of sexism. They should, however, suffice to demonstrate the immense array of questions that present themselves once we have critically examined the existing literature for sexist problems.

It is not easy to accept the idea that well-established ways of looking at the world may be inherently flawed, as the hero of our first chapter, the Square from Flatland, found when he was bodily lifted by his guide, a Sphere, out of his two-dimensional homeland to look at it from the third dimension:

An unspeakable horror seized me. There was a darkness; then a dizzy, sickening sensation of sight that was not like seeing; I saw a Line that was no Line; Space that was not Space; I was myself and not myself. When I could find voice, I shrieked aloud in agony, "Either this is madness or it is Hell." "It is neither," calmly replied the voice of the Sphere, "it is Knowledge; it is Three Dimensions: open your eye once again and try to look steadily."

I looked, and, behold, a new world!

If, like the Square, we dare to open our eyes and look steadily at the world as it presents itself from the perspective of both sexes, we will find a new richness in what we thought were familiar and well-charted grounds. Introducing the perspective of women into a previously androcentric frame of reference opens up infinite research possibilities. Looking at men as gendered beings – and not as humanity pure and simple – makes us understand them differently and more realistically. By embracing the principles and practices of nonsexist research, we too can behold a new world.

Appendix: Nonsexist Research Checklist

Type of Problem	Description of Problem	Text References: Description/Examples	Text References: Identification/ Resolution
	Research Component: Title		
Overgeneralization	Title generalizes content of study when in fact research has been carried out on only one sex	3.3, 3.6	7.4
Based on sexist concept	Title reflects and/or contains a sexist concept (see below)	3.2.2, 3.3	7.4
Based on sexist language	Title contains sexist language (see below)	3.2	7.4
	Research Component: Language		
Overgeneralization	Sex-specific terms used for generic purposes	3.2.1	7.5
Overspecificity	Generic terms used for sex-specific purposes	3.2.2	7.5
Double Standard	Nonparallel terms used for females and males	5.2.1	7.5
Androcentricity	One sex consistently named first	2.3.1	7.5
Double Standard	One sex consistently discussed in the passive mode, the other in the active mode	5.2.2	7.5
	Research Component: Concepts		
Androcentricity	Ego constructed as male in concepts that are presented as general	2.2.2, 2.3.2	7.6.1.1

Androcentricity	Concept expresses relational quality from the perspective of one sex only	2.2.2, 2.2.5, 2.3.2	7.6.1.1
Androcentricity	Concept demeans women	2.3.2	7.6.1.2
Overspecificity	Concept defined as sex-specific when it is applicable to both sexes	3.4	7.6.2
Double Standard	Concept classifies the same attribute differently on the basis of sex	5.3.1	7.6.3.1
Double Standard	Concept identifies a behavior, trait, or attribute with only one sex when in fact it is or may be present in both sexes	5.3.2	7.6.3.2
Double Standard	Concept or conceptual pair ascribes a different value to traits more commonly associated with one sex	5.3.3	7.6.3.3
Sex Appropriateness	Concept based on the notion of "sex-appropriate" behavior, traits or attributes	6.2	7.6.3.4
Familism	Concept attributes individual properties to families of households	6.3.3	7.6.4
Sexual Dichotomism	Concept attributes human capacities to one sex only	6.4.2	7.6.5

Research Component: Research Design

Frame of Reference

Androcentricity	Study designed from a male perspective	2.2.1, 2.3.3	7.7.1.1
Androcentricity	Female behavior assessed against male behavior, which is taken as the norm	2.2.4	7.7.1.1

Choice of Research Question

Androcentricity	Women excluded from research design even when the research question affects both sexes	2.2.3	7.7.1.2

Type of Problem	Description of Problem	Text References: Description/Examples	Text References: Identification/Resolution
Gynocentricity	Men excluded from research design, especially in areas concerning family and reproductive issues	2.3.3, 5.4.1	7.7.1.2
Double Standard/ Sex Appropriateness	Both sexes included in research design but different research questions asked about females and males	5.4.1, 6.2.1	7.7.1.3
Choice of Research Instrument			
Double Standard	Different research instruments used for the two sexes	5.4.2	7.7.2.1
Sexual Dichotomism	Research instrument divides males and females into discrete groups and assigns human attributes to each of them	6.4.3	7.7.2.2
Variables Examined			
Androcentricity	Variables related to women's specific situation in two-sex studies not adequately taken into account	2.3.3	7.7.3
Sex of Participants in the Research Process			
Gender Insensitivity	Study does not take into account the fact that female and male subjects may react differently to comparable situations	4.5	7.7.4

Gender Insensitivity	Study does not take into account the fact that male and female researchers and research staff may elicit different responses from human subjects	4.5	7.7.4
Gender Insensitivity	Study does not take into account the fact that data obtained from informants and authors of statements (whether written, oral, audiovisual, or other) are likely to vary by sex	4.5	7.7.4
Unit of Analysis			
Familism	The family used inappropriately as smallest unit of analysis	6.3.2, 6.3.3	7.7.5
Comparison Groups			
Gender Insensitivity	Noncomparable groups of females and males used	4.6	7.7.7

Research Component: Methods

Research Instrument Validation			
Androcentricity	Research instrument validated for one sex only but used for both sexes	2.3.4	7.8.1
Sample Composition			
Overspecificity/ Gender Insensitivity	Researcher fails to report on sample composition by sex	3.5.2, 4.2	7.8.2
Questions and Questionnaires			
Overgeneralization	Questions use sexist language	3.5.1	7.8.3

Type of Problem	Description of Problem	Text References: Description/Examples	Text References: Identification/Resolution
Sample Composition			
Androcentricity	Questions do not allow for total range of possible answers for both sexes	2.3.5	7.8.3
Sex Appropriateness	Questions premised on notion of sex-(in) appropriate behavior, traits, or attributes	6.2.1	7.8.3
Choice of Research Instruments			
Sexual Dichotomism	Research instrument stresses sex differences with the effect of minimizing the existence and importance of sex similarities	6.4.4	7.8.4
Other-Sex Opinions			
Gender Insensitivity	People (including experts) asked about behaviors, traits, or attributes of members of the other sex, and such information treated as fact rather than opinion	4.4	7.8.5
Coding Procedures			
Double Standard	Identical responses coded differently by sex	5.4.3	7.8.6
Research Component: Data Interpretation			
Androcentricity	Findings interpreted within male frame of reference	2.2.5	7.9.1
Androcentricity	Forms of female subjugation, abuse, or restriction seen as trivial	2.2.4	7.9.1

Androcentricity	Forms of female subjugation, abuse, or restriction seen as normal or defended in terms of cultural or ethnic tradition	2.2.4, 2.2.6	7.9.1
Androcentricity	Victim rather than perpetrator made responsible for the crime	2.2.5	7.9.1
Overgeneralization	General conclusions drawn from an all-male (or all-female) sample	3.6	7.9.2
Gender Insensitivity	Data collected (or available) for both sexes but not analyzed by sex	4.3	7.9.3
Gender Insensitivity	Interpretation of sex similarities or differences fails to take the different social positions of the sexes into account	4.6	7.9.3
Sex Appropriateness	Sex-specific roles accepted as normal and desirable	6.2.2, 6.2.3	7.9.4

Research Component: Policy Evaluations and Recommendations

Gender Insensitivity	Failure to take into account the fact that policies have different impact on the sexes due to the historically grown differences in the position of the sexes	4.3, 4.7	7.10.2
Double Standard/ Sex Appropriateness	Same circumstances evaluated differently on the basis of sex	5.6.1, 6.2.2	7.10.2
Double Standard	Differential treatment by sex hidden behind ostensibly nonsexual distinction	5.6.2	7.10.2

Index

Abbott, Edwin A., *Flatland* 1
ability grouping 55, 61
abstracts 55
abuse 77, 142, child abuse 38, sexual abuse 38, wife abuse 31, 32, 75
activism 59
adolescents 76, 94, 95, deviance in 95
adultery 29, 30
adventure stories 121
agriculture, women's role in 73, 74
alternative motivational schemes 26
American Journal of Psychology 66
American Political Science Association Award 73
androcentricity 4–6, 19–45, androcentric bias 74, 80, androcentric choice of variables 151, androcentric concepts 139, androcentric formulation of research questions 148, androcentric frame of reference 146, in data interpretation 158, and double standards 87, 91, and gender insensitivity 79, in language 40, in the validation of research instruments 154
androgyny 122
Anglo-Saxon England, concubinage in 25
anthropology 122
Aries, Philippe 29

asymmetrical concepts 90, 142
authors of statements 77

baseline data sets 45
beauty, quantification of 66
bedroom community, suburb as a 26, 40, 139
Bernard, Jessie 80
"big blob" theory of sexism 3
blaming victims 146, 158–60, blaming women 34; *see also* mother-blaming
breadwinners 90, 162

cellar lad 79
Chagnon, Napoleon, *Yanomamo: The Fierce People* 31, 32, 75
character attributes 119
checklist 134, 170
child abuse: *see under* abuse
childcare 108, 109, 113
childlessness 54–56, 140, 166, 167; *see also* infertility
chivalry, women's privileges during period of 22
Christiansen-Ruffman, Linda 69
citizen (as a nonsexist term) 146
citizen contractors 58
coding procedures 96, double standards in 158

communists 51, 52, 57, 155
comparison groups 153
complex double standards 98, 100, 101
concepts, sexist 138–145, androcentric
    40, 139, asymmetrical 90, 142, based
    on sexual dichotomism 144,
    familistic 144, misogynist/misandrist
    140, overgeneral 56, 140, premised on
    a double standard 89, 141, premised
    on notions of sex appropriateness
    143, premised on unequal treatment
    of equal attributes in the two sexes
    89, 141, value-laden 91, 142
concubinage 25, 26
construction of ego as male 139
consumer (as a nonsexist term) 146
consumer surplus 50
contacting 59
contactor 59
context awareness 91
context blindness 91
coping inhibitors 72
coping resources 71, 72, 168
cruelty 30, 31, mental 30, physical 30, 159
cultural subjectivism 13

Daly, Mary, *Gyn/Ecology* 39
data interpretation 158–162,
    androcentricity in 158, double
    standards in 93, 97, gender
    insensitivity in 67, 160,
    overgeneralization in 60, 160, sex
    appropriateness in 161
de Beauvoir, Simone 20
decontextualization 78–80, and gender
    insensitive data interpretation 161
department heads 44, 156
derived sexist problems 4
desexed terms 14, 15
desexing of language 124
development of moral judgment
    (Kohlberg's model) 43
deviance, adolescent 95
division of labor 111–114, 156
divorce 78, 146, 152, 161, grounds for 29,
    30
double standards 4, 7, 9, 85–102, in
    coding procedures 158, concepts
    premised on 89, 90, 141, in data
    interpretation 93, 97, 161, in language
    86, in policy evaluation and
    recommendations 98–102, 164, in
    research methods 92, research

questions based on 148, 149
dressmaker 121
dual perspective 45
dysphoria 8

earner, primary 91, 101, 102, 117, 142,
    164, secondary 91, 101, 102, 117, 142,
    162, 164
earnings differentials 32–34, 70, 80
Economic Council of Canada 32
Edmonton Area Study 110
education 33, 34, educational
    expectations in Israel 55, 61,
    educational mobility 55, educational
    outcomes 61, participation in 78
elderly 72, 116, 167, 168, elderly sick role
    55, 60, 61, as a nonsexist term 146
Ellis, Havelock 86
emotional commitment 12
emotionality 119
employer discrimination hypothesis 79,
    80
encoding 67
equal attributes, unequal treatment of
    141
equal benefits, assumption of 117
equal pay for equal or equivalent work
    32, 34
equatorial westerlies 133
estrogen 119
exogamy 24
experimental subjects 66
experimenter 76–78, experimenter's
    confederates 77
expert 12

familism 4, 8, 76, 114–118, familistic
    concepts 144
family (as a generic term) 52
family 114, 115, 148, behavior studies 42,
    decision-making in 76, family/work
    conflict 110, head of 89, income 117,
    144, 152, as the smallest unit of
    analysis 114, 152, studies 148,
    support systems 116, 144
fathers 6, 54, 93, 109, 113, attendance of
    at birth 112, fathering role 113,
    father's tongue 56, psychological
    functioning of 93
Fee, Elizabeth 11, 12
female invisibility: *see* gynopia
female-male differences in participation
    73

female perspective 45
female subjugation 39, 159
feminism 77
fertility 54, 56, 140, 166, 167, rates 167
field dependence 91, 142
field independence 91, 142
fishing 121
Flatland 1, 2, 168
Flatland, Edwin A. Abbott 1
footbinding 39
formulation of questions and
    questionnaires 43, 50, 57, 148, sexist
    bias in 155, 156
frame of reference 145, androcentric 146
free trade 81
freedom of speech, attitudes towards 51,
    52
French Revolution 56

gender apartheid 119
gender differences in productivity 21
gender dysphoria 121, 122, syndrome
    120
gendered people 45
gender insensitivity 4, 6, 65–82, in data
    interpretation 160, familism 8, 114,
    144, in policy evaluations and
    recommendations 162, in reporting
    on sample 155, in research process
    151, 157
gender-neutral terms 15
generational boundaries, dissolution of
    36, 37
generic terms 49, 52, 54, 146
genital mutilation 39
gerontologists 115
grammar and grammatical modes 87,
    137, grammatical structure of
    scholarly writing 89
group cohesion 23–25, 40, 42, 139, 146,
    167, among early hominids 151
group membership 23
guidelines for nonsexist research
    129–164, 166
Gyn/Ecology, Mary Daly 39
gynocentricity 5, 20, 154, gynocentric
    concepts 40, 139, in formulation of
    research questions 148, incipient 20
gynopia 5, 20, 27

heads of department 144, 156
heads of household 70, 71, 89, 90, 138,
    141

Herman, Judith 38
historians 28, 29
Hobsbawm, Eric 29
hominid groups 25, 151, hominid
    evolution 23
homogamy 80
homosexuals 52, 57, 120
hopscotch 121
household 115; *see also* heads of
    household
housewives 109
housework 108, 110
human capital 167, literature 21
hunting (as an exclusive male activity) 24
husband sharing 24, 41

imbalance of knowledge 55
incest 36–38, 77, 159, taboo 24
inclusive fitness 23–25, 167
income security system 100, 101
independence 119
individual (as a nonsexist term) 146
industrialization 78, 79
industry, participation of females in 79
infertility 77; *see also* childlessness
infidelity, female 75
intergroup warfare 5, 22–24, 40, 139, 146,
    166, 167
interviewers 77
Israel 55, 61

joint utility functions 117, 152
joint-utility maximizing unit 118
Journal of Voluntary Action Research 69
journalistic fraternity 50
judicial decisions, sexism in 98

Keller, Evelyn Fox 13
keywords 55
Klinefelter's syndrome 93
Kohlberg's model of the development of
    moral judgment 43

Lapita, migration of the 133
leaders, expressive 43, instrumental 43
leadership capacity 119
Lineland 1, 2
love stories 121

MacDonald Commission 100
male childlessness 54
male dominance 158, 159

male fertility 54
male guardian 94, 95
male mobility 55
male perspective 45
man (as a generic term) 155
manipulative sensuality 35
mankind (as a generic term) 49
marginal individual 50
marginal productivity theory 21
marriage 78, 152, 161, marriage
    asymmetry hypothesis 79, 80
masculinity 13, masculinity-femininity
    scales 120, 150, 157
masochistic woman 140
maternal deprivation 90, 91, 142
maternal employment 108, 109
men's experience 49
Messing, Karen 12
methods, sexism in 154
microeconomics 21
migration patterns 97, 133
Mincer, Jacob 28
Minnesota Multiphasic Personality
    Inventory (MMPI) 120
misandrist concepts 41, 140
misogyny 5, 20, 34, misogynist concepts
    140
moral judgment, development of
    (Kohlberg's model) 43
mothers 6, 36, 54, 55, 93, 109, 113, 136,
    mother-blaming 38, 90, 92, 109, 146,
    mother-child relationships 34, 35,
    mother-sister dyads 37, mother-
    tongue 56, 63, 140, psychological
    functioning of 93
motivation, structure of 27
mutilation 159

natural selection 27
Newfoundland migration patterns 70, 97
Nie, Norman 73, 95
noncohabitation 29-31
nonexpert 12
nonparallel terms 86, 136
nonpositional goods 27, 28
nonsexist content 3
nonsexist language 3
nonsexist policies 74
nonsexist scholarship 3
nonsexist society 3
non-significant finding 123
null hypothesis 123

object 12
objectivity 11-14, in research 12
office holders 44
old age 72; see also elderly
Ontario Law Reform Commission 99, 100
opinion polls 43
opposite-sex siblings 37
optimization of family resource 117, 152
ostensive definition 53
other-sex opinions 157
out-migration 70
overgeneralization 4, 6, 15, 48-62, in data
    interpretation 160, in language 28,
    overgeneral concepts 140
overspecificity 6, 57

parents 6, 36, 53-55, 76, 136, parental
    tongue 56, parent-child relationships
    34, 35; see also fathers; mothers;
    single parents
participants in research process, sex of
    76, 151
passive mode 87, 89
paternal deprivation 90, 91, 142
paternal support 113
patient (as a nonsexist term) 146
perceptual isolation 67
perpetrators 147
person (as a nonsexist term) 146
Pierson, Ruth 28
policy consequences 73
policy evaluations and
    recommendations, double standards
    in 98, 164, gender insensitivity in 163,
    recommendations premised on
    notions of sex appropriateness 112,
    sexism in 162
policy formation 118
policy research 98
policy studies 117, 162
political activism 59
political participation 78, 161, in America
    73, 95
polyandry 41, 139
polygyny 24, 25, 40, 41, 139
Polynesians, migration of 133
positional goods 27
prelearning 67
Prentice, Alison 28
primary school students, Israeli 61
primary sexist problems 4
primitive man 23, 41, 146
primitive societies 87, 88

probability model 123
production methods 79
productive work 142
progesterone 144
psychological disorders 7,8
psychopathology 92,93,113

qualitative interviews 43
questions, exact wording of 50,
    formulation of 43,50,57,148

racial-ethnic groups 21
racists 51,52
referents, theoretical and empirical 140
Reinharz, Shulamit 20
Renaissance 21
reporting on sample, gender
    insensitivity in 155
reproduction 52,148
research 92,130–164, androcentricity in
    40,41, formulation of research
    questions 43,92,145,146,148,155,
    gender insensitive research 70,
    neglecting sex of participants in 151,
    objectivity in 12, sexism in 3,4,14,15,
    76
research design 67, androcentricity in
    41,151, based on sex
    appropriateness 108, sexism in
    145–154, sexual dichotomism in 119,
    120
research instruments 94, choice of 149
    (sexual dichotomism in) 150,
    validation of 42, (androcentricity in)
    154
research subjects 12,76,78,151
researcher 76, sex of 77
return migration 70
rhesus monkeys 67,69
Royal Commission on the Economic
    Union and Development Prospects
    for Canada 81

Safilios-Rothschild, Constantina 73,74
schizophrenogenic mother/father 90,91,
    142
Schreiner, Olive 86
scientific rationality 12
secondary analyses 159
seductive behavior 34–38
sensitivity 119
sequencing of the sexes 40
seven-nation study 58

sex appropriateness 4,8,107–114,143,
    148,149, in data interpretation 161
sex blind policy evaluation and
    proposals 81
sex composition 155
sex equality 162
sex identity 143,161,162
sex of participants in the research
    process 76
sex roles 113,143,161,162, in primitive
    societies 87, sex role transcendence
    113
sex-specific situations 15
sex-specific terms 49
sexist bias in the formulation of
    questions 155
sexist concepts 138–145
sexist language 14,15,28,40,49–55,134,
    136,137,156
sexual abuse: *see under* abuse
sexual assaults 146
sexual dichotomism 4,9,119–125,144, in
    choice of research instruments 150,
    in research methods 156
sexually identified stimuli 77,78
siblings 37,38,55, "sibsize" 55
Sierra Leone 74
simple double standards 98–100
single parents 52,53,55,76, single parent
    families 52,53
social ascription 21
social class 94,95
social commitment 12
social sanctions in primitive societies 87
social status 7
social stratification 26,148,166,167
social theory 21
society, concept of 26
sociobiology 40,41
socioeconomic status 94–96,149
Spaceland 1
spatial location memory 67,68
Square, The 1,2,168,169
Stiehm, Judith Hicks 73,95
stimulus probability 67
Strong Vocational Interest Blanks 96
structural functionalist literature 21
student-body composition 62
suburb as a bedroom community 26,40,
    139
support system 152
surrogate motherhood 98–100,164
survey data, validity of 50

survey research 43
suttee 39,137

taboos 88, incest 24
target dyads 37
test of significance 123
test statistic 123
testosterone 119,144
titles 55,135
toddlers 35
tolerance 57,156
training 33

unattached individual 89
unemployment 97, insurance 91,117,
    unemployed employable 101
unequal treatment of equal attributes in
    the two sexes 141
union members 28
universal suffrage 56,140
universe, three-dimensional 2
universe, two-dimensional 2
unproductive work 142
unwed father/mother 90,142
urbanism 57
utility function 27

value-laden concepts 91,142
values 13

variables, androcentric choice of 151
Verba, Sidney 73,95
verbal ability 66
Vickers, Jill McCalla 12
victimization 34,89,147
violence 142
voluntary organizations, participation in
    69
voter 50

wage differentials: *see* earnings
    differentials
warfare 23,31; *see also* intergroup
    warfare
widow-burning: *see suttee*
wife abuse: *see under* abuse
wife sharing 41
wives 26
wives' labor force participation 110
women in primitive societies 87,88
women's experience 49
work, women and 32,33,43,44
worker (as a nonsexist term) 146
work-family conflict 149

Yanomamo: The Fierce People, Napoleon
    Chagnon 31,75
"you", use of the word 50

About the Author

Margrit Eichler is Professor of Sociology at the Ontario Institute for Studies in Education. She has written and lectured widely on the subject of nonsexist research and is the author of several books, including: *The Double Standard: A Feminist Critique of Feminist Social Science* (1980) and *Canadian Families Today: Recent Changes and Their Policy Consequences* (1983). Professor Eichler received her Ph.D. from Duke University in 1972 and has served in various capacities as an advisor to the Canadian government on the status of women.

FROM BOOK IDEA TO BESTSELLER:

What You Absolutely,
Positively Must Know to
Make Your Book a Success

Michael Snell
Kim Baker
Sunny Baker

PRIMA PUBLISHING

For Patricia and all the other book lovers
of the world who turn their passion into a
successful career in the publishing business.

Library of Congress Cataloging-in-Publication Data

Snell, Michael.
    From book idea to bestseller : what you absolutely, positively must know to make your book a success / Michael Snell, Kim Baker, Sunny Baker.
        p.   cm.
    Includes index.
    ISBN 0-7615-0630-6
    1. Authorship—Marketing.   I. Baker, Kim, 1955–   .   II. Baker, Sunny.   III. Title.
    PN161.S64   1997
    808'.02—dc21   96-51455
                                                                                              CIP
97 98 99 00 01 02 HH 10 9 8 7 6 5 4 3 2 1

Printed in the United States of America

How to Order
Single copies may be ordered from Prima Publishing, P.O. Box 1260, Rocklin, CA 95677; telephone (916) 632-4400. Quantity discounts are also available. On your letterhead, include information concerning the intended use of the books and the number of books you wish to purchase.

Visit us online at http://www.primapublishing.com

Contents

Acknowledgments   v

Dreams Do Come True   vii

1 What Really Happens in Book Publishing Today:
*An Overview of the Changing Landscape of Publishers,
Conglomerates, Agents, and Booksellers*   1

2 What Smart Authors Do Before They Propose a Book:
A Start-Up Kit for the Aspiring Author   25

3 How to Write a Book Proposal:
*A Step-by-Step Guide for Turning Any Idea
into a Business Plan*   48

4 How to Find and Work with an Agent:
*An Action Plan for Building a Profitable Relationship
with an Agent*   80

5 How to Sell Your Proposal Yourself:
A Blueprint for Finding a Publisher   122

6 How to Evaluate a Publisher:
A Series of Initial Questions   151

7 How to Negotiate and Understand a Contract:
*A Tour of the Important Clauses in a
Publishing Agreement*   171

8 How to Work with a Publisher:
*The Process of Writing the Book and Getting
into Print*   210

9 How to Promote Your Book:
The Tools of Marketing and Publicity   246

10 How to Build a Successful Career As an Author:
*A Career Map for Long-Term Personal and
Financial Fulfillment*   296

Appendix: Proposal Templates   325
Resources for Writers   395
Index   409

Acknowledgments

We've always hated those long-winded acceptance speeches at awards banquets when the recipients thank everyone from their spouse and parents to their family dog. So, we'll keep our thank-yous mercifully brief and bestow our heartfelt gratitude on all the family members, writers, teachers, publishers, editors, and booksellers who have contributed so much to our success in the wonderful world of book publishing. We particularly thank James F. Leisy, founder of Wadsworth Publishers, who taught us deep respect for all authors, and Sheryl Fullerton, the best developmental editor in the world, who keeps reminding us that we always have a lot more to learn.

Dreams Do Come True

We have worked as writers, book developers, editors, and literary agents for a combined total of over fifty years, and during our careers we have pretty much seen it all, from the twelve-year-old-girl who submitted a little crayon-illustrated booklet she wrote about the death of her sister to the handwritten memoir of the eighty-seven-year-old poultry inspector from Wisconsin.

Whether they write to us, phone, e-mail, or fax us; whether they approach us at a cocktail party or after one of our publishing workshops; and whether they are young, old, male, female, black, white, or brown, all these would-be authors share a dream: to write and publish a book. Their motivations vary. Some long for fortune and fame; some yearn to touch the lives of their fellow humans and change the world; and some merely follow an impulse they find irresistible, satisfying, and cathartic. In the end, most of them fail to realize their dreams, not because they have nothing to say, but because they do not take the time to learn and master the step-by-step process of turning an idea into a publishing success.

We have written this book to take the mystery out of the process for the aspiring nonfiction book author. If you scan the book reviews at the back of *Publishers Weekly*, the journal of the publishing industry, you will find forthcoming books broken down into two categories: fiction and nonfiction. Both categories require both art and engineering—that is, both inspiration and craftsmanship—but they differ in dramatic ways. Novelists create complete "works of art," which they or their agents submit to the handful of publishers who dominate the fiction marketplace, while nonfiction authors fashion book proposals that might appeal to a great many houses, both large and small. Since writing and publishing a novel does not lend itself to a step-by-step process, we have chosen to limit this book to the nonfiction book, detailing a clear program that can enable anyone with a good idea to fulfill the happy dream of getting published.

In the pages ahead you will not only follow the steps in that clear program, you will also watch countless others use it successfully. You will meet such people as:

- Ollie Stevenson, the dynamic young black career counselor in Beverly Hills, who saw her dream come true with the publication of *The Color Blind Career*.

- Peter Lehndorff, the seventy-five-year-old Austrian anesthesiologist, whose lifelong passion for helping people cope with chronic pain resulted in *60-Second Pain Relief*.

- Sara Bernstein, the precocious twelve-year-old from Scottsdale, Arizona, whose royalties from her published book, *HAND CLAP!*, will help pay for her college education.

- Emmett Murphy, a respected management consultant in the prime of his career, who established himself as an important author with three books in six years: *The Genius of Sitting Bull, Forging the Heroic Organization,* and *Leadership IQ.*

- Sally Edwards, a world-record holder in triathlons and other endurance sports, who turned her passion for fitness into *Heart Zone Training.*
- Craig Hickman, the business strategist who launched a ten-book career as an author with the bestselling *Creating Excellence.*
- Myrna Milani, veterinarian and pet psychologist, whose first book, *The Weekend Dog,* inaugurated a twelve-year, five-book stint as America's leading authority on the human-companion animal bond.
- Paul Coleman, the psychologist and family therapist who helped thousands of people overcome adversity with *Life's Parachutes.*
- Pamela Gilberd, entrepreneur and mother of seven, who toured the country promoting *The Eleven Commandments of Wildly Successful Women.*
- Brian Tarcy, a young freelance writer who became a much-sought-after book collaborator after writing *Profit Secrets of a No-Nonsense CEO* with turnaround expert Gary Sutton.
- Jeanette Smith, former newspaperwoman, whose *The Publicity Kit* has, in its second edition, become the bible on the subject.

All of these successfully published authors, and the others you will encounter in this book, mastered our program which begins in Chapter 1: What Really Happens in Book Publishing Today. Here, you will gain a broad perspective of the world in which your proposed book must make its way. Next, in Chapter 2: What Smart Authors Do Before They Propose a Book, you will see how to develop your ideas and prepare yourself to create a convincing "business plan" for your book. Chapter 3: How to Write a Book Proposal walks you through each important element of a winning proposal and includes a successful model proposal for one of Myrna Milani's books.

If you plan to work with a literary agent, Chapter 4: How to Find and Work with an Agent gives you the knowledge you need to contact, select, and work happily with a good agent. For those who decide, instead, to approach publishers directly, Chapter 5: How to Sell Your Proposal Yourself provides a blueprint for successful self-marketing to publishers of all sorts and sizes.

Regardless of the method you use to locate your publisher, you will need to know how to choose the right house and how to negotiate an advantageous contract, the subjects of Chapters 6 and 7.

Chapter 8: How to Work with a Publisher covers all the important steps between signing a contract and receiving copies of your bound book, then Chapter 9: How to Promote Your Book teaches you what you need to know about the art of publicity and promotion. Finally, Chapter 10: How to Build a Successful Career as an Author provides a map for achieving long-term personal and financial fulfillment.

At the end of this book you will find a useful Resource section and Appendix. Resources for Writers annotates the vital resources every nonfiction writer should include in his or her writing library, while the Appendix offers two model proposals for two very different kinds of books. These "templates" can help you shape your own convincing proposal.

Does getting published sound like a lot of work? It is. By the time you have shaped a complete book proposal, you may feel, as Davis Young, author of *Your Company's Good Name*, felt: "Writing the proposal was harder than writing the book. If I knew in the beginning what I know now, I would have had second thoughts about going forward!" Go forward he did, and he reaped the immeasurable joy that comes from seeing his idea transformed into a bestseller.

It's a long journey from here to there, so what do you think? Shall we get started?

—Michael Snell, Truro, Massachusetts
—Kim and Sunny Baker, Miami, Florida

(Agent Mike Snell can be reached at the Michael Snell Literary Agency, P.O. Box 1206, Truro, MA 02666. Kim and Sunny Baker can be contacted by e-mail at kimbaker@aol.com or through their agent, Michael Snell.)

CHAPTER ONE

What Really Happens in Book Publishing Today:

An Overview of the Changing Landscape of Publishers, Conglomerates, Agents, and Booksellers

When you imagine the offices of a major New York publishing house, what picture leaps to mind? An erudite young editor in tortoiseshell-rimmed glasses carefully scanning the book proposals that flood across her desk, hoping to find the next bestseller? Try this instead: an overworked, underpaid young woman with a degree in comparative literature from Radcliffe struggling to move a mountain of proposals from one side of her desk to the other, giving each a few minutes before assigning an assistant the task of returning the material with a form rejection letter stating, "While we find this work admirable, it does not fit our current publishing plans." Then a proposal for a new book on Vincent Van Gogh catches her eye. She falls in love with it, shares it with her fellow editors, then presents it to an editorial acquisitions meeting, recommending that her publisher should offer a contract to the author.

The story ends happily, no? No. Irving Stone's first book was, in fact, about Van Gogh, and he offered it first to Alfred

A. Knopf. According to Stone, "They never opened it; the package with the manuscript got home before I did." When he took it to Doubleday, he found to his delight that everyone there liked it. Then, to his chagrin, the publisher rejected the book because the sales department insisted, "There is no way to sell a book about an unknown Dutch painter." Fifteen rejections later, the book finally did win a contract; the book, *Lust for Life*, published in 1934, went on to sell over twenty-five million copies.

In some respects, book publishing has changed little over the years. In some ways, however, it has changed radically. Fifteen years ago you could come up with a good idea for a book and sit down with a typewriter and a box of paper, and write a first draft, a synopsis, and a resumé which you would submit to a likely publisher. Twelve months and three rejections later, you might attract a willing publisher who would offer you a contract with a modest advance. A year later you would find your book on the shelf of a local bookstore. With luck, in another year you might receive a positive royalty statement and a small check. As one editor said in those days, "Writing books is a slow way to make a fast buck."

All that has changed. Today you must not only dream up a good idea for a book, you must create a complete business plan for it, with the help of a literary agent if you're lucky. Many agents will not even consider taking on unpublished writers. In any case, you immerse yourself in the published competitors, positioning your book as a unique product in a crowded marketplace, detailing who will buy the book and why. You will probably use a personal computer to "desktop publish" a beautiful book proposal, which you or your agent will sell aggressively and simultaneously to as many as five appropriate publishers. Within three months, you may receive a contract offer, and if you're writing on a hot topic, you must submit a publication-ready manuscript within six months. Six months later, copies of your book will appear in the major bookstore chains such as Barnes & Noble, and in another six months you will either receive a sizable check or learn that all your books have been returned unsold to your publisher. As one publisher put it recently, "A book these days either makes it big or it doesn't make it at all."

Seven factors have greatly altered book publishing over the past fifteen years, and in order for you to become the one writer out of six who "makes it big," you need to understand how the game works. You may not like the new rules of the game, but you cannot hope to succeed as a book author unless you learn to play by them in a thoroughly professional manner.

THE SEVEN NEW RULES OF THE BOOK PUBLISHING GAME

Despite all the takeovers, mergers, and downsizing that have occurred in book publishing during the past decade, a record number of new titles came into the marketplace in 1996. Hardly a niche exists in which there are not dozens of books competing for a book buyer's attention. Whether you're writing about relationships between men and women or business management, about Chinese geomancy or preparing lowfat meals, your book will compete not only with established books but also with all the proposals on similar topics that are circulating among publishers every day.

The glut of books and proposals on any given topic has created an environment in which publishers, agents, and writers

have come to think of the book as a product much like any
other consumer product. "Who will buy this book?" "What
other books has this customer bought?" "Why will people buy
it?" Editors expect you to answer these questions for them in
your book proposal. Since they do not know your market
niche as well as you should, they expect you to be an authority
on its needs.

In this age of publicity and promotion, the answers to these
questions hinge increasingly on the author-as-promoter. Successful authors such as Covert Bailey (*Fit or Fat*) and John
Gray (*Men Are from Mars, Women Are from Venus*) seize every
opportunity to draw attention to their books. It's no longer
enough to be promotable (e.g., to carry yourself with aplomb
on the *Oprah Winfrey Show*); you must be a promoter (e.g.,
aggressively push for media attention anywhere, any way, all
the time).

As books become products and authors become promoters,
the need for project development and packaging increases.
More than ever, authors must brainstorm a catchy title, package their ideas in an attention-getting way, and develop stunning proposals. The best literary agents now spend more time
on these activities than they do on negotiating contracts.

Once a strong proposal lands on an editor's desk, it
becomes a topic for discussion in a series of acquisitions committee meetings where executives, editors, marketing managers, salespeople, and publishers debate its viability as a
candidate for that publisher's list. No longer can an editor
buy a book and tell the marketing department to sell it; nowa-
days an editor must seek consensus among (or permission
from) those who will be responsible for bringing the book
to market.

This may sound awfully bureaucratic, and it is. The continuing conglomeration of publishers has resulted in fewer but bigger houses with complex decision-making processes; even smaller independent presses weigh every acquisition carefully. In most cases, decisions are made not by single editors but by groups of people, some of whom do not even read what they publish. "It's turning into the automobile industry," observes one veteran agent. "We'll soon have three big publishers selling tons and tons of titles."

Finally, the rise of sprawling bookstore chains and the advent of the super-bookstores have completed the evolution from what was once an idealistic and literary profession into a hard-nosed, market-driven industry. If the chains and superstores don't get behind a new book, that book will be doomed before the printing presses even start to roll.

These rules may, on the surface, seem like challenges that run counter to the artistic side of writing a book. But let's

---

The Seven New Rules of the Book Publishing Game

1. Compete for readers.

2. Think in terms of product.

3. Act like a promoter.

4. Develop and package the project.

5. Design your proposal for a committee decision.

6. Understand the changing landscape of book publishing.

7. Turn the chains and superstores into allies.

explore how you can turn them into opportunities for successfully getting published.

Compete for Readers

Emmett Murphy, a leading management consultant specializing in healthcare reorganization, had been working for several years on a rather academic manuscript for a book on leadership. Although his ideas seemed both fresh and practical, he had not considered the fact that business book editors had grown weary of the subject. As one editor put it, "I see a dozen leadership proposals a week, so don't even bother sending me another one. I'll just send it back unread." Emmett eventually overcame that objection with an unusual title and a compelling proposal package, but for now put yourself in the editor's shoes and ask yourself this one simple question: "Does the world really need another book on this subject?"

That may strike you as a harsh question, designed to convince you to abandon your project, but in fact it is meant to stimulate you to think hard about what you have to offer your intended audience that it hasn't heard from another writer. It should also force you to research your competitive environment more thoroughly. These exercises can result in stronger project development and packaging, because any author can come up with a new way of thinking and talking about a subject, even if hundreds of other writers have explored it over the years. Start your exploration of the competitive environment by haunting the shelves of a major full-scale bookstore. As you ask yourself the questions listed in the following box, you will begin to think like a competitor.

How Can I Compete Effectively for Readers?

- Can I list a dozen successfully published titles in my market niche?
- Have I analyzed the strengths and weaknesses of the competitors?
- Have I looked back ten to fifteen years at earlier competition?
- In what specific unique ways have I framed or approached this subject?
- Can I focus my book, its title, and its packaging to display my unique approach?
- Have I asked editors, agents, and booksellers for their thoughts about the need for new books on my topic?
- Have I examined publishers' catalogs to find out about forthcoming books in my field?
- Can I position my book to strike a responsive chord with readers? For example, how does my approach respond to media coverage of my topic?

Keep in mind two important points about "competition." When it comes to selling toothpaste, each product competes directly with the others, but in the marketplace of ideas, a given book competes both directly and indirectly with other titles. For instance, a book on using heart-rate monitors to design a fitness program not only competes directly with other heart-rate monitor books, it competes indirectly with all fitness books, whether they discuss measuring heart rates or not, because those books will cover some of the same basic information on fitness. For a new book on any subject, the competition spectrum might look like this:

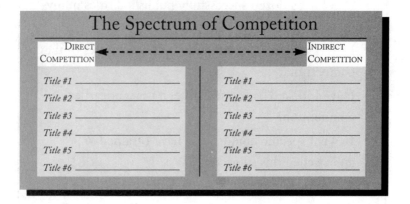

The author of the heart-rate monitor book would list direct competitors, such as Sally Edwards' *Heart Zone Training*, as well as indirect competitors, such as Bob Greene's *Make the Connection.*

Where does your title lie on the spectrum? First of all, bear in mind that when you compete for a reader's dollars, you not only argue that your target reader will buy your book instead of all the other alternatives, you must present a convincing case for why that reader will add your book to her or his library. In most market niches, readers do not buy just one book; they buy several over the years. People who buy political books usually own three or four, and people who purchase diet books usually end up owning a dozen.

Second, don't count on an editor knowing much about the competitive environment for your book. If she has published a couple of books in the area—and even if she focuses her time on the niche, publishing five or six new books a year— she may know her own list intimately, but will know little about the bestsellers on other publishers' lists. She expects *you* to be the world's most credible authority on both your own subject and your book's major competitors.

In this era of conglomeration, there are fewer editors publishing more books each season, and their goals force them to act more like "traffic cops," buying proposals and putting manuscripts into production, than as editors who edit and develop projects. There are almost no Maxwell Perkinses who will spend countless hours shaping the work of a promising young Hemingway, the way Max did. Editors today cannot afford to sign up promising, but undeveloped talent. Not only do their job descriptions exclude them from project development, but faster production schedules have kept them from even acquiring those skills. By thoroughly and persuasively positioning your book against its competitors, you will make the editor's job much easier when she presents your proposal to an acquisitions committee meeting whose members will know far less than she does about the direct and indirect competition.

Think in Terms of Product

"No!" you may shriek in protest. "Books are the embodiment of ideas, tools to touch peoples' lives, to change the world. My book is my life, my soul!" While every author needs that sort of idealism and motivation to deal with the often frustrating task of getting published, in a world of increasingly bottom-line-oriented, market-driven publishers, where hard-nosed marketing people wield the most power, the successful author couples that idealism with equally hard-nosed marketing savvy.

When Emmett Murphy began working with an agent on his leadership book, his agent advised him to think long and hard about what he called the "need-benefits equation." Does a very real need exist for your information? How, precisely, will your target audience benefit from your information? You can also think in terms of problems and solutions. Will your book solve a pressing problem that readers experience in their lives?

Emmett answered those questions forcefully, arguing that America lacks authentic leadership role models and tends, instead, to worship celebrities and those with financial power. He could, he believed, solve that problem and fill that need with a unique and proven leadership development program he had refined over the years.

Marketers who push any product, even something as mundane as dishwashing detergent, sell solutions to problems—products or programs that provide tangible benefits to consumers. "Lemon Bright will leave your dishes sparkling clean and your hands as soft as a baby's bottom," they insist. Book marketers strive to do the same, promising that a new book on investing money or on using a popular software program or on strengthening a marriage will benefit readers in tangible ways: they will make more money, operate their computers more productively, or enjoy a more satisfying relationship.

Often, the best way to make your ideas seem tangible to editors and, eventually, to readers is to present them as a program. Imagine yourself standing in front of a tent urging passersby to spend twenty dollars to come inside and hear your presentation. To get them to part with their money, you must offer something that they need—or think they need.

Solving the Needs-Benefits Equation

- What need does my book address?
- Who, specifically, needs what I am offering?
- Does my book solve a problem?
- For whom does my book solve a problem?
- Can I write a one-sentence sales pitch for my book that makes its benefits or solutions clear to editors, agents, and readers?
- Have I organized my ideas into a program from which readers will gain tangible benefits?

Never assume that your pitch will automatically strike a nerve. You must work hard to convince people that they will leave the presentation happier, wealthier, slimmer, or more effective. In short, your pitch and your program must drive home the needs-benefits equation.

As you ponder the need for your book, you should evaluate your motivation for writing a book in the first place. One top editor in New York always looks for what she calls "balanced motivation," by which she means a combination of idealism and a desire to make money. "I am drawn to authors who have a burning passion," she says, "because only writers with passion can change peoples' lives. But the writer also needs to channel that passion in a way that convinces people to pay to read it. I don't measure a book's success in terms of dollars but in terms of how many people it has touched. If it touches no one, it hasn't sold. If it benefits a lot of people, it makes money automatically. Idealists need this foot on the ground;

they need to think in terms of a product people will buy. Incidentally, the purely greedy usually fail, too, because when you strip away the hype you find they have little of substance to offer."

Act Like a Promoter

Emmett Murphy is a gifted salesman. He immediately realized that he should analyze the competition for his leadership program and think of his program as a marketable product. Once he did so, he put all his salesmanship behind the project. When his editor introduced his book to the sales staff, Emmett unveiled a fifteen-minute video presentation that captured the spirit of his book. Once his book came out, he attended book signing events at bookstores, appeared on numerous radio and television shows, conducted workshops and seminars, and seized every opportunity to attract attention to himself and his book.

It's no longer enough to be promotable—to be an attractive, articulate author who can tour the country at a publisher's expense, talking to reporters and shaking hands and signing books. These days publishers look for promoters—people who will work tirelessly to get their message out to the world regardless of, or even despite, what the publisher itself does or doesn't do to promote the book.

If you ask one hundred recently published authors if they are happy with their publishers' promotional campaigns, ninety-five will say that their publishers could have done a lot more to promote their books. The five happy authors, it turns out, never sat back waiting for book promotion to happen; they made it happen themselves.

Several years ago, Callan Pinkney published an exercise book called *Callanetics* with William Morrow. Coming into a saturated market, the book languished for months, but Callan, rather than sitting home and complaining that her publisher wasn't doing enough to promote her book, seized control of her own destiny and sought every opportunity, no matter how small, to draw attention to her program. After countless appearances on radio shows in Des Moines and Worcester, she finally wrangled an appearance on *The Oprah Winfrey Show*, where her passion, her program, and her lively personality enchanted the audience. The next day orders for fifty thousand books flooded into her publisher's sales office, igniting a strong run on the *New York Times* bestseller list.

For successful authors, promotion is a way of life. They believe so deeply in what they offer readers that they blow their own horns before, during, and after they sign a publishing contract. Their book proposals make it clear that not only will they eagerly participate in their publishers' promotional campaigns, but they have already led the effort and always will.

Later in the book you will learn the nuts and bolts of book promotion. At this stage, however, you want to prepare yourself for that activity by reading articles in newspapers and magazines that profile current authors. You can even track down local reporters and begin forming relationships with them by offering yourself or your ideas as a subject of local interest. Authors make news everyday. Try to analyze how they do so, and begin doing it yourself. It's never too early to begin sowing the seeds of self-promotion that will flower into headlines once you get your book successfully into print.

Salespeople are made, not born. You don't need the looks of a Tom Cruise or the voice of a Dan Rather or the energy of a Martha Stewart, but you do need to act like a promoter—someone who cares so passionately about your ideas that you will do whatever it takes to make people aware of them. Many new authors feel very uncomfortable with this role, but they will feel even more uncomfortable with failure. Regardless of how uncomfortable you may feel about doing it, remember that if you don't blow your own horn, nobody else will.

The Book Promoter's Ten Commandments

1. Learn about publicity. (See Chapter 9: How to Promote Your Book.)

2. Write an imaginary press release for your book.

3. Meet reporters in your region.

4. Study feature articles in magazines and newspapers about authors and their books.

5. Submit Op-Ed pieces on your subject to local newspapers.

6. Study how successful authors promote their books.

7. Create a twelve-to-fifteen-minute audio or video presentation of your ideas.

8. Offer free seminars, workshops, or public speeches on your subject.

9. Include your promotional accomplishments and plans in your book proposal.

10. Remember that you can never over-promote good ideas.

Develop and Package the Project

After struggling for months with titles and the best way to package his leadership program, Emmett Murphy began to feel that he had hit a brick wall. Then his agent asked him, "Emmett, when you're consulting with clients or making a speech, is there something you say that wakes people up and gets them on the edge of their seats?" Emmett didn't even pause to think about it. "Yes," he said. "They really respond when I compare our leadership crisis to Custer's last stand. We're surrounded by the enemy, and if we don't get our act together, we're gonna get massacred."

The agent liked that, but he suggested that the book needed to deliver a more positive message. "What about the leader who *won* the Battle of Little Big Horn?" he asked. It turned out that Sitting Bull, chief of the Sioux Nation, was an exceptional leader, a true American legend. Thus was born the title and the packaging concept for Emmett Murphy's eventual bestseller, *The Genius of Sitting Bull: Seven Strategic Lessons for Today's Business Leaders* (Prentice Hall).

Whatever the subject of your book, dozens of other authors have written about it before. Can you come up with a fresh title, an exciting metaphor, fresh language for talking about your subject? Authors, agents, and editors spend more time agonizing over this question than any other, because answering it can spell the difference between "just another book on the subject" and one that "breaks out of the pack." Brainstorming can provide the necessary breakthrough.

The best titles and packages often come from surprising sources, and the stunning ones usually result from the most free-wheeling and outrageous brainstorming. A few years ago,

Brainstorming Titles and Packaging

- Study what language has worked in past book titles and in the media.

- Visit bookstores to look at successful titles and packages in both your niche and other niches.

- Construct lists of words and metaphors that no other author has used when writing about the subject.

- Think "outside the box," letting your imagination run wild and remaining open to anything that pops up, even the far-out and weird.

- Consider how marketers in nonbook fields have come up with winning product names and packages.

- Try out new ideas for titles and packages on numerous people.

- Remain open to suggestions from professionals in book publishing.

Roger Connors and Tom Smith were struggling to come up with a title and a packaging concept for their program on how to become more accountable for results in one's life. Since the abstract concept of assuming personal responsibility did not ignite much excitement—even though the authors perceived a crying need for it and had built a successful consulting practice around this program—they felt their book needed something to which readers would respond instantly. The title finally emerged at a dinner party, where a young artist sat listening to the author's agent discussing the problem. "What's this book really about?" she asked. "It's about the fact that individuals possess the power to succeed, but too often look to others for results or blame others when they fail to get the results they want," responded the agent. "Oh," said the artist, "That's like the characters in *The Wizard of Oz*. They thought the wizard could give them what they wanted, but they learned that only they could do it." Voila! *The Oz Principle* (Prentice Hall) was born at that dinner table and went on to become a bestseller in both hardcover and paperback.

Design Your Proposal for a Committee Decision

Emmett Murphy's proposal for *The Genius of Sitting Bull* received three contract offers within a month because it gave acquisitions committees exactly what they needed to understand and believe in the book. In the next chapter, you'll walk through the art of proposal writing step by step, and in the appendices you'll see two model proposals that can guide your own proposal writing. But for now just think about the people at the publishing houses who will determine the fate of your book.

The process generally works as follows. The editor receives your proposal and eventually decides whether to send it back or to take a closer look at it. If you have worked through an agent, the latter will probably occur because the agent knows whether a particular editor publishes your kind of book and whether he or she is looking for a new product in your market niche. Let's say that the editor reads the whole proposal, still likes it, and shows it to a few other editors. If they all like it, your proposal becomes an agenda item for an editorial meeting attended by a few editors, an executive editor or editor-in-chief, and people from marketing and sales. If the marketing people like it, the editor leaves the meeting and begins assembling a mountain of paperwork that includes sales estimates, production costs, schedules, profitability goals, advances, and royalties. Then another meeting convenes and, if all the numbers make sense, the committee votes on whether to offer a contract. Even then, the editor may need to convince a top executive, usually the publisher, to sign off on the project.

This means that you're writing your proposal not for your intended audience, but for literary judges (editors), marketers (marketing managers, sales managers, publicists), and businesspeople (executive editors and publishers). In some cases, the publishing house may include another person in the deliberations, asking for the opinion of a buyer at a major bookstore chain. That person may not know books from mouthwash, having been working until last year as a product manager at Procter and Gamble, but since bookstore chains account for eighty percent of sales, his or her reaction to your book can make or break its chances in the market.

Before you write the first word of your proposal, you should think about the players who will vote on whether to offer you a contract (see next page).

There is a downside and an upside to this decision-making process. On the downside, racehorses designed by committee proverbially end up looking like camels or even platypuses. Editors continually complain about the endless meetings that consume their days; they take time, they devolve into pointless discussions and debates, and they do not always result in good decisions. On the upside, however, acquisition decision-making meetings can build consensus—a unified vision of an

The Committee Players

- **Editor:** Usually a word- and book-lover, perhaps with a degree in English, who has little if any background in your subject area.

- **Marketing Manager:** Sometimes called a Project Manager, this person is responsible for the overall strategy of bringing books to the market.

- **Sales Manager:** Someone with sales experience in the field, who manages the sales staff that calls on bookstores or oversees a direct-mail program.

- **Executive Editor or Editor-in-Chief:** The person who manages a group of editors; usually has many years of editorial experience, and carries financial responsibility for the list.

- **Publisher:** The president of the group; functions as a general manager, with primarily business concerns and responsibilities.

- **Booksellers:** Those who determine what goes on bookstore shelves and who try to move books off the shelves and into consumers' hands.

important new product. When enthusiasm for a book builds, that—more than anything else—can determine a book's ultimate success. Though it never appears in a publishing agreement, the enthusiasm of all the players in the publishing game makes all the difference between a moderate seller and a runaway bestseller.

Understand the Changing Landscape of Book Publishing

Emmett Murphy signed a contract with Prentice Hall, but his royalties come from Blockbuster Video. Some years ago, Simon & Schuster bought Prentice Hall, then itself became part of Paramount Communications (yes, that's Paramount Pictures, the moviemaker), which was a unit of Gulf & Western. Recently Viacom, Inc. bought Gulf & Western; among other entities, Viacom operates Blockbuster Video.

David Duncan, author of the classic baseball novel, *The Brothers K*, published with the house whose name is synonymous with the great American pastime, Doubleday (as in Abner Doubleday, the grandfather of professional baseball), but his advance and royalty checks originate in Germany, home of Bantam-Doubleday-Dell's parent company, Bertlesmann, AG.

Merger mania has swept through big-league publishing, and you need a scorecard to keep track of the shifting relationships, takeovers, downsizings, and new imprints announced in *Publishers Weekly* every week. Of course, an active literary agent keeps abreast of all these machinations and can tell you whatever you need to know about the changing landscape. However, any author can and should keep track of major developments in the industry. After all, the way the industry works will influence your decisions about designing your book for particular publishers or signing with a particular house.

At a later stage in your growth as an author you will want to consult the annotated list of references and resources in Resources for Writers at the back of this book, but, at this point, while you are beginning to shape your ideas and

Raising Your Industry IQ

- **Publishers Weekly.** Originally designed for book-sellers, this industry magazine contains advertise-ments, feature articles, and book reviews that can expand an author's knowledge of book publishing. Each weekly issue focuses on a category (such as Mystery, Fiction, Business, or Children's Books), and the big spring and fall issues offer a roundup of books coming out that season. An annual subscription costs around $150, so you may want to consult "PW" at your local library.

- *Literary Agents.* Agents not only read *PW,* they meet and talk with editors and publishers every day. A good agent can educate you about the industry with-out boring you with unnecessary details and technical information.

- **Jeff Herman's *Writer's Guide to Book Editors, Pub-lishers, and Literary Agents*** (Prima). While *Literary Market Place* (LMP) has long served as the phone directory for the publishing industry, Jeff Herman's book offers the more qualitative information that authors find extremely valuable.

your proposal, the following activities will help you increase your industry intelligence.

Conglomeration dominates the contemporary landscape of publishing. On the negative side, conglomeration has all but eliminated the independent, privately-owned major publishers and has created all the button-down, bottom-line bureaucratic problems that plague any immense organization. On the positive side, however, these enterprises pack a lot of marketing muscle and can invade a market with tremendous firepower. In addition, small upstart publishers have sprung up to fill the gaps neglected by the Goliaths, and these Davids add titles to the bestseller lists every year. More personable, more responsive, quicker to make decisions and to produce and market books, they represent an increasingly attractive alternative to the New York juggernauts. You'll learn a lot more about them in Chapter 5: How to Sell Your Proposal Yourself.

Turn the Chains and Superstores into Allies

If you visit the Compass Rose bookstore in Orleans, Massachusetts, you'll find a small section of business books, including Emmett Murphy's *The Genius of Sitting Bull* and Roger Connors and Tom Smith's *The Oz Principle*. Traveling down the road a few miles to Hyannis, you can stroll into the Barnes & Noble superstore, where you will find a whole aisle devoted to business books, and not just the big sellers but small niche titles you'll never see at the Compass Rose.

As with many recent developments in book publishing, the advent of the chains and superstores prompts shouts of both "Yay!" and "Boo!" from authors and book lovers. "Yay!" for the fact that even books with limited or specific interest find their way onto the bookshelf, and "Yay!" for the opportunity they afford for aspiring authors to conduct more extensive market research. Yet "Boo!" for the fact that the big guys have been steadily putting the little guys out of business and decreasing the chance for books of local and regional interest

to gain any shelf space at all. You can cheer or decry this phenomenon all you want, but if you ignore it, you do so at your
peril. Respect it, and you put yourself ahead of the game.
Why not turn what might seem like a problem into your own
personal research laboratory?

The Superstore Research Lab

- Haunt the section of the superstore that displays
  competitors in your niche.

- Spend time in all of the store's sections looking for
  ideas that can help you package your project for your
  own niche.

- Introduce yourself to the superstore's personnel; ask
  them about bookselling and request that they share
  with you publishers' catalogs, which promote forthcoming titles.

You can also do yourself, other authors, and independent
booksellers a big favor by ordering books you want from
small bookstores. One reason the superstores have flourished
is that most people don't special-order books. They hear
about a book on *The Oprah Winfrey Show*, then go to the
bookstore, but if they don't see that book they buy something
else or go home empty-handed.

PLAYING THE GAME

By this point you should be gaining an appreciation for
book writing and publishing as a business—a business like any

other, in which success hinges on an understanding of such basic issues as customers, markets, products, packaging, promotion, and selling. Does this mean that the thrill has gone out of the literary life, that creating a masterpiece has been reduced to a paint-by-numbers activity, that a bottom-line business mentality has shoved aside graceful prose and high-minded goals? Not at all.

The book business has grown more businesslike, but every day committed writers propose important ideas that caring publishers shepherd through the system and that enrich and entertain an expanding audience of people who cherish the feel and smell and companionship of a brand-new book.

In the pages ahead, you will learn how you can play the game by the new rules, and how you can win the game. The business has changed and will continue to change, but the rewards of authorship remain the same: a small portion of immortality that comes from touching the minds of others, and the tremendous self-fulfillment that attends the birth of a brainchild.

CHAPTER TWO

What Smart Authors Do Before They Propose a Book:

A Start-Up Kit for the Aspiring Author

Getting published is like starting a business. Suppose you have come up with an idea for a new wristwatch that displays temperature as well as time. You'll become an expert on wristwatches, research the market and competition, develop the skills to build your device, create a business plan, fashion a prototype, seek funding for your operation, construct a manufacturing facility, and then start producing and selling your ThermoWatch. With luck, the world will beat a path to your door.

The same steps apply to getting a book published. You begin with an idea for a new book on a subject dear to your heart—let's say a collection of TV-free activities parents can do with their kids. You become an expert on the subject through research, education, and experience; you study all the available books on the subject in an effort to understand the need for a new book and how you might fill that need; you hone your writing ability; you write a book proposal; you submit that proposal to agents or publishers; you win a contract and funding; you write the book; and finally you uncork a bottle of champagne to celebrate its publication. With luck, a promotion-minded publisher, and your own tireless promotional effort, book buyers will beat a path to bookstores and turn your book into a bestseller. Steve and Ruth Bennett followed these steps faithfully when they wrote *365 TV-Free Activities that You Can Do with Your Child* (Adams Publishers), and over 500,000 copies have been sold to date.

This chapter explores the start-up steps in this process—everything smart authors do before they write their book proposals. As with any new enterprise, eventual success depends on painstaking planning.

THE SIX START-UP STEPS

In the pages ahead you will meet six authors who faithfully followed the six start-up steps every smart author takes.

- Retired computer documentation writer Richard Whalen turned a lifelong dream into a reality when he published *Shakespeare: Who Was He?* with Greenwood Press.

- Sally Edwards, an accomplished triathlete and entrepreneur, published her sixth book, *Heart Zone Training*, with Adams Publishers.

- Management consultant Craig Hickman published his tenth book, *The Fourth Dimension*, with John Wiley & Sons.

- William Green, a journalism professor with no medical training, convinced Plenum Publishing Corporation to issue *Fatigue Free*, his book on Chronic Fatigue Syndrome.

- Career counselor Ollie Stevenson, one of the few young black women in her profession, placed *101 Great Answers to the Toughest Job Search Problems*, her first book on career problem-solving, with Career Press.

- Davis Young, president of a corporate public relations firm, published his first book, *Your Company's Good Name*, with AMACOM.

These six very different people published successfully with six very different publishers, but they all followed the same six start-up steps.

The Six Start-Up Steps

1. Develop expertise.

2. Establish market need.

3. Become a writer.

4. Link up with experts and writers.

5. Learn about publishers and agents.

6. Build credentials.

Start-Up Step 1: Develop Expertise

In this age of electronic media, more people than ever dream of writing and publishing a book. Every accomplished cook thinks he can assemble a great cookbook, any successful dieter believes she can reveal the truth about weight loss, and all excellent parents know in their hearts that they can impart the best advice on raising beautiful children. However, out of every 100 skillful cooks, newly slim dieters, or proven parents, 99 fail to fulfill their dreams of getting published, most often because they neglected to turn their amateur interests into professional expertise. Getting published requires more than a passing acquaintance with a subject; it demands a level of knowledge that convinces agents, editors, and readers that this author has become demonstrably authoritative on that subject.

Does this mean that you must have graduated from the California Culinary Institute before you can presume to write a cookbook? Not at all. Many successful cookbook authors, such as Jeff Smith who wrote the bestselling *Frugal Gourmet* series, learned what they know "on the job." Or, like Sunny Baker and Michelle Sbraga who published *Lemon Tree Very Healthy* and *The Pasta Gourmet*, they taught themselves everything about a particular aspect of culinary art.

Richard Whalen offers an instructive example of the "self-taught expert." Having developed a passion for Shakespeare's work during his career as a software documentation manager at IBM, Richard grew obsessed with the question of the playwright's true identity. When he retired, he turned his hobby into a new career, embarking on a research endeavor every bit as arduous as any Ph.D. program. He read every research monograph on the issue, he joined and eventually became president of the Oxford Society, and he invested countless hours in preparing himself to discuss and debate his subject with even the most dedicated and influential scholars. As a result, this self-made expert landed a contract with Greenwood Press, a top scholarly publisher, and saw his book, *Shakespeare: Who Was He?* go through several printings and arrive at a cherished position in the literature of the field. To aspiring experts on any subject, Richard would pose these questions:

- What do I *really* know about my subject?
- What *don't* I know about my subject?
- Have I researched my subject thoroughly?
- Have I read all the important articles and books on my subject?
- Do I attend meetings, conferences, and discussion groups devoted to my subject?
- Have I met, corresponded, or talked with other local, regional, and national experts on my subject?
- Can I write and submit for publication newspaper, magazine, or journal articles on my subject?
- Can I honestly describe myself as an *expert* in this subject area?

Even if you have earned a Ph.D. in your subject or have worked for years in a field related to your subject, you should still ask yourself the above questions. No matter what your background, you must shape your credentials in a way that convinces agents, editors, and, ultimately, readers that you know what you're talking about.

If you were to set about building a Victorian house, you would not just look at some pretty pictures in an architecture magazine or tour a few examples of the style, you would immerse yourself in the entire history and practice of the craft. You might be an architect, but you could hardly expect someone to hire you to design a Victorian house if you have devoted all your time to designing contemporary homes. English teachers advise their students to "write what you know about." The smart author turns this admonition around, "Know what you write about."

Start-Up Step 2: Establish Market Need

Regardless of the source of your expertise, it will get you nowhere unless you connect it with a genuine need in the marketplace.

With each season's new book releases, you will find an astonishing range of topics.. A recent issue of *Publishers Weekly* proves this point: Bison Books advertises *Basketball: Its Origin and Development;* Pocket Books promotes *365 Ways to Make Love;* University of Oklahoma Press presents *Native People of Southern New England 1500-1650;* Avery Publishing Group introduces *Healing Teas;* and Prima Publishing announces *Camping with Kids in California.*

Such titles might lead you to assume that a market exists for any book idea, especially the one so dear to your heart. Maybe. Maybe not. While some reader somewhere will surely pay good money for information on a topic as offbeat as the history of the potato chip, finding a publisher for that book may turn out to be difficult or even impossible, especially if some publisher recently published the "bible" on that topic.

To rephrase George Orwell, "All ideas are equal, but some ideas are more equal than others." Consider the two extremes that can exist in the marketplace. On one hand, there are subject areas, such as healthful eating or making love, that are saturated with titles. To a publisher, that sort of glut spells both good news and bad news. While a plethora of books on a subject indicates a broad, perennial appetite for information on it, the heavy competition makes it difficult to break a new book out of the pack. On the other hand, there are untested niche markets, such as the market for an autobiography of an unknown individual. A field in which no book has been published is, again, both good news and bad news from a publisher's perspective. While a gap may clearly exist, there may be a good reason for that gap; perhaps only the author's friends and family would buy a book on that subject.

Does this mean that you should play it safe somewhere in the middle? Not necessarily. *Books in Print* might list 500 titles on your subject, but that does not preclude book number 501. Every season, a new book on an old subject bursts onto the bestseller list, as the *Martha Stewart Cookbook* did in 1996. Likewise, every season witnesses a breakthrough book on a subject that no one could have imagined before, in the way that Allan Bloom's *The Closing of the American Mind* and Edward Hirsch's *Cultural Literacy* did a few years back.

Sally Edwards created a breakthrough when she published her sixth book, *Heart Zone Training*, with Adams Publishers. A professional athlete and one of the first women to compete in triathlons, Sally had developed expertise over the years. She had a master's degree in kinesiology from the University of California, she was a competitive athlete, and she had published five fitness books in a relatively crowded market. Her latest book, however, explored brand-new territory. Having seen the popularity of heart-rate monitor wristwatches (devices that monitor a person's heart rate continuously) in Europe and among Olympic athletes, she decided to bring this new information to an American audience. "I was a little surprised," she confesses, "when Bob Adams snapped up my proposal because he usually publishes into well-established niches. But he caught the vision. He understood the potential in a market that could go from zero to half a million in six months." Sally would encourage all aspiring book authors to use the Market Need Analyzer.

The Market Need Analyzer

- *Who* needs information on my subject?
- *What* new information do they need?
- *How many* people need this information?
- *Why* do people need this information?
- *Where* do people currently get this information?
- *When* will people respond to information on my subject?

In Chapter 3: How to Write a Book Proposal, you will find detailed tips on conducting market research, but for now, notice how these questions mimic those a good reporter asks when covering a story: who, what, why, where, and when. Too many authors forget to ask, "How many?" thinking that every living soul simply must need their book, when in fact that is not the case. Others forget the importance of *timing*, proposing something too far ahead, or too far behind, the course of public interest. Authors who pursue the illusion that their book will be "all things to all people" usually end up proposing something that amounts to "nothing for no one."

How quantitative should you make your market need analysis? The answer is: as quantitative as it needs to be in order to entice a publisher who worries over the paradox of focusing a book on a specific market need, yet making that book broadly appealing as well. In other words, you need only prove that you have focused *narrowly enough* for your book to appeal to an identifiable audience, and that you have made it as *broadly* appealing to that audience as possible.

Start-Up Step 3: Become a Writer

Once you couple your expertise with a genuine market need, you must then make sure you possess or acquire the tools needed to get the job done: you need to become a writer.

Every editor and agent has received a phone call like this:

"Hello, my name is Ishmael, and I am writing a book about whales."

"Hello, Ishmael. Are you a writer?"

"Oh no. I'm a whale expert."

"That's nice. But in order to write a book you must, unfortunately, actually *write* the book."

Going back to our example of the person wanting to build a Victorian house, imagine a similar conversation between the would-be designer and a prospective client:

"Hello, my name is Victoria, and I will design you a house."

"Hello, Victoria. Are you an architect, contractor, or carpenter?"

"Oh, no. I just love Victorian houses."

"That's nice. But in order to design a house you must, unfortunately, actually know how to *create architectural drawings*."

A variation on the scenario goes like this: after the polite introductions, the caller answers the question, "Are you a writer?" by saying, "Of course I am. I've been writing all my life!" Who hasn't? We all learn to "write" in elementary school, but how many of us can claim to write *professionally?* How many people who have begun to play the cello would claim a chair with the New York Philharmonic? Some aspiring authors assume they can write simply because they can power-up a word processor, while others suffer the illusion that they can master the craft overnight. That's like assuming that owning a Stradivarius makes you a string virtuoso.

Does this mean that you should give up your dream of writing just because you've spent your life working as a butcher or baker or candlestick maker? No, provided you are willing to invest some time in learning the craft of writing or linking up with a collaborator who can close the gap between your inexperience and a professionally acceptable prose style. Experts in many areas have managed to become at least minimally accomplished writers, and some have gone on to win literary prizes—for example, paleontologist Stephen Jay Gould or longshoreman Eric Hoffer.

Bestselling business book author Craig Hickman became an accomplished writer, though it took him ten years of self-schooling. For his first book, *Creating Excellence* (New American Library), he depended heavily on the writing and editing assistance of a professional collaborator. Then he gradually picked up those skills himself on books two through nine. By his tenth book, he no longer needed writing assistance and delivered production-ready manuscripts to his publisher. "Maybe I'm a slow learner," laughs Craig, who graduated at the top of his class from the Harvard Business School, "but becoming a writer was a lot harder than becoming a management expert."

No two writers follow the same path as they acquire and develop their skills, but all professional writers would agree that to do so you should "go to school."

Schools for Writers
- Writing courses at local colleges
- Continuing education programs
- Writers' conferences
- Personal writing coaches or teachers
- Informal writers' groups
- Textbooks on writing
- Agents, editors, collaborators, developmental editors, and ghostwriters
- Self-education via analytical reading and a willingness to revise, revise, revise

You will find a list of recommended resources for your writing education in the back of this book, but whatever program you choose, never forget that writing is hard work; the harder you work, the better a writer you will become. It never gets easier, even after the tenth book, because a good writer constantly sets higher and more ambitious goals after each project.

Some writers, and even some writing instructors, don't think that writing can be taught; it can only be learned. In this regard, the last element on the Schools for Writers list can contribute the most to your development as a writer: write, revise, write, revise, write, revise .... Good writers read other good writers but, unlike people who read for the sheer pleasure of it, they read analytically, trying to figure out exactly how the author achieved that absorbing effect on the page. Good architects don't just admire a beautiful house, they analyze the elements that contributed to its style.

Start-Up Step 4: Link Up with Experts and Writers

Few masters of any craft live in a vacuum; they share their skills and knowledge with others. In the case of writing a book, this sort of sharing takes on added meaning. If you lack necessary expertise in a subject, not only can you learn by linking up with an expert in the field, you can form a partnership wherein your desire and writing ability and that person's expertise create a complementary joint venture. The converse holds true as well. If you possess world-class expertise but lack necessary writing skills, you can establish a collaboration by linking up your knowledge with the capabilities of a professional writer.

"With" has become a popular word in publishing circles. Lee Iacocca wrote his bestseller "with William Novak;" Colin Powell wrote *My American Journey* "with Joseph Persico;" and Gary Sulton wrote *The Profit Secrets of a No-Nonsense CEO* "with Brian Tarcy." Far from a negative in the minds of agents, editors, and readers, a collaboration can be a big plus, resulting in a better book than if the expert or the writer had chosen to go it alone.

An interesting example of a writer joining forces with experts in order to get a book published comes from the case of Bill Green, author of *Fatigue Free* for Plenum. Bill Green taught journalism at Ohio State University and had only interacted with the medical profession as a patient. Having suffered from Chronic Fatigue Syndrome throughout graduate school, Bill decided to apply his state-of-the-art research skills to gaining a full understanding of his ailment. At the end of a four-year investigation into the subject, he discovered that he had learned more about it than any single doctor he interviewed. Even the doctors encouraged him to publish his findings.

Wisely, however, Bill sought the active involvement of specialists in the treatment of Chronic Fatigue Syndrome, which resulted in a foreword by Ralph N. Wharton, M.D., from the Columbia-Presbyterian Medical Center in New York, and book jacket endorsements from three other leading experts at the National Center for Chronic Fatigue, the Ohio State University Medical School, and a research hospital in Minnesota.

Bill Green's story underscores the value of creative partnerships on book projects. To weigh the degree to which you might benefit from such link-ups, put yourself realistically and conservatively through the Expertise and Writing Ability Grid.

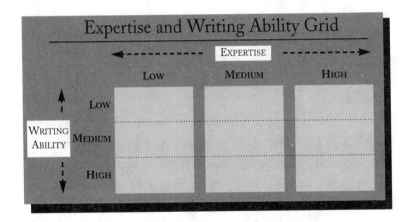

If you rate both your expertise and writing abilities as low, you face an enormous challenge because you must shape yourself up in two areas at once. Conversely, if you rate both your expertise and writing ability as high, you can confidently proceed on your own with little or no assistance. Of course, most mortals fall short of the ideal. The author with high expertise and medium writing ability may benefit most from a developmental editor, while the author with high writing ability and medium expertise surely must spend more time linking up with experts. The high-low combinations may argue for collaboration or co-authorship, when the author shores up either low expertise or low writing ability with more of a full-fledged partner.

Other sorts of partners include researchers, illustrators, photographers, ghostwriters (collaborators who do not receive credit), technical advisors, developmental editors, copy editors, and contributing writers or editors. Test the working relationship as you create your proposal, then put it in writing. Depending on the degree of involvement, your partner's name may or may not appear on the book contract. If the name does appear, shares of income should be spelled out. If not, you should both sign a work-for-hire agreement wherein the partner transfers to you all rights to the work in exchange for a specified payment, paid out according to an agreed-upon schedule.

This brings us to a final caution about co-authorship and collaboration. As with any relationship, opposites attract and the happiest "marriages" result from complementary skills. Two experts working on a project or two writers working on a project can run into difficulties that can result in divorce. It's like cleaning a really dirty window. If two people try to clean the same pane at the same time, they'll invariably end up poking each other with their elbows, getting irritated and angry, and even abandoning the job. However, if one wipes off the heavy grime while the other follows with the Windex, the work runs along smoothly toward a gleaming result. The best book project partnerships usually follow such a division of labor.

Start-Up Step 5: Learn About Publishers and Agents

Chapters 4, 6, and 8 discuss in detail how to work with agents and publishers, but at this point you should grasp a few basic rules about these unique professions. Underline the word *professions*.

Many new authors cling to the illusion that agents are cigar-chomping, fast-talking, wily foxes who can charm publishers out of the combinations to their safes, and that publishers are tweedy, erudite literary aficionados who sit at their desks searching for the next great masterpiece or runaway bestseller.

In reality, the typical agent today has worked in publishing for many years, acquiring, developing, and marketing books, before setting up shop as an independent agent. Take Sheryl Fullerton, for example.

After a distinguished career in college textbook publishing at Wadsworth, where she progressed from production editor to developmental editor to editor-in-chief over the course of fifteen years, Sheryl felt restless. She also knew that she had gained valuable knowledge about turning book ideas into bestsellers, so she struck out on her own and established Sheryl Fullerton Associates in San Francisco. What does she do during a typical day? "It's seventy-five percent development," she explains. "Finding the right publisher and negotiating a good contract is simple, provided you have the right stuff." By "the right stuff" she means a proposal that she and her author have slaved over to make it as valuable as possible. "I do pretty much what I did at Wadsworth," she observes. "I look for bright people with good ideas, strong credentials, and some writing ability, then I work with them to shape their ideas into both convincing business plans and compelling manuscripts." She concludes by paraphrasing what real estate agents say about selling homes: "They say it all comes down to three variables: location, location, location. Well, in agenting it all comes down to development, development, development. Real estate developers do it with dirt, we do it with ideas."

The typical acquisitions editor today has worked in publishing for several years, and while he or she may have graduated from college with a degree in English and dreams of publishing the great american novel, the editor has become a businessperson who is rewarded more for marketing savvy than wordsmithing. If agenting comes down to development, then editing comes down to marketing.

Richard Staron, senior editor at Macmillan Spectrum, would describe his normal day as a series of marketing decisions. "It doesn't matter much if I like the author and fall in love with his proposal," he explains, "If the sales and marketing folks don't like the book, it's a dead duck." Remember, in this era of conglomeration and downsizing, fewer editors are publishing more books. They can no longer afford to take the time to develop talent. Not only has development disappeared from their job descriptions, but many simply lack these skills, which have fallen outside the publishing industry and onto the shoulders of authors and agents.

Ollie Stevenson finally got published after she learned about those realities. Her query and initial material intrigued an agent, but her ideas for a comprehensive career guide needed a lot of development before it could make its way in a crowded market. "Working with my agent was like going to school," she recalls. "He said my material was an explosion of good ideas, whereas it needed to become a laser beam." Under her agent's guidance, Ollie fashioned her ideas into a laser beam—a unique package of career advice published as *101 Great Answers to the Toughest Job Search Problems.* "That title came from my editor at Career Press," she says. "Everything we talked about was marketing, marketing, marketing. As a novice author, you may think of your book as a gift to your readers, but you soon discover that you must wrap it up in an appealing package." Ollie would recommend that authors approach agents and publishers with an understanding of their professional roles in today's publishing industry.

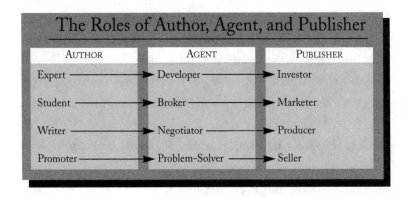

The Roles of Author, Agent, and Publisher

AUTHOR	AGENT	PUBLISHER
Expert →	Developer →	Investor
Student →	Broker →	Marketer
Writer →	Negotiator →	Producer
Promoter →	Problem-Solver →	Seller

You'll learn more about these roles in later chapters, but at this point you should think about your role as student. You may know everything in the world about butterflies, and you may write like an angel, but you are a novice when it comes to book publishing, even if you've published a number of successful books. Your agent and editor can't teach you anything about butterflies, but then you can't teach them anything about their jobs. Listen, learn, and be a good student. As one veteran agent puts it, "I look for clients with a good set of ears. That's why I find it so hard working with academics. Somehow, fifteen minutes after getting tenure they go deaf. They're so used to telling other people what's what, they forget that they still have a lot to learn themselves, especially when it comes to something as unique and strange as the world of book publishing."

Start-Up Step 6: Build Credentials

Expertise and writing ability will get you into the stadium, but only your credentials will get you onto the pitcher's mound. In the old days, an author would build a successful career as, say, an astronomer, publishing articles in learned journals then capping her career with a book, the culmination of a lifelong climb up the professional ladder. These days an earnest astronomer might publish a book early on in her career, using it as a stepping stone to advance her professional standing.

This brings us to another of those paradoxes so prevalent in book publishing: it's easier to sell a second or third book than a first book, but even Stephen King had to get that first book published somewhere. Publishers respect track records, and the only track record that really matters is previous sales success. Having published two or three books won't make selling your fourth book any easier if your earlier efforts flopped in the marketplace. Eighty percent of all authors find themselves in that predicament because only one out of every five published books goes on to make money beyond the initial advance.

The odds seem depressing for both first-time and experienced authors. An agent takes on one out of fifty projects that come to the office; editors buy one out of twenty-five of the proposals that land on their desks; and only one out of five of those turns a profit. So what's an author to do—give up the dream and ride forlornly off into the sunset?

No. Despite the cruel odds, there is one way in which you can give your career a big boost: build credentials that turn your expertise and writing ability into professional accomplishments. With a lot of patience and perseverance, plus a little luck, those accomplishments will give you a chance to take the pitcher's mound in Yankee Stadium.

Davis Young proves the point. As the president of a nationally respected corporate public relations firm in Cleveland, and as a skilled writer of press releases, he possessed the expertise and writing ability to propose a book on managing a company's reputation asset. But he didn't stop there. Over the years, he deliberately wrote and published articles on the subject in magazines and trade journals, until his author's biographical sketch included a long list of publishing credentials. "It was part of my long-range strategy," he says. "I tried to figure out what, besides my position and experience in the field, would impress editors, and I thought that having published lots of articles might do the trick." It did. AMACOM snapped up his proposal for *Your Company's Good Name* partly because the editor was so impressed by his credentials. Davis would recommend that any author, new or experienced, devise a credential-building strategy.

In addition to strengthening your credentials, this strategy can create surprising opportunities. Most editors are avid readers, and often they pick up on a magazine or newspaper article and pursue the author to write a book on the subject of the piece.

A Credential-Building Strategy

1. Make a list of magazines, newspapers, and journals that publish articles on your subject.

2. Obtain publication guidelines from targeted periodicals.

3. Tailor short pieces on your subject to those guidelines.

4. Submit articles to as many periodicals as possible.

5. Set a goal of four to six published articles before you complete your first book proposal.

This happened with Amy Dascyzn, who had created *The Tightwad Gazette*, a newsletter which she published and distributed from her home in Vermont. The success of her little operation attracted national publicity, including a feature article in the *New York Times*. No fewer than three editors for major New York publishers contacted Amy to see if she might collect her advice on living cheaply into a book. Diane Reverand, then at Villard, a subsidiary of Random House, snared the project, which went on to become a bestseller in both its original and revised versions. For Amy, publishing in a small way led to big-time success. What attracted Diane and the other editors? Besides Amy's pluck and persistence, it was her self-made track record and amazing motivation.

What motivated Amy Dascyzn? A mixture of idealism (she deeply believed in helping people on tight budgets), a desire for fame (she loved getting publicity for her work), and a wish to make money (she approached her work in a businesslike way).

GETTING MOTIVATED

Motivation pulls all of the six start-up steps together. Back in Chapter 1, we talked about the importance of motivation when we discussed solving the needs-benefit equation. Let's revisit that aspect of getting published in terms of what you do before you write your book proposal.

Ask yourself why you have developed expertise in a subject, why you feel inspired to fulfill a need in the marketplace, why you wish to become an author, why you enjoy linking up with experts and writers, why you want to learn about publishers and agents, and why you work so hard to build your credentials. To answer these questions objectively, apply the Motivation Gauge, asking yourself what drives your urge to get published.

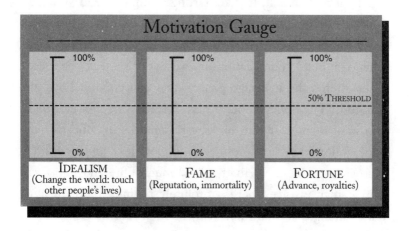

Like writing, motivation may not be teachable, but it is learnable. Be honest with yourself. If you cannot honestly say that you are motivated by a balanced mixture of idealism, fame, and fortune, consider ways in which you can bring more harmony to what drives you. If idealism drives you too much, you probably won't pay enough attention to an agent's or editor's marketing concerns. If a desire for fame rules your heart, you probably won't worry enough about the needs of your readers. And if fortune preoccupies you, you will probably think so much about marketing that you'll not deliver as much substance as a really good book requires. That's another publishing paradox: the only good book is a book that sells, and the only books that sell are really good books, written by people who balance their idealism, their yearning for fame, and their hunger for fortune.

Undertaking a Labor of Love

Getting published is like starting a business, but it's also much more than that. It's like starting a family. Glenn Weadock, author of several "Bulletproof" computer software books, compares the process to having a baby. "There's the dating phase, when you build your relationship with your subject," he muses, "then there's the marriage phase when you commit body and soul to it. The honeymoon can last several years, but eventually you want a child. It can take several months to conceive your book, followed by nine months of development, and a period of excruciating labor. No matter how much time and effort and pain it may involve, there's absolutely nothing more thrilling than holding that brand-new baby book in your hands."

Most new authors look back on the process of getting published and jokingly say, "If I'd known how much labor was involved, I would have thought twice about doing it." All new parents understand that feeling, but like Glenn and all the other authors you have met in this chapter, the result makes all the labor worthwhile. You've invested two or three years of your life shaping your proposal, writing your manuscript, and suffering through the details of production and manufacturing, then one bright spring day you open a cardboard box containing ten author's copies of your new book, and you sit at your desk in awe. Your ideas have finally taken on a life of their own.

CHAPTER THREE

How to Write a Book Proposal:

A Step-by-Step Guide for Turning Any Idea into a Business Plan

Experienced authors know that getting paid for their work depends as much on patience and perseverance as it does on creativity. According to a popular publishing legend, one aspiring author submitted a story entitled *How I Made Love to a Bear* to *Reader's Digest*, and promptly received a form rejection. He rewrote the story a little and resubmitted it with the title *How I Made Love to a Bear in an Iron Lung*. Again, *Reader's Digest* rejected it. Unwilling to take no for an answer, the author rewrote the story yet again, retitled it *How I Made Love to a Bear in an Iron Lung for the FBI* and resubmitted it to the magazine, only to get a third rejection. Finally, he didn't bother to rewrite at all but just lengthened the title to *How I Made Love to a Bear in an Iron Lung for the FBI and Found God.* Two weeks later he found a letter of acceptance and a check in his mailbox. The author persevered until he had the right "collateral" to get the "loan" he wanted.

If getting published is like starting a business, then selling a proposal to a publisher is a lot like going to a banker for a loan. In fact, publishing contracts define advances as loans, albeit interest-free, which the author must pay back out of future royalties. Imagine stumbling into a banker's office, all dusty and disheveled, with a shakily sketched map to the Lost Dutchman Mine. "Invest in my dream!" you cry. The banker would probably throw you out of his office. Now suppose you stroll into that same office, fish a leather pouch from your vest pocket, and scatter a dozen gold nuggets on the desk. The banker would be reaching for his checkbook.

When you or your agent submit your book proposal to publishers, you are offering that document as collateral against a loan. The more collateral you offer, the larger the loan for which you can qualify. Publishers don't hand out advances for far-fetched, speculative projects, and they don't offer a figure off the top of their heads. Your ability to land a contract and a sizable advance will depend on the perceived value of your proposal and the sales estimates it generates from the publisher's marketing department. This cold, hard fact should stimulate you to invest as much blood, sweat, and tears into writing your proposal as you will into writing the book itself.

Agents see it every day. Betty Lou holes up in her garret for a year furiously creating a manuscript for *How to Market a New Product*. Finally, she submits a query letter and a book synopsis to the Garcia Vega Literary Agency. Jerry Garcia asks to see a proposal, which Betty Lou promptly slaps together. Assuming that Jerry still sees merit in the project, he puts Betty Lou through the proposal-writing process outlined in this chapter. Three drafts later, Jerry agrees to submit the proposal to editors, and Betty Lou heaves a sigh of relief. "If I had known how hard it would be to write a good proposal," she complains, "I never would have started this project in the first place." Of course, that complaint turns to joy when McGraw-Hill offers a contract and a $10,000 advance for the book. "I know how to market a product," Betty Lou says at her publication party a year later. "So why didn't I practice what I preach when I started my career as a book author?"

Why, indeed? Experienced authors do not write books then hope to interest publishers in them. They write strong proposals that can attract the publishing commitment and funding that will enable them to write their books.

DEVELOPING THE PROPOSAL

Before we set about examining the elements of a good proposal, consider the following parable, which offers a wonderful lesson to all aspiring authors. Long ago, a mighty king ruled over a great and powerful nation. Wisely, he did not rest easily with his country's accomplishments and sought constantly for all the new ideas and advancements that would keep him, as well as his kingdom, prospering over all rivals. As time passed, that quest became harder and harder, until one day the king summoned his most learned scholars, skilled artisans, and fiercest warriors and issued the proclamation: "Go forth and find me the newest ideas, the most inventive devices, the most advanced weapons. Bring them back to me and I shall reward you handsomely."

So commanded by their king, the scholars, artisans, and warriors went forth throughout the land, searching high and low for everything new under the sun. They combed the countryside north and south, east and west, until they had located every new idea, invention, and armament.

The king held an audience with all of his subjects and considered each item in turn. First, the chief scholar expounded on a new philosophy of governance, proclaiming it the most up-to-date idea in the land. The king frowned. "That is nothing new to me. Tell me something I don't already know." The scholar retreated in embarrassment.

Next, the king's master architect strode forth, unfurling a blueprint for an extravagant new castle. "That's just a fancy version of what I already have," observed the king. "Show me something I have never seen before." The architect joined his colleague, the scholar, in disgrace.

Finally, the commander of the army marched triumphantly to the throne. "Sire," he announced, "behold the most devastating weapon ever pressed into battle." As a dozen officers rolled forth a huge and cumbersome catapult, the king began shaking his head. "We have been using smaller machines like this for over fifty years; why can't you bring me something *new?*" The commander slunk off to join his humiliated peers.

"For the sake of my kingdom, for the sake of my soul," bellowed the king, "can no one in this vast kingdom bring me just *one truly new thing?*"

As all of the king's wisest men bowed their heads in embarrassment, a small voice came from the assembled throng: "May it please your highness that I come forward?" To the astonishment of all, a young boy, in the tattered garments that bespoke his humble peasant background, dashed forward.

"Hah!" shouted the king's chief scholar, "This ragamuffin insults the king with his impudence! Soldiers, take him away!"

"Silence!" commanded the king, amused at the boy's boldness. "Let him show me something new."

The young peasant boy crept to the king's side, unfolded a red silk scarf, and gently placed a tiny blue egg in his master's palm. As the king cradled this surprise offering, a tiny beak poked through the shell, and soon a baby bird sat quivering in the king's hand.

The look of bewilderment on the king's face slowly gave way to a broad smile. "Yes," he mused, "the most humble among us has shown us the *one* new thing under the sun."

The moral of the story? Approach this undertaking in all humility and draw upon your deepest wellspring of creativity. Humility and creativity will help you fashion the nine key elements of your book proposal into a masterpiece much stronger than the sum of its parts.

Putting Your Proposal in Perspective

Before you set to work on your book proposal, you should contemplate the publishing environment in which your proposal will sink or swim. Hundreds of book proposals flood editors' desks each year, and only a small fraction of them win contracts. Although editors reject many proposals because the authors' material lacks market appeal or strong writing, they turn down most because the author has not portrayed his or her material properly.

The following tips, while they do not ensure success, will increase the chances that editors will thoroughly and fairly evaluate your proposal. It surprises most new authors that editors do not sit at their desks reading book proposals in an eager search for the next bestseller. To the contrary, most editors maintain a list of "kiss-offs" that allow them to reject a proposal and get it off their desks. As in selling anything, the author must anticipate and head off the standard objections.

Editors' Standard Objections

- **"This is a magazine article, not a book."** This type of rejection usually stems from an incompletely developed outline for the book. *Have you proposed 250 to 300 manuscript pages?*
- **"People will not buy a book on this subject."** In this case, the author has not properly positioned the book. *Have you compared your book to successfully published competitors?*
- **"The author lacks credibility."** Editors look for credentials in the subject area. *Have you presented a strong biographical sketch?*
- **"The material is not well written."** Many authors make the mistake of placing less emphasis on the quality of writing in the proposal than on actual sample material from the book. *Does your proposal reflect your best writing?*
- **"There is too much competition."** Perhaps the author has not supplied enough detail about the new book's uniqueness. *Have you stressed your book's uniqueness compared with competitors?*
- **"The book does not suit our current publishing program."** The author or agent has submitted the idea to the wrong house. *Have you determined which publisher regularly issues books on this subject?*
- **"The market is too small."** This signals either an inadequate evaluation of the market or an inability to establish an eager audience. *Have you quantified your potential audience?*

- **"We already plan to issue a book on this subject."** The manuscript promises too little uniqueness, or it has come into the market late. *Have you thoroughly researched the market for your book?*
- **"Readers are no longer interested in this subject."** The book trails rather leads a trend. *Have you built forward-looking features into your book?*
- **"Get yourself an agent."** Editors expect agents to filter out unworthy proposals. *Does your agent specialize in the sort of book you propose?*

Most editors ask the same questions about a book idea:

- "What's it like?" (it must appeal to a proven book-buying audience)
- "How's it different?" (it must complement, rather than duplicate, what already exists)
- "Why is the author ideally suited to write this book?" (he or she must know the subject and must write well)
- "Will the manuscript live up to the promise of the proposal?" (the sample must prove the author's ability)

A good proposal answers these questions clearly and compellingly.

THE NINE KEY ELEMENTS
OF A BOOK PROPOSAL

Strong proposals that win publishing contracts always contain nine key elements. As you walk through these elements

The Nine Key Elements of a Good Proposal

1. The Cover

2. The Title Page

3. A Brief Synopsis or Executive Summary

4. The Contents Page

5. The Book Description

6. The Author Profile

7. Book Contents and Specifications

8. Chapter Summaries

9. Sample Chapter (usually optional for established authors)

in the pages ahead, you will see how one author—veterinarian Myrna Milani—implemented them. You will also find two other model proposals in the Appendix of this book that can serve as templates for your own proposal.

Proposal Element 1: The Cover

Perhaps people shouldn't judge a book by its cover, but they do. So do editors. Since you want your project to leap out of the pile of proposals stacked in an editor's "In" box, you should create a professional-looking cover, including a graphic image, the title/subtitle of your book in attractive type, and your name. A strong cover lifts the proposal out of the pile and says, "Read me!"

For her proposal, Myrna Milani borrowed a graphic from a greeting card, which she color photocopied:

Example of a cover graphic for a book proposal.

Proposal Element 2: The Title Page

This element repeats the book title, subtitle, and author's name, and adds the agent's name, address, and phone number if the book is being represented by an agent. Like covers, titles can make a big difference. Good titles strike a nerve in the potential reader. If you mentioned just your title to ten people browsing the section of the bookstore in which your book would be stocked, would they both understand its subject and feel excited by it? In most cases a catchy title and clarifying subtitle work best:

- *High Inside: The Memoirs of an Ex-Baseball Wife*
- *The Oz Principle: Tapping the Power of Accountability in Organizations*
- *Whisper in His Ear: Improving Your Sex Life with X-Rated Fantasies*
- *Tight Ships Don't Sink: Profit Secrets of a Maverick CEO*
- *The Genius of Sitting Bull: Thirteen Heroic Strategies for Today's Business Leaders*
- *Life's Parachutes: How to Land on Your Feet During Trying Times*

Although Myrna reproduced part of her cover image on the title page, that isn't necessary (See the next page.).

Proposal Element 3:
A Brief Synopsis or Executive Summary

This one- to one-and-a-half-page "sales pitch" for your book, written like book-cover or jacket-flap copy, stimulates editors to read your proposal. It should not only enable editors to "hold your book in their mind's hand," but it should also drive home the need for the book and the tangible benefits it delivers or the pressing problem it solves. A strong executive summary appeals to the publisher's marketing

The Four Percent Solution:

*A Six-Month Program for Finding—and
Launching a Lasting Relationship with—Your Ideal Dog*

by
Myrna M. Milani, D.V.M.

Author of
The Weekend Dog, The Invisible Leash, and
The Body Language and Emotion of Dogs

Michael Snell Literary Agency
P. O. Box 1206
Truro, Massachusetts 02666-1206
(508) 349-3718

people, who play a major role in acquisitions decisions. A tightly written and convincing summary compels the editor to read the rest of the proposal, while a rambling, unconvincing one prompts a swift rejection. Imagine that you have only thirty seconds to convince a committee to buy your book.

Brief Book Synopsis

The *Four Percent Solution: A Six-Month Program for Finding—and Launching a Lasting Relationship with—Your Ideal Dog* synthesizes what scientists and successful dog owners know: The human-canine bond forms during the first six months (a mere four percent of the average dog's life), and that the quality of that bond will determine whether owner and pet will experience a lifetime of joy or a few years of misery that might even end with the animal's abandonment or demise.

In her highly regarded The Weekend Dog, Dr. Myrna M. Milani, a recognized authority on the human-canine bond, taught people who only saw their dogs evenings and weekends how to create quality relationships with their pets. In this latest book, she shows a new generation of readers how to use their knowledge of the bond to find their perfect pet and successfully integrate that animal into even the busiest household.

The Four Percent Solution will appeal to owners who

- would like to own a dog, but aren't sure their busy lifestyles can accommodate one.
- experienced a less than perfect relationship with a previous dog, but still long for a pet.
- already own a dog and are thinking about adding another to the household.

The book offers readers in a fast-paced world a six-month program that takes into account their own and their dog's unique personality and situation. It teaches them:

- How their own feelings, beliefs, and needs affect their choice of, and relationship to, a particular animal.
- How to choose the best dog to match their needs, based on its breed, early experience, and other behavior- and health-influencing factors.
- How to create the most comfortable environment that will meet both the dog's and the owner's unique needs.

Other essential new dog owner topics include:

- The most practical training method for the new dog.
- The most enjoyable human-canine exercise program
- The healthiest canine food and feeding schedule
- The most effective medical approach to insure wellness

Because it emphasizes the uniqueness of the bond that forms the foundation of every human-canine relationship, The Four Percent Solution provides the kind of solid information that will enable readers to find and enjoy their perfect dogs for a life-time.

Proposal Element 4: The Contents Page

This element allows an editor to turn to the sections of the proposal with ease. You can place it before or after the executive summary. A "knock-out" executive summary up front works well for some writers and some books.

Proposal Contents

The Book	page 1
The Market	page 8
The Author	page 10
Book Contents	page 12
Brief Chapter Summaries	page 13
Sample Chapter	page 35

Proposal Element 5: The Book Description

This three- to seven-page summary develops your "quick pitch" more fully. A compelling synopsis does not recapitulate the book's contents in detail (your chapter summaries will do that); it positions your book in the market by answering these questions:

- *Who* will buy it?
- What *other books* has the audience bought in the past?
- *Why* will the audience buy your book instead of the competitors' books?

Begin your book description with a concrete example or anecdote that brings your subject to life and draws the editor into your material. Compare and contrast your book to successfully published titles. Stress the need for the book and its benefits, as well as problems and solutions your book addresses and solves. If possible, offer sales figures, statistics, and other quantitative arguments that establish a wide audience for the material.

Notice that Myrna has broken her synopsis into two separate elements. The first, The Book, focuses on her book's content and organization; the second, The Market, deals with audience and competition. Since the latter considerations usually figure greatly in a publisher's decision about acquiring a new project, it often makes sense to separate and stress your market/audience/competitive analysis. The boldface in Myrna's synopsis did not appear in her proposal, but has been added to draw your attention to its strengths.

The Book

Four eight-week-old Doberman pups receive a joyous welcome when they take up residence in four different American homes. Two years later, beloved family pet Roscoe suddenly drops dead of heart failure while playing fetch with the kids, Kildair is lauded for his exceptional work as a therapy dog, Kayla keeps her owners both exhausted and broke treating her chronic medical problems, and Fang mauls a Girl Scout during the annual cookie drive.

Although a casual observer might consider what happened to those four owners the luck of the draw, readers of *The Four Percent Solution* discover that these results reflect the quality of the human-canine bonds formed during the animals' first six months, a mere 4% of the average canine life span. The early experiences of a specific owner and a specific pet, not luck, made the difference. Although some owners do luck out,

---

every year millions of them abandon, give up, or euthanize their pets, or live with them in less than fulfilling relationships.

In today's world, complex owner lifestyles, breeding practices that multiply the number of canine disorders, and a dizzying array of behavioral and medical approaches all challenge the quality of the human-canine relationship. These factors all argue for a new, bond-based approach to dog ownership, one that applies the best science and common sense to those crucial first six months of human-canine interaction. By wisely using this time, readers and their dogs will gain a lifetime of beneficial returns from their four percent investment.

Unlike other books on the market, *The Four Percent Solution* focusses on the intimate world of the human-canine bond—the biolog- ical, psychological, and environmental factors that define a relation- ship—and how it affects the relationship for good or ill. Without this knowledge, even the most longed-for, seemingly perfect, pedigreed pup may become a misfit; with it, even an adult stray of the most questionable origins can become a healthy, well-behaved best friend for life. By presenting the latest scientific data and a broad spectrum of case histories representing both human and canine points of view, the book shows readers how to analyze themselves, a prospective pet, and those critical aspects of their lives that will exert the greatest influence on their relationship with a dog.

To accomplish this goal, *The Four Percent Solution* first takes an inti- mate look at the human half of the human-canine equation. Psychologist and canine behaviorist William Campbell only half-jokingly suggests that, by law, anyone who wants to own a dog should undergo extensive psycho- logical evaluation. He proposes this after spending thirty years dealing with all the problems that result when owners project their most inti- mate—and often bizarre!—beliefs on their pets. Because scientific studies of the bond prove that our beliefs affect our dogs' physiology as well as their behavior, smart owners will take their beliefs into account when selecting and introducing a new dog into their household. Otherwise they could join the ranks of those fearful owners who are attracted to or create fearful dogs, or of those fearful owners with heart disease whose fearful dogs develop similar medical problems, too. Had Fang's owners read Chap- ter One, they would have realized how their attitudes toward animals put them on a collision course with any dominant animal, and especially the canine ball of energy who raced up to them at the breeder's.

Chapter Two shows readers how to evaluate a dog in terms of its breed- ing, personality, and previous experiences, all of which can enhance or erode a quality relationship. The increased numbers of purebred animals available from a wide range of sources have given rise to several phenom- ena that can undermine an animal's sense of self and function, as well as distort once reliable breed characteristics. While always a concern, these can prove particularly problematic for potential dog owners with complex lifestyles. It's one thing to admire the qualities that make a field golden retriever a joy to watch; it's quite another to fulfill the special needs of such an animal in a fast-paced urban or suburban environment. Had Roscoe's owners realized the prevalence of inherited heart problems in certain Doberman lines, they surely would have asked questions beyond those specifically related to his kid-safe temperament before they chose him.

In Chapter Three, *The Four Percent Solution* examines how dog and owner relate to their physical space, the third component of the bond. All behaviorists rank establishing and protecting a territory as the strongest canine drive. Unfortunately, as our lives and environments become more complicated, satisfying this innate drive can generate crushing pressure on the dog. Kayla's retired owners chose her because they wanted a dog who would protect their home in a newly gentrified urban area. However that responsibility so overwhelms their shy pet, she chews herself raw when left alone.

Once readers learn how to analyze the most critical human, canine, and environmental components of the bond and find the dog most likely to succeed in their particular situation, they then begin sorting through the many, increasingly sophisticated and often conflicting contemporary approaches to training, nutrition, exercise and medical care. Research reiterates what Hippocrates declared ages ago: No treatment will work unless the patient believes in it. Recent studies further expand that basic premise: Pet owners won't train, feed, exercise, or medicate their animals consistently if any aspect of these procedures bothers them. The Four Percent Solution explores each of these subjects in depth, with the express purpose of helping readers select those approaches that will best meet their and their dog's needs.

When Dr. Milani wrote *The Weekend Dog* over a decade ago, behaviorists classified the majority of canine behavioral problems as isolation behaviors, those which occurred when previously stay-at-home owners entered the workforce or pursued other activities that left the naturally social dog home alone. Because the lack of a human-centered pack structure now claims the number one problem slot, *The Four Percent Solution* devotes an entire chapter to helping prospective dog owners avoid this detrimental phenomenon. Regardless what training technique an owner uses, it can't and won't work consistently unless the dog perceives the trainer (or any person) as dominant. Unfortunately many people perceive the establishment of a dominance hierarchy as conferring "superior" and "inferior" or even "villain" and "victim" roles on humans and canines. In reality, nothing could be further from the truth. Those people who truly assume the leadership role in their human-canine packs never resort to force of any kind. Conversely, those who do the most yelling and "disciplining" invariably have failed to assume a true leadership position, leaving the dog no alternative but to fill this void. While always a major concern, the need for a human-centered pack becomes especially critical when owners add a second dog to their household.

Once the dog knows who's the teacher and who's the pupil, owners need to decide what they want to teach the dog and how. Numerous books, videos, and individuals stand ready to help everyone create a well-behaved pet. Unfortunately, however, many dog owners pick a program with little or no consideration of whether it fits their particular relationship with that particular dog. Because every failed program makes later training more difficult and exacerbates rather than solves any problems, owners with little time or complex lifestyles can't afford to jump from method to method. *The Four Percent Solution* helps readers sort through the major options, using their intimate knowledge of themselves, their dogs, and their environments to pick the one that will work best for them and their pets. Does it really matter whether the dog can come, sit, heel, and hold a down/stay? Only if a need for those skills exists for that particular human-canine combination in their particular environment.

The book next takes a critical look at some old standards and new entries in the training arena, the success of which demands intimate knowledge of the bond between owners, their dogs, and their environments before they use them. Electronic devices can produce seemingly miraculous results when used to train a stable dog in a stable relationship in a stable environment. Lacking these prerequisites, however, those same miracle devices can lead to hellish results for human and canine alike: "Invisible" fences may increase aggression, while shock collars may produce circling and other neurotic behaviors in all but the most well-adjusted animals, hardly the results these owners had in mind when they sought an easy solution to their problems. Recommendations from veterinarians to treat behavioral problems with psychotherapeutic drugs touted by the human medical community increase by leaps and bounds. Two days on Prozac and Fang stops chasing the letter carrier: Should his owners consider him cured? Not at all.

The next two chapters explore how the choices owners make regarding canine nutrition and exercise also affect their relationships with their pets. The once simple act of feeding the dog can become a very involved, time-consuming, and expensive matter for those who haven't taken the time to consider this aspect of dog ownership beforehand. Fortunately, however, problems related to feeding more commonly arise from our failure to grasp a few basic concepts and how they they specifically and intimately relate to us and our pets. Once we master these, we can determine which one of all those regular, premium, all-natural, and therapeutic diets will work best for us and our dogs. Had Kayla's and Fang's owners understood the bond-

basics of canine nutrition and feeding, they wouldn't have given their pets food treats, yet for entirely different, but equally crucial, reasons.

Applying that same logic, the chapter on exercise shows readers how to analyze a particular dog's activity needs in terms of their own needs and their specific environments. Although this chapter discusses how to find and maintain a dog whose exercise needs best match the owner's, it also describes a wide range of exercise options that enable even a human couch potato to find happiness with an active canine.

The penultimate chapter of the book explores human and canine health as these affect the relationship for better or worse. Kayla's owners compound their dog's problems because they strongly believe in homeopathy and other forms of alternative medicine, but pursue a traditional course of treatment for their pet because they erroneously assume such veterinary alternatives don't exist. However, their negative feelings about the medication cause them to administer it haphazardly, and Kayla gets worse instead of better. Given the increased variety, sophistication, and cost of veterinary care, contemporary owners need solid bond-related health information to create and maintain the long and healthy relationships they desire.

In its final chapter, *The Four Percent Solution* summarizes the material in the preceding chapters in the form of a series of self-help exercises and check lists readers can use to evaluate all aspects of their relationship with a prospective or existing pet. Not only does this material give prospective and new dog owners a solid understanding of their starting point, it provides them with a convenient and reliable way to detect and respond to any changes that may occur over the years.

By presenting case histories of humans and animals successfully and not-so-successfully grappling with some of the most complex and intimate contemporary human-canine issues, *The Four Percent Solution* enables readers to develop a clear and intimate image of the kind of relationship they want—and realistically can create—with a dog. Given that information, they then can select the dog that best meets their needs, or initiate any changes in themselves and/or their environments that will best allow them to experience this ideal. All too often people endure less than fulfilling relationships with their pets because they select a dog based on the out-dated, romantic notion, "I'll know him when I see him." That might have worked when Mom or someone stayed home all day to care for the animal, and when breeders bred purebreds for functions that demanded physical and behavioral soundness, and only people who could fulfill those animals' functions owned them. However, we live in a much different world now. In today's world, the owners who enjoy the most rewarding relationships with their dogs are those who enter the relationship with the most knowledge.

After years of discussion and commiseration about the many negative effects created by well-meaning, but naive gurus and dog owners who romanticize rather than understand the human-canine bond, the author's dear friend, trainer Job Evans, confided that he wanted to write a dog book entitled *Love is Not Enough*. Naturally, editors found the title much too negative, and Job died before he could fulfill his dream. Nonetheless the same problem persists, and *The Four Percent Solution* addresses it head-on. **Far from ignoring the role of love, the book shares the secret every successful trainer, behaviorist, and dog owner knows: Without that intimate, practical, and relevant knowledge of the bond and how it works, the love between owner and dog cannot and will not last.**

THE MARKET

Like Elizabeth Thomas' *The Hidden Life of Dogs* (Houghton-Mifflin, 1993) and other descriptive texts, *The Four Percent Solution* embodies Dr. Milani's experiences, in her case those gleaned from more than twenty years in veterinary practice, over half of them devoted to the human-animal bond and behavioral problems. Unlike Thomas' book, however, Dr. Milani's offers intimate views into the hidden lives of a wide variety of dogs and their owners. Like the many books on canine psychology, such as Warren Eckstein's *How to Get Your Dog to Do What You Want* (Villard: 1993), Bruce Fogel's *Know Your Dog: An Owner's Guide to Dog Behavior* (Dorling Kindersley, 1992), Michael Fox's *Understanding Your Dog* (St Martin's Press, 1992), and Desmond Morris' *Dogwatching* (Crown, 1993), *The Four Percent Solution* delves into the mysteries of the canine psyche. However, unlike them, it presents this material in the context of the human-canine bond, revealing how it affects all aspects of the dog's existence, not just its behavior. Like the training texts by Job Michael Evans (*People, Pooches, and Problems;* Howell, 1992), Carol Benjamin's *Surviving Your Dog's Adolescence* (Howell, 1993), and the Monks of New Skete's *The Art of Raising a Puppy* (Little, Brown and Company, 1991), the book offers specific information for those seeking to resolve or prevent problems with their dogs. Unlike these books, it focusses on those intimate human-canine-environment issues that can undermine even the most well-conceived training program. Like texts written by other veterinarians, such as William Kay's *Complete Book of Dog Health* (Macmillan, 1985), Terri McGinnis' *Well Dog Book* (Random House, 1991), and Carlson's and Giffin's *The Dog Owner's Home Veterinary Handbook* (Howell, 1992), *The Four Percent Solution* discusses some of the most recent medical advances. Unlike these books, however, it addresses these issues as they affect the relationship between the owner and the dog.

A large and eager need exists for Dr. Milani's unique bond-based approach. During a recent discussion of her *The Weekend Dog* on the internet, not only did people around the country request the book but, according to Charlene Woodward, the force behind Direct Book Service's *Dog & Cat Book Catalog,* many also expressed a desire for an updated version of the book. When Dr. Milani contacted Ms. Woodward and discussed the contents of *The Four Percent Solution,* Ms. Woodward expressed no doubts that the book would fill a void that currently exists in the dog literature. Considering the *Dog & Cat Book Catalog* prides itself on locating and carrying every dog book in print, *The Four Percent Solution* could receive no greater endorsement.

Where other books describe the best—and sometimes the only—way to select, train, feed, exercise, or medically treat a dog based on their authors' experience, *The Four Percent Solution* provides readers with the knowledge to make these same decisions based on their own needs and those of that one particular dog they want to live with happily ever after.

Proposal Element 6: The Author Profile

This one- to two-page biographical sketch must establish two sets of credentials: the author's subject expertise and his or her writing ability. Do not include an academic *vitae,* but write more of a press release that makes you sound promotable, presentable, and knowledgeable. Editors will find any previously published work of interest, especially if it sold well. Include sales figures, reviews, media coverage, or any other salient market tests of your previous work. In this age of hype, publishers want to know not only that an author can handle a media appearance, but will work tirelessly to promote the book. The happiest authors never sit back and wait for the publisher to make things happen; they take the initiative to draw attention to their work.

Myrna included *all* her credentials as an expert on the subject, as a writer, and as a promoter of herself and her books.

THE AUTHOR

Dr. Myrna Milani received a Bachelor of Science degree from Capital University (Columbus, Ohio) in 1968 and a Doctorate in Veterinary Medicine from the Ohio State University, College of Veterinary Medicine in 1972. Following a year as a full-time academic advisor to pre-veterinary students at the university, Dr. Milani entered private veterinary practice in Keene, New Hampshire. Her interest in the relationship between humans and animals as it affects the health and behavior of both led her to write four books for the general public:

- *The Weekend Dog* (Rawson/Scribners, 1984; Signet paper, 1985)
- *The Invisible Leash* (New American Library, 1985; Signet paper, 1986)
- *The Body Language and Emotion of Dogs* (William Morrow, 1986; Quill, 1993)
- *The Body Language and Emotion of Cats* (William Morrow, 1987; Quill, 1993)

The latter three books were voted best in their categories by the editors of *The Reader's Catalogue,* which lists the 40,000 best books in print. *The Body Language and Emotion of Dogs* has been used as a textbook for collegiate courses in the human-canine bond and pet-facilitated therapy and replaced *The Weekend Dog* on trainers' reading lists when the latter proved difficult to locate. Dr. Milani recently completed a bond-based veterinary text, *The Art of Veterinary Practice: A Guide to Client Communication* which was published in Spring, 1995 by the University of Pennsylvania Press.

Throughout her career Dr. Milani has taught numerous courses: Biology, Anatomy and Physiology, Animal Behavior, and Bioethics on the college level, and courses in the human-canine and the human-feline bond for the general public. In addition to advising private behavior/bond clients, she also serves as a consultant to non-profit and for-profit organizations regarding animal-related issues. As a function of her work as a spokesperson for the KalKan Corporation, she discusses canine and feline care and behavioral problems with thousands of owners and professionals at shows and events. She has been interviewed numerous times regarding various aspects of the human-animal bond on the "Today" and "NBC Nightly News" shows, and for "The Miami Herald," "The Los Angeles Times" and "The New Yorker Magazine," API and Reuters news services and Rodale Press, among others. Her radio work runs the gamut from three-hour listener call-in marathons in San Francisco and Indianapolis, to in-depth interviews on programs such as the syndicated "Charlie Citrine Show," to more academically oriented segments for various public radio stations nationwide.

Dr. Milani has spoken to a wide variety of public and professional organizations on pertinent aspects of the human-animal relationship, and delivered the keynote address to the Sheba International Veterinary Congress in Vienna, Austria in 1988. While a member the executive board and president of the New Hampshire Veterinary Medical Association, she worked with the state legislature and provided testimony to insure uniform licensing and quality veterinary standards throughout the state. She currently enjoys a close working relationship with veterinarians nationwide who call her regarding behavioral or bond problems, and who refer clients to her. The eclectic nature of her studies of the human-animal bond have led her to develop a network of trainers, breeders, psychologists, wildlife experts, and other professionals with whom she routinely shares personal observations and material. Dr Milani serves vice-president of B. R. Smith and Associates, a small business and veterinary practice consulting firm in Charlestown, New Hampshire.

Proposal Element 7: Book Contents and Specifications

This one-page "bird's-eye view" of the book lists chapter titles only. Pay as much attention to the quality of these titles as you did to the quality of the book title itself. They should be catchy, lively, clear, and enticing. The title/subtitle format often works well here, too.

At the bottom of the page or on the next page, include the book's specifications: projected manuscript length or number of words, format (hardcover, quality paperback, mass market paperback), and anticipated delivery date (for example, six months after contract). Publishers determine a book's format by estimating maximum revenues. In a market in which book buyers are not price-resistant, such as the one for professional books on business and investing, the publisher can achieve maximum revenue with a high-priced hardcover book; a mid-priced quality paperback may sell the greatest number of copies; and, where price resistance runs high, the lowest-priced mass-market format may make more sense. Anticipate the format for your book. You can also specify the form of delivery (i.e., hard copy or on computer disks). Notice how Myrna's chapter titles follow a consistent pattern.

BOOK CONTENTS

Introduction

Chapter One — In a Mirror Dimly: The Dog Owner's Sense of Self and Function

Chapter Two — A Universe Apart: The Canine Sense of Self and Function

Chapter Three — Inner and Outer Spaces: The Human and Canine Sense of Place

Chapter Four — A Meeting of Minds: Pack Structure, Leadership, and the Human-Canine Relationship

Chapter Five — Training a Keeper: Singular versus Combined Image Training

Chapter Six — Techno-Shock: Controversial Training Techniques and Their Effect on the Relationship

Chapter Seven — Nouveau Nutrition: Canine Dietary Delights and Demons

Chapter Eight — The New Millennium Work-Out: Multidimensional Human-Canine Exercise

Chapter Nine — Well and Good: Canine and Human Health as it Affects the Relationship

Chapter Ten — Bond Check: Routine Maintenance for a Healthy Relationship

Specifications: Hard cover and/or quality paperback

Length: 350 pages

Delivery Date: Nine months after receipt of contract

Proposal Element 8: Chapter Summaries

The chapter summaries provide a "worm's-eye view" of the book's organization. Do not present a conventional outline, but summarize each chapter in one, or at most two, pages. If your book contains twelve chapters, try to limit this section to twelve pages, remembering that while this section affords you an opportunity to display your writing skill, you should summarize, rather than condense, your chapters. Open each summary with an enticing example or anecdote (one paragraph), summarize the chapter's content (one paragraph), and highlight the chapter's features (perhaps in a bulleted list). Outlines can be boring, so you will want to make yours as interesting as possible, as Myrna has done.

BRIEF CHAPTER SUMMARIES

Introduction

Systems engineer Marty Murphy decided she wanted a dog the day a co-worker announced the birth of a litter of wire-haired dachshund pups. When Marty went to see the litter that evening, she immediately claimed the only pup with black ears, and christened her Frieda. During the next two months, Frieda experienced interactions with humans and other animals that shaped her behavior for life. Marty spent this same period learning to operate her new high performance, ultra-fast, single lens reflex camera so she could record every minute of her first wonderful days with Frieda. She also bought a mountain of dogs toys and eight different kinds of puppy food and treats, all of which came highly recommended by co-workers and friends. When the Big Day finally arrived, Marty and Frieda commenced a four-month spree of programs that affected virtually all aspects of the pup's life and their relationship. By the time Frieda reached six months of age, she still chewed the furniture, and rarely ate her dog food or came when called. For her part, Marty was getting a little tired of hearing the breeder say, "That's just the way doxies are," every time she asked for help.

> *The Four Percent Solution* proposes that prospective dog owners spend two months preparing themselves and their households mentally, physically, and emotionally for this big event, and then four months selecting the right animal and getting off to a good start with it. That way by the time the pup reaches six months of age, they'll be well on the their way to a solid, lasting relationship rather than still trying to iron out the wrinkles. Adult dogs also benefit from this approach because it enables new owners to respond to the animal consistently. Because lack of owner consistency contributes to many of the problems for which adult dogs are abandoned or given up, this helps insure the animal's success in its new home. Although six months may seem like a long commitment for busy people, it's a mere four percent of the average dog's life span, and that's nothing compared to how long the memory lingers when owners must give up or put down an animal for preventable problems.

Proposal Element 9: Sample Chapter

Unless your book contains radically different types of chapters (for instance, theory in some, applications in others), you need only submit one complete sample chapter. Pick a chapter that puts your book's best foot forward—a central or unique chapter (usually not Chapter 1) that displays both your writing talent and your book's special benefits to readers. An author can write a brilliant proposal and then fail to prove that the manuscript will live up to its promise. Likewise, strong samples seldom overcome a weak proposal. Few writers submit anything that has undergone less than four or five thorough revisions.

We could not take the space to reprint Myrna's sample chapter, but if you want to see how it appeared in the book, you can look at the published book, finally titled *Dog Perfect* (Contemporary Books). Myrna's hard work paid off when Contemporary Books offered her a lucrative contract.

PACKAGING THE PROPOSAL

Authors hate to think that readers judge a book by its cover, but these same authors lie awake at night worrying that their publisher will mess up their book's cover. Think of editors as readers, and package your proposal so that it is easy and exciting to read. Since editors often read on trains or at home, they appreciate the handiness of a spiral-bound proposal.

Some authors include their photo, if it's of press-release quality, at the end of the Author Profile. There, too, you can insert copies of relevant media coverage or previously published magazine or newspaper articles on the same subject as your book. Since publishing involves excruciating attention to detail, pay close attention to the quality of every detail in your proposal. Quality comes before quantity *and* schedule. Take your time, polish every component of your proposal, and never rely on friends and family to judge its worth. You may find yourself going over three or four drafts with your agent.

Tips for Authors of Practical, Self-Help, and How-To Books

This perennially robust market has grown so competitive that authors must work especially hard to succeed in it. Almost any area of human activity (sex, money, health, business, pets, psychology, family) lends itself to treatment in such a book, and almost anyone with any experience in one of them longs to publish a book. When acquiring such a book, editors look especially hard at an author's subject-area credentials. If the author possesses broad knowledge but no professional status, such as a Ph.D. or M.D. to support it, a foreword or endorsement by professionals can add credibility. By the same token, an advanced degree from a prestigious school will never overcome a poorly developed proposal or a badly written sample chapter. Some authors require the collaboration of a developmental editor, rewriter, or ghost-writer, but many can learn to present their ideas attractively by following a few basic guidelines.

Ten Percent Theory, Ninety Percent Practice Many would-be authors of self-help, how-to books fail because they present their material as a dissertation rather than as an easy-to-follow step-by-step program. Readers do not want to know *why* they should follow the author's advice; they want to gain benefits immediately, before the end of Chapter 1. Convert your theories into numbered lists or rules; offer applications in the form of checklists, self-tests, and exercises; provide examples that motivate, illustrate, and reinforce your concepts. We will say more about examples later.

Anglo-Saxon Spoken Here Most experts have written dissertations or papers for peers or colleagues, but readers of popular books disdain highfalutin lingo and jargon. Use common, everyday English—short, simple sentences and paragraphs. Avoid passive constructions (much favored by scientists and doctors) in favor of a vigorous, active prose style. You can easily convert passive forms ("the book was eagerly read by Michael") to active ones ("Michael eagerly read the book"). And you can alter overly Latinate expressions to their Anglo-Saxon equivalents (not "descent was effected from the arboreal habitat by the quadruped," but "the squirrel climbed down from the tree").

Chapter Organization This may seem artificial, but you can save yourself a lot of time by organizing your book and each of its chapters according to a formula. A conventional book contains twelve to fifteen chapters; each chapter runs twenty-five to thirty manuscript pages, and contains five to seven key ideas presented in logical sequence. The key ideas become chapter subheads, each spanning four to six pages. If you propose a ten-page chapter, either you've underdeveloped it or the material belongs in another chapter. Likewise, if you propose a forty-five-page chapter, you've either overdeveloped it, or part of it belongs somewhere else. The current fad for books with lots of short chapters (say, fifty five-page chapters), simply plays a variation on this theme, with what would have been a subhead in a conventional book becoming a whole chapter in the new format. Whatever your own particular preferences, strive for consistency.

Chapter Templates It helps to develop a consistent format for each chapter. With some variation, the following model works well for most books:

1. **Open with an engaging example, case study, or anecdote.** Remember that this audience learns best when it can grasp a concrete example through visualization and relating to someone actually *doing* something. Grab your reader's attention with something interesting. People remember stories that help them remember your points. *Present the concept you've illustrated briefly and clearly.* Be sure to define the concept, especially any uncommon or special words. *Introduce and reinforce all concepts with examples.*

2. **Involve the readers in the concept by inviting them to apply a checklist, administer a self-test, or perform an exercise.**

3. **Move on to the next concept in the same manner, but avoid discussing too many concepts per chapter.** Five to seven concepts will usually suffice.

4. **Conclude with a summary of what the reader should have learned from the chapter.** Additional self-tests or exercises may work well here, too.

5. **Use examples.** These can make or break a book. The most skillful authors employ a wide variety of examples, paying some attention to geographical, racial, and sexual balance in order to give the book its broadest possible appeal. Types of examples include:

   • **The short anecdote,** possibly even a joke—something that engages the reader's attention or makes a point memorably.

   • **The short series example.** Two or three quick examples in a row can add diversity and range of application. These run less than a short paragraph apiece (compared to the anecdote that might consist of a sentence or even a parenthetical phrase).

   • **The recurring example.** An example running through a discussion can add a "plot" element to the chapter. A strong example can become like an old friend, and it can reduce the constant need for the author to provide background for examples. These can even turn into full-fledged case studies.

   • **The case study.** Such lengthy examples can appear in one chapter or broken up among chapters or sections.

They can provide the most detail and can even become role-playing cases in which readers can test or apply what they've learned.

- **Hypothetical examples.** If an author knows a subject thoroughly, a composite or hypothetical example can sometimes illustrate the point more aptly or precisely than something based faithfully on experience. In any case, the examples must ring true to the reader.

Market Research Anyone can browse through a bookstore and see what publishers currently offer, but a wise author looks at the history and the future of the market. Many good books appeared years ago, then disappeared, but still can provide instructive models. Publishers' catalogs announcing forthcoming publications, available in bookstores, shed light on upcoming titles. Study books in unrelated fields, because some of the most stunning successes come from transferring a winning format or approach from one subject to another. Regardless of your specific field, look at all sorts of how-to books that have made the bestseller charts over the years.

Particularly troublesome for aspiring authors is the fact that publishers may already have books on a certain topic under contract or in production. Here, your agent can perform a valuable service because he or she has gained some knowledge of what the market will probably look like in a year or two, when your book will finally be available.

The Eternal Paradox Every month, it seems, a new diet or exercise book makes the bestseller lists. How do readers distinguish among all these books? Success for the self-help author usually rests on solving a riddle: Editors want the comfort of knowing that a steady book-buying audience has always existed for this subject (better sex, more money, healthier children), but they also want the confidence that a new book will *add to* the existing literature rather than merely repeat it. This means that an author must place tremendous emphasis on the portion of the book synopsis that positions the book in its market. You must convince editors that your book may look like a lot of others, but it offers something no other does. Failing to do so will usually result in a series of rejections!

MAINTAINING THE PATIENCE OF JOB

Once you've polished your proposal, you will be entering the sometimes fascinating, often frustrating, and always challenging world of agents, editors, publishers, and booksellers. The chapters ahead will walk you through that world as you learn how to find and work with an agent, how to market your proposal yourself, how to understand and negotiate contracts, how to work with a publisher, how to promote your published book, and how to build a successful career as an author. That world will test your patience, your perseverance, and your creativity. Prepare yourself for rejection. It happens to every author.

You might suffer the harshest form of rejection, as the poet A. Wilbur Stevens did when a hoped-for-publisher returned to him not his beloved manuscript but a little pile of ashes. Or you may receive an excruciatingly polite rejection, as one writer did when his manuscript came back from a Chinese economic journal with this note: "We have read your manuscript with boundless delight. If we were to publish your paper it would be impossible for us to publish any work of a lower standard. And as it is unthinkable that, in the next thousand years, we shall see its equal, we are, to our regret, compelled to return your divine composition, and to beg you a thousand times to overlook our short sight and timidity."

Whether harsh or polite, flattering or stupid, all the rejections you collect will put you in the good company of Irving Stone, Julia Child, Margaret Mitchell, and, believe it or not, Stephen King. Like them and countless other authors, the patience of Job—and a well-drafted proposal—will see you through to successful publication.

CHAPTER FOUR

How to Find and Work with an Agent:

An Action Plan for Building a Profitable Relationship with an Agent

In his little promotional pamphlet, "The Truth About Literary Assistance," published in 1933, literary agent Lawrence R. D'Orsay ("Builder of Literary Careers Since 1919") promised aspiring writers the moon and the stars. He would critique their work, revise it line by line, type the revision, and submit the results to editors, all for a flat fee of thirty dollars for a fifty-thousand- to seventy-five-thousand-word manuscript, and thirty-five dollars for a seventy-five-thousand- to one-hundred-thousand-word manuscript.

That sounds like a bargain when you consider that an agent today may critique a book proposal and guide the author's revisions until it has reached a point where editors might consider it, then market the results and negotiate a contract, for a hefty fifteen-percent commission. Given a typical advance of ten thousand dollars, the agent pockets fifteen hundred dollars, and if the book sells twenty thousand copies at twenty dollars a copy, accumulating royalties of ten percent per copy (forty thousand dollars less the ten thousand dollar advance, for a net of thirty thousand dollars), the agent puts fifteen percent of that income, another forty-five hundred dollars, in the bank.

That six thousand dollars sounds like a lot. You might think, "Couldn't I save that money by eliminating the agent?" Before you take that route, though, you may want to inform yourself more about what an agent does to earn that commission. Why does anyone need an agent? Before you answer that question or make the decision to represent yourself to the publishing world, consider the Bakers' experience.

Kim and Sunny Baker sold their first book—a humorous restaurant review guide for the Seattle area—entirely on their own. Kim developed a few sample pages on his Macintosh computer and innocently presented it in person to local publishers. The first two showed Kim the door, but the third, David Tatelman of Seattle's Homestead Books, instantly liked the idea and told Kim he'd offer a contract the next day.

When David put the offer on the table as promised, the Bakers assumed it was fair and legal. Like most new authors, they were so excited about getting a book—any book— published that they just signed on the bottom line without negotiating advance terms, expense money, or copyright. Fortunately, David is an honest fellow and put together an equitable contract.

The naïve approach worked for the Bakers' first venture into publishing. Then, after completing their dining adventures, the Bakers came up with an idea for a book on marketing communications for small businesses; it demanded a house with national distribution. Homestead, strictly a local enterprise, lacked the deep pockets for producing and marketing such a book. Given their first success, the Bakers enthusiastically mailed off their proposals to twenty large publishing houses, complete with cover letters and stamped, return envelopes. When they couldn't obtain the name of an editor, they simply mailed the packages to the "editor in charge of business books."

Sadly, none of the publishers or nameless editors expressed any interest in the Bakers' next and bigger project. Courteous (sanitized might be a better word) rejection letters filled the mailbox for a fortnight. Some publishers failed to respond, in spite of the return postage. The Bakers took to heart the story of the author who submitted one of Hemingway's masterpieces to a publisher in jest, only to have it curtly rejected as "not suitable for this house at this time." They had discovered the cardinal truth in selling a proposal to a large publishing house without representation:

Even if the idea is timely, the proposal compelling, and the market clearly defined, unagented proposals from unknown authors generally end up in the "slush pile."

That's when the Bakers decided to get an agent. After a few queries to prospects, they found Mike Snell in Truro, Massachusetts. Mike, who possessed a strong background in several fields relevant to the Bakers' interests, showed the Bakers how to construct a more compelling proposal. He knew what publishers and editors wanted to see, he had established contacts in every major house, and he spent time brainstorming with them on the phone. Another important factor in the Bakers' decision to work with Mike was his simple, straightforward business approach: he didn't require lengthy, binding contracts or up-front fees.

After Mike reviewed the Bakers' proposal in detail, he suggested reorganization of the topics and further focus on the target audience. Once the Bakers redrafted the proposal, Mike submitted the package to editors at five houses. About six weeks later, the Bakers deposited their first advance check. It was originally titled *Getting the Word Out* and was published by John Wiley & Sons as *How to Promote, Publicize, and Advertise Your Growing Business.*

The Bakers started with a little restaurant review guide, some experience writing promotional copy for computer products, and a couple of magazine articles written for trade magazines. On the recognition and credentials meter, they were clearly not Carl Sagan and Jane Goodall. For an agent with Mike Snell's experience, however, building their limited background into a viable writing career proved more than possible.

Now, twenty-two books later and still pumping the word processor, the Bakers wouldn't consider a writing life without Mike. And its not just their experience that supports their loyalty. They know how the publishing game works, how editors come to consider manuscripts, and what an agent can do for a writer. So before you decide to represent yourself, answer two fundamental questions: "Why does using an agent make sense for most new authors?" and "Do I have what it takes to represent myself?"

WHY USING AN AGENT MAKES SENSE
FOR MOST NEW AUTHORS

Most agents would agree with Mike Snell's advice to competent new authors: "Representing your own work to publishers turns out like the surgeon who takes out his own appendix with a rusty can opener. You might get the job done, but you'll create a lot of unnecessary pain and probably make a bloody mess of it."

Jeff Herman, author of *Writer's Guide to Book Editors, Publishers, and Literary Agents*, reminds aspiring authors: "No author is born published." After all, approximately sixty thousand new books reach store shelves each year, and brand-new authors have written many of those books. With the right agent, you can maximize your chances of joining that select group.

Unless your name rings bells in the canyons of Manhattan, getting your proposal past the slush pile at a major publishing house requires more than a solid presentation. You need the visibility a good agent commands. This holds especially true when you consider the everyday experience of an acquisitions editor at a major publishing house.

Most editors at publishing companies are not sitting at their desks eagerly waiting for new manuscripts to arrive. Those FedEx packages, boxes, and dog-eared envelopes arrive by the bushel every working day from all over the country in such quantities that the editors don't even try to read them all. At best, editors throw unagented submissions into the corner and give them a quick glance when attempting to clean up their offices. At worst, the editors practice "hoops" as they throw unagented proposals at the round file. In fact, some houses' policies prohibit editors from even considering unagented or unsolicited submissions.

Countless unagented proposals arrive from unknown, would-be Stephen Coveys and Betty Eadies every month. Most of those manuscripts end up in the slush pile because authors have no idea whether they've got the right editor (that is, whether the subject fits the editor's list or interests) or even the right publishing house. Unagented authors send in their manuscripts full of hope and the belief that what they've got is truly what the world needs now. But editors know otherwise. Extremely busy editors look for reasons not to read manuscripts; they have to have a compelling reason to consider a project, even if theoretically it is perfect for their publishing program.

When a harried acquisitions editor comes across a package from Bob, the good agent, this gives the editor the one good reason she needs to consider the proposal. If dependable, credible Bob sent the package, she should look at it seriously. The editor has acquired eight books from Bob in the last few years and has turned a profit on most of them. The editor respects Bob's judgment. She knows that Bob carefully screens writers, submits only good-quality ideas, and weeds out the *prima donna* novices who would be a pain to work with. Because she's worked with Bob before and knows she will do so again in the future, she wants to maintain high levels of mutual respect and good feeling.

The relationship between editor and agent can pave the way to the client-writer's success. With Bob's letterhead attached to the proposal, the beleaguered acquisitions editor automatically moves that project from the slush pile to the give-it-a-good-look pile. That simple move across the desk represents the most significant step toward getting a contract offer on a book. *That move means that the editor will actually open the package and seriously consider the proposal.* And that's where it all starts.

Your unagented book proposal, like the Bakers' unagented proposal, will probably be rejected by the major publishing firms without so much as a cursory read. Still, just as there are good reasons to have an agent, there are many valid situations in which you can represent yourself. If you only expect to write a single book, or if you intend to get your book published by a

---

Do I Have What It Takes to Represent Myself?

- Do I know the best publishing houses in my subject area?

- Do I have established relationships with receptive editors in the appropriate publishing houses?

- Do I know the types of projects the editors usually buy and why?

- Will editors recognize my name when my proposal arrives?

- Do I know what to insist on or delete from a publishing deal?

- Do I fully understand the legal ramifications of the standard clauses and options in a complex publishing contract?

- Do I have enough knowledge about publishing to negotiate a deal for myself, including distribution percentages and royalty levels?

small, regional, academic, or specialty press, representing a book on your own may make sense. (Chapter 5 explains how to market your proposal without an agent.)

Of course, some authors simply prefer to do things on their own or have forged the contacts that make an agent unnecessary. Alfred Glosbrenner, a noted computer book author, used an agent once. But because he knows most of the computer book editors and publishers on a first-name basis, he found that he really could represent his books himself.

In many cases, however, reasons beyond oblivion in the slush pile may preclude you from successfully agenting yourself to the publishing world. Thus, before you decide to represent yourself to a publisher—even a small or specialized house—you should honestly answer the seven questions on the previous page about your ability to sell your book on your own.

If you cannot truthfully answer "yes" to at least four of these seven questions, you will probably benefit from representation by a good agent. And even if you have answered all seven questions positively, you'll still probably benefit even *more* from a good agent's representation because that means you are a talented professional who should spend all your time writing and developing ideas not marketing them. Having a good agent as a partner could free you up to do just that.

THE PROFILE OF A GOOD AGENT

You need to take time to find the right representation. Don't sign with the first agent willing to represent your book unless you know that agent makes sense for your project and career. Bad representation can cause as many problems as no representation. The wrong agent can add bureaucracy, expense, and complexity to your career. Even worse, the wrong agent can limit your career potential instead of expanding your horizons.

The match between author and agent functions like a strong marriage. A good agent becomes a partner in your career as a writer, just as Mike Snell and the Bakers formed a lasting relationship based on compatible personalities and publishing interests. In your search for a good agent, look for someone with these twelve core traits:

1. **Knowledge of publishing.** An informed agent knows the difference between hot book topics and cold ideas (within a range of topics) and stays on top of the movers, shakers, and ripples in the ever-changing publishing scene.

2. **Professional recognition.** The agency name for most professional agents appears in all of the major directories (*Literary Market Place, Writer's Digest,* and *Writer's Guide to Book Editors, Publishers, and Literary Agents*). Many competent agents present seminars on publishing and maintain active roles in professional organizations related to writing, editing, and publishing (such as the Author's Guild, American Society of Journalists and Authors, and/or the Association of Authors' Representatives).

3. **Editorial contacts.** A well-connected agent can name four or five editors at major houses who take on your kind of book (with at least one recent sale to most of these).

4. **Satisfied author-clients.** A confident agent will gladly put you in touch with author-clients (typically no more than two or three) who will be willing to share their experiences with you regarding the agent's skill and performance.

5. **Responsive communications.** A worthy agent responds promptly to initial queries (within one to two weeks) and author-client submissions (within three to four weeks). Such an agent also provides clear and specific criticism and suggestions, usually through preprinted guidelines and/or sample proposals.

6. **Good literary sense.** A well-read agent likes books, reads them, and filters out your strong book ideas from the weak ones. He or she works with you to develop or refine your ideas and proposals.

7. **Negotiating skill.** A competent agent has a realistic grasp on what you should be paid for your project (and what the market should and will bear), and will negotiate advance dollars and contract terms on your behalf. Usually a well-chosen agent will get a bigger advance and royalty terms than you could get on your own. An experienced agent's knowledge of contracts facilitates smooth, fair, and understandable deals.

8. **A record of sales successes.** The exemplary agent can cite half a dozen (or more) books she or he has sold recently, with at least one in the general subject area of your book.

9. **Interest in author-clients' careers.** A concerned agent demonstrates interest in your long-range career as an author. The agent also expresses interest in all the different kinds of books you might write. Working with your well-formulated ideas and sound writing skills, a loyal agent can help develop a career for you as an author. If you are a novice in publishing, a good agent will also be willing to act as your mentor and guide. You, in turn, should be willing to listen to good advice and heed

(possibly decades of) experience. After all, an experienced agent will have sold many more books than you.

10. **Marketing savvy.** An adept agent has a clear idea of the markets and distribution opportunities for your book. Such an agent also details a strategy for developing, marketing, and negotiating on your behalf and knows which editor and house to send your package to as market interests shift and publishing fortunes wax and wane.

11. **Good business sense and fair business practices.** A capable agent details your financial relationship with the agency, with or without a formal, written agreement. Furthermore, a fair agent charges no fees for initial evaluation of material (except an SASE).

12. **Personal chemistry.** A compatible agent sounds on the phone like someone you will enjoy working with. The energy between an author and a good agent radiates accord.

For the years of experience, valuable contacts, worldly advice, marketing savvy, and negotiating skills, an agent typically earns fifteen percent of every dollar you make on your books. This percentage applies to the advance, subsequent royalties, and other rights sold on the work. An agent who possesses the twelve traits of good agents *earns* that fee.

Unfortunately, not all agents are good agents. Anyone with a business card and a telephone can claim to be a literary agent. As with politicians, some agents are smooth talkers but weak on action. Some agents would rather watch *Leave It to Beaver* reruns than get on the phone and pitch your book. Some agents depend more on blind luck to place a book than on panache and marketing strategies. Such a so-called agent may take fifteen percent of your royalties without offering any credibility, expertise, or effort on your behalf.

You may need to interview multiple agents before you find the person with the right match of skill, integrity, interest, and energy to handle your work. The search for an agent demands a well-executed plan to filter the good from the bad.

You'll also need to sell yourself to potential agents in much the same way you'd sell your idea to a publisher. Agents and publishers ask many of the same questions about you, your proposal, and your ability to complete the book. Once you find appropriate representation, you'll probably stay put unless your proposals repeatedly fail to sell or the agent decides to retire.

HOW TO ACHIEVE
HIGHLY EFFECTIVE REPRESENTATION

You will discover that finding the right agent involves a lot more than merely looking in Jeff Herman's guide or in *Literary Market Place* and choosing someone with a nifty name, like Swifty Lazar. If you're unpublished, many agents won't even consider you as a potential client.

In many ways, the issues and processes involved in securing representation from a good agent resemble those involved in choosing a place to live. You want to feel safe and secure, to enjoy adequate space for your personal lifestyle, and to match location, services, availability, price, and style to your unique needs.

To find the optimum combination of traits in an agent, you can follow seven proven steps to securing and maintaining appropriate representation. Writers can take these at any stage of their careers and for any level of representation. This process takes time and effort, since there are almost as many agents as editors in the publishing business. Still, if your book is worth publishing and you remain patient and persistent, you will find that competent agent willing to represent your work enthusiastically to the right editors at the right publishing houses.

The Seven Steps to Securing Highly Effective Representation

1. Understand the type of representation you need.

2. Research the agencies.

3. Query potential agents.

4. Match the agent's style to your needs.

5. Establish business terms and get to work.

6. Build the partnership.

7. Review your relationship regularly.

Agent Quest Step 1:
Understand the Type of Representation You Need

Finding an agent starts with understanding your own strengths and weaknesses as a potential client. Are you a one-book author or do you want to establish a career as a writer? Do you possess credentials that will impress the agent? Can you prove your ability to complete projects on time and as specified? How much help do you need as a writer? Is your project a one-time blockbuster that needs immediate, high-dollar representation, or do you intend, like most authors, to start with one or two good ideas and build from there to form a career? Are you willing to accept advice and criticism? You'll need to answer these questions before an agent will even consider representing you. Your answers to these questions will also help determine the type of representation you need.

After weighing your own strengths and weaknesses, you need to compare your career interests with the nature of various types of agency. Be aware of these general categories of agents and agencies when evaluating your representation needs: the wolves and sloths, the independents, the multiple-agent firms, and the agents of the rich and famous. A satisfying relationship hinges on matching your skills, goals, and credentials to the category of agent that will best represent your projects.

Wolves and Sloths Although it is not always easy to do, you should avoid the wolves and the sloths at all costs. This category includes agents who take on any project for an up-front fee and those who charge for dubious editing and other questionable expenses, such as "literary development." The category also includes agents without contacts and those with good intentions but no experience in publishing. Distinguishing a wolf or sloth from a legitimate, hard-working agent demands effort. Many first-time writers have trouble differentiating legitimate credentials from hype. Take your time. Ask questions. Follow the guidelines offered here.

While the marginally legitimate members in this category may clean up your proposal, they'll probably clean out your pocketbook too. Recognize these agents by their overzealous willingness to take you on as a client and the fact that they charge you for everything, right down to the paper clips. Don't

Reading Fees May Be Legitimate

Note that some legitimate, accomplished agents charge new authors a *reading fee* to discourage unpolished submissions by wanna-be writers. This practice is often on the level. The willingness to pay for a reading establishes the commitment level of the would-be author. The fee is often returned if the agent agrees to represent the work. The reading fee should fall within industry standards (four hundred dollars or less at this writing). Furthermore, you should obtain actual advice and written commentary in exchange for the fee. Otherwise, steer clear and look for someone who will read your work without the charges.

be fooled by sales pitches and promises. These vanity agents will waste your time and money. Such an unscrupulous agent may ultimately tarnish your reputation through association.

The wolves and the sloths offer little in the way of useful advice. When you ask agents in this category about their publishing contacts and successes, and as you check references with other authors, the successes will typically be minimal and the references few or non-existent. Should any agent refuse to provide references, assume the worst and find someone who can document his or her credentials.

Independent Agents   Independent agents include experienced individuals and couples working on their own to represent a select group of authors. Many of these agents prefer independence simply because they like working on their own. Others have chosen independence because they have recently left a position at another agency and want to build their own company over time. Independent agents are often more open to handling unpublished authors than are larger agencies, but not always. Some independents have prestige authors in their stables and handle only a limited number of select writers.

Often the match between a competent independent agent and a new author provides distinct advantages for both. Many new independents are former editors (or agents) from large companies, who, after investing years meeting and working with people in the book trade, decide to get away from the office politics and strike out on their own. Since they boast vast experience and numerous contacts, this kind of "novice" could turn into a loyal, helpful, and resourceful partner in a new author's career.

Mike Snell exemplifies the editor turned independent agent. After his employer accepted his plan for a whole new publishing division and granted approval to proceed with the project, company bosses handed the reigns to another senior editor. Frustrated by this turn of events and confident that he could run his own company, Mike quit his job of thirteen years and started the Michael Snell Literary Agency.

One advantage of working with an independent is the personal contact and attention you'll enjoy. The disadvantage is that a single agent may not be able to provide the range of services or diversity of connections of a large agency. Some independents are lawyers, but many are not. Thus, an independent agent may not have immediate access to legal advice when contracts go awry.

There are lawyers who claim to be agents, but many of these know more about the contracts than they know about selling books. If you choose an attorney as an agent, make sure that agenting is the first priority, and the legal expertise only an added benefit of the relationship. Rather than taking a commission, non-agent lawyers typically charge by the hour, so working with such a person may prove pricey as well as useless.

Multiple-Agent Firms   Multiple agent firms range from small partnerships of two or three agents to large corporations that employ hundreds of junior and senior staff, concept developers, and lawyers. Typically, but not always, the larger agencies look for established writers or celebrity clients with proven track records. The operational expenses of larger agencies demand that they take on only that type of client.

Many multiple-agent firms (and a few elite independents) won't touch a book advance of less than $25,000 to $50,000 or more because of the overhead involved in representing a book. It basically takes the same amount of time and expense to pitch a ten-thousand-dollar book as it takes to sell a million-dollar blockbuster.

Occasionally a senior agent in one of the larger agencies takes on new authors as a way of building a client base. More commonly, an unpublished author who approaches a mega-agency will be assigned a newer and less experienced representative at the firm. Of course, this person may be highly motivated and an excellent salesperson. This could present a win-win opportunity for both careers. In general, don't expect much time from senior agents in larger firms unless your ideas glow and your bankability screams for attention.

The main advantage of working with multiple-agent firms is in their resources and contacts. Large agencies almost always retain a lawyer or two for interpreting complex contract clauses and resolving disputes. The number of agents allows the agency to represent a wider range of titles than a single independent agent can. And the name of the agency alone may carry notable clout with editors and publishers. However, most writers limit their projects to a few topical areas, so the range of contacts may not always translate into better representation (money, service, or expertise) for your work.

On the downside, the representation agreements with larger firms tend to be more complex. If you sign with a multiple-agent firm, make sure you insert an escape clause to be activated in the event that your agent leaves the firm. Also, verify that the agent you are considering can legitimately claim the successes of his or her clients, and that those achievements are not due to the work of another agent in the firm. Remember, it simply doesn't matter if Gloria the agent at Megahouse Agency consistently procures million-dollar deals for her authors unless Gloria herself represents you.

In the end, you should base your decision to be represented by an independent agent or multiple-agent firm on the *person* handling your work as well as on the reputation and services of the agency as a whole.

Agents for the Rich and Famous   Some independent agents and multiple-agent firms simply won't deal with clients or projects that don't command six- or seven-figure advances. Unless an idea is blistering hot (and proprietary) and the author's mass appeal reaches the proportions of Colin Powell's, unpublished authors simply shouldn't waste their time with these agents. These agents represent ideas, stories, or reputations with established dollar signs in front of them. They are not interested in your career, unless you *already* have the clout (or the story) to make them lots of money.

You can recognize these agents by their client list. If you are comfortable with the company, great. Go for the gold. If not, try an independent or a multiple-agent firm that handles new, unpublished talent. There are many good independents and multiple-agent firms out there that are eager to take on sincere new authors.

If the agent you choose handles less notable clients than does the William Morris Agency, that's okay. Remember, even if the hottest agent at William Morris offers to sign you up as a client, that person might not have time to represent your best interests. It doesn't matter how prestigious your agency looks on paper if the agent handling your work doesn't spend time representing your projects and honing your career.

Agent Quest Step 2: Research the Agencies

You might launch your research for appropriate agents with a reading of the most recent edition of Jeff Herman's *Writer's Guide to Book Editors, Publishers, and Literary Agents.* This book contains not only names and addresses of agents, but also a narrative description of each agent's background and publishing history.

Other credible sources for agent listings include the annual publications *Literary Market Place, North American Guide to Literary Agents,* and *Poets and Writers Guide.* These sources are available in the reference section of most libraries—or better yet, buy a copy of your own. *Writer's Market* also offers a guide to agents, and several other books include listings of literary agencies.

Of course, some good agencies do not appear in any of these sources. Some successful and fully booked agents who don't want a suitcase of submissions from unpublished writers choose to avoid inclusion in the reference publications. Thus you might meet an author who swears by an agent whose name never appears in any of the books. This doesn't necessarily mean that the agent is one of the wolves or the sloths, but it does mean that you should check out the agent's sales record and references with the utmost care.

Screening Factors for Possible Agents   As you review the listings, you'll note that many agencies are located in the heart of the publishing mecca (Manhattan). But don't be prejudiced by an agent's address in the listings. An office in Manhattan is not a prerequisite to success for an agent, no matter what the Manhattanites may tell you. Location may be a plus if you find a suitable agent near your home who can work with you on a more personal level, but location is only a secondary concern. The most important criteria for including an agent on your "possibility" list are the answers to the following questions; the information is generally available in the standard reference guides suggested previously.

As a new author, you need an agent who will work hard and long to obtain an advance on a first book. Most good agents for new writers will do this, because the smart agent knows that while you may accept $5,000 for your first book, with your hard work and the agent's direction, the next project will bring in much more. Further, many agents accept low

Questions to Ask About an Agent

- Does the agent handle new and unpublished authors?
- Does the agent handle the topics you wish to write about?
- Does the agent handle the genre of book you intend to publish?
- Is the agent's client load acceptable?
- Is the agent selective?
- Does the agent document recent successes with appropriate publishers?
- Does the agent charge reading and development fees? Are they appropriate?

advances for books that they know will sell steadily and reap royalties over the long haul.

If the agent listing indicates "published authors only," simply don't bother. The only exception applies when you obtain a personal introduction or referral to the agent through a client or editor who also knows (and likes) your work.

In addition to finding the agencies that handle *new and unpublished authors*, you'll need to find agencies with expertise in the category of books (or other publications, such as CD-ROMs or software) in which you want to publish. As you peruse the agency listings, you'll notice that agents specialize in genre *and* subject matter, just like publishers and editors do. Some agents handle fiction or nonfiction exclusively. Others handle only screenplays. Some handle only children's books. Some agents handle multimedia publications, syndicated columns, and/or magazine articles as well as books.

A few agents maintain broad portfolios. If you hope to publish in diverse areas, this type of agent might suit you best. Still, beware of independent agents who claim to handle *everything*. Agents tend to build their contacts with specific types of publishers and editors. No agent can form useful contacts in all publishing areas in an industry that produces over sixty thousand disparate titles every year.

The fourth screening factor in your agency research involves the workload of the agent. Most listings indicate the average number of new and existing clients handled by an agent each year. Obviously, an independent agent with two hundred existing clients can devote less time to your career than one with only twenty clients. The number of new clients the agency takes on each year also says something about the agent's selectivity (or desirability). Query any prospective agent about workload. Make sure the person has time to represent you.

Some of the listings present the number of new clients signed as a percentage of submissions. You want your agent to be fairly selective because it helps their credibility with editors. Selective agents filter submissions so that editors can avoid trudging through the slush piles on their own.

The next screening attribute for a potential agent, and a very important one, is evidence of placement successes. To be successful for you, an agent has to have a steady record of multiple sales. The incompetent agent can't list such references. Most agencies boast about their most notable recent placements in their agency profiles in the standard publishing references and writers guides. Consider both the type and

---

Looking for an Agent? Find Another Author

Other writers are a great source of agent information. If you don't personally know any writers, you can often meet them at writing workshops, seminars at local colleges, and bookstore signings. If you have an account with an online service such as America Online, try entering the Writer's Forum chat rooms and asking for a recommendation. You'll need to explain in a line or two the nature of the book and see what comes up. Try this over several days, since the mix of users changes by the hour. You can also ask to be assigned a writing career mentor. This service is free except for connect time. In the Resources for Writers at the end of this book, you will find listings for writing organizations, World Wide Web sites, and Internet newsgroups that may be able to help in your research for a suitable agent.

---

caliber of publishers where the agent has placed these books. Are these the same kinds of houses that might publish your books? If not, that agent is probably not a top candidate. Also, check the publication dates. If the agent hasn't placed anything notable in the last year, his or her reputation among editors may be waning.

Finally, you should be able to determine from the listings whether the agent charges fees for reading proposals or assisting new authors. Try the non-fee agents first, unless you have personal recommendations or other reasons to use a fee-based agent.

After considering the research and screening criteria, you should create a potential agent list of five to ten independent agents or multiple-agent firms. Include some of each on your list if possible.

Agent Quest Step 3: Query Potential Agents

After developing a list of possibilities, you should query the potential agents in much the same way you would query a publisher. You can do this in a number of ways, but always do it in writing, not on the telephone. Mike Snell prefers getting a query letter with a one-page synopsis and outline of the book. Other agents want to see a sample chapter or complete proposal along with the query letter. Some agents specifically request that you limit queries to a one- or two-page letter or a letter and concept outline. Read the agency listings carefully before you send off your query package. Some agencies accept—even prefer—faxed or e-mailed queries. Most do not.

Regardless of the format, the query to the agent should include four fundamental pieces of information:

1. a concise, focused description of your project concept
2. your background and credentials
3. your need for representation
4. your telephone number *and* address (yes, many submissions arrive without them)

Remember, the query has one purpose: to get the agent to ask for more information about you and your book.

For those agents who prefer to see proposals and writing samples, submit your best shot at a finished proposal and maybe even a sample chapter from the book. If you have them, include two or three clippings of your best magazine articles or other evidence of your writing ability, such as awards or publicity clippings. The sample material should support the fact that you are a professional ready and willing to do the work necessary to break into book writing.

Your proposal may still need honing and polish, but a good agent will be able to see a diamond in the rough—as long as it's not too rough. The letter on the following page inspired Mike Snell to respond the moment he read it. You should strive for the same clarity and impact in your own submissions to prospective agents.

Notice that the author limited the query to one page, enclosed an SASE (self-addressed stamped envelope for a response or a return of the material), and stated his business clearly and interestingly, focusing on the book's content, title, audience, and competition. He also established his credentials both as a subject-matter expert and a writer. If someone referred you to the agent, mention the person's name. This can help get attention for your query.

Initial submission materials to agents should be neat and simple. There's no need to invest in laser-printer stationery and fancy envelopes. A showy presentation will not cover up a weak idea or poor craftsmanship. Furthermore, if the idea is good, the fancy trappings are simply not necessary at this point. If the agent wants to dress up your proposal at a later date, that's a decision you and the agent should make together.

Never phone an agent before you send a query. The best agents are busy people, and a phone call without a prior query

Malcolm Preston
235 Gull Road
Stinson Beach, CA 90167

Michael Snell
Michael Snell Literary Agency
P.O. Box 1206
Truro, MA 02666-1206

Dear Mr. Snell:

I obtained your name from Jeff Herman's *Writer's Guide to Book Editors, Publishers, and Literary Agents.* From your listing, I see that you handle pet books and "welcome new authors."

I have been working on an innovative book on housebreaking dogs based on my twenty years of experience as a professional trainer of both household pets and show animals. *The Sixty-Minute Guide to Housebreaking Your Dog* should appeal to new dog owners who work away from home during the day but want to get their new pet off to a good start as easily and quickly as possible.

In addition to my work as a dog trainer, I have published over two dozen articles on the subject in the *San Francisco Chronicle, Dog Fancy,* and the *San Jose Mercury News.* Two of my clients' golden retrievers have won championships at the Westminster Dog Show in 1989 and 1992.

I would love to send you a proposal for my book, including a comparison to four direct competitors and a full sample chapter. If you would like me to follow any specific submission guidelines, I will happily do so. Please let me know if this project interests you via the enclosed SASE.

Sincerely,

Malcolm Preston

Malcolm Preston

letter may start your relationship off on the wrong foot. Send the package Priority Mail (not overnight) to ensure quick arrival. Don't expect an immediate response; these are rare.

You will probably need to submit your proposal to five or more agents before one expresses an interest in your work. It is perfectly ethical to submit your query to multiple agents at one time, but do not mention this in your query letter. When you hear from an agent or from more than one agent, submit the requested material exclusively to one agent at a time, following the rule that multiple queries are okay, but multiple submissions are not. If several agents ask to see the material, arrange them by priority, submit to one, allow a month for evaluation, then submit to another, and so on.

If you receive no response to your query after four weeks, call or fax the agents. Who knows? Maybe the agent or the post office misplaced your letter and no one has seen it. Perhaps the agent has been confronting tigers in the jungle. Maybe the incoming pile has grown a mile high. Be friendly and inquisitive rather than confrontive; anger and irritation don't breed desire to work with a new author.

If an agent responds to your query with suggestions, take them to heart even if the agent isn't interested in representing you. If you receive disheartening comments about your writing or your idea, be critical of your submission. Go to the bookstores and do more homework about the field. Hone the writing. Step back. Try again.

If you thoroughly screened for agency interests, posed an attractive, timely book idea, and wrote a strong query letter, within two or three weeks you will get a call or letter from one or two agents interested in representing your project.

Agent Quest Step 4:
Match the Agent's Style to Your Needs

Once you've got an agent interested, you'll be confronted with the challenge of evaluating the agent in a telephone conversation. When talking to a potential agent about representing your work, consider the attributes you'd want in a business partner and look for the twelve traits of all good agents discussed earlier. Look also for evidence of honesty, intelligence, clear communications, and genuine interest in your book.

Ask questions relating to every trait on your list. Cover all the issues that concern you. The questions you forget to ask now may haunt you later. Write down the answers. If you aren't clear on an issue, call back and ask for an explanation.

The prospective agent should seem comfortable answering your questions on the phone. The phone is likely to be your most important means of communication with your agent, so you must be able to talk together on the phone with understanding, clarity, and respect.

A face-to-face meeting over lunch often helps when selecting an agent if you happen to work in the same area or are planning a visit. However, in this age of electronic communication, you don't need to hop on a plane if your prospective agent works in New York and you write in Elko, Nevada. The Bakers have worked with Mike and Pat Snell for over five years, and they have yet to meet them in person. (It's about time, but they can't decide who owes whom lunch.) Phone, fax, mail, and e-mail provide sufficient opportunity for exchanging information and establishing relationships between publishing professionals.

If only one agent expresses interest in representing your work, don't simply sign the agency agreement because you think it's your only choice. Be sure you're satisfied—and pay attention to your doubts. Make sure the agent is a good agent for you. The agent-author relationship outlasts most editor-author relationships. Since it represents one of the most permanent professional relationships in a writer's life, the time taken at this point to assure a good match results in future payoffs for both parties. Rushing into a contract with an agency is like meeting your future spouse at a bar after a night of partying. The initial passion may lead to quick vows—but the lust soon gives way to disillusionment and a complicated divorce. If the agent doesn't seem right, you may want to repeat the screening process in search of a few more candidates, or you may even consider representing your book on your own. (Read Chapter 5 first.)

After establishing rapport on the phone, screen out the promises from the realities. Michelle Sbraga, now a successful cookbook author, was enticed by an agent who rejected her original ideas but promised her a $50,000 advance if she would develop a proposal for a gourmet guide for recreational vehicle owners. In disbelief, but hopeful, she submitted a proposal to this "agent" after several weeks of long nights in front of her word processor. The agent praised the draft, suggested no revisions, and sent it out to his "hot contacts."

The book proposal was rejected by every major house in the country. With no explanation about the failure of this book, the agent suggested trying a cookbook on crêpes. Michelle politely declined. Fortunately, she had not signed the three-year contract that would have obligated her to an extended relationship with this fellow. Later, she discovered that the agent had never sold a cookbook and was just trying to explore the publishers for editorial contacts.

After considerable background-checking this time, Michelle agreed to sign a contract with a new agent. This person sold two proposals within a few months. Yes, the advances weren't as high as $50,000, but the books have earned handsome royalties for her over the years. She continues to sell one or two new books every year. With the agent's help, Michelle is growing her career in a sensible, deliberate way with realistic expectations.

The moral to the story? No agent can promise that your book will sell, or guarantee a specific amount of money for your efforts. If the agent weaves fantasies about immediate wealth and fame, and never mentions the risks, go elsewhere.

Before you decide that an agent suits you, talk to the agent's other author-clients if possible. A secure agent will provide the names and phone numbers of references who can answer your questions about working relationships, industry knowledge, contract skills, support level, financial records, and contacts. Ask the references tough questions. You should always ask the clients what they like *and* dislike about the agency's representation.

Two other key traits to verify include the business sense and financial practices of the agent. Most agencies (though not all) handle their client's advance and royalty checks. A few agents are slow to turn this money around to their clients. If your agent files for bankruptcy, you may not receive your money but you will still be on the hook to write the book. For this reason, query both the agent and the agent's clients about payment history, financial condition, escrow accounts, and record-keeping.

Remember, you're not choosing a best friend, but a partner in your career. You need to ask about the contractual terms of working together. Some agents use a handshake or a simple written agreement consisting of little more than a promise to try to sell your books for a specific commission. Other agents require a multi-page agreement that barely falls short of indentured servitude.

Always be sure to ask about the commission percentages the agent expects. Although the most common rate (at this writing) is fifteen percent, some agencies have sliding scales, different percentages for domestic and international sales, and other schemes for determining their commissions.

As you talk to a potential agent, make sure that the traits of negotiating skill and salesmanship reveal themselves in the demeanor and diplomacy of the person. The trait of marketing savvy emerges when the agent talks confidently, in business language, about markets, audience, competition, strategy, and distribution. If you don't hear any of these words, beware. Finally, if all the other traits are evident, assess the chemistry between you. At this point, you should feel that you can work well together and enjoy frequent contact. If you have any doubts, try talking to some other agents.

Agent Quest Step 5:
Establish Business Terms and Get to Work

Once you decide on the agent who will represent your books, you need to establish the agreement and operating procedures between yourself and the agency. The range of contractual relationships between writers and independent agents is as diverse as the personalities involved. The representation agreements of the independent agents range from casual (or non-existent) to complex. Review the representation terms in detail before you allow any agent to represent your work.

The Bakers found Mike Snell's agency agreement and operating procedures appealing. There's no written agreement—just mutual promises to give the best they have. In return, Mike gets fifteen percent of every dollar the Bakers receive on their books, not including production fees. He does not charge for mailing, supplies, or copies. He does not retain fiduciary responsibility for distributing the Bakers' advances and royalties. Instead, he includes a clause in the publishers' contracts that provides that his fifteen percent goes directly to him, and the authors' eighty-five percent goes directly to them. This gives the authors a direct trail to their publisher should anything happen to Mike, and it releases Mike from filling out hundreds of 1099 tax forms and account reports for his clients.

The Bakers and Mike use mail and telephone to communicate. The Bakers send their ideas, and Mike responds to them with praise, criticism, and advice, as appropriate. If Mike doesn't wish to represent a certain project, the Bakers can sell it on their own. (They have done this with three books.) Mike suggests ideas and provides leads based on his contacts with editors. As a team, Mike and the Bakers even write books together (this one for instance). With few ups and downs, they have created a mutually rewarding relationship.

Mike is not typical among agents, however. Most agents will want to formalize an agreement with you in writing. There's nothing wrong with this. In fact, most new authors feel elated to " sign" with an agency. Before you sign, however, make sure that the agreement is legal, tenable, and clear. The agreement should protect your interests, as well as the agent's.

The Agency Agreement   Most agents use a letter of agreement, similar to the one shown on page 113. An agreement with an agency, whether written or not, should delineate the following:

- The term of the agreement
- The works and the rights (i.e., third-party, television, resale) covered by the agreement
- The services the agent will perform
- The services you will provide as an author
- The amount the agent will receive for services
- The expenses the agent pays and the expenses you will pay
- The way any money will be handled
- The process for payment of the author and the agent
- The way accounting will be handled (if applicable)
- The ways in which either party may terminate the agreement

Almost anything can appear in a formal agent's contract, so you might ask an attorney experienced in publishing to review the one you are considering. At the very least, show the agreement to an experienced author. Remember, the terms should all be somewhat negotiable; the document must work for both author and agent. As with a publishing contract, your time of greatest leverage is before you sign it.

If all the personality, reference, business practice, and other agent traits seem in line, then agree to the agent's terms and undertake your first project together on a trial basis. This works best if you have developed a complete book proposal beforehand. Just make sure your agreement includes an appropriate

(SAMPLE) LETTER OF AGREEMENT
(Courtesy of the Sheryl B. Fullerton Associates
Literary Agency)

Date_____

You have asked me to serve as your sole and exclusive literary agent. I am happy to do so on the following terms and conditions:

1. (a) I shall counsel and advise you professionally and shall market all your literary rights throughout the world, including but not limited to publishing, motion picture, stage, radio, electronic media, and television rights, in all the literary material that you submit to me during the term of the agency.

   (b) The term "literary material" includes any material that you may now, or at any time during the term of this agreement, own or to which you have any right, title, interest, or control, including, but not limited to, literary, dramatic, and musical material, books, plays, dramas, stories, episodes, scripts, recordings, motion pictures and radio and/or television or electronic media programs, formats, and outlines. We have specifically agreed to exclude previously published works, including all works that might be sold to Business McGraw-Hill.

2. I agree to exercise reasonable commercial efforts in marketing your literary material and promoting your professional standing. I retain the right to render my services to anyone else in any capacity, even if their work may compete with yours, and to appoint others to assist me in fulfilling this agreement, including subagents.

3. I agree to submit to you any offers received. No agreement shall bind you without your consent and signature, such consent not to be unreasonably withheld.

4. I shall be entitled to receive from the publisher my full agency commission of fifteen percent of all money due to you as advances or royalties on sales of the work(s). If I appoint a subagent, or if another agent represents your literary material, the combined commission for all such co-agents shall not exceed twenty percent. I will also be entitled to be reimbursed for the full amount of direct out-of-pocket expenses I incur on your behalf, such as telephone, postage, and reproduction expenses, such expenses not to exceed $150/year unless you approve them. I will submit a bill to you for such expenses, and you agree to pay me within thirty days of your receipt of royalties or advances.

5. My term as exclusive literary agent for your work begins today and extends for at least one year. The agreement will continue until either of us gives the other sixty days prior written notice of our intention to terminate it. If, within six months after the date of termination you, or an agent representing you, enters into a contract for the sale of literary rights with respect to which I had been negotiating before the termination, I will receive half of my regular commission once a contract is concluded with a publisher. I agree to disclose fully in writing all contacts made on your behalf before the termination notice was given, and to initiate no new contacts on your behalf once either of us gives notice.

6. Each of us represents and warrants that we are free to enter into and fully perform this agreement and that we do not have nor shall have any contract or obligations which conflict with any of its provisions and that you own and are

---

free to dispose of all rights in the work subject to this agreement. You agree to indemnify me and hold me harmless against any loss, damage, claim or expense if you as the author fail to comply with the terms of this agreement or any publishing contract on which I have represented you.

7. This agreement constitutes the entire agreement between us, and may be changed only by a written instrument signed by both of us. This agreement shall be governed by the laws of the State of New York pertaining to contracts entered into and to be performed within that state.

Sincerely,

_____

Sheryl Fullerton for Sheryl B. Fullerton Associates

Agreed and Accepted:

Author: _____

Dated: _____

---

cancellation clause in case your initial experience with the agent doesn't work out for some reason.

Agent Quest Step 6: Build the Partnership

The first project together parallels the first year of a marriage. You must both get comfortable with each other's personalities, idiosyncrasies, and responsibilities. A few misunderstandings may erupt along the way, but unity eventually prevails and productivity comes forth.

As a new author, it pays to listen to your agent and make the suggested changes to your proposal. Your agent may advise changes to the proposal that differ from those specified in this book. Some agents prefer slightly different formats, but it's usually a matter of preference, not substance. In general, the content will look similar to what you've seen in this book. If you don't agree with the requested changes, or think the agent lacks inspiration for the project, ask questions and make suggestions of your own.

Be professional—nothing less, nothing more. You should expect the same from the agent. If you don't feel you're getting what you need, let the agent know sooner rather than later.

Again, the author/agent relationship functions as a business partnership, although some collaborations have led to close friendships and even a marriage or two. An agent does not shoulder responsibility for your writing; only you can do that. Your agent helps sell books and build your credentials as an author. Agents are not counselors or baby-sitters. If you need kudos, go to your friends. If you want candid advice on the salability of an idea, trust your agent.

The agent you have selected should be someone you would feel comfortable working with in an office environment. If that model doesn't work for you, think of your agent as a next-door neighbor with whom you cut the lawn, rake the leaves, and shovel the snow. A win-win situation arises from cooperation and a clear division of labor.

If you don't seem to be hitting it off, and if you've really given it your best shot to make the working relationship a positive one, then discuss your dissatisfaction with the agent and, if necessary, send a certified letter of termination and begin another search for representation. Your termination letter should specify that all projects under consideration have reverted to your ownership. Should the agent demand payment for services, phone calls, or other expenses that you agreed to pay in the agency agreement, pay up when the final accounting arrives.

In most cases, you and your agent will agree when the proposal can go out to publishers. At this point, the agent takes over. The proposal goes to appropriate editors in publishing houses the agent selects (sometimes with your input). The agent will use an experience-based approach that he or she feels is best for the particular book. In the ensuing days and weeks, the agent should keep you up-to-date on responses from publishers. You may be asked to speak with an editor before a deal comes together. This happens occasionally, since some editors want to "feel you out" to see if you're really as knowledgeable and cooperative as the agent claims.

Ask the agent how to respond when editors call and what you should talk about. Normally, you shouldn't talk to the editor about advances or contract terms, even if the editor tries to draw you into such discussions. These are the agent's responsibility. Just politely respond that your agent will be happy to talk about the contract terms.

Agent Quest Step 7:
Review Your Relationship Regularly

Your agent provides the key to unlocking the heavy doors of the largest publishing companies. Assuming that you have selected a good match for your projects, chances are favorable that your first book will see the light of day.

Your agent is (or should be) on your side should a dispute erupt with an editor. You agent will provide advice on correcting the situation and counsel you on how to handle demanding editors and unresponsive publishers. You should also listen to the agent's advice. This doesn't mean that you should give in when you think the agent is wrong, but it does mean that you should listen.

As a client, you also assume ongoing responsibilities to your agent. Provide the agent with all your ideas for review. Reward the agent's success on your behalf with professional loyalty. Be available when your agent needs to talk to you. Be responsive. Again, it's a professional relationship; act accordingly. Keep the agent informed of your schedule and progress (and problems). If you talk with editors, make the agent aware of any important issues.

As you work with your agent, you may feel that you're getting the "I've got to run now" brush-off. This attitude prevails among good agents because they're too busy deal-making to talk at length. Unless your call deserves special attention, your agent needs to keep the phone available in case a deal comes through. So don't get hurt that your "friend" doesn't have time to chew the fat or shoot the bull. Instead, hope that the agent's next call is a publisher offering a deal on your book.

After a profitable book or two, you may begin thinking that you could make more if you had a different agent—maybe one of those for the rich and famous. Sometimes changing agents works. However, before you decide that your recent success deserves greener pastures (i.e., bigger advances or a larger agency), remember that many a writer has changed agents in hope of increasing the advance levels on books, only to long for the advice and treatment of the first agency.

To keep agency-client relationships in top shape, hold a serious career strategy discussion with your agent every year. Talk to the agent frankly about what you have done and what you would like to do. Ask the agent what he or she thinks you can do to build your career.

Sometimes agents lose interest in a genre or subject matter. If you submit high-quality proposals but get only meager offers, consider changing agents. But before you do, ask your present agent what has gone wrong. If no credible explanation materializes, or if the agent seems truly negative, then suggest that the time may have come to part paths. Keep it as friendly as possible. Since the book business is comparatively small, burning bridges never makes sense. Besides, if you change your mind and want to go back to your former representative, it's much easier if you left on friendly terms.

AVOIDING COMMON MISTAKES WITH YOUR AGENT

As you begin forging a relationship with a literary agent, you will discover that you have entered the strange world of publishing, where art, passion, and emotion merge with craft, business, and common sense. To ensure a successful long-term relationship with your agent, avoid these ten common mistakes:

1. **You phone a prospective agent instead of submitting a query letter.** As one agent observed, "You can't judge talk, but only the words on the page."

2. **You confess that you've sent queries to twenty agents.** The agent's response? "I'm so swamped with

would-be authors that I can't afford to go on a fishing expedition. I'll just keep the stamp on the SASE."

3. **You submit proposals to more than one agent at a time.** See the agent's response to #2. Plus, expect the agent to think, "Why should I invest my expertise in a project if another agent might reap the rewards?"

4. **You refuse to follow the agent's guidelines for submission.** The agent's reaction? "If the author can't follow these simple instructions, why would the author respond to an editor's intelligent instructions later on?"

5. **You demand that the agent send your proposal to a specific publisher without justification.** The agent responds, "I've spent my life figuring out which editors at which houses buy what kind of books, and this author wants me to send a book on fly fishing to a publisher that does only gardening books. Maybe this author isn't worth my time, since he thinks he knows how to do it on his own."

6. **You tell your agent that only a huge advance will interest you.** A good agent knows that "advances don't sell books." A $2,000 advance looks paltry in light of $20,000 in royalties, and a $20,000 advance that the book's sales never recover is a failure for all concerned.

7. **You tell your agent that you're going to hire a lawyer to review the contract he sent.** Most agents will say, "Keep in mind that cousin Buddy knows real estate law, but not publishing law. It might be more trouble than help."

8. **You fire your agent after four rejections.** The persevering agent knows that "the fifth or tenth or fifteenth

publisher may snap up the book." And it takes only one editor—the right one—to make your success.

9. **You throw in the towel after ten rejections.** Every agent looks for feedback as much as for a contract offer. As one put it, "I've sold dozens of books where the author and I went back to the drawing board and overcame the objections we heard the first time around."

10. **You approach a new agent with exactly the same proposal your original agent couldn't sell.** The new agent comments, "If the other agent sent the material to only two or three editors, I might consider it. But, if twelve turned it down, it obviously needs work. Has the author *learned* anything?"

Before you move on to the next chapter and learn how to sell your book idea directly to publishers, ponder these words by Lawrence D'Orsay, whose advice sixty years ago still rings true:

> Perhaps the most discouraging thing that confronts the writer, whether professional or beginner, is to have his manuscript rejected without any reason being given. Editors simply attach a printed rejection slip: no matter if the story is really good, if it does not happen to suit the requirements of that particular editor at that moment. It is sent back with identically the same rejection slip that accompanies a story with no merit at all. The author, left in the dark, wishes he could turn to some competent person for advice.

That might serve as the best definition of a good agent: a competent person willing to give advice. When you find that kind of representation, hold on tight!

CHAPTER FIVE

How to Sell Your Proposal Yourself:

A Blueprint for Finding a Publisher

Michael J. Murphy, a clinical psychologist employed by the Massachusetts Department of Corrections, worked a day job and a night job. By day, he counseled young people who had tangled with the law; by night, he divided his time between nurturing his own children and pursuing his passion for writing. Over the years he had published essays, notably in the bestselling book *Chicken Soup for the Soul,* and he dreamed of publishing his own book on fathering. Most of the troubled kids he met during the day ended up in the criminal justice system because they lacked good fathers.

After assembling a proposal for a book of essays on what it takes to be a good father (a proposal much like the one you saw in Chapter 3), Michael went in search of a publisher. Having decided to proceed without the help of an agent, he approached small publishers on his own and eventually found Health Press in Santa Fe, New Mexico. Imagine his joy when the publisher sent him finished copies of his brand-new book, *Popsicle Fish: Tales of Fathering.*

Every year, thousands of aspiring authors like Michael create their own publishing success because they faithfully follow two rules of the game: first, make every component of the proposal count, including the cover; second, get your proposal to a receptive editor at the right time. When marketing your book idea yourself, your success will depend on heeding both of these precepts and on following the detailed guidelines found in this chapter.

PREPARING THE PROPOSAL FOR SUBMISSION

Before you even think about submitting a proposal to an editor, review Chapters 2 and 3. Follow the guidelines closely. Make certain that every aspect of your proposal is clear, concise, and complete. Take your time, revisiting your material until you feel satisfied that every word conveys your intentions; only then should you submit your work to selected publishers.

The proposal you submit should exude quality and professionalism. As with people, the first impression matters a lot. The following tips will help you fashion a proposal every bit as compelling and professional as those shaped by experienced authors and agents. (Refer to the sample proposals at the back of the book for examples that follow these recommendations.)

Type Tips

The professional presentation of your proposal starts with an easy-to-read typeface. Be sure to number each page and include a table of contents. If you use a computer (we suggest that you do), choose a simple, readable typeface such as

---

Guidelines for Preparing Your Proposal for Submission

1. Write a clear, concise, complete proposal. (Refer to Chapters 2 and 3.)

2. Format the text in a simple, easy-to-read typeface. Incorporate only those illustrations and design elements that enhance the presentation.

3. Develop a color cover for the proposal.

4. Make five clear copies of the proposal on quality paper. (Copy on only one side of each page.)

5. Bind the proposal with coil or plastic binding. Include a clear plastic cover to protect the proposal if possible.

Times, Helvetica, Avant Garde, Garamond, Futura, or Palatino. If you use a typewriter, the typewriter's typeface is fine as long as you use a fresh ribbon.

The art of typography takes years to master, even for professional graphic designers. Avoid complex typography unless you boast graphic design skills among your accomplishments. A straightforward, well-written, visually simple proposal will appeal to an editor more than an over-designed, cluttered, and amateurish one.

Avoid display (decorative) typefaces and script fonts unless you know how to use them. Especially avoid using the Zapf Chancery font that comes with all laser printers. You may feel drawn to it because it's the only "fancy" font at your disposal, but be forewarned: Zapf Chancery and similar fonts are overused and hard to read. If you doubt the impact or readability of a typeface, opt for simple rather than decorative.

Don't set general text in all capital letters or italics. Also avoid excessive use of boldface type. Save boldface and italics for really important words and sentences—or don't use them at all.

You should also avoid using more than one typeface in your proposal unless you know how to choose complementary styles. If you employ word-processing software on a computer, you can use different sizes for headlines. Set the body copy (paragraphs) of the proposal in eleven- to thirteen-point type. Don't use smaller type that's tiresome to read. Set the headlines in sixteen- to eighteen-point type.

Double-space the entire proposal and leave wide margins. Editors like to use the white space for notes and comments. With a word processor, choose double spacing or set the *leading* (the space between lines) at eighteen to twenty-four points.

Design Tips

A well-crafted proposal on crisp white paper generated with no more than an old Selectric typewriter will satisfy an editor's eye more than one printed with a laser printer on colored paper.

Only include pictures or illustrations that are absolutely essential to your text. Be wary of using figures that may appear amateurish or unnecessary. If you plan to incorporate copyrighted images, you must eventually obtain written permission to do so.

As mentioned in Chapter 3, always add a colorful cover with a large attractive title. If you lack knowledge about designing in color, stick to two basic colors: black or dark gray and a second color (such as red or blue). The cover should catch the eye but not jar the emotions. Many authors add a good-quality photograph or illustration that reinforces the book's content and style.

The substance of a proposal always takes precedence over pretty pictures and fancy type. Still, professional page design can set your presentation apart from the ordinary. If you want to really wow 'em, you can add running heads, rules, photos, charts, and illustrations to the proposal pages using desktop publishing techniques. The sample proposals in the Appendix were created at home on basic computers using easy-to-learn software programs. Get a book on desktop publishing to help you. If you prefer the help of a real person, you can take classes in desktop publishing at most community colleges, or you can hire the services of a graphic designer (which can be less expensive than you might think).

Mailing and Reproduction Tips

Another step in putting your best foot forward is the successful arrival of the proposal at the editor's office. "Successful arrival" means intact and without spots from rain, dog-earing of the corners, or other damage. Protecting your proposal with cardboard protectors on both sides and a wrapping of bubble-pack takes care of most incidental damage, but avoid overpacking. You don't want to make an editor work too hard just to open the package.

Paper and Copies Never send a proposal that *looks* photocopied. The copy you send must look close to an original, with no black streaks, glitches (small black specks), or smudges from the copy machine. If the proposal appears to be a fifth-generation copy, your target editor will assume that it has been rejected by every other press in the nation before it reached his desk.

Never submit a carbon copy to an editor. Even in this era of computers and photocopiers, editors still complain about smudged carbon-copy proposals arriving with penciled-in edits. You can't afford to appear sloppy or amateurish, and nothing adds a professional look more surely than a good word processor. If you suffer from computer phobia, bear in mind that today's machines and software take little more than an hour to master. If you want to make money from your nonfiction writing, you should become expert in the use of a word processor.

Type, photocopy, or print onto good-quality paper. Larger stationary stores sell special paper (thicker, whiter, and more opaque) for use with laser printers. Such paper remains crisp through repeated thumbing. Never use cover-weight, textured, or colored papers for the body of your proposal. (You can get away with very light gray or a pale cream, but white commands more authority and generally costs less.) Never reproduce your proposal using tractor-fed computer paper.

If you use a computer, print your proposal with a laser printer. At the very least, use a good-quality ink-jet printer with 300 or 600 dots per inch (dpi) resolution. Avoid dot-matrix printers, and never submit a handwritten proposal (unless your last name is Grisham).

Copy or print on only one side of the paper. This makes the document easier to read and copy. Editors often photocopy proposals for distribution to management and fellow editors.

Color covers can be copied on color copiers or printed on a color computer printer. Avoid low-resolution (less than 300 dpi) color ink-jet printers because the ink fades and the images are fuzzy.

Never send off the proposal with marks or handwritten corrections. Yes, it's probably acceptable to add a missing period on page 23, but in all other cases fix and reprint the offending pages.

After printing, make your copies at a copy store (such as Kinko's) which uses high-resolution, state-of-the-art copiers. In every city, *service bureaus* and many copy shops provide color copying services. Also, look under *Typesetting* or *Desktop Publishing* in the *Yellow Pages* and obtain several price quotes and samples before you use duplication services.

Binding   Have the proposal bound with a plastic comb or a metal spiral. The binding should allow the proposal to open flat for easy copying. We add a sheet of clear plastic on the front and back of the proposal for protection. The binding with plastic protectors or lamination can be done at any copy store and at most large office supply stores.

Never submit a proposal in a three-ring binder or a folder with metal tabs; the binder adds too much bulk, and the folder format makes copying difficult. For the same reasons, don't add plastic tabs to your proposal. In most cases, the finished proposal shouldn't be more than fifty pages long; a document of that length doesn't need tabs.

Once you have written, polished, and packaged your proposal, you are ready to send it out into the world, where editors will look at it with a critical, even skeptical, eye.

Finding the Right Editors

Authors who decide, for whatever reason, not to work through an agent with good contacts must identify the publishers and editors that may buy the sort of books they have proposed. As mentioned in Chapter 4, if you work with an agent you don't need to worry about finding the right publishers and editors; your agent will do that. Your agent will also guide you in assembling your book proposal for submission to editors. However, if you decide that working with an agent isn't right for you, then you'll need to market the book to publishers as if you were an experienced literary agent.

Choosing publishers and editors for your submission list is much like investigating the market for your book or choosing an agent. You must match the prospective publishing houses to your project. Chapter 6 provides information to help you ask the right questions when evaluating prospective publishing houses—questions that can also help you identify appropriate publishers in the first place.

Go to bookstores and libraries to find recently published books that appeal to the same people who would read your book. The publishers of these books may be likely publishers for your work as well. The source books recommended for finding an agent can also be used to identify suitable publishers and editors. Start with Jeff Herman's *Writer's Guide to Book Editors, Publishers, and Literary Agents* (Prima), or a current edition of *Literary Market Place, Publisher's Directory,* or *Writer's Marketplace.* The listings in these books include general submission information, as well as the names and addresses of some editors.

After identifying appropriate publishing firms, you must send your proposal to specific, named editors. Without a name on your submission, an administrative assistant may "reject" your proposal simply because there was no addressee, or it may float right into a slush pile and never get read at all.

In addition to looking in the standard publishing source books, you might obtain editors' names from other authors or by reading the personnel announcements in the Writer's Guild newsletter. (Of course, you have to be published to join the Guild.) You may also find editors' names in the acknowledgment pages in published books, where authors have thanked those who have helped them succeed. A few presses put the editor's name on the copyright page.

Finding editors' names can be tough because the busiest editors keep a low profile, and most publishing houses shield their editors from unknown callers; unpublished writers frequently call to propose hopeless projects or to argue about recent rejections. Getting editors' names from the reference publications can also prove problematic because the listings age quickly as people move from job to job and publishing houses merge, are sold, or even change names. Thus, you need to verify editorial information and publisher's addresses before you mail your submissions. (This points to a key advantage of using an agent. It's the agent's job to keep track of who's who in the publishing world.)

Make a quick phone call to the prospective publishing firms and tell the receptionist you want to verify that John Doesteski, Senior Acquisitions Editor, will be in this week to receive your proposal. Ask to verify the spelling (and pronunciation) of Mr. Doesteski's name. If the name gets spelled back to you, it confirms that the editor still works there. The editor's title should be verified as well, in case of a promotion or job transfer. Also ask for the person's direct phone number. If that person has left, ask for the name of the new editor.

Such a phone call serves two important purposes. First, the call confirms the editor's existence. Second, the call informs you that the person is in town. This is important because you don't want to submit to someone who is on vacation or just getting back from vacation. An editor returning from a two-week vacation on Maui may sort through the tall submission pile with an eye on the wastebasket. Wait until the person settles back to work before you send in your package. Remember: timing plays a huge role in the publishing world.

SUBMITTING YOUR PROPOSAL

Armed with three to five photocopied, bound proposals and a hit list of ten to twenty editors at hot publishing venues, you're almost ready to submit the proposal packages. (Remember: even though you have more prospects, don't send out more than five proposals at a time.) Now all you need is a cover letter.

The Cover Letter

Your proposal must go out with a personalized, convincing, one-page cover letter to the editor. The letter should be brief and focused. In no more than three or four paragraphs, be certain to mention the title of the book, explain why the project is important, describe who you are, and note how the proposed book fits into the publisher's catalog. If you make simultaneous submissions (which is a good idea), do not mention this in the cover letter, because that fact alone may cause a rejection.

Avoid too much hype. Let the proposal speak for itself. Although you must provide a brief, credible reason for why you are uniquely qualified to write this book, resist the temptation to boast about yourself. Study the sample cover letter that Sunny Baker and Michelle Sbraga used to sell *Lemon Tree Very Healthy*. This letter and the proposal literally sold the book overnight. Amazing? Yes. Unheard of? Not with a strong proposal package submitted to just the right publisher.

With cover letter attached, each proposal should be mailed in a red, white, and blue U.S. Postal Service Priority Mail envelope or a good-quality mailer. Priority Mail makes it look like you spent the extra money for Federal Express even though it costs just three dollars (at this writing) to send a two-pound package. Attractive mailings and Priority Mail imply a sense of urgency. When you use Priority Mail, you get two- or three-day delivery for little more than the cost of regular First Class mail. If you mail proposals via Third Class or other economy methods, you communicate to recipients less concern about timeliness.

Never send a proposal with the possibility that it will arrive with postage due or other charges from an overnight service. Check with the Post Office or with your carrier if you aren't sure, and always double-check the publisher's address.

The SASE   There are two schools of thought about using SASEs (self-addressed stamped envelopes): the conventional view, and the unconventional view. The conventional view holds that editors receive so many queries and proposals that they usually disregard all but the best if the author fails to

Baker & Sbraga
2501 S. DOBSON • MESA, AZ • 85283 • 602-555-1212

July 9, 1997

Jane Doe, Editor
Seven Seas Press
P.O. Box 1234
New York, NY 10023

Dear Ms. Doe,

No pantry is complete without fresh lemons. Lemons are as important as fresh vegetables and herbs in today's health-conscious cuisine. In season, lemons are a deal across the nation. Thousands of Americans boast of prolific lemon trees in their backyards. But, while lemons are plentiful, the lemon recipes are not.

For these and other reasons, lemons deserve a book of their own. *Lemon Tree Very Healthy* puts a wealth of great lemon recipes and household applications for lemons in one volume. It is the ultimate source for information on this incredible fruit.

Michelle Sbraga is a nouvelle cuisine instructor in Phoenix and the proud owner of two mature lemon trees. Sunny Baker is an established author of trade books, a self-made gourmet, and former owner of the Food for Life natural restaurant in Santa Cruz, California. Together, Michelle and Sunny bring a passion for healthy food that permeates the pages of this fun, informative compilation of tasty lemon recipes. John Wincek, a gourmet cook in his own right and an illustrator for Disney projects, captures the book's spirit in pen and ink.

Enclosed is a complete proposal for *Lemon Tree Very Healthy*, including an overview, market analysis, detailed outline, and a few sample recipes. We'll wait for a few days before calling to see how you want to proceed.

Best regards,

Sunny Baker   *Michelle Sbraga*
Sunny Baker and Michelle Sbraga

include an SASE. Some authors want all of their material back; others only want a reply. The former enclose a larger envelope with correct postage, the latter send a regular business envelope or postcard. Though agents expect SASEs from prospective clients, they do not send SASEs with their submissions because editors know them and will return proposals as a professional courtesy.

This leads to the unconventional view of SASEs. Now, authors marketing their own work may decide that this practice only provides the publisher with a convenient mechanism for quick rejection. Here's why a return mailer may undermine your marketing efforts:

- Return mailers peg you as an unpublished writer. Yes, SASEs are standard in most magazine writing and when querying a syndicate, but published book authors almost never use SASEs. They expect a phone call from an interested publisher, or to have the proposal returned at the publisher's expense.

- A harried editor attempting to clean out the slush pile may return your proposal via the return mailer without a serious glance at the contents. It's like greasing the rails of a roller coaster—the more oil, the faster the drop.

- The postage money spent on the SASE can be better used for copying and mailing additional proposals to other publishers.

- The returned proposal(s) may become dog-eared and should not be reused. (You *never* want to clue an editor into the fact that your magnum opus has previously been rejected!) Therefore, it doesn't matter whether you get the proposal back.

If you want a quick reply but not an automatic rejection, enclose a self-addressed, stamped number-ten business envelope or a self-addressed, stamped postcard. This will get you a brief response without investing in the return postage for the complete proposal package.

How Many Proposals Should You Send?

Send your first mailing to those top five or six editors or publishers on your list of ten to twenty candidates. If you get rejections from any of these prospects, immediately send a proposal to the next editor/publisher on your prospect list. Don't send multiple submissions to different editors at the same imprint. If the idea has any merit, it will be passed around the office.

If you're lucky enough to get negative feedback on your rejected submissions, take the comments seriously. Use the insights to prepare an improved presentation. Persistence counts. So does humility. Go back to your proposal to see if you can improve the presentation. (If you have an agent, he or she will probably provide insights at this point.) Then send the revised proposal to some different editors. Don't give up. It may take submission to twenty publishers before the proposal reaps a positive response. It may also take multiple revisions of the proposal until you hit the right house and editor at the right time.

Finally, there are some things you should avoid doing at all cost when you submit your proposal on your own. The list of "Don'ts" includes:

- Never tell an editor up front how much money you want for the book. Agents can do this, but authors must not. You should only negotiate after an initial offer has been made.

- Never tell an editor how much work you put into the proposal or how important the project is to you and your family. The effort invested in the proposal should be obvious, and the editor already knows that you want to get the book published.

- Never tell an editor that a friend read the proposal and liked it a lot, no matter how socially or politically important that friend may be. Yes, you should have critics read the proposal before you submit it to editors, but you don't need to let the editor know that you did what every smart author always does anyway.

- Never tell the editor that the proposal has been rejected already or that the editors who looked at it previously did not understand the audience or the idea. This only raises a red flag in the editor's mind about the market for the title. Let the proposal be rejected or accepted on its merit alone. An editor who has both interest and questions will contact you for clarification.

ACCEPTANCE AT THE PUBLISHING HOUSE: FROM PROPOSAL TO CONTRACT

The path from proposal to contract offer varies from publisher to publisher. The process can be quick and expedient or slow and drawn out, depending on the publisher, the market for the book, and countless other factors. In most cases, patience is not only a virtue after mailing off your proposals; it's a necessity.

Chapter 1 detailed the committee approval process that your proposal is likely to traverse on its way to acceptance. From the author's point of view, the result of the process is always predictable: you get either an offer or a rejection. If you're working through an agent, the process works the same way.

Most proposals go through these steps at the publishing house:

1. **Arrival.** If the submission bears an editor's name, it will be routed immediately to the intended recipient. Your unagented proposal may be relegated to the editor's slush pile unless it catches the editor's attention for some reason. Agented proposals may avoid consignment to slush-pile status if the editor has been expecting the submission. Proposals lacking an addressee may be returned, discarded, or routed to a junior editor or administrative assistant; you may never learn the fate of such a submission. Some publishers send a postcard or form letter acknowledging receipt of a proposal. Because of the volume of submissions, most send nothing.

2. **The First Review.** The editor reviews the agented proposals first, and then glances at the "over-the-transom" submissions. Remember, any unagented proposal is deemed an over-the-transom submission, commanding as much status as a mouse in the basement. Interesting and well-written proposals (even the over-the-transom variety) are put aside for a second, in-depth reading. The editor

stacks the rest in the "out" pile for return or "recycling."
The out pile towers above the slim stack of proposals put
aside for a second reading.

3. **Serious Consideration.** Solid proposals are taken seriously when the editor finds time to study them closely.
Keep in mind that the editor looks for reasons to dismiss
each submission, weighing whether a book fits in with his
or her line of books and considering the likely manage-
ment/committee reaction to the title. Author credentials
are taken into account, as is the cost of producing (designing and printing) the book. Those few proposals that fit
the editor's niche are put aside for even more serious consideration, or they may be referred to a colleague for
another point of view.

4. **A Call of Interest.** If the proposal continues to spark the
editor's interest, and if you are an unknown author, the
editor may call to get more information on the project.
Editors commonly use this approach with unagented writers to weed out hard-to-work-with "prima donna" writers.
They may also test your depth of knowledge on the topic
and query your motivation for writing the book. Your positive attitude, willingness to work with the editor, and
friendly but intelligent responses to questions provide the
key to leaping this hurdle without tripping over your good
intentions. If you have an agent, the agent gets this first
call of interest. Occasionally the agent will suggest that the
editor speak with you as well.

5. **Working Up the Numbers.** If the editor still likes the
idea after talking with you, the editor "works up the
numbers" on the project to determine the break-even and

profitability points. This may also happen before the preliminary get-to-know-you phone call. The work-up justifies (or disproves) the economics of the book. The editor considers these questions: How much will it cost to produce the book? How many copies will sell in the first year? How much advance does the project command? (Editors almost never reveal their numbers to authors.) If the numbers "work" (i.e., the book seems to be a good risk), then the proposal moves to the next step. If not, you'll get a rejection letter or phone call.

6. **The Committee Meeting or Management Review.** Depending on the size and organization of the publisher, by now the book is either slated for an offer or on its way to an editorial committee meeting. At the committee meeting, your would-be editor makes a case for your book. Committee members review photocopies of your proposal and the profit analysis worked up by the editor. Depending on the editor's political clout and the convincing argument presented by your proposal, the group votes to accept or reject your book. Occasionally a project will be sent back for further review or editorial changes before a final decision at a later meeting. If the meeting runs longer than planned, discussion about your book may be bumped to a subsequent meeting, next week or next month. (Remember: patience, patience.)

If a positive consensus is reached on your proposal, your editor assembles an offer for the book and presents it to you verbally. Details of the book's format and contract terms—hardcover, softcover, number of pages, type of illustrations, royalty rates, delivery date, and all the other issues described in Chapters 6 and 7—will now be discussed.

The Publishing Process

Arriving at the publisher, your nonfiction book is routed to its addressee. Unagented proposals enter the slush pile.

An editor (or an assistant) gives your project a cursory glance and either dismisses it or puts it aside for a second look.

Strong proposals are read in depth. The editor attempts to think up reasons for rejection.

An interested editor will phone you or your agent for more information. Sound knowledgeable *and* cooperative!

The editor assembles a spreadsheet analysis of the cost of developing, producing, printing, and promoting your book. If the numbers work, then the editor takes the next step.

An editorial committee reviews your project and makes a "yes" or "no" decision.

An offer with a contract proposal is made to you, either directly or through your agent. Most offers are negotiated to increase the advance and/or royalties.

At this point, the metamorphosis is complete. Your proposal has been transformed from a book idea into a contract offer. Congratulations! Your status has also changed. You're about to become a published author. Now, before you sign the contract, you must determine whether the publisher and the offer make sense for your career and your book. (Refer to Chapter 6 and Chapter 7.)

Incidentally, if you receive multiple offers on the same proposal, you may want to ask an agent to help you negotiate the deal. Many agents will eagerly take you on as a client at this point. Reread Chapter 4 for more information on choosing an agent.

The review and contract wrangling process can leave you in suspense for weeks. Nothing can speed it up except an occasional polite call to the editor to find out how the paperwork is progressing. Don't go to work on a book based on a verbal offer until at least a written letter of understanding arrives from the publishing firm. Once in a while, internal changes within a publishing house can kill a book if the sponsoring editor moves on to other pastures. Remember, if it's not in writing, it's not a legal and binding offer. Once the contract is signed, then it's appropriate to go to work in anticipation of the first advance installment.

WHAT *NOT* TO DO
AFTER SUBMITTING A PROPOSAL

After submission, experienced authors play their cards carefully to give the proposal the best chance of acceptance. Remember that a slow acceptance always beats a quick rejection. Therefore, never apply too much pressure or look desperate for an offer. You should also avoid making these five common mistakes after submitting your proposal:

1. Phoning and Bugging the Editor. Do not call up and bother an editor until at least two weeks have elapsed after submission. And when you do call, make it polite and brief; all editors are busy with projects and buried in work and negotiations. The only exception to this rule occurs when you have proposed a time-sensitive topic, such as a biography of Saddam Hussein begun on the opening day of the Gulf War.

If you hear nothing within sixty days it means one of the following:

- The editor hasn't looked at your project because it's buried in the pile of over-the-transom submissions. Or the editor left for Katmandu and hasn't seen it yet.

- The editor rejected your book and didn't let you know that fact.

- The proposal lies somewhere between review and acceptance, as discussed earlier.

- The package has been rerouted to another editor. This change of ownership restarts the waiting game's clock, since the new person needs time to get to the submission.

A phone call will confirm one of these scenarios. If the proposal has not been read, a call may motivate a busy editor to dig it out and read it. Call again in another couple of weeks if you still hear nothing.

2. Whining and Complaining. Avoid penning whiny follow-up letters if a book doesn't sell. Passionate pleas for response may alienate you from an editor who was otherwise interested in your project. Editors see complainers as potential trouble; they will pass on projects from such authors even if they like the ideas. Editors confronted with a "problem author" make mental notes to ignore future submissions as well.

3. Creating Organizational Conflict with Multiple Submissions. Never submit the proposal to multiple editors within the same house in hopes that sheer group force will sell it. This can cause a political rift if more than one editor expresses interest in your book. It can also work against you because one editor may like it and another may think it's inappropriate for the house. This may sink your book when the editorial committee meets. Again, there's nothing wrong with simultaneous submission to more than one publishing house, but *never* submit multiple copies to the same division within a house. Submitting to separate imprints within the same mega-houses is acceptable—if the imprints have separate editorial and marketing staffs. Thus, its okay to submit a proposal to an editor at Random House and one at Villard (both imprints of the same company), but not acceptable to submit to different editors within the Business Division of McGraw-Hill.

4. Making a Premature Second Submission. Do not submit another project to the same editor until the first project has completed the review process. If it's your first sale, don't submit a second project until you complete the first manuscript to the publisher's satisfaction. Never confuse your editor with multiple ideas or alert your publisher that you might be biting off more than you can chew.

5. Letting Rejection Slow You Down. If a project fails to sell immediately or is rejected, instead of sulking around in your bathrobe waiting for the phone to ring, use the time profitably. Submit the proposal to other houses, propose another book, or sell a magazine article based on the book idea by rewriting the sample chapter. In this age of books as commodities, persistence is often as important as talent. If you understand the steps and criteria presented in this book and stick to them, you'll eventually sell a book and get it published.

WHAT ABOUT SELF-PUBLISHING?

A handful of exceptional cases can create a myth that does more harm than good to aspiring authors. Yes, Wes Roberts successfully self-published *Leadership Secrets of Attila the Hun*, selling several thousand copies on his own, but the book did not become a bestseller until HarperCollins picked it up and reissued it. But 99.9 percent of self-published books don't sell enough copies to attract the interest of a HarperCollins. Those 99.9 percent of self-published books end up accomplishing little more than soothing an author's vanity and draining his or her savings account.

Self-publishing doesn't make sense in most cases, especially for a first book. Still, because the publishing process can be arbitrary and time-consuming at conventional houses, authors have increasingly looked to self-publishing their books as an alternative to giving publishers all the power over the success or failure of their ideas.

Self-publishing is both difficult and easy. It's easy if you have the money to invest, and difficult if you lack the time and the know-how to get the book into the hands of readers.

To be a successful self-publisher, you'll need the following elements:

- funds for publication
- knowledge of production, marketing, and fulfillment
- both the expertise and the time to distribute and promote your book

As a self-published author, your can get your book printed regardless of its quality or market size. This is both a blessing and a curse. You can also make decisions about title, cover, length, size, and price that are otherwise generally the domain of publishers. Your self-publishing results depend on you (and your money) alone. You become not only author, but publisher, salesperson, and promoter. Without full-time effort and dedication, your self-published tome will remain unceremoniously boxed in the garage. Of course, the ultimate reward of self-publishing is that you get to keep all of the profit on your book—if there is any.

Only consider self-publishing if you have experience in publishing or if you can effectively sell your book through the mail without spending a fortune on expensive ads. The tools of public relations (explained in Chapter 9) and some small ads in carefully chosen magazines and newspapers, along with some targeted direct mailings, should be enough to sell your book without bankrupting you. If you choose this approach, don't forget to take sales tax into account; otherwise, the state in which you live may come after you for it. You should also charge for postage and handling in addition to the sales price of the book, or set a price that covers these costs. If you handle the distribution on your own (you could hire an outside fulfillment house if you have the money), you'll also need to keep copious records of your transactions and be ready to accept returned books at a loss.

Books that sell well through the mail and via other self-publishing distribution schemes (such as infomercials and seminar sales) sometimes do get picked up by major book distributors. A few self-published authors even get contract offers from conventional publishing houses after a book has established its marketability.

Craig Hosada's amusing *Bare Facts Video Guide* (a reference source that details the content and location of nude scenes by star and movie) was once sold exclusively through mail order. After a period of successful sales, book distributors and bookstores took notice. Craig still offers the book through the mail, but he also has distributors that handle the book for retail consumption. He financed a house and a comfortable lifestyle on this previously "unpublishable" idea.

If your self-published effort is picked up by a distributor (known also as a *disti*), the company will help promote and distribute your books to retail booksellers. Make sure you set a retail price high enough so that you can afford to sell the book wholesale (which is about fifty percent off the retail price) with enough profit left over to make the sale worthwhile.

The Risky Waters of Self-Publishing

Success stories like Craig Hosada's inspire many authors to consider self-publishing as an option. But self-publishing is fraught with risk and complexity. For every successful self-publisher, ninety-nine other authors lose their shirts. Before you decide to publish a book on your own, get some advice and some capital. Even Craig Hosada (now in the process of writing the fifth edition of his *Bare Facts Video Guide*) laments his biggest mistake in publishing the first edition: not securing enough capital to get through the first year.

To sell five thousand copies of a book in one year, the expense for printing and production could be twenty-five thousand dollars or more, plus an additional ten thousand dollars or more for promotion, and another ten thousand dollars for miscellaneous distribution (mailing and packaging) expenses, for a total outlay of forty-five thousand dollars. Of course, if the book sells for twenty-five dollars a copy, then that five thousand copies could reap an income of one-hundred-twenty-five thousand dollars—and a potential profit of eighty thousand dollars. To ever enjoy this kind of success, however, you'll need to work full time at selling the book—and there's no guarantee that you'll sell even one copy.

If you can't sell your book to an established publishing house, and if you really think it will sell to your target audience, be sure to consider all the costs involved in the production and printing of the book before you jump into the publishing game. Also consider the time you'll spend on paperwork: you will need to secure your copyright, get an ISBN (International Standard Book Number) for the book if you want to sell it retail, and have your business licenses and accounting methods in order. In the Resources for Writers, you will find a list of books on self-publishing that can help you through this maze.

Vanity or Subsidy Publishing

From idea to printed book in customers' hands, self-publishing involves handling the entire process (and expense)

yourself—a method not to be confused with "vanity" or "subsidy" publishing, wherein a "publisher" charges you to "publish" your book. At one extreme, you'll find vanity presses
that amount to little more than overpriced print shops. These
publishers won't promote your book, and, most importantly,
may require you to purchase copies from them to resell, even
after you've paid for the printing. Some of these firms promote their services in ads at the back of magazines, and even
on matchbooks. Beware of any publisher that runs ads asking
for submissions. No conventional, quality publisher solicits
books this way because they already have too many over-the-
transom submissions without inviting more.

Rather than going to an unscrupulous and expensive vanity
press, consider going the self-publishing route and hiring a
book promoter to handle the project for you. Unless you plan
a lavish promotion, this method will cost about the same as a
vanity press and *you*, not the publisher, own the copies and
distribution rights.

Keep in mind that few bookstores carry titles printed by
vanity presses, and putting the name of a known vanity press
on your publishing resumé may be the kiss of death when
approaching conventional publishers (unless you've actually
sold a lot of copies of the book).

A variation of the vanity press is the subsidy publishing
house, where you pay part of the cost of publishing and marketing your book. Some subsidy arrangements are legitimate.
Subsidy publishing may be an option if the house has documented successes and real editors. Look for a subsidy publisher
with an effective marketing department and fair terms. Ask the
same questions you'd ask of other publishers, as detailed in
Chapter 6. Before you sign on the bottom line, check the pub-

lisher's references with authors who have done business with the house. Some subsidy publishers have established distribution channels and decent reputations; others do not.

At a conventional house, the publisher is taking a risk with your book by using the company's time and money to produce, print, and promote the project. At vanity and subsidy presses, the money being spent is partly, mostly, or all yours. Therefore, there's little risk to the publisher if it fails to promote and sell your book. When dealing with a press that you pay, read the contract terms carefully. Get everything, including promotion and distribution plans, spelled out in the contract.

WAKING UP A WANNA-BE, GOING TO BED AN AUTHOR

Michael Murphy woke up every morning for three months hoping for a miracle—that a publisher would fall in love with *Popsicle Fish*. One Friday afternoon, the phone finally rang. Health Press offered a contract, and Michael Murphy went to bed that night an actual, bona fide author.

It happens every day. Jim Wilfong woke up a wanna-be every morning for four months before the phone call came with an offer from Career Press to publish *GLOBALINK*, his book on international trade. "It was a lot like going fishing," he recalls. "At first I thought all I had to do was amble down to the creek with my bamboo rod and a rubber worm. But as I got to know more about the publishing business, I learned I needed better bait and to find a lake full of hungry fish." After months of hard work, Jim created the right bait: a beautiful proposal that could serve as a model for any aspiring book author. And he dropped that appealing bait in the right lake, with a publisher who specializes in cutting-edge books for entrepreneurs. Even then, it took a while for the fish to bite because it had eaten its fill. Career Press did not need more titles in May, but it was eager for new ones in August.

Your own publishing success story will probably come as Michael's and Jim's did. You'll work, work, work on your book. You'll search, search, search for a hungry fish. You'll wait, wait, wait for a nibble. And in the end, you, too, will catch your dream: you'll wake up a wanna-be and go to bed an author.

How to Evaluate a Publisher:

A Series of Initial Questions

When you envision a hot-shot negotiator, do you picture someone with the thick hide and toughness of a rhinoceros, the silver tongue of a meadowlark, and the tenacity of a pit bull? True, those qualities may help people get what they want by the end of a negotiation, but the really smart negotiator relies, more than anything else, on a good set of ears, as the following little tale illustrates:

A young woman planning a dinner party approaches the greengrocer with her order, saying, "I'll take fifteen pounds of potatoes, fifteen pounds of tomatoes, and fifteen pounds of onions."

The grocer smiles and shakes his head. "Well, young lady, I have plenty of new red potatoes, and the ripest red tomatoes you've ever seen, but I ran out of onions an hour ago."

"Oh, I see," replies the young woman. "In that case, I'll just take ten pounds of potatoes, ten pounds of tomatoes, and ten pounds of onions."

Patiently, the grocer repeats, "I can sell you all the potatoes and tomatoes you want, but I am fresh out of onions."

The customer seems to ponder the grocer's words before she insists, "Well, then, just give me five pounds of potatoes, five pounds of tomatoes, and five pounds of onions."

Exasperated, the grocer thinks for a minute then says, "Let me put it to you this way. What happens if you take the 'toes' off the end of 'potatoes'?"

"Why, you get 'potay.'"

"Correct. And what happens if you take the 'toes' off the end of 'tomatoes'?"

"You get 'tomay.'"

"Absolutely right. Now, what happens if you take the 'bloom' off the end of 'onion'?"

"Don't be silly. There is no 'bloom' in 'onions.'"

"That's what I've been trying to tell you all along. There's *no bloomin' onions!*"

The moral of this story for the author entertaining a contract offer from a book publisher? You must understand what the publisher can and cannot give you contractually, and you must ask only for what you can reasonably expect to receive.

If you have proposed a small paperback on a narrow subject like *The Insider's Guide to Housebreaking Your Dog*, as did Audrey Carr and Lou Ellen Davis, then you cannot expect a one-hundred-thousand-dollar advance. But you can expect a top royalty rate escalating from seven percent to ten percent after twenty thousand copies are sold. The publisher may not project sufficient first-year sales to earn back a huge advance, but it will still offer a standard, or even better-than-usual, royalty rate. On the other hand, if you have published two books on management that have sold over fifty thousand copies each, you might reasonably expect a fifty-thousand-dollar advance for your third book on the subject—a level Craig Hickman attained with *The Productivity Game.*

Regardless of your subject area and track record, however, you should focus on the five other factors listed in the following section before you argue with a publisher about the sixth factor, advances and royalty rates; these first five factors contribute more to successful long-term sales (and to your income) than do the numbers that appear in the publishing agreement. Of course contract terms are important, but a book that fails to sell a lot of copies renders those numbers meaningless.

The artful negotiator asks six key questions when considering a contract offer from a publisher, listening carefully to the publisher's answers to these questions. If you feel comfortable with the answers, you can feel confident that you have gotten the best deal possible. If not, you may sign the publisher's contract anyway, hoping for the best, but you will always wonder whether you made the right decision.

THE NEGOTIATOR'S SIX CRITICAL QUESTIONS

Contracts don't manufacture books, *publishers* do; royalty rates don't edit manuscripts, *editors* do; option clauses don't create a good environment for a new book, the *publisher's list* does; the words *acceptable to the publisher* appear in a contract, the word *vision* never does; advances don't sell books, the *marketing* team does; a piece of paper doesn't guarantee success, only an *effective partnership* can create a climate in which that might happen.

That longed-for event finally arrives: your agent or an editor calls you up and utters those magic words, "I have a contract offer for your book." Do you immediately ask for fifteen pounds of onions? No, you ask these six critical questions:

1. Is this the right publishing house?
2. Can I work with this editor?
3. Does the publisher share my vision for the book?
4. Will my book fit the publisher's list?
5. What marketing plan has the publisher devised?
6. Do the contract terms make sense?

If the answers to the first five questions satisfy you, the answer to the sixth will fall naturally into place. Let's examine each question in order before we walk through the clauses of a typical publisher's agreement in Chapter 7.

Evaluating the Publishing House

Imagine that you have proposed a new book, *Women-preneuring*, that will offer women practical advice on starting and growing a business. You may have marketed the book to publishers yourself, or you may have joined forces with a good literary agent. In either case, the same questions should occupy your mind as you work your way toward signing a contract. In publishing, where so much depends on people and relationships, nothing appears black-or-white but instead reflects varying shades of gray. Nevertheless, as we follow this hypothetical case to its conclusion, let's pretend that you enjoy the luxury of choosing between two dramatically different options. Here, for example, suppose that two hypothetical houses have offered you contracts: Busy Bee Books in Tucson, Arizona; and MacDougal, Inc., of New York.

While an experienced agent can tell you a lot about these two publishers, you can conduct a good deal of research on your own. Your investigation might include consulting these resources:

- Recent catalogs (often printed for the spring and fall seasons)

- Bookstores (especially the superstores and chains)

- Other authors (agents and editors can suggest names)

- Directories (*Literary Market Place* and *Writer's Guide to Book Editors, Publishers, and Literary Agents*) list subject areas and numbers of titles in print and published each year

In our hypothetical case, you might uncover the following facts:

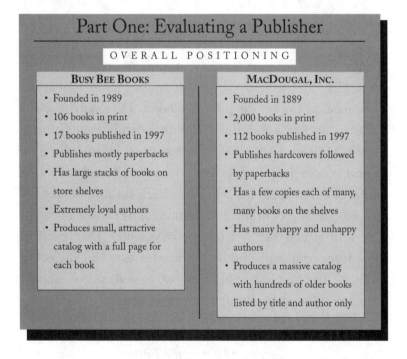

Part One: Evaluating a Publisher

OVERALL POSITIONING

BUSY BEE BOOKS	MACDOUGAL, INC.
• Founded in 1989	• Founded in 1889
• 106 books in print	• 2,000 books in print
• 17 books published in 1997	• 112 books published in 1997
• Publishes mostly paperbacks	• Publishes hardcovers followed by paperbacks
• Has large stacks of books on store shelves	• Has a few copies each of many, many books on the shelves
• Extremely loyal authors	• Has many happy and unhappy authors
• Produces small, attractive catalog with a full page for each book	• Produces a massive catalog with hundreds of older books listed by title and author only

From an objective point of view, the two houses differ dramatically. On one hand, you see a younger, smaller, steadily growing publisher; on the other hand, you see a major conglomerate with a long history in the marketplace. Bigger is always better, no? No. Look at the houses from a subjective point of view. Would you feel more confidence in a publisher for whom your book might be a top priority, or in one where your book might get lost in the bureaucracy and sheer volume a big conglomerate must maintain?

However, bigger might be better if the larger house can put more marketing muscle behind its new books. Which would do more for your book, a mighty marketing machine with strong credibility among booksellers, or a leaner, meaner marketing staff hell-bent on building its own credibility with every new book?

Two different authors of books much like *Womenpreneuring* compared two different houses and came to opposite conclusions. Vicki Montgomery went with smaller, more nimble and more focused Career Press for her book, *The Smart Woman's Guide to Starting a Business of Her Own*, while Pam Gilberd, author of *The Eleven Commandments of Wildly Successful Women*, chose large, venerable Macmillan (a subsidiary of Simon & Schuster) as her publisher. Each author brought her own unique desires to the deliberations and reached a conclusion with which she felt most comfortable. That comfort arose from contemplating both objective data and subjective feelings. The same combination of considerations should come into play when getting to know an editor.

Getting to Know the Editor

Once you have formed an impression of the publishing house, you will want to find out about the editor with whom you will be working. Like houses, editors come in all shapes and sizes, from the fresh-faced, young, eager, and ambitious recently promoted editor at MacDougal, Inc. to the seasoned veteran at Busy Bee Books. At MacDougal, Joelle's enthusiasm (see the box on page 159) may make up for a small resumé of published successes, but at Busy Bee, Seymour's experience may count for more in a world where sound business judgment carries the day.

Again, your agent can tell you a lot about working with a particular editor, but that should not prevent you from forming your own impression and making your own judgment. If you have been marketing your book yourself, you will automatically get to know your prospective editor; if not, then you can tell your agent you want to talk to the editor before you consider signing a contract. Since the editor proposes becoming your partner, you want to know as much about that person as possible. Look for these attributes:

- Experience: How many successful books has this editor brought to market?
- Stability: How many jobs has the editor held? Does the person function as an assistant, associate, senior, or executive editor? How long has he or she held the present position?
- Knowledge: Does the editor offer good suggestions about improving your book?
- Temperament: Do you enjoy talking with this person?
- Enthusiasm: Does the editor care deeply about your subject and your book?
- Clout: Do the editor's supervisors and colleagues in production and marketing respect this person's judgment?

The smart negotiator knows that the quality of an author's relationship with an editor can do more to ensure successful publication than all the legal clauses in a formal document. Good editors not only add value to the manuscripts they acquire, they serve as their authors' champions throughout the publishing process, igniting the support and passion of management, production, and marketing people who will join the partnership as the project moves from a manuscript to a bound book.

Let's look again at our hypothetical case. While you have uncovered a few objective details about both editors, your half-hour conversation has yielded more subjective impressions than cold, hard facts. Seasoned experience is always better, no? No. Think about this as entering into a publishing marriage. Would you feel more inclined to tie yourself to someone who brings a lot of experience to the union but strikes you as relatively cold and dispassionate, or would you opt for the enthusiasm of an ardent lover? On the opposite side of the coin, would you rather hitch yourself to a business partner who runs the show, or to someone who wields relatively less power in her company?

In the case of *Womenpreneuring*, you might also weigh another factor. Which editor more deeply relates to your subject: a woman who brings a feminine perspective to bear on the project, or a man who has actually started a business of his own?

When Myrna Milani proposed her first book, *The Weekend Dog*, two editors offered contracts: a bright young editor at Putnam, and one of the most respected, experienced women in the industry, Eleanor Rowson, then at Scribners. An inexperienced newcomer herself, Myrna decided that she felt most confident going with experience. In contrast, Paul Coleman chose youthful enthusiasm over a lengthy track record when he sold his first book, *The Forgiving Marriage*, to Stacy Prince at Contemporary Books. So did Diane Lusk, when she signed up her book on day-care, *Nothing But the Best*, with a new editor and soon-to-be-mom, Randy Ladenheim at Morrow. In all of these cases, the authors came to believe that their publishers and editors fully embraced their vision of what their book could accomplish in the marketplace.

Part Two: Evaluating a Publisher

THE EDITORS

EDITOR: SEYMOUR (BUSY BEE BOOKS)	EDITOR: JOELLE (MACDOUGAL, INC.)
• Published three *New York Times* Bestsellers at a New York house before starting his small house in Tucson • Has been an editor/publisher for 30 years and has run Busy Bee for seven • Believes you can write a great book with little help • Quiet, confident, easygoing, aloof • Likes your proposal a lot	• Has published only a dozen books so far but has a blockbuster (she hopes) coming out next fall • Worked for Random House as an assistant before landing this job two years ago • Makes a lot of suggestions, some of which delight you, some of which seem off-the-wall • Talks fast, has a bubbly personality, is highly personable and informative • Has fallen head-over-heels in love with your proposal

Determining the Vision

Your complete and well-organized proposal gives prospective editors a clear idea of the book you intend to write, but what if an editor envisions a book quite different from the one you have been holding in your mind? While you want an editor who will make good suggestions for improving and adding value to your manuscript, you don't want to find yourself in the disturbing situation where, after you have signed a contract and written your book, the editor expects something radically different from what you want or can deliver.

The successful author remains flexible and open to suggestions, but maintains a certain backbone as well. Likewise, a smart editor tries to challenge an author and help stimulate greater creativity, but knows when to back off and respect an author's expertise on the subject matter.

In order to ensure a good match between your vision of your published book and that of a prospective editor, you can pose these questions, either directly or through your agent:

- What do you like best about my proposal?
- What do you like least about my proposal?
- What do you want me to do differently?
- Do you approve of the proposed length and format for the book?
- Will you read two to three early chapters to make sure I'm on the right track?
- Do you expect changes in the writing style?

The author of *Womenpreneuring* could hear dramatically different answers to these questions:

Part Three: Evaluating a Publisher

EDITORIAL APPROACHES

SEYMOUR'S APPROACH (BUSY BEE BOOKS)	JOELLE'S APPROACH (MACDOUGAL, INC.)
• I like the emphasis on practical, how-to advice. • I don't like so many long examples. • I want more lists and tips. • I'd like to keep the paperback under 200 pages. • I can't edit the manuscript until it's complete. • I want you to make it even more "folksy."	• I like your examples. • I don't like lists of "dos and don'ts." • I want even more examples. • I'd like to expand the page count to 300 for hardcover. • I want to get the first two chapters perfect before you complete the manuscript. • I'd prefer a more businesslike style.

You've uncovered two different visions, but with which can you live most comfortably? Regardless of your personal preference, at least both editors have thought about how your book should read. One author might, as Tom Gorman did when considering Pocket Books for *Multipreneuring*, prefer the editor who shared his vision at the outset. Another might, as Emmett Murphy did when contemplating Wiley for *Leadership IQ*, favor the editor who felt the book needed radical rethinking before it could make its way successfully in the marketplace.

Given the subjectivity that comes into play when an author and an editor discuss their vision for a book, both parties should invest a certain amount of trust and confidence in one another's perspectives. An editor cannot teach you much about your subject; you cannot teach an editor much about publishing. The best resolution occurs as the two parties forge a vision that takes both content and market realities into account. Once a match has been forged between your vision and the publisher's vision, you can turn your attention to weighing the publisher's list.

Weighing the List

Every plant requires a special environment in which to thrive. Blueberry bushes like to keep their feet wet, while geraniums like to dry out between waterings. Crabgrass and tulips make bitter enemies, while marigolds and petunias get along quite happily. Pachysandra loves shade, tomatoes demand sun. A book does not exist in a vacuum but in an environment, surrounded by all the other books on the list. Good companions support each other, while orphans lead a lonely and often desperate existence.

This holds especially true for books, when the surrounding list can lend a lot of interest and indirect support. If, for instance, the house has published numerous successful books for entrepreneurs and small business owners, the company's executives, editors, and, most importantly, marketing people know the subject area quite well, have demonstrated their ability to penetrate this market niche, and have built credibility with booksellers and book buyers. Should you worry that a publisher with a strong list in a particular subject might publish books that would conflict with or compete with your book for sales? That can happen, but most publishers try hard to distinguish their titles from one another and would rather not compete with themselves. If your book would hurt sales of an existing title, you will probably not receive a contract offer from its publisher, a fact that accounts for most rejections of an otherwise excellent proposal. When you are gathering information about the publisher's list, you can consult:

- Bookstore buyers (who know the past history and upcoming lists)
- Publishers' catalogues (which advertise forthcoming titles)
- Your agent (who may know about many recently acquired titles that do not yet appear in catalogues)
- Your editor (who knows the publisher's long-term strategic goals in various subject areas)
- Authors (who may be working on future titles for the publisher)

Returning to *Womenpreneuring*, your investigation might yield information about your two prospective publishers' lists as seen on the next page.

This comparison poses something of a dilemma for the new author. On one side you see Busy Bee with a robust, ongoing interest in publishing books for your target audience. On the other you find the former powerhouse MacDougal, which has lost some of its momentum lately, but which seems intent on recapturing its prestige in this area. Moreover, authors have jumped ship in both directions. Both houses' books have a similar physical appearance, though Busy Bee tends to favor

Part Four: Evaluating a Publisher

BUSY BEE BOOKS	MACDOUGAL, INC.
• Publishes only self-help books	• Has combined four inhouse imprints that publish business books in order to focus more heavily on the subject
• Half the list deals with small business topics and women's issues	• Lost some of its dominance in recent years by publishing in many unrelated areas
• Plans to publish 12 (out of 15 to 20) books a year for the small business market	• Has announced its rededication to the market niche
• Continues to revise three books that have been bestsellers on finance, accounting, and marketing strategies	• Plans to publish 36 new titles (out of 100 to 120) a year for small business
• Recently signed a well-known author who previously published with MacDougal	• Has signed up three authors who previously published with Busy Bee

paperback originals, while MacDougal pushes the traditional approach of issuing hardcovers, followed by paperbacks if the hardcovers sell well enough to justify doing so.

Two recent authors made different decisions when faced with a similar dilemma. Mike Snell and the Bakers decided to go with Prima Publishing for this book you're reading, rather than with a major New York publisher, because they felt their book fit the Prima list where it would make an ideal companion to Jeff Herman's *Writer's Guide to Book Editors, Publishers, and Literary Agents*. The larger house boasted a longer list of books for writers, but none of them had sold as well as

Herman's book, which will appear in new editions every two years for many years to come. However, Pete Richman, author of *The Insider's Guide to Growing a New Business*, went with Macmillan Spectrum, an imprint of a large conglomerate that has expressed its intention to dedicate itself to the market for small business books, rather than with a smaller house that has made huge inroads in that market recently. Pete liked the idea of "getting on a fast elevator in a tall building," as he put it. "I saw risks on both sides, but I gambled that Macmillan possessed the resources to get a book in the game in a big way."

One author chooses to be a big frog in a small pond, another chooses to be a small frog in a big pond. Either strategy can pay off, provided the author consciously places the bet, knowing full well the position of the new book on the list. Both a leader and a follower can win big. However, neither author will have gambled wisely unless the chosen publisher has fashioned a marketing plan that will bring the book to the attention of booksellers and book buyers.

Assessing the Marketing Plan

For a publisher who issues from ten to one hundred books a year, every new product enters a horse race, running for a spot on the publisher's list and for space on the bookstore shelves. Regardless of the size of the advance to the author, the publisher devises an initial marketing plan but adjusts it as the book takes shape and moves into production. A publisher probably won't throw good money after bad, however, so the book with a fifty-thousand-dollar advance may turn out so surprisingly bad that the publisher will reduce its marketing budget, while the book with a twenty-five-hundred-dollar advance may turn out so amazingly well that the publisher will boost its budget considerably.

Conventional wisdom once held that a big advance would automatically ensure a big marketing effort, but in this era of fierce competition for the book buyer's dollars, a savvy publisher will put a lot more money on the horse that looks fastest when the race actually begins.

Initial marketing plans usually sound quite vague, with the editor saying something like, "We have developed a system for marketing and sales, and we'll give your book all the attention we can afford." In your discussion of marketing plans with your agent or editor, you can, however, try to understand the basic system the publisher employs. Unlike marketers of toothpaste or breakfast cereal, book publishers have historically followed, rather than led, their products to market. While Procter & Gamble will spend a fortune on advertising a new mouthwash to launch its marketing campaign, Simon & Schuster will promote the book to booksellers, then follow up with more promotion if the book starts to fly off the shelves. Most publishers believe that advertising does not sell books to a skeptical consumer, but that reviews, publicity, feature articles, talk-show interviews, and word of mouth do. In a world of "lead, follow, or get out of the way," you want a publisher who will at least lead your book to market with a promotional campaign designed to generate reviews, publicity, magazine and newspaper articles, talk-show interviews, and word-of-mouth recommendations.

To get a feel for a publisher's marketing system, ask about recent triumphs. Publishing professionals love to tell "war stories" about their successes. You can also urge your agent or editor to share with you some specific marketing achievements for recent titles. Examine such items as:

- Recent press releases (generated by in-house or freelance publicists)
- Published reviews of recent titles (especially in national publications)
- Feature articles in magazines and newspapers (both regional and national)
- Lists of recent author tours and radio and television interviews (drive-time radio shows have become popular)
- The author's marketing questionnaire (usually given to authors after they have signed a contract)
- Booksellers' responses (What do they think of the publisher's sales organization? Do they find them knowledgeable and credible?)
- Sales figures (How many copies have comparative titles sold in their first year? Their second and third years?)

The author of *Womenpreneuring* might construct the following comparison between the two houses' typical marketing strategies. See the box on the following page.

If you put both these houses behind the same book, which one will win the race? With Busy Bee you might reasonably count on selling twenty-five thousand copies, but with Mac-Dougal you might end up at the bottom of the scale with twenty-five hundred. But what if MacDougal can sell one-hundred-fifty thousand, a record Busy Bee has not yet reached?

Like so many of the issues surrounding a decision about signing with a publisher, subjective factors may count for

Part Five: Evaluating a Publisher

MARKETING COMPARISIONS

BUSY BEE BOOKS	MACDOUGAL, INC.
• Assigns an outside publicist to each new title	• Employs two in-house publicists to handle the whole list every season
• Gains a few reviews of paperbacks but generates many feature articles in magazines and newspapers	• Consistently garners reviews and feature articles in major newspapers and magazines
• Prefers radio drive-time talk shows and sends a few authors on limited promotional tours	• Tours only two to three authors each season, focuses on national television talk shows
• Consistently sells 20,000 to 40,000 copies of a new book	• Sales figures range from 2,500 to 250,000 copies for a new book
• Obtains author information during face-to-face meetings	• Sends authors a 12-page marketing questionnaire
• Uses a commissioned salesforce that bundles titles from 23 publishers	• Maintains a 23-person permanent sales staff

more than objective ones. If the publisher's marketing people fall in love with you and your book, you'll get maximum support, but if they merely feel confident that they can do reasonably well with your book, you may receive little more than routine attention. Publicity budgets, for example, reflect the publisher's initial expectations, so a small budget reveals low expectations, while a large one signals high expectations. Though a publisher will not set a book's promotional budget until after it goes into production, you can get a ballpark idea for what the publisher usually budgets for a book like yours.

Sally Edwards chose Adams Publishing over a larger house for *Heart Zone Training* because she saw merit in the fact that Adams employs as many publicists as editors, while Glen Woodcock went with McGraw-Hill for *Bulletproofing Your PC Network* because he felt that such a leviathan could penetrate the market more effectively than one of the many smaller, more agile computer book publishers.

Putting the Business Relationship in Perspective

The author of *Womenpreneuring* might, as you've seen throughout the discussion of negotiation, opt for Busy Bee or MacDougal in any or all of the first four categories, but regardless of the choice she makes, once she has settled on the house, the editor, the vision, the list, and the marketing plan, she can now consider the contract itself and the important clauses it contains.

But before we explore that sometimes bewildering, often intimidating subject in the next chapter, let's step back a moment to view the larger picture of your relationship with your prospective publisher. If you ask the first five critical questions (listed on page 154) and probe relentlessly until you get answers, you run the risk of striking your publisher as something of a pest. After all, strong relationships grow out of trust, and a detailed "prenuptial agreement" may seem to the intended spouse as distrustful. It certainly can rob the future marriage of some of its romance.

Therefore, as you ask the penetrating questions and *listen* carefully to the answers, try to maintain an atmosphere of trust—one in which you assume that you and your publisher share one basic common goal: to publish the best possible book as soon as possible—one that will sell as many copies as possible for as long as possible. Belief in that common goal will do more than anything else to help you win the best contract terms and smooth the bumps that inevitably arise in any marriage. When you expect the best from other people, they usually try to fulfill or surpass your expectations; when you expect the worst, they usually fulfill those expectations, too.

One spring day in 1995, a meeting took place that illustrates the positive possibilities of business collaboration. The potential partners in a book project—an expert on leadership skills, an editor from a major New York publishing house, and an agent/book developer—met at a seaside resort to hammer out a publishing plan. As they sat on a blanket gazing out at the incoming tide, two things happened: the outline for the book began to take form, and, more importantly, a deep and lasting friendship was born. The book, *Leadership IQ*, burst onto the *New York Times* bestseller list a year later, but the partners—Emmett Murphy, Janet Coleman, and Michael Snell—won much more than a publishing triumph from their day at the beach: they gained a trusting friendship that no amount of money can buy. As you grow as a book author, you, too, will make many friends in the publishing world, and in the end these relationships will matter at least as much as any contract terms or financial rewards.

CHAPTER SEVEN

How to Negotiate and Understand a Contract:

A Tour of the Important Clauses in a Publishing Agreement

Publishing contracts vary from the fifty-plus-page Simon & Schuster document, with all its rambling legalese, to the two-page letter of agreement used by some smaller publishers that simply and clearly sums up the understanding. While the basic boilerplate clauses in the standard four- to six-page agreement used by most publishers cover the same basic elements as the longer and shorter ones, the variable terms (advances and royalty rates and shares of subsidiary rights income) can differ widely. Consider two cases at either end of the spectrum.

Twelve years ago, two authors signed contracts with two publishers for two very different books. The first, Danielle Torrez, the ex-wife of Boston Red Sox pitcher Mike Torrez, went with Putnam after a fairly intense bidding war among several major houses. The second, Arnold Goldstein, a noted business attorney, accepted a contract from small Enterprise Publishing. In the first case, publishers saw a hot property in the baseball wife's sexy memoir. In the second case, Ted

Nicholas, the crafty entrepreneur who ran Enterprise, saw a good match between the lawyer's book of business agreements and his own bestselling *How to Start a Corporation for Less than $50.*

The lengthy Putnam agreement provided a substantial advance of fifty-thousand dollars, a fifteen-percent hardcover royalty rate based on the publisher's selling price of twenty dollars, and better than fifty-percent shares of the sale of film and foreign translation rights. The two-page Enterprise contract contained a preprinted, non-negotiable royalty rate of five percent for mail-order sales on the list price of fifty dollars and a tiny advance of one thousand dollars. If it sold fifty-thousand copies, Danielle's *High Inside* would earn $150,000 in royalty income; if Arnold's *Basic Book of Business Agreements* sold the same quantity, he would earn $125,000. Surely the formidable Putnam would do even better than that with its headline-making exposé, and surely little Enterprise would not do even that well with its limited airline magazine advertising.

The bottom line, five years later: the baseball memoir not only did not sell enough copies to earn back its advance, it never made it into paperback or film. The book of business agreements, however, went on to sell 750,000 copies, not one of them through a bookstore, reaping a huge windfall for both the author and the publisher.

The two cases represent extremes in the two most important facets of contract negotiation: the agreement itself and the negotiation of terms in the agreement. Regardless of the size of the publisher and the complexity of its customary contract, you cannot expect to alter the rest of the contract as much as you can influence the income-generating terms; and to accomplish the latter, you may need some leverage. Because Danielle possessed unique experience in her subject, and in light of the fact the publishers were dying to sign her to a contract, her agent brought a lot of leverage to the bargaining table. Arnold's agent lacked any leverage with his book, because the publisher figured any good business attorney could assemble it and the publisher was not desperate to acquire the book. As it turned out, the dozens of hours of negotiation with leverage did not create success for Danielle, but the fifteen minutes spent reviewing and signing his contract fattened Arnold's bank account.

Before you contemplate the art of negotiation with leverage, you should first grasp the fundamental clauses that appear in most publishers' contracts.

A TYPICAL PUBLISHING CONTRACT

If you examined contracts from one hundred publishers, you would discover that seventy-five percent of them look quite a lot like the following one. As you read through it, bear in mind that the publisher wrote it primarily for its own benefit, and that it dwells on "worst case" scenarios (i.e., it deals more with what might go wrong in the legal relationship than with what might go right). Later, as you study the explanation of the various clauses and, finally, as you embark on negotiating your own contract more to your advantage, keep in mind the fact that none of the legal language captures the fundamental goal you want to hammer out with your publisher: bringing out the best possible book as soon as possible and selling as many copies as possible for as many years as possible.

Agreement made _____ _____, 199__, between Palomino Hill, Inc., Career and Personal Development Division, with offices at 113 Sylvan Avenue, Englewood Cliffs, N.J. 07632, hereinafter called the "Publisher," and _____, whose address is _____, hereinafter called the "Author."

THE AUTHOR AND THE PUBLISHER AGREE THAT:

A. Grant of Rights. The Author will write for publication a work tentatively entitled _____ (the "Work"). The Author hereby grants and assigns exclusively to the Publisher all rights in the Work throughout the world, including but not limited to all copyrights (and renewals, extensions, and continuations of copyright) in the Work and in all derivative works, in all languages, media and formats, including without limitation electronic versions, under the Publisher's own name and under other imprints or trade names, together with all exclusive rights granted to an author under the copyright laws of the United States, foreign countries, and international copyright conventions; and the right to grant these rights or any part of them to third parties. The Author grants to Publisher the right to use or authorize the use of the Author's name and likeness in connection with the Publisher's exercise of the foregoing rights.

B. Delivery of Manuscript. The manuscript, containing sufficient text and illustrations, which together will make a book of approximately _____ printed pages in a _____ inch trim size, will be delivered by the Author in final form and content acceptable to the Publisher, in its sole judgment, by _____. Time is of the essence in connection with the Author's delivery hereunder.

C. Royalties. Unless otherwise specifically provided in paragraphs 8, 9, or 10 of this Agreement, the Publisher will pay the Author a royalty of 10% on sales of the Work, based on the actual net cash received by the Publisher, except that on copies sold by the Publisher direct to the consumer (through coupon advertising, radio or television advertising, direct mail circularization, mail or telephone orders, any of the Publisher's book club divisions or institutes, or other direct sales to consumers), the Publisher will pay the Author a royalty of 5%, based on the actual net cash received from such sales of the Work.

D. Payments. The Publisher will report on the sale of the Work in March and September of each year for the six-month period ending the prior December 31 and June 30 respectively. With cash report of sales, the Publisher will make settlement for any balance shown to be due.

E. Paragraphs 1 through 21 inclusive, on Pages 2–4 following, are part of this Agreement as though placed before the signatures.

_____   Palomino Hill, Inc.

Author

                                                By: _____

_____

Social Security No./Federal Tax ID No.

1. Submission of Work/Acceptance/Proofs. The Author will deliver the manuscript in typewritten form, in duplicate, double-spaced on 8½" x 11" sheets on one side only, and on computer disk or in other electronic format as agreed to by the parties. The Author will retain a copy of all material on disks delivered to the Publisher. The manuscript will be in proper form for use as copy by the printer and the content will be such as the Publisher is willing to publish. If the Author is unable or unwilling to deliver the Work on time, or if the Work is not acceptable to the Publisher, in its sole editorial and marketing judgment, in length, form or content, the Publisher may terminate this Agreement and recover from the Author any monies paid to or on behalf of the Author in connection with the Work. Unless this Agreement has been terminated and until such sums have been repaid, the Author may not have the Work published elsewhere. After acceptance of the Work, upon request, the Author will read and correct the successive proofs in duplicate and promptly return one set of proofs to the Publisher. The Author will be responsible for the completeness and accuracy of such corrections. All costs of corrections and alterations in the proof sheets (other than those resulting from printer's errors) exceeding 10% of the cost of typesetting shall be borne by the Author, and the Publisher shall have the right to deduct or offset such charges from payments otherwise due the Author.

2. Other Items for the Work. Together with the manuscript, the Author will supply a title page; preface or foreword (if any); table of contents; complete and final copy for all illustrations, charts, diagrams, and forms (if any) properly prepared for reproduction; and, when requested by the Publisher, an index, a bibliography, or list of sources of material. In the event that the Author does not prepare these items, the Publisher may have them prepared, and the cost of such preparation will be offset against the Author's royalties. All artwork may be used by the Publisher in any work and manner without compensation. The Publisher shall not be liable for damages, if any, resulting from the loss or destruction of the manuscript, or other such material, or any part thereof.

3. Author Warranty and Indemnification. The Author warrants that the Author has full authority to make this Agreement, that (except for material in the public domain or material for which permission has been obtained by the Author from the copyright owner) the Work shall be original; the Author is the sole owner of the Work and all rights in the Work; and the Work will not infringe any copyright or trademark or violate other property rights or contain any scandalous, libelous, or unlawful matter or any formula or instruction that may cause harm or injury. The Author will indemnify and hold the Publisher harmless from and against all claims, suits, costs, damages, and expenses, including reasonable attorney's fees that the Publisher may sustain or incur by reason of any breach or alleged breach of any of the foregoing representations and warranties. The Publisher shall have the right to assume and control the defense or settlement of any such claim, and the Author will cooperate and provide reasonable assistance; and until such claim or suit has been settled or withdrawn, the Publisher may withhold from sums due the Author under this or any other agreement between the parties an amount reasonably sufficient in the Publisher's judgment to cover these liabilities. Notwithstanding any request by Publisher for change or substantiation, nothing in this Agreement shall be deemed to impose upon the Publisher any duty of independent investigation or relieve the Author of any of the warranties given or obligations assumed by the Author hereunder. The provisions of this paragraph shall survive the termination of this Agreement.

4. Permissioned Material. The Author will not include in the Work any material from other copyrighted works (including material from prior publishers, and co-authors or contributors who do not have separate agreements with the Publisher) without the Publisher's consent and the written consent of the owner of such material. The Author will be responsible for obtaining such written consents at the Author's expense. These consents shall be in a form and content acceptable to the Publisher, consistent with all rights granted to the Publisher in this Agreement and shall be submitted to the Publisher together with the manuscript for the Work.

5. Editing and Publishing Details. The Publisher will have the right, with respect to the Work, including reprints, revisions, and new editions, (a) to edit the Work; (b) to publish the printed Work in one or several volumes and in a style deemed suitable by the Publisher as to paper, printing, and binding; (c) to produce other versions of the Work in formats and media to be determined by the Publisher; (d) to fix or alter the title, cover, packaging, and the prices at which the Work shall be sold and the quantities printed or produced; and (e) to determine the methods and means of advertising, marketing, and selling the Work.

6. Author Copies. The Publisher will furnish six copies of the Work to the Author without charge. Should the Author desire additional copies for the Author's personal use and not for resale, they will be supplied at a 40% discount from the retail list price. No royalties will be paid on such purchases. If the Author purchases copies of the Work for resale, the Author shall be entitled to purchase such copies in accordance with the Publisher's standard Special Sales discount schedules.

7. Revisions. (a) The Author agrees to revise the Work, upon the request of the Publisher, if the Publisher considers it in the best interest of the Work. The provisions of this Agreement shall apply to each revision of the Work by the Author as though the revision were the Work being published for the first time under this Agreement. The Author shall provide the manuscript for the revision within the reasonable time requested by the Publisher. (b) Should the Author be deceased or unable or unwilling to provide a revision acceptable to the Publisher within the reasonable time requested, the Publisher shall have the right to have the revision prepared by another person and charge the amounts paid to the revisor against payments due or that may become due to the Author for sales of the revised edition, except that the Author's royalty for the first revision prepared without the Author's participation shall not be less than 50% of the royalties otherwise due hereunder, and the Author's royalty for the second revision prepared without the Author's participation shall not be less than 25%. The Author shall have no right to royalties on any subsequent revision. The Publisher reserves the right to continue to display the Author's name and likeness and the

Continues

Continues

name and likeness of the revisor(s) in revised editions of the Work and in promotional materials. (c) In the event that the term the "Author" includes more than one person, paragraph 7(b) shall apply only to any of the author(s) who is deceased or otherwise unable or unwilling to provide an acceptable revision within the time required by the Publisher. In such case, the Publisher may, at its election, have the revision prepared by the remaining author(s), on their own or with assistance from other revisor(s), who may also be designated as Author. In either case, the Publisher may charge amounts paid to the revisor(s) against the non-participating author's royalties, subject to the minimum royalty terms in paragraph 7(b). The publisher reserves the right to continue to display the non-participating Author's name and likeness and the name and likeness of the revisor(s) in revised editions of the Work and in promotional materials.

8. Other Royalties: (a) The Publisher may itself publish; broadcast by radio; make recordings, or mechanical or electronic versions; publish book club and microfilm editions; make translations and other versions; show by motion pictures, television, or cable syndicate; quote and otherwise utilize this Work (in whole or in part, alone or in combination with other Works) and material based on this Work (the "subsidiary rights"), or permit others (including affiliates of the Publisher) to do so. If the Publisher or any of its affiliates exercises such subsidiary rights, the Publisher will pay the Author a royalty of 5% of the actual net cash received from such use. If the Publisher grants any subsidiary rights to third parties, the license fees and/or royalties received by the Publisher from such grant shall be divided equally between the Publisher and the Author. (b) On copies of the Work sold by the Publisher at a discount of more than 50%, irrespective of market or means, the Author shall be paid a royalty of 5% of the actual net cash received by the Publisher, except for sales as set forth in paragraph 9(f). (c) On copies of the Work sold outside of the United States, in English or a foreign language, the Publisher shall pay the Author a royalty of 5% of the actual net cash received from such sales. (d) Upon any sale or licensing of any copies of the Work or part of the Work for which a royalty is not otherwise specified in this paragraph, the Author shall receive a royalty of 5% of the actual net cash received by the Publisher for such use. If the use of a Work falls into more than one category set forth in this Agreement, the Author shall be entitled to the single highest applicable royalty.

9. General Royalty Terms: (a) As used in this Agreement, the term "actual net cash received" by Publisher shall mean the amounts actually received by the Publisher from the sale of the Work, not including taxes and freight. (b) If the Publisher excerpts, packages, or sells the Work together with or as a segment of another product, in determining the actual net cash received for the Work for purposes of calculating royalty payments, the Publisher will allocate to the Work that portion of the receipts which the Publisher determines to be the Work's fair value to the entire period sold. (c) Any royalties payable to the Author shall be subject to a reasonable reserve for returns established. (d) The Publisher may deduct from any amount due the Author under this or any other agreements between the parties any amounts that the Author may owe the Publisher for unrecouped advances, previous overpayment of royalties, subsequent returns, or charges payable by the Author. (e) No royalty shall be payable for: returns, copies of the Work for the physically or visually handicapped. (f) No royalty shall be payable for copies of the Work sold at or about the Publisher's manufacturing cost plus royalties; (g) If the balance due the Author for any settlement period is less than fifty dollars, no report or payment shall be required of the Publisher until the next settlement period at the end of which the balance has reached fifty dollars. (h) The Author's right to audit or bring claim with respect to any royalty period shall be limited to a two-year period following the issuance of the report set forth in paragraph D.

10. Booklet. The Publisher shall have the right to publish a booklet based on the Work, not exceeding five thousand words and consisting of excerpts from the Work or a condensation or abridgment thereof, for use as a premium or for sales in quantity. On any sales of such booklet, the Publisher will pay the Author a royalty of 5% of the actual net cash received from such sales.

11. Electronic Versions Defined. As used in this Agreement, electronic versions shall mean any and all methods of copying, recording, storage, retrieval, or delivery of all or any portion of the Work, alone or in combination with other works, including in any multimedia work or electronic book; by any means now known or hereafter devised, including, without limitation, by electronic or electromagnetic means; by analog or digital signal; whether in sequential or non-sequential order, on any and all physical media, now known or hereafter devised including, without limitation, magnetic tape, floppy disks, CD-I, CD-ROM, laser disk, optical disk, IC card or chip, and any other human or machine readable medium, whether or not permanently affixed in such media, and the broadcast and/or transmission thereof by any and all means now known or hereafter devised.

12. Discontinuing Publication. When the Publisher decides that the public demand for the Work no longer warrants its continued manufacture, the Publisher may discontinue manufacture, declare the Work out of print, and destroy any or all films, plates, books, and sheets without liability to the Author. In such event, and only after one year from the first publication of the Work, Author may request in writing that all rights granted to Publisher hereunder shall be assigned to Author. Publisher shall have six (6) months from receipt of such written request to notify Author in writing of its intention to put the Work back into print. If Publisher fails to so notify Author within this six (6) month period, all rights granted to the Publisher hereunder shall be assigned to the Author, provided that all materials including artwork prepared by or at the expense of the Publisher (see paragraph 2) shall remain the Property of the Publisher, and discontinuance shall not affect the Publisher's right to sell the existing inventory of the Work or the rights of any party to whom the Publisher has previously granted any subsidiary right or license to the Work. If there is more than one Author under this Agreement, the Authors shall own the reverted rights jointly, unless otherwise provided below.

13. Competing Publications. The Author agrees that during the term of this Agreement, the Author will not contract for, publish, or furnish to any other publisher, any work on the same subject that will conflict with the sale of the Work. The provisions of this paragraph shall not apply to articles of less than seventy-five hundred words published in magazines or journals.

14. No Publication. Notwithstanding anything contained herein to the contrary: (a) In no event shall the Publisher be obligated to publish the Work if, in its judgment, the Work contains libelous or obscene material, or its publication would violate the right of privacy, common law or statutory copyrights, or any other rights of any person. In such event, the Publisher shall be entitled on demand to the return of all monies advanced to the Author hereunder, and to terminate this Agreement, in accordance with paragraph 1 above. (b) If the Publisher, in the exercise of its editorial and marketing judgment, decides not to publish the Work after acceptance thereof, the Publisher shall give written notice to the Author of its decision. Upon such notice, (i) all rights granted to the Publisher hereunder shall revert to the Author except that all materials including artwork prepared by or at the expense of the Publisher (see paragraph 2) shall remain the Property of the Publisher, (ii) the Author shall be entitled to retain any payments previously made by the Publisher to the Author under this Agreement as full compensation, and (iii) neither party shall have any further liability to the other under this Agreement or otherwise, except as set forth in any other Agreement between the parties.

15. Option. The Author grants to the Publisher the option to publish the Author's next book-length work upon the same terms as those contained in this Agreement. The Author shall deliver a proposal and sample chapter for the new work to the Publisher and the option may be exercised by the Publisher by written notice to the Author within 60 days after receipt.

16. Joint Authors. For purposes of this Agreement, all authors are collectively referred to as the "Author." Whenever the term the "Author" refers to more than one person, those persons will be deemed to share equally in the royalties and expenses arising under this Agreement, unless a different division is set forth on the lines below. Notwithstanding the foregoing, royalties shall be divided as follows: _____. Unless otherwise indicated in this Agreement, the rights and liabilities of the Author are joint and several, except that the Publisher shall be entitled to exercise its rights or remedies against or with the responsible Author.

17. Assignment. The Publisher may assign this Agreement in whole or in part. The Author may assign this Agreement only upon the prior written consent of the Publisher, except that the Author may assign the right to receive any payments hereunder, upon written notice to the Publisher and under such reasonable conditions as the Publisher may require. This Agreement shall be binding upon the parties hereto, their heirs, successors, permitted assigns, and personal representatives.

18. Law and Jurisdiction. This agreement shall be governed by the laws of the state of New York applicable to contracts made and fully performed therein and the parties agree that in any action or proceeding arising under or relating to this agreement, they shall be subject to the exclusive jurisdiction of the federal and state courts sitting in New York County, New York. In any such action, service of any papers by certified mail, return receipt requested, shall be sufficient, as will all other means provided by law.

19. No Waiver. No waiver of any term or condition of this Agreement or of any breach of this Agreement shall be deemed a waiver of any other term or condition or any later breach, nor shall publication or continued publication or payment by the Publisher following notice or claim of facts which, if true, would constitute a breach of warranty, representation, or agreement of the Author, constitute or imply any waiver by the Publisher of any defenses, rights, or remedies.

20. Binding Agreement. This Agreement represents the complete understanding of the parties with respect to the subject matter. No other representation shall be binding upon the parties. This Agreement may not be changed except by a writing executed by the Author and Publisher.

21. Advance. The Publisher agrees to make an advance payment of royalties to the Author of $____, payable as follows: $____ upon signing this Agreement and $____ upon submission of a complete and acceptable manuscript provided, however, that the Publisher shall retain for its own account the first $____ otherwise due the Author under the terms of this Agreement. Should the Author not deliver a complete and final manuscript acceptable to the Publisher, the Author shall repay the unrecovered portion of the total advance upon demand. The provisions of this paragraph shall not apply to revised editions of this Work, except that the Publisher may deduct any unrecovered portion of the advance from monies due the Author on sales of future editions.

22. Agent Clause. The Author hereby authorizes and appoints Mike Snell of Michael Snell Literary Agency, P. O. Box 655, Truro, MA 02666, Federal ID# 04-2724996 to act as his agent and to collect and receive all sums of money payable to him under the terms of this Agreement, and the receipt by such person shall be a valid discharge in that respect. Michael Snell Literary Agency receives 15% of all such monies (as divided in paragraph 16). Such person is hereby fully empowered to act on behalf of the Author in all matters in any way arising out of this Agreement, and is hereby designated as the Author's agent upon whom notices regarding this Agreement may be delivered. The designation of such person as agent shall survive the incapacity (physical or mental) or death of the Author, and may be terminated only upon written notice to the Publisher signed jointly by the Author (or his heirs, executors, administrators, successors, or assigns) and by such agent.

Your publisher's contract may differ from this one in length, organization, and amount of legalese, but certain key clauses appear in virtually every publishing agreement. The first page summarizes the basic components of the understanding between the publisher and author, while the subsequent pages amplify that understanding. Your own needs and circumstances may also differ from the typical author's, but the following explanation should help you understand basic terms and position yourself to negotiate reasonably with your publisher.

Grant of Rights Clause

A. **Grant of Rights.** The Author will write for publication a work tentatively entitled _____ (the "Work"). The Author hereby grants and assigns exclusively to the Publisher all rights in the Work throughout the world, including but not limited to all copyrights (and renewals, extensions, and continuations of copyright) in the Work and in all derivative works, in all languages, media and formats, including without limitation electronic versions, under the Publisher's own name and under other imprints or trade names, together with all exclusive rights granted to an author under the copyright laws of the United States, foreign countries, and international copyright conventions; and the right to grant these rights or any part of them to third parties. The Author grants to Publisher the right to use or authorize the use of the Author's name and likeness in connection with the Publisher's exercise of the foregoing rights.

This clause defines the essential relationship between the publisher and the author. Most publishers will agree to obtain necessary copyrights in the author's name, rather than the publisher's name. However, the publisher will almost always want world rights to the book because it wants to exploit as many income opportunities as possible. If you wish to retain certain rights, you can try to negotiate changes in this clause A. An author may, for example, wish to retain rights to an electronic version or to foreign translations if the publisher cannot exploit those rights itself. Your agent can help you determine your publisher's capability and track record in this area. Bear in mind that the working title will probably change before the book goes into production. For instance, Wiley eventually published the Bakers' *Getting the Word Out* as *How to Promote, Publicize, and Advertise Your Growing Business.*

Delivery Clause

B. **Delivery of Manuscript.** The manuscript, containing sufficient text and illustrations, which together will make a book of approximately _____ printed pages in a _____ inch trim size, will be delivered by the Author in final form and content acceptable to the Publisher, in its sole judgment, by _____. Time is of the essence in connection with the Author's delivery hereunder.

Agreements may specify length in terms of manuscript pages, number of words, or printed book pages. In any case, the specified length represents a target, not an ironclad requirement. The publisher may accept a longer or shorter manuscript, if it feels it can profitably sell that book, but it will probably insist that a manuscript that is much longer than specified be cut back because the publisher cannot turn a

profit on an eight-hundred-page book that was originally expected to come in at five hundred pages.

No phrase in the contract matters as much as "acceptable
to the Publisher." All your years of labor will amount to nothing if the publisher finds your submitted manuscript unacceptable for any reason. Ask your publisher to clarify what it
means by "acceptable," possibly with an insertion such as this:

> If, within thirty days of receiving the manuscript, the Pub-
> lisher notifies the Author that the manuscript is unsatisfac-
> tory, the Author shall have thirty days after receiving such
> notice within which to make those changes the Author and
> Publisher agree are necessary. If those changes do not ren-
> der the manuscript satisfactory, or if the Author fails to
> make such changes in the time provided, this agreement
> shall be terminated by the Publisher's notice to the Author.

Early submission of initial chapters, though not necessarily
a formal part of the agreement, can help ensure that the publisher will find the final manuscript acceptable. The delivery
date, like the length, is a goal rather than a "drop-dead deadline," but you should agree to a date that you know you can
meet. Publishers begin scheduling and budgeting for books as
much as two seasons in advance of publication, so a delay can
cause a publisher grief. If you discover that you cannot meet
the delivery date, ask for an extension *in writing.*

Royalties Clause

C. **Royalties.** Unless otherwise specifically provided in paragraphs 8, 9, or 10 of this Agreement, the Publisher will pay

the Author a royalty of 10% on sales of the Work, based on the actual net cash received by the Publisher, except that on copies sold by the Publisher direct to the consumer (through coupon advertising, radio or television advertising, direct mail circularization, mail or telephone orders, any of the Publisher's book club divisions or institutes, or other direct sales to consumers), the Publisher will pay the Author a royalty of 5%, based on the actual net cash received from such sales of the Work.

Since the royalty rate determines your future income, you want the best possible rate. Publishers calculate royalties in one of two ways: either multiplying the number of books sold by the net cash received for each book (i.e., list or catalogue price minus discounts) times the royalty rate, or multiplying the number of books sold by the list price times the rate. No publisher will alter its accounting procedure for a single author, but most publishers who base royalties on "net proceeds" will offer higher royalty rates for higher sales figures. For example, they might offer ten percent on the first five thousand copies sold, twelve percent on the next five thousand copies sold, and fifteen percent on all sales over ten thousand copies. Compare the two sets of calculations in the box on the next page.

Royalty rates for paperback originals will run lower than for hardcover books because the publisher reaps smaller profits from that format. Paperback rates range from five to eight percent for list price publishers, and from seven to fifteen percent for net-proceeds publishers. Publishers who market their books via direct mail will seldom increase the royalty rate beyond five percent, but bear in mind that even the net-proceeds publisher will be selling these books at the full

Proceeds: The Art of the Deal

	NET PROCEEDS	LIST PRICE
	(10%, 12½, 15%)	(10%)
Price	$24.95	$24.95
Net	14.97 (assumes 40% discount)	24.95
Sales	15,000	15,000
Royalty	7,485 (10%)	
Royalty	9,356 (12%)	
Royalty	11,287 (15%)	37,425 (10%)
Total	$28,068	$37,425

undiscounted list price (e.g., a book selling for fifty dollars at a five percent royalty rate will earn two dollars and fifty cents per copy sold).

Payment Clause

D. **Payments.** The Publisher will report on the sale of the Work in March and September of each year for the six-month period ending the prior December 31 and June 30 respectively. With cash report of sales, the Publisher will make settlement for any balance shown to be due.

Most publishers render royalty statements and pay any royalties due twice a year. In many cases, these clauses will appear before the signature lines. Some successful authors have incorporated themselves and will use a corporate tax ID number rather than a Social Security number. If so, the publisher may demand a personal guarantee of performance, usually in the form of a one-page amendment to the contract, which makes the author personally responsible and liable under the terms of the agreement.

Amendment Clause and Signatures

E. Paragraphs 1 through 21 inclusive, on Pages 2–4 following, are part of this Agreement as though placed before the signatures.

Palomino-Hill Direct, a division of Palomino-Hill, Inc.

_____   _____
Author   Social Security No./Federal ID No.

By:_____
   Eugene F. Brissie
   Vice President/Editorial Director

You sign here (or, in some cases at the end of the contract), providing your Social Security number (or corporate tax ID number) for tax reporting purposes. An officer of the company, not usually your editor, will sign on behalf of the company after you return the contract with your signature. The publisher will sign and process the agreement, then send you (and your agent) copies for your file. Advance checks usually arrive four to six weeks after that, sometimes sooner.

Submission Clause

1. **Submission of Work/Acceptance/Proofs.** The Author will deliver the manuscript in typewritten form, in duplicate,

double-spaced on 8½" x 11" sheets on one side only, and on computer disk or in other electronic format as agreed to by the parties. The Author will retain a copy of all material on disks delivered to the Publisher. The manuscript will be in proper form for use as copy by the printer and the content will be such as the Publisher is willing to publish. If the Author is unable or unwilling to deliver the Work on time, or if the Work is not acceptable to the Publisher, in its sole editorial and marketing judgment, in length, form or content, the Publisher may terminate this Agreement and recover from the Author any monies paid to or on behalf of the Author in connection with the Work. Unless this Agreement has been terminated and until such sums have been repaid, the Author may not have the Work published elsewhere. After acceptance of the Work, upon request, the Author will read and correct the successive proofs in duplicate and promptly return one set of proofs to the Publisher. The Author will be responsible for the completeness and accuracy of such corrections. All costs of corrections and alterations in the proof sheets (other than those resulting from printer's errors) exceeding 10% of the cost of typesetting shall be borne by the Author, and the Publisher shall have the right to deduct or offset such charges from payments otherwise due the Author.

Since publishers increasingly use the author's disks to drive typesetting, be sure to find out exactly what electronic format your publisher requires.

If your relationship with your publisher falls apart for any reason, you cannot approach another publisher with your material until you have secured a formal termination of this agreement. In most cases, that involves a "conditional release," specifying that if you sign with another publisher you must repay any outstanding advance out of proceeds you receive from the new publisher. When an author demands termination, the publisher understandably expects the return of any advance money it has paid; when a publisher moves to terminate an agreement, however, it will often allow the author to retain the advance (the portion paid on signing the agreement, for example).

The ten-percent limit on the costs of corrections and alterations in proof sheets protects the publisher from an author deciding to rewrite a book after the publisher has set it into type. That can be prohibitively expensive—as much as two dollars per change. So make all your revisions and changes before the manuscript has been put into proofs. Some publishers will raise the limit to fifteen percent, and those who set a five-percent limit will usually allow you to change it to ten percent.

Artwork and Other Items Clause

2. **Other Items for the Work.** Together with the manuscript, the Author will supply a title page; preface or foreword (if any); table of contents; complete and final copy for all illustrations, charts, diagrams, and forms (if any) properly prepared for reproduction; and, when requested by the Publisher, an index, a bibliography, or list of sources of material. In the event that the Author does not prepare these items, the Publisher may have them prepared, and the cost of such preparation will be offset against the Author's royalties. All artwork may be used by the Publisher

in any work and manner without compensation. The Publisher shall not be liable for damages, if any, resulting from the loss or destruction of the manuscript, or other such material, or any part thereof.

A good picture may be worth a thousand words, but it can also cost a thousand dollars. Though your publisher may agree to pay a certain amount to have your artwork created, in most cases the author must supply any photographs or artwork, or pay out of royalties for the publisher to provide it. In any case, try to restrict your art program to *essential* drawings or photos, eliminating any "window dressing" or "art for art's sake." You may want to stipulate that only artwork "created by the publisher" may be used by the publisher in any other work without compensation to you.

Many authors dislike the drudgery of compiling an index, so publishers will happily do it themselves, charging the author's royalty account between three hundred and fifteen hundred. A publisher may agree to pay for the index itself, but that will probably mean a smaller advance for the work.

Warranty and Indemnification Clause

3. **Author Warranty and Indemnification.** The Author warrants that the Author has full authority to make this Agreement, that (except for material in the public domain or material for which permission has been obtained by the Author from the copyright owner) the Work shall be original; the Author is the sole owner of the Work and all rights in the Work; and the Work will not infringe any copyright

or trademark or violate other property rights or contain any scandalous, libelous, or unlawful matter or any formula or instruction that may cause harm or injury. The Author will indemnify and hold the Publisher harmless from and against all claims, suits, costs, damages, and expenses, including reasonable attorney's fees that the Publisher may sustain or incur by reason of any breach or alleged breach of any of the foregoing representations and warranties. The Publisher shall have the right to assume and control the defense or settlement of any such claim, and the Author will cooperate and provide reasonable assistance; and until such claim or suit has been settled or withdrawn, the Publisher may withhold from sums due the Author under this or any other agreement between the parties an amount reasonably sufficient in the Publisher's judgment to cover these liabilities. Notwithstanding any request by Publisher for change or substantiation, nothing in this Agreement shall be deemed to impose upon the Publisher any duty of independent investigation or relieve the Author of any of the warranties given or obligations assumed by the Author hereunder. The provisions of this paragraph shall survive the termination of this Agreement.

In four words: "Don't break the law." Ever. Period. Then this clause never comes into play. Some publishers include authors in their liability insurance, but even so any kind of lawsuit spells disaster for all concerned. The publisher places the liability on the author's shoulders, but in reality the publisher stands to lose both its investment in, and its profits from, a book forced off the market by an adverse legal judgment. If you do not plagiarize anyone else's work (or even your own from another work), and if you do not libel or defame another person, no one can successfully sue you.

Permissioned Material Clause

4. **Permissioned Material.** The Author will not include in the Work any material from other copyrighted works (including material from prior publishers, and co-authors or contributors who do not have separate agreements with the Publisher) without the Publisher's consent and the written consent of the owner of such material. The Author will be responsible for obtaining such written consents at the Author's expense. These consents shall be in a form and content acceptable to the Publisher, consistent with all rights granted to the Publisher in this Agreement and shall be submitted to the Publisher together with the manuscript for the Work.

Your audience wants to read what you have to say, not what others have said. Avoid the need for permission to quote, using only those small amounts of material from other sources that fall within the concept of "fair use" (a sentence or short paragraph from a published work). Gathering permissions not only takes a lot of time, but those charging permission fees can add immeasurably to your cost of manuscript preparation.

Editing Clause

5. **Editing and Publishing Details.** The Publisher will have the right, with respect to the Work, including reprints, revi-

sions, and new editions, (a) to edit the Work; (b) to publish the printed Work in one or several volumes and in a style deemed suitable by the Publisher as to paper, printing, and binding; (c) to produce other versions of the Work in formats and media to be determined by the Publisher; (d) to fix or alter the title, cover, packaging, and the prices at which the Work shall be sold and the quantities printed or produced; and (e) to determine the methods and means of advertising, marketing, and selling the Work.

Authors tend to worry about many of the details, especially interior and cover design, but if you have chosen a good publisher, you can rely on their expertise to do a good job in producing a handsome book. Again, as with acceptability, a strong working relationship with your publisher will allow for your input and suggestions along the way.

Author Copies Clause

6. **Author Copies.** The Publisher will furnish six copies of the Work to the Author without charge. Should the Author desire additional copies for the Author's personal use and not for resale, they will be supplied at a 40% discount from the retail list price. No royalties will be paid on such purchases. If the Author purchases copies of the Work for resale, the Author shall be entitled to purchase such copies in accordance with the Publisher's standard Special Sales discount schedules.

Most publishers will boost the number of author's free copies to twelve or even twenty-four. Remember that these are for your personal use and that your publisher will probably send free copies to reviewers, opinion shapers such as talk show hosts, and important figures in the field. If you plan to sell a lot of books yourself at workshops, seminars, or public appearances, you can usually ask for a better than forty percent discount on these books, up to fifty-five percent for one thousand copies or more.

Revisions Clause

7. **Revisions.** (a) The Author agrees to revise the Work, upon the request of the Publisher, if the Publisher considers it in the best interest of the Work. The provisions of this Agreement shall apply to each revision of the Work by the Author as though the revision were the Work being published for the first time under this Agreement. The Author shall provide the manuscript for the revision within the reasonable time requested by the Publisher. (b) Should the Author be deceased or unable or unwilling to provide a revision acceptable to the Publisher within the reasonable time requested, the Publisher shall have the right to have the revision prepared by another person and charge the amounts paid to the revisor against payments due or that may become due to the Author for sales of the revised edition, except that the Author's royalty for the first revision prepared without the Author's participation shall not be less than 50% of the royalties otherwise due hereunder, and the Author's royalty for the second revision prepared without the Author's participation shall not be less than 25%. The Author shall have no right to royalties on any subsequent revision. The Publisher reserves the right to continue to display the Author's name and likeness

and the name and likeness of the revisor(s) in revised editions of the Work and in promotional materials. (c) In the event that the term the "Author" includes more than one person, paragraph 7(b) shall apply only to any of the author(s) who is deceased or otherwise unable or unwilling to provide an acceptable revision within the time required by the Publisher. In such case, the Publisher may, at its election, have the revision prepared by the remaining author(s), on their own or with assistance from other revisor(s), who may also be designated as Author. In either case, the Publisher may charge amounts paid to the revisor(s) against the non-participating author's royalties, subject to the minimum royalty terms in paragraph 7(b). The publisher reserves the right to continue to display the non-participating Author's name and likeness and the name and likeness of the revisor(s) in revised editions of the Work and in promotional materials.

Again, in four words: "Revise your own book." If you won't or can't, the publisher can proceed on its own, as this clause prescribes. The wise author who does not want to do this work and retain full control over the work will bring on board a "junior" co-author before the publisher decides to do it itself.

In whatever manner a new author takes over, the original author's share of income might drop from revision to revision like this: 75%/25% for a second edition, 50%/50% for a third; 25%/75% for a fourth; 100% to the new author after that.

Other Royalty Clause

8. **Other Royalties:** (a) The Publisher may itself publish; broadcast by radio; make recordings, or mechanical or

electronic versions; publish book club and microfilm editions; make translations and other versions; show by motion pictures, television, or cable syndicate; quote and otherwise utilize this Work (in whole or in part, alone or in combination with other Works) and material based on this Work (the "subsidiary rights"), or permit others (including affiliates of the Publisher) to do so. If the Publisher or any of its affiliates exercises such subsidiary rights, the Publisher will pay the Author a royalty of 5% of the actual net cash received from such use. If the Publisher grants any subsidiary rights to third parties, the license fees and/or royalties received by the Publisher from such grant shall be divided equally between the Publisher and the Author. (b) On copies of the Work sold by the Publisher at a discount of more than 50%, irrespective of market or means, the Author shall be paid a royalty of 5% of the actual net cash received by the Publisher, except for sales as set forth in paragraph 9(f). (c) On copies of the Work sold outside of the United States, in English or a foreign language, the Publisher shall pay the Author a royalty of 5% of the actual net cash received from such sales. (d) Upon any sale or licensing of any copies of the Work or part of the Work for which a royalty is not otherwise specified in this paragraph, the Author shall receive a royalty of 5% of the actual net cash received by the Publisher for such use. If the use of a Work falls into more than one category set forth in this Agreement, the Author shall be entitled to the single highest applicable royalty.

This contract, both here and in clause A, lumps all subsidiary rights together, here dividing income fifty-fifty or providing a set royalty rate for certain sales. Other contracts break out subsidiary rights separately. In any case, only concern yourself with those opportunities for income that are likely to arise with respect to your particular book. If your book will not become a television miniseries, don't argue to retain that right or to gain a better than fifty-percent share of income from it. But if your book will appeal to a European or Asian audience, try to keep foreign translation rights if your Publisher does not plan to sell them itself, or, if it does, argue for a better than fifty-percent share of income, perhaps somewhere between sixty-five and eighty percent.

General Royalty Terms

9. **General Royalty Terms:** (a) As used in this Agreement, the term "actual net cash received" by Publisher shall mean the amounts actually received by the Publisher from the sale of the Work, not including taxes and freight. (b) If the Publisher excerpts, packages, or sells the Work together with or as a segment of another product, in determining the actual net cash received for the Work for purposes of calculating royalty payments, the Publisher will allocate to the Work that portion of the receipts which the Publisher determines to be the Work's fair value to the entire period sold. (c) Any royalties payable to the Author shall be subject to a reasonable reserve for returns established. (d) The Publisher may deduct from any amount due the Author under this or any other agreements between the parties any amounts that the Author may owe the Publisher for unrecouped advances, previous overpayment of royalties, subsequent returns, or charges payable by the Author. (e) No

royalty shall be payable for: returns, copies of the Work for the physically or visually handicapped. (f) No royalty shall be payable for copies of the Work sold at or about the Publisher's manufacturing cost plus royalties; (g) If the balance due the Author for any settlement period is less than fifty dollars, no report or payment shall be required of the Publisher until the next settlement period at the end of which the balance has reached fifty dollars. (h) The Author's right to audit or bring claim with respect to any royalty period shall be limited to a two-year period following the issuance of the report set forth in paragraph D.

Only two of the phrases in this clause should cause much concern: "reserve for returns" and "this or any other agreement." The return of unsold books from booksellers has become a nettlesome problem for most publishers, so they try to account for possible returns. What is "reasonable"? Ten to fifteen percent makes sense; twenty to forty percent does not. Therefore, try to insert a specific number that defines "reasonable."

"This or any other agreement" permits what the industry calls "joint accounting." If you plan to write more than one book with this publisher, strike this clause. Otherwise, the publisher can credit positive income from your first book to the unrecovered advance on your second book, and vice versa.

Whenever you feel that your publisher has cheated you out of income, you can audit the publisher's accounting records, but this usually costs more than it recovers. If you have chosen a reputable publisher, you can probably trust their accountants and competence, but since humans and machines can make honest mistakes, always study your royalty statement. Your agent or editor can help you read royalty statements, which differ radically from house to house and often seem to defy logic.

Booklet Clause

10. **Booklet.** The Publisher shall have the right to publish a booklet based on the Work, not exceeding five thousand words and consisting of excerpts from the Work or a condensation or abridgment thereof, for use as a premium or for sales in quantity. On any sales of such booklet, the Publisher will pay the Author a royalty of 5% of the actual net cash received from such sales.

Publishers rarely publish booklets, but ask your publisher if it plans to do this.

Electronic Versions Clause

11. **Electronic Versions Defined.** As used in this Agreement, electronic versions shall mean any and all methods of copying, recording, storage, retrieval, or delivery of all or any portion of the Work, alone or in combination with other works, including in any multimedia work or electronic book; by any means now known or hereafter devised, including, without limitation, by electronic or electromagnetic means, by analog or digital signal; whether in sequential or non-sequential order, on any and all physical media, now known or hereafter devised including, without limitation, magnetic tape, floppy disks, CD-I, CD-ROM, laser disk, optical disk, IC card or chip, and any other human or machine readable medium, whether or not permanently affixed

in such media, and the broadcast and/or transmission thereof by any and all means now known or hereafter devised.

This publisher, like so many these days, hopes to cash in on the increasing popularity of electronic dissemination of ideas. Much debate has erupted in the industry over the future of "electronic publishing." Ask your publisher about its current and future plans. Some publishers will insist on keeping electronic rights, even if they lack the ability to exploit them; others couldn't care less. Most authors need not worry excessively about the channel of distribution since whatever the future holds, authors who create content will receive payment regardless of the channel through which that content flows. Plagiarism can and does occur in new media, such as the Internet, and it will take some time for publishers, authors, and agents to ensure that they receive proper compensation for intellectual property.

Discontinuing Publication Clause

12. **Discontinuing Publication.** When the Publisher decides that the public demand for the Work no longer warrants its continued manufacture, the Publisher may discontinue manufacture, declare the Work out of print, and destroy any or all films, plates, books, and sheets without liability to the Author. In such event, and only after one year from the first publication of the Work, Author may request in writing that all rights granted to Publisher hereunder shall be assigned to Author. Publisher shall have six (6) months from receipt of such written request to notify Author in writing of its intention to put the Work back into print. If Publisher fails

to so notify Author within this six (6) month period, all rights granted to the Publisher hereunder shall be assigned to the Author, provided that all materials including artwork prepared by or at the expense of the Publisher (see paragraph 2) shall remain the Property of the Publisher, and discontinuance shall not affect the Publisher's right to sell the existing inventory of the Work or the rights of any party to whom the Publisher has previously granted any subsidiary right or license to the Work. If there is more than one Author under this Agreement, the Authors shall own the reverted rights jointly, unless otherwise provided below.

Any marriage can come to an end, and this clause details the terms for an eventual divorce when the book goes out of print. As with clause 1, you must obtain a formal termination of the agreement before you can publish the work elsewhere, but in no event do you owe the publisher any unearned advance money.

Non-Competition Clause

13. **Competing Publications.** The Author agrees that during the term of this Agreement, the Author will not contract for, publish, or furnish to any other publisher, any work on the same subject that will conflict with the sale of the Work. The provisions of this paragraph shall not apply to articles of less than seventy-five hundred words published in magazines or journals.

Authors often express concern that this clause prohibits them from writing and publishing anything else on the subject or from using their ideas in classrooms, workshops, seminars, or public presentations. However, "non-competition" clauses apply strictly to the copyrighted work in question, not to ideas, and they aim to protect the publisher from an author publishing a book that actually robs sales from the original work. Many successful authors aid the sales of a book by drawing public attention to their work, and many others boost sales of one book on a subject with a new and different book on that subject. Multiple book authors should consult their agents and editors to make sure that a new project does not compete with, but creates a synergy with, a previous publication.

No Publication Clause

14. **No Publication.** Notwithstanding anything contained herein to the contrary: (a) In no event shall the Publisher be obligated to publish the Work if, in its judgment, the Work contains libelous or obscene material, or its publication would violate the right of privacy, common law or statutory copyrights, or any other rights of any person. In such event, the Publisher shall be entitled on demand to the return of all monies advanced to the Author hereunder, and to terminate this Agreement, in accordance with paragraph 1 above. (b) If the Publisher, in the exercise of its editorial and marketing judgment, decides not to publish the Work after acceptance thereof, the Publisher shall give written notice to the Author of its decision. Upon such notice, (i) all rights granted to the Publisher hereunder shall revert to the Author except that all materials including artwork prepared by or at the expense of the Publisher (see paragraph 2) shall remain the Property of the Publisher, (ii) the Author shall be

entitled to retain any payments previously made by the Publisher to the Author under this Agreement as full compensation, and (iii) neither party shall have any further liability to the other under this Agreement or otherwise, except as set forth in any other Agreement between the parties.

This clause, like clauses 1 and 12, provides for possible termination of the agreement.

Option Clause

15. **Option.** The Author grants to the Publisher the option to publish the Author's next book-length work upon the same terms as those contained in this Agreement. The Author shall deliver a proposal and sample chapter for the new work to the Publisher and the option may be exercised by the Publisher by written notice to the Author within 60 days after receipt.

Should you allow the publisher an option on your next book? Most publishing agreements contain option clauses which are, in most cases, "toothless" (i.e., they do not restrict an author unnecessarily from marketing new book ideas). Publishers include such clauses because they feel that, having cultivated and developed an author, they should deserve the right of first refusal on future work.

Seldom will a publisher refuse to strike the clause entirely or agree to reword it in a way that both gives the publisher a chance to keep working with a prized author and permits a successful author some flexibility if the relationship should sour over time.

Beware of the unacceptable option clause:

> Author agrees not to offer any other full-length work for
> publication prior to the delivery of the Literary Work in final
> form and that the Publisher shall have the first opportunity
> to consider the Author's next (i.e., written after the Literary
> Work) full-length work for publication on mutually satisfac-
> tory terms. If, within 60 days following submission of the
> final manuscript for such work to the Publisher, or within
> 60 days after publication of the Literary Work, whichever
> shall be later, Publisher and Author are unable in good faith
> to agree upon terms for publication, the Author shall be free
> thereafter to submit such next work to other publishers.

This clause restricts an author unduly because it forces the
author to wait until after publication of a current work before
submitting a new idea, and it requires a manuscript rather
than a proposal.

Such a clause can be made acceptable:

> The Author agrees to submit to the Publisher a book pro-
> posal for the Author's next book before offering rights on
> the next book to another Publisher. The Publisher shall
> notify the Author within 60 days after receipt of such pro-
> posal whether it desires to publish the next book. If the
> Publisher within such period notifies the Author that it
> does wish to publish the next book, the parties shall nego-
> tiate in good faith with respect to the terms of such publi-
> cation. If within 30 days thereafter, the Author and the
> Publisher are unable to agree to such terms, the Author
> may offer rights to the next book to other publishers.

Sometimes an option clause concludes with "topping privileges," stating that the publisher can match any other offer for a next work. That can work to an author's advantage, since it provides a way to ensure top dollar for a future work while continuing a relationship with a current publisher.

If a publisher refuses to offer a contract for a next book under the terms of an option clause, then that cancels the clause entirely for any and all books the author may write in the future.

Joint Authors Clause

16. **Joint Authors.** For purposes of this Agreement, all authors are collectively referred to as the "Author." Whenever the term the "Author" refers to more than one person, those persons will be deemed to share equally in the royalties and expenses arising under this Agreement, unless a different division is set forth on the lines below. Notwithstanding the foregoing, royalties shall be divided as follows: _____.

Unless otherwise indicated in this Agreement, the rights and liabilities of the Author are joint and several, except that the Publisher shall be entitled to exercise its rights or remedies against or with the responsible Author.

An author working with one or more co-authors should have determined during the proposal-writing stage exactly who will do what on the book, assigning accurate percentages to each author. Co-author relationships often change as a project proceeds, and co-authors can be dropped, added, or reassigned percentages with a formal addendum to the contract, which the publisher will supply. From a publisher's point of view, the makeup of the author team matters less than the resulting work. Pick a spokesperson from your group to handle communications with your editor (and agent), and never ask your editor to settle any disputes that may arise among your team members. Your agent can, however, provide some "marriage counseling" when needed.

Assignment Clause

17. Assignment. The Publisher may assign this Agreement in whole or in part. The Author may assign this Agreement only upon the prior written consent of the Publisher, except that the Author may assign the right to receive any payments hereunder, upon written notice to the Publisher and under such reasonable conditions as the Publisher may require. This Agreement shall be binding upon the parties hereto, their heirs, successors, permitted assigns, and personal representatives.

In the event of a takeover or merger, a publisher's books and contracts remain intact as its assets. This means your contract is sold to the new owner along with all other assets. Some authors assign royalties to relatives or non-profit organizations, but they make sure to do it *before* they sign the contract. Otherwise, the IRS may frown on what might seem to them to be a tax dodge.

Law and Jurisdiction Clause

18. Law and Jurisdiction. This agreement shall be governed by the laws of the state of New York applicable to contracts made and fully performed therein and the parties agree that in any action or proceeding arising under or relating to this agreement, they shall be subject to the exclusive jurisdiction of the federal and state courts sitting in New York County, New York. In any such action, service of any papers by certified mail, return receipt requested, shall be sufficient, as will all other means provided by law.

Most American publishing legal precedents have occurred in New York, where most publishers operate. Your publisher may stipulate that its home state's laws apply. Regardless, any legal action must occur in that state, not your home state, which can pose a problem if three thousand miles separate the two of you.

No Waiver Clause

19. **No Waiver.** No waiver of any term or condition of this Agreement or of any breach of this Agreement shall be deemed a waiver of any other term or condition or any later breach, nor shall publication or continued publication or payment by the Publisher following notice or claim of facts which, if true, would constitute a breach of warranty, representation, or agreement of the Author, constitute or imply any waiver by the Publisher of any defenses, rights, or remedies.

All this really means is that any alteration to this agreement does not alter the rest of the agreement, and that the contract remains in effect even if a lawsuit against the author should arise for any reason.

Binding Agreement Clause

20. **Binding Agreement.** This Agreement represents the complete understanding of the parties with respect to the subject matter. No other representation shall be binding upon the parties. This Agreement may not be changed except by a writing executed by the Author and Publisher.

Many agents and authors ask editors to outline in a memo certain understandings, such as a general marketing plan. However, such a memo or letter does not bind the publisher to honor it unless it has been included formally in this agreement, usually in an addendum. Since this contract will bind you to your publisher, make sure you can live with every sentence in it. Contracts can be amended later, of course, but you should assume that what appears in this contract will not change except in an emergency, such as death, illness, or an act of God.

Advance Clause

21. **Advance.** The Publisher agrees to make an advance payment of royalties to the Author of $____, payable as follows: $____ upon signing this Agreement and $____ upon submission of a complete and acceptable manuscript provided, however, that the Publisher shall retain for its own account the first $____ otherwise due the Author under the terms of this Agreement. Should the Author not deliver a complete and final manuscript acceptable to the Publisher, the Author shall repay the unrecovered portion of the total advance upon demand. The provisions of this paragraph

shall not apply to revised editions of this Work, except that the Publisher may deduct any unrecovered portion of the advance from monies due the Author on sales of future editions.

Publishers typically pay advances in two installments, though they may insist on three or four in the case of a large advance (fifty thousand dollars or more). Advances represent an interest-free loan the publisher can recover though earned royalties. When calculating an advance, the publisher will weigh your "collateral" (your proposal), estimate conservatively how many copies the book will sell in six to twelve months, and offer a sum less than the royalties the book may earn in that period. For instance, an editor might project sales of seventy-five hundred copies in the first year of publication for a book carrying a list price of twenty dollars (a net of twelve dollars for a net-proceeds contract). A ten-percent royalty note would generate royalties of nine thousand dollars. The advance offer would probably then fall between five thousand and seventy-five hundred dollars. Sometimes this clause contains "joint accounting" language that allows a publisher to recover advances from this or *any other* book the author publishes with that house. You should always look for—and eliminate—such language so that a money-losing book does not rob royalties from a money-making one.

Agent Clause

22. **Agent Clause.** The Author hereby authorizes and appoints Mike Snell of Michael Snell Literary Agency, P. 0.

Box 655, Truro, MA 02666, Federal ID# 04-2724996 to act
as his agent and to collect and receive all sums of money
payable to him under the terms of this Agreement, and
the receipt by such person shall be a valid discharge in
that respect. Michael Snell Literary Agency receives 15%
of all such monies (as divided in paragraph 16). Such person is hereby fully empowered to act on behalf of the
Author in all matters in any way arising out of this Agreement, and is hereby designated as the Author's agent
upon whom notices regarding this Agreement may be
delivered. The designation of such person as agent shall
survive the incapacity (physical or mental) or death of the
Author, and may be terminated only upon written notice
to the Publisher signed jointly by the Author (or his heirs,
executors, administrators, successors, or assigns) and by
such agent.

Whether or not you have signed an agency contract, your
formal financial relationship with your agent becomes a part
of the publishing agreement. The typical clause provides for
the agent to receive and distribute monies, as this particular
clause does, though some agents prefer that they and their
authors receive their shares directly from the publisher.

NEGOTIATING WITH LEVERAGE

The scope of this book does not allow for a course on how
to negotiate, but you can do yourself a big favor if you
observe the following six rules when discussing contract terms
with your publisher.

Six Rules for Successful Negotiating

1. Behave like a friend, not an enemy. The contract you
end up with cannot capture the spirit of partnership that
creates a successful book. Approach discussions with the
attitude that you will capture more flies with sugar than
you will with vinegar.

2. Ask questions before you offer answers. Almost everything in a contract can be changed, but no publisher will
change everything in a contract. Probing questions will
elicit areas where your publisher can make changes and
those where it cannot.

**3. Focus on what really matters to you, not on trivial
issues.** If you ask for ten changes, you may get five, but
you may get the five that matter least. Argue over the five
that concern you the most and remain willing to give up on
the five that worry you the least.

**4. Know the difference between compromise and cooper-
ation.** Despite the wisdom of so-called "win-win" negotiations, many compromises represent a loss for both parties.
If two contract terms mean a lot to you, prepare yourself to
give in on one and stand firm on another. Sometimes you
come out ahead, winning all of A and losing all of B, instead
of losing half of both A and B.

5. Emphasize collateral, not dreams. Your proposal and
your talent mean more to a publisher than your ambitions
and aspirations. No better leverage can come into play
during negotiations than the tangible assets you offer the
publisher.

6. **Think long-term, not short-term.** Concentrate on those elements of your relationship with your publisher that will contribute most to long-range success. A book that wins a big advance but doesn't sell many copies will not help your career as an author, but a book that receives a small advance and becomes a bestseller will make you money and position you to make even more money with new books downstream.

Once you have worked out an acceptable contract, don't hesitate. Sign on the dotted line and get busy writing a great book.

SIGNING ON THE DOTTED LINE

Congratulations! You've found the right publishing house, you've decided you can work with your editor, you feel that your publisher shares your vision of the book, you see a nice fit between your book and the house's list, you like the marketing plan your editor has outlined, and you have worked out the best possible contract terms with the publisher. Sign the contract, put it in a drawer, and never think about it again. That may sound glib but, in fact, nine times out of ten you'll never need to look at that piece of paper again. And besides, now you can focus all your attention on the words that *never* appear in a contract but that do more than all the contract clauses in the world to make a book a success: enthusiasm (both yours and your publisher's), creativity (both yours and your editor's), respect (the foundation of a profitable working relationship), and effort (the hard work it takes to surpass your own, your publisher's, and your audience's highest expectations).

A wonderful example of the triumph of enthusiasm, creativity, and effort occurred in the early 1970s, when a Los Angeles textbook publisher launched an important new ethics textbook by a renowned philosopher at an Ivy League school. Editor Richard Stone (not his real name) sent the contract to author Joshua Weinstein (also an alias) and received it back within a week. Copies went into the publisher's and the author's files. Weinstein wrote the book, Stone edited and published it, and the book went on to sell over a hundred thousand copies over the years. The author happily cashed his royalty checks until one day he decided to review the clause in the contract that governed revisions because he had decided to bring aboard a junior co-author. Imagine his astonishment (not to mention Mr. Stone's) when he discovered that the inside two pages of the document were blank! He had signed a contract that committed no one to anything, but that fact did not hamper the eventual success of the book because the author and the publisher built a fine working relationship based on trust, not on some legal gobbledygook on a piece of paper. That philosophy may sound a bit too optimistic to authors who have gotten embroiled in legal problems with their publisher, but it does provide the perfect transition to the next chapter, How to Work with a Publisher.

CHAPTER EIGHT

How to Work with a Publisher:

The Process of Writing the Book and Getting into Print

Perhaps the most famous author/publisher arrangement was that between Ernest Hemingway and his editor for twenty years at Scribners, Maxwell Perkins. Midway through that long and productive professional liaison, Hemingway wrote a letter to Perkins, apologizing for one of his typical angry outbursts over a decision the publisher had made. "Please remember that when I am loud-mouthed, bitter, son-of-a-bitching, and mistrustful," Hemingway wrote, "I am really very reasonable and have great confidence and trust in you."

An author's relationship with a publisher follows the phases of a marriage: courtship, a formal contract, a honeymoon, a period of hard work to solidify the bond, the birth of one or more children, and, all too often, divorce. Like any good marriage, the quality of the relationship hinges on mutual respect, and, as Hemingway put it, confidence and absolute trust.

Once you have concluded the courtship and contract stages discussed in the previous chapters, you will enter the period of hard work that leads to the birth of your brainchild. The period breaks down into phases: completing an acceptable manuscript for your acquisitions editor; working with your publisher's production department as it turns your manuscript into a bound book; and coordinating your promotional activities with those of your publisher's marketing department. This chapter will explain the first two phases of working with a publisher in detail, while the next chapter focuses on the third phase.

COMPLETING AN ACCEPTABLE MANUSCRIPT

The first phase—working successfully with a publisher—requires four things from you:

1. Ongoing communication with your editor on progress toward completion of the manuscript

2. Dependable execution of contractual requirements

3. A responsive attitude

4. Patience

To understand what can go wrong when an author ignores these requirements, consider the fate of Joel Levine (an alias).

After signing a contract with Placid Publishers, Joel locked himself in a cabin in Montana and started pounding the keys on his typewriter. Six long weeks of fourteen-hour days later, he had a complete manuscript and triumphantly mailed the 490-page achievement to his acquisitions editor, Jennifer Stone (also an alias). Anticipating praise and congratulations from Jennifer, Joel called New York a week later to see what his editor thought of the book. Jennifer was in a meeting. The administrative assistant who took the message assured Joel a speedy return call. Two days went by, and no call. Joel called the editor again. Similar response. This went on for a full month.

In utter frustration, Joel called the editor's boss and demanded to speak with someone who knew what had happened to his manuscript. He wanted to know when he could expect to see the printed book. That same day, an angry Jennifer phoned Joel to explain that the manuscript had arrived four months earlier than expected. She hadn't had time to look at it yet, and assured the impatient author that she'd get to it as soon as possible.

Inside Joel fumed, but he saw no option but to wait for his editor's response. Six weeks later, he received a call from the editor's administrative assistant who asked Joel to send another copy of the manuscript—this time double-spaced, along with a copy on a computer disk, as specified in the contract.

When he learned that the administrative assistant had misplaced the original manuscript, Joel called the editor in a panic, threatening to sue the publishing house if the company didn't compensate him for his lost work. You see, Joel hadn't used a computer—and he had sent his only copy of the manuscript to the editor.

The editor retorted that if Joel couldn't deliver the appropriately formatted copies of a complete and acceptable manuscript by the contracted due date, the publisher would cancel the contract. To add insult to injury, she informed Joel that in that event he must return the advance he'd received (and already spent).

Joel went on to rewrite the book (on a computer this time) within the two weeks remaining in the schedule. The book was eventually accepted and printed, but not without bad feelings on both sides of the relationship. Joel never worked with that publisher again.

Although this may sound like an extreme case, it really happened. In order to avoid alienating your editor and others in the publishing firm as Joel did, you should learn to communicate with your editor before you complete the book; ask questions about format, process, and expectations; and learn how to submit a manuscript that's suitable for your publisher.

Acceptance of your book for publication depends on the delivery of a complete manuscript in appropriate format and on schedule as specified in the contract. In order to do this, you need to know the process your material will go through on its way from first review to approved submission. You also need to be aware of what you can realistically expect from your editor and publisher—and what you shouldn't expect. With realistic expectations, you'll get your book into production without undue frustration or delay.

Follow the Guidelines

To facilitate the acceptance of your manuscript, before your manuscript reaches the production department you must follow the publisher's guidelines. You or your agent should always ask your editor about style guide preferences and submissions guidelines *before* you prepare your manuscript for submission.

A style guide specifies preferences for grammar, punctuation, and word usage. Some publishers specify a standard style guide, typically *The Chicago Manual of Style*, as their house style. (Invest the fifty dollars and get a copy for yourself.) Other publishers employ their own house styles for grammar, hyphenation, and punctuation and are happy to provide you with a copy.

Submission guidelines include the publisher's preferences for the word processing (or typewritten) format of the manuscript, heading levels, page numbering, the specifications for numbering figures and illustrations, and the number of copies to be submitted. To get you started, your acquisitions editor may provide a document that details the publisher's manuscript preparation requirements. These guidelines vary in complexity from a list of acceptable word processing formats to a 150-page book on manuscript preparation, including information on hyphenation, word usage, heading levels, typefaces, paper, copying, editorial cycles, and even instructions for eliminating sexist words from your writing.

Each publisher uses different guidelines, so don't expect uniformity in the requirements of publishers. Ask before you blunder. The format you mastered at Random House may prove totally unacceptable for your book at Wiley. Some publishers leave the manuscript formatting to your judgment. Others want you to follow their standards—to the letter.

Failure to adhere to the publisher's specific manuscript submission guidelines may mean that you'll have to do substantial revision before the publisher will accept the manuscript. In extreme cases, the publisher may even reject the manuscript for failure to adhere to the format. Even if you prefer another style guide, say *The Chicago Manual of Style* as opposed to *Words Into Print*, your publisher expects you to follow the style of the house, not the style of your choice.

Sometimes this can be negotiated (through your agent); most times it can't.

The guidelines reproduced on the following pages from Prima Publishing, the publisher of this book you are holding in your hands, illustrates what you might expect from your own publisher. In order to implement these guidelines successfully, you must acquire and learn to use the tools of the author's trade.

Master the Tools of the Trade

Publishers expect you to be a professional. That means using the best available tools for preparing your manuscript. The days of writing with scratchy pencils on yellow legal paper died in the 1960s. Publishers no longer accept manuscripts written in longhand. Even typed (as opposed to word-processed) submissions are, at best, frowned upon by the few houses that still accept them. The era of the chattering typewriter withered in the 1980s as the efficient word processor evolved into a technology affordable to the less-than-wealthy writer. Because many publishers typeset their books directly from disk, most publishers expect—and some demand—that you use a standard word processing program on an IBM compatible or Apple Macintosh computer.

Today's publishers prefer computer disk submissions along with hard copy printout. The reason is simple: because most books are typeset electronically on computers, a typed manuscript must be completely retyped by the publisher. This costs money, wastes time, and introduces errors into the text.

With the ability to make changes and edit freely while saving multiple revisions in case an idea doesn't pan out, word-processing software on a modern personal computer allows

PRIMA PUBLISHING
AUTHOR GUIDELINES

Thank you for your interest in Prima Publishing. We ask that you follow these guidelines when preparing your manuscript and also suggest that you familiarize yourself with our current publications. This will give you an idea of the kinds of books we publish and the approach we take in presenting information to our readers.

Prima draws its strength from the collaborative efforts of its authors and staff. In the initial stages of the project, the author will receive preliminary direction from an *acquisitions editor* and, if needed, from a *developmental editor.* Once the manuscript has been received, a *project editor* will guide the author through the remainder of the production process, which includes author review of copyedits and page proofs. Feel free to call your editor at any time to discuss questions about style, mechanics, or manuscript appearance.

First Things First
The most important point to keep in mind as you work on your manuscript is to *always write with your readers in mind.* Who are they? Why will they want to buy your book? How much do they know about your subject matter? You will develop a relationship with your reader through your writing.

You must develop a well-balanced manuscript. Take the time to form a well-organized outline and table of contents. Your readers should find elements within your book that enlighten or persuade them, in a style that is clear and easy to follow. The book must be clearly organized with its parts connected logically to one another. Chapters should be as consistent in length as possible. Be concrete, direct, and efficient. Compose your sentences carefully. Make your prose readable, interesting, informative, and *lively*—banish the passive voice, use active verbs as much as possible, avoid overusing the passive verbs "is" and "are," avoid excessive prepositions, use adverbs sparingly, and use the pronouns "you" or "I" (rather than third-person constructions) whenever appropriate.

Manuscript Preparation
Submit to Prima *two* hard copy printouts of your manuscript that adhere to the following guidelines:

- Use clean, white, good quality 8½" × 11" paper.
- Double space and use a ragged right (not justified) margin.
- Indent the first line of each paragraph with a single tab—do not use extra line spaces ("hard returns") between paragraphs.
- Leave at least a one-inch margin on all sides.

- Indicate levels of heads with boldface type or italics that will avoid any misinterpretation by the copy editor or compositor. First-, second-, and third-level heads should appear different from one another.
- Use a clean, readable font, such as 12-point Courier or Times.
- Do not apply design styles—do as little formatting as possible. All text in your manuscript should appear in the same typeface. (You may use bold and italics, but don't change font style, point size, or use any software graphics programs.) Please do not use boxes, rules, or word-processor-formatted bulleted lists (see section on bulleted lists). Do not embed graphics of any kind within the text.
- Label each page with a header or footer that shows (1) book title, (2) chapter number, and (3) page number.

Disk Preparation

You must submit a 3½-inch floppy disk that contains an exact duplicate of your printed manuscript. The word-processing software Prima requires for text submissions is *Microsoft Word for Windows* (version 2.0 or 6.0). If you choose to use another word-processing program, you must be sure you can save your files in the Microsoft Word for Windows format. (Most current versions of word-processing software allow you to save your files in a number of formats.) Contact your software manufacturer's technical support or your editor at Prima with any questions regarding software.

As you prepare your disk, please keep in mind the following:

- Save each chapter as a separate file (i.e., as one document), labeled numerically in the order in which it appears in the manuscript, with the ".doc" extension used for Microsoft Word files (for example, "ch01.doc," "ch02.doc," "ch03.doc," etc.).
- Resist the temptation, passed down through generations of typewriting classes, of typing two spaces following each sentence (after periods or other terminal punctuation). There should never be more than one space between words *or* sentences.
- Separate columns with a single tab only. Do not worry if tables do not align perfectly—that will be fixed easily during typesetting if you follow this rule.
- Do not lay out (design) your manuscript. Do not format *any* text beyond the use of italics or, where absolutely necessary, boldface. Use the same, clean, readable font throughout. Levels of heads should be differentiated with capitalization and italics, etc. (see "Heads and Subheads," below).
- Always double space your text and format the right margin so that it is ragged (not justified). Do not use any hard returns at the end of a line unless you are starting a new paragraph.
- Label each disk with your name, the book's title, and the name and version number of the word-processing program used.

When you ship your manuscript and disk to Prima, do not use the U.S. Postal Service; use a traceable shipper such as Federal Express, DHL, or Airborne. Ship to your acquisitions editor at the following street address and include our tracking phone number (916-632-4400):

Prima Publishing
3875 Atherton Road
Rocklin, CA 95765

Special Elements in Your Manuscript

Contact your editor at Prima if you have any questions regarding manuscript appearance, structure, or style. Our job is to work with you to ensure that the final product meets with our, and *your*, satisfaction.

Heads and Subheads

Each chapter should open with introductory text that provides the reader with an overview of the topics to come. Following this brief introduction, it is wise to use headings and subheadings to break up the chapter into logical blocks of information that the reader can assimilate quickly. Think of headings and subheadings as sign posts that direct the reader quickly to a specific topic.

The main topics of each chapter should be discussed under first-level heads. Secondary points within a main heading should be discussed under second-level heads, and so forth. Each level indicates the relative weight, or scope, of the topic. As mentioned earlier, differentiate levels of headings through type appearance (for example, THIS IS A FIRST-LEVEL HEAD, This Is a Second-Level Head, *This Is a Third-Level Head*). Also, try never to stack heads without intervening text.

Lists

It is sometimes desirable to assemble short, cogent points into lists. The most common forms of lists are bulleted and numbered.

Bulleted lists are used to indicate a series of options, such as points in a theory or categories in a group. Although most current word-processing programs are capable of automatically creating bulleted lists, please do not use this feature; use hyphens or asterisks only, not bullets. Formatted bullets are often lost when the text is imported into the page layout software.

Numbered lists are used for items that should appear sequentially. As for bulleted lists, please do not use your word-processor's feature for automatically creating numbered lists.

Do not indent your lists or apply any formatting beyond hyphens, asterisks, or numbers. Avoid the use of tabs in lists.

Figures, Illustrations, and Other Artwork
All artwork must be delivered as camera-ready copy (CRC) or, if possible, in an electronic file format. Submit photographs as black-and-white or color glossy prints, slides, or as transparencies.

Electronic artwork should be submitted in one of the following file formats: TIF, GIF, PCX, or PICT (Mac). Make sure all electronic files are named appropriately (for example, "fig04-01.tif" would be the first figure in Chapter 4; "fig06-02.tif" would be the second figure in Chapter 6, etc.). *Do not embed any figures, illustrations, or other artwork within the text of your manuscript. Always submit artwork as separate files.*

Within the text files, figures must also be numbered sequentially throughout each chapter (for example, "3.1, 3.2, 3.3" for figures in Chapter 3). Every numbered figure must be referenced in the body text:

> The distinctive look of Lincoln's handwriting (see Figure 3.3) has been attributed by some researchers to physical ailments.

During page layout, each numbered figure will then be set at the top or bottom of the page on which it is referenced, or as close to the text reference as possible. Unnumbered artwork, usually small illustrations (no larger than one inch deep), can sometimes be placed in text directly after their references.

Each numbered figure usually requires a brief, descriptive caption. Place each caption on a separate line after the paragraph in which the figure is referenced:

> Figure 2.3. An example of Lincoln's distinctive handwriting.

Place your artwork in separate envelopes for each chapter. Make sure that all figures and envelopes are numbered and that their numbers correspond with those in the manuscript.

Footnotes
Do not use your word-processing software's footnote feature to create footnotes. Formatted notes can be lost when the text is imported into the page-layout program. All footnotes should be gathered into an electronic document labeled "notes.doc" and separated by chapter number:

> Chapter 1
> 1. Daniel Patrick Moynihan, *Family and Nation* (New York: Harcourt Brace Jovanovich, 1986).
> 2. See Alvia Branch, James Riccio, and Janet Quint, *Building Self-Sufficiency in Pregnant and Parenting Teens* (New York: Manpower Demonstration Research Corporation, 1984).

Chapter 2
1. See Kennedy's article, "The State, Criminal Law, and Racial Discrimination," Harvard Law Review, April 1994.
2. See my review of Derrick Bell's *Faces at the Bottom of the Well* on pp. 289–292 of this book.

When designating placement of footnotes within text, enclose numbers within square brackets: [1] Note that footnote numbers follow periods, as shown below. Please *do not use superscript formatting:*

The researchers found that their white blood cells were not able to inhibit the growth as efficiently as cells from patients who did not have the antigens in their blood.[1] When patients receive antibiotics, the level of cells increases and their blood system functions more smoothly.

Tables
Although tables should be typed directly in text, note that because of page-layout considerations, they will probably be placed at the top of the next new page. Therefore, assign each table a number with which it may be referenced in text:

See Table 5.1 for a comparison of the Democratic and Republican parties on fiscal matters.

Each table should have a title and, where appropriate, column headings. Use only *one tab* to separate columns, do not use spaces or multiple tabs.

As with small illustrations, *brief* tabular matter need not be numbered and can sometimes be set directly after its reference in text:

The U.S. dollar amounts and the Canadian equivalents for the four books described are as follows:

$12.95 U.S.	$17.95 Can.
$14.95 U.S.	$20.95 Can.
$17.95 U.S.	$24.95 Can.
$19.95 U.S.	$27.95 Can.

Do not border or box tables even if they will eventually be typeset that way. Embedded design elements present difficulties during the typesetting of your book.

Recipes
When preparing recipes, keep in mind the following:

- Supply a complete list of recipe titles organized by chapter.
- On your disk, save recipes within each chapter file; *do not save individual recipes as separate files.*
- Every recipe must have a title.

- If your recipe has a headnote (a brief commentary or introduction for that recipe), place it after the recipe title.
- List the ingredients in the order in which they will be used.
- Give the precise amount or quantity of each ingredient.
- Specify if items are peeled, cubed, grated, or chopped, before or after they are measured (for instance, "1/4 cup parsley, chopped" is a different amount than "1/4 cup chopped parsley").
- Always include the number of servings each recipe will yield.
- An excellent reference for cookbook writers is *Recipes into Type,* by Joan Whitman and Dolores Simon (HarperCollins, 1993).

Permissions

It is the author's responsibility to obtain written permissions and to pay any required fees for all previously copyrighted material included within his or her book. The use of brief excerpts from other publications is protected under the fair-use provision of copyright laws. However, please note that although a paragraph from a 400-page work may fall within fair use, a few verses from a six-stanza poem probably do not. The length and nature of the original work is the determinant for what is, and what is not, fair use.

Be forewarned that publishers are increasingly charging fees for the right to reproduce copyrighted material. Unless other arrangements have been made, the payment of these fees is the responsibility of the author. For this reason, we strongly urge you *not* to exceed the fair-use provision. Attached is a copy of Prima's "Permission to Reproduce" form for your reference. Begin seeking permissions early on—the process can take months. Signed copies of permissions letters for all copyrighted material must be submitted with your manuscript. Prima will not begin the publishing process until we receive all necessary permissions.

For more information, refer to the copyright section in the fourteenth edition of *The Chicago Manual of Style* (available at any library).

Summary

If you adhere to these guidelines, your book will pass through our hands quickly and end up on bookstore shelves in great shape. All these rules boil down to a few simple principles:

- Have a clear idea of where you're going.
- Keep it simple.
- Number everything clearly and logically so it can't get out of sequence.
- If you have any questions, *ask.*

Remember, you are not alone. The creation of a book is a team effort, and you are the most valuable player. We at Prima look forward to receiving your completed manuscript.

Publisher

Dear Permissions Editor:

I am writing to request permission to reprint the following material from your publication:

Author, title, date of publication. Include page numbers or issue number where material appears, if possible.

This material is to appear as it was originally published as it appears below [or with changes noted] in the following work, which Prima Publishing is currently preparing for publication:

Title of your work, author, approximately. number of pages.

This book is scheduled for publication in [**month, year**] in [**hardcover, paperback**] form at an approximate retail price of [**$00.00**] in a press run of [**0,000**] copies.

I am requesting nonexclusive world rights to use this material as part of my work in all languages and for all editions. If you are the copyright holder, may I have permission to reprint the material described above in my book? Unless you request otherwise, I shall use the conventional form of acknowledgment, including author and title, publisher's name, and date.

If you are not the copyright holder, will you kindly indicate where I should write to request reprint permission.

Thank you for your prompt response to this request. A duplicate copy of this letter is enclosed for your convenience.

Sincerely,

your name

The above request is approved on the conditions specified on the understanding that full credit will be given to the source.

Approved by: Date:

you to focus on writing instead of preparing the manuscript. If you *must* use a typewriter, get modern and buy one with a spellchecker, a full-sized display for editing your work as you type, a disk drive that saves disks in MS-DOS format, and the ability to format type through the use of an ink-jet printing head instead of keys or wheels. At this writing, such a machine costs three hundred dollars or less at discount office supply stores.

The Heart of the Writer: The Word Processor For computer-based writers, the choice of word processor is key to effective writing. While bare-bones word-processing software, such as the version included in Microsoft Works, will get you by for most writing, you may want something more powerful for book-length projects; a one-hundred-thousand-word manuscript will choke most inexpensive word processors and may crash your system. You can keep your book's chapters as separate files, but by keeping one contiguous file you will find it easier to restructure, fine-tune, and check for consistency. You can also automatically generate a table of contents and a rough, "first pass" index this way. However, a huge file can slow down your processor, and you also run a greater risk of losing everything if the file becomes corrupted. A full-blown word processor includes the following tools that any writer will find useful:

- **Powerful and thoughtfully designed style sheet functions.** A style sheet incorporates a series of settings for everything from paragraphs to multiple headlines. With one key-click, you can elevate twelve-point text to a twenty-four-point bold headline throughout the manuscript.

- **The ability to format and track footnotes easily.** Even if you don't need this ability now, who knows? You might need it in the future. Basic word processors lack this feature.

- **A spellchecker with a large dictionary.** The best spell-checkers find replacement words phonetically. Without this capability, you must enter a spelling that's very close to the actual word, or the spell checker will offer several useless suggestions if any at all.

- **A useful thesaurus with a large number of alternative words.** It's so much easier to have a computer look up a word's relatives with one command than to thumb a moldering paper thesaurus with the pages falling out!

- **The ability to see your document on-screen as it will print.**

- **A powerful find/change capability.** Your word processor should be able to locate words by their formatting as well as by spelling.

- **A split-screen option.** This allows you to view two separate sections of the open document at the same time. It's a powerful tool for axing redundant sections, looking for inconsistencies, and adding a thought to one section while writing another.

- **Conversion routines.** Your word processor should have the ability to convert word processing files saved in other popular word processing file formats.

Choosing a Word Processor   With more than one hundred word processors out there, which one should you pick? This number includes the freeware and shareware programs available from online services and writer's clubs, most of which aren't worth bothering with for all but the most cash-strapped authors. At this writing, the standard in the publishing world is Microsoft Word on both the Macintosh and IBM (Pentium) platforms. Since your publisher probably uses it, your choice of MS-Word provides full compatibility with most publishers. This compatibility ensures that complex elements in your manuscript, such as boxed text and footnotes that must flow and appear on the correct page, look the same on your screen as on your publisher's.

Runners-up to Word include the powerful Nissus for Macintosh and AmiPro for Windows. WordPerfect, once the most common word processor, is fading away through the failure of the company to keep it up-to-date. The same goes for WordStar—once the leading product on computers everywhere—which has faded quickly into oblivion.

Writing on a computer is easiest when you can see all or most of a full page at one time. For that reason, most full-time authors work on large monitors or portrait-style ones in which the monitor is taller than it is wide. A big monitor makes editing easier and results in less time spent scrolling. While large monitors were once hopelessly expensive and often incompatible with an existing computer (especially on the IBM PC side), a seventeen-inch unit can be had for several hundred dollars, and hook-up problems on new Macs and PCs are largely a thing of the past. Ask your equipment dealer to help you solve any problems that crop up.

WHAT SHOULD YOU SUBMIT?

If you write on a computer, submit one hard copy and one disk copy. Submit the disk copy on a 3½-inch floppy disk using either IBM PC or Macintosh format. Your publisher may ask for the file in a word processing format different from the product you use. Ask your publisher what format they prefer, and accommodate them if possible.

Most publishers prefer disks with relatively simple formats. Don't use a lot of different fonts, fancy styles, or symbols. Typesetters must modify or strip out these elements on their systems, so simpler is better.

Some publishing contracts stipulate that authors submit two hard copies of the manuscript; most publishers want just one hard copy and a disk. A new hard copy can easily be printed from the disk should that become necessary. Make a photocopy of the manuscript before submission, or print another copy for yourself.

For the typewriter user, make four copies and submit the original plus a copy to your publisher. Keep one copy, and give the other to friends living in another building. While it's unlikely that the submission will be lost *and* your house or office burn down, it could happen, as it did to novelist and Nobel Prize laureate Toni Morrison. Keep in mind also that publishers are infamous for losing manuscript pages. You will want a second copy so that you can resubmit missing pages. One incompetent house lost an author's entire edited manuscript. It turned up some months later in an empty office! (They lost another from the same author several months later that never did turn up.)

Pictures, Illustrations, and Charts

Make sure you've included all the elements that are to go in your manuscript, including footnotes, bibliography, resource lists, charts, tables, and sketches for illustrations or figures that the publisher will render into final form. Many publishing contracts call for the author to submit final versions of figures and illustrations, with the proviso that they will redo them at the author's expense if they don't accept what you've submitted. Since most authors can't provide reproduction-quality versions of even simple figures, you're better off making sure that your contract does not call for you to pay for rendering. In that case, you simply submit a clear sketch of the figure or diagram, which the publisher will turn over to a staff person in the production department to render into final form, often using a computer. If you really want to create the artwork yourself, be sure you get clear instructions from the publisher on house style and other requirements so that you don't waste your time creating something that will ultimately have to be redrawn.

Submit all photos and illustrations (whether final or conceptual) with your manuscript. Label them with a sticker on the back for easy identification. Number each piece of artwork and insert this number in the manuscript where the picture should go. Protect photos with tissue paper. Thirty-five-millimeter slides should be stored in protective envelopes taped to stiff backing paper. (Tape the covering, not the slide!) Film should be handled like slides, with a protective holder and backing.

Send manuscripts containing irreplaceable documents (photos, original artwork, etc.) via an overnight service such as Federal Express. *Do not use the postal system.* The risk is simply too great that important items might get lost or misrouted. Submitting your book via a registered courier that can verify delivery is also useful; the book might get misrouted within a large house, or the editor might quit and someone else could assume that your book is an over-the-transom submission and relegate it to the back burner.

The most important thing to keep in mind as you submit your manuscript and its accompanying materials is completeness. When anything is missing—whether text, a bibliographic entry, a date, or a figure—the publisher will have to come back to you for it, which could delay your project, cause last-minute problems, or result in an incomplete book. You get the picture. Your best insurance for a happy experience in working with the people who produce your book is to turn in everything in final form and ready to go. Production people love conscientious, tidy authors who make it easier for them to keep the book on schedule and within budget.

HOW LONG SHOULD IT TAKE?

New authors assume that writing the first draft of a book takes a year or more. While this may hold true for books that require extensive research and development, it's not true for most nonfiction projects. Notable exceptions include academic works and masterpieces of critical thinking, such as *Gödel, Escher, Bach: An Eternal Golden Braid*. Few publishers will even wait a year for an author to complete a general nonfiction book. Most nonfiction books are scheduled for delivery within six to nine months after signing the contract.

The time required to write a book depends on the nature of the book and your experience and ability as a writer. To make a good living writing books, you must streamline the process so that you can write a good 250- to 300-page manuscript in about two or three months. Does this sound impossible? It's not. A professional writer working a regular forty-hour week can easily accomplish this rate of production. This includes time for editing and proofreading. On a highly productive day, most writers churn out five thousand to eight thousand words of unedited text. An average book contract specifies an eighty-thousand-word book. Theoretically, a book could be produced in ten days with an extra two days for editing, keeping the time to less than a fortnight. In practice, few writers can knock off a good book without careful and deliberate research, thought, and revisions that may ultimately take less time than repairing something written hastily.

Some nonfiction books take longer because the project scope is more complex. These include:

- A first book, because you lack the experience acquired after penning several books.

- Books that require extensive research, such as investigative journalistic and scholarly books.

- Textbooks that require exercises, an instructor's guide, many pictures and charts, references, and extensive glossaries. Of course, you'll get help from the publisher with this type of book, and it will go through many review cycles.

- Books that require you to provide a large number of charts and illustrations.

- Books that require substantial rewriting and reorganization because your writing skills are weak. These may take forever. Hire an editor to help you sort out such a project.

The Proposal as a Template

The proposal you sold to the publisher should serve as your template for writing the book. Although few projects follow the outline to the letter and some, often on the editor's suggestion, digress significantly, for most books the publisher expects to receive the manuscript you outlined in your proposal.

Sometimes, as writing proceeds, the chapter outline in the proposal doesn't work as well as it should or a new idea pops up that wasn't previously considered. Minor changes and reorganization are permissible, but you should discuss any major changes with your acquisitions editor. If the house bought an apple and you unexpectedly deliver an orange, your manuscript may get rejected.

During the writing of this book, for example, the authors decided to eliminate a proposed section of answers to the most common questions authors ask. Rather than waiting until they completed the manuscript, they discussed their decision with their editor, who agreed that it would be redundant to the text and add unnecessary length to the finished work.

WORKING WITH A PUBLISHER'S PRODUCTION DEPARTMENT: THE SUBMISSION AND ACCEPTANCE CYCLE

As you proceed to work on your manuscript, on your own or with your writing partners, you should keep your editor aware of your progress and your completion schedule. If, for any reason, the delivery date differs from the date on your contract, let your editor (and agent) know of the new dates. As with bill collectors, if you're a cooperative author and you maintain contact, most houses will accommodate a later delivery date.

If you submit a complete manuscript, most trade publishers have a fairly short manuscript editing cycle. The publisher wants to get the book into print as quickly as possible, especially when a topic is timely or competition is heavy. For example, the number of books about the Internet grew from one in 1993 to about forty by 1994.

Longer cycles are associated with textbooks and books published by academic presses. As mentioned earlier, textbooks require extensive review by outside experts. Academic presses move slowly because they view their books as less commercial products than do mainstream houses. Where the length of time allowed from contract to manuscript delivery may be in months with a mainstream house, two years is not unusual in academic publishing, especially if extensive research or long, hard thought are necessary to create a worthy book.

In this era of desktop publishing, when a completed manuscript can be readied for press in less than a day, most publishers still take six months to a year to produce a book after acceptance because it takes that long to gear up the marketing machinery. One author, delivering a book completely typeset and ready for the printer, discovered eleven months later that the book would not be available for at least another sixty days because the lists for the next two seasons were full and the publisher could not possibly schedule this new book any earlier.

An author can do little to speed up the production process. Even a book that arrives early has nowhere to go until the publisher is ready to put the book into production and slot it for an upcoming list. While your title might be physically ready for production, your publisher needs to coordinate the manufacturing with internal promotional programs. The publisher needs time for its sales and channel-marketing specialists to develop promotional campaigns and to approach all potential buyers, from bookstores to book clubs, before it takes the work to the market. All this takes time, especially if the bureaucracy established in most large houses slows the process even further.

Who Produces Your Book?

After acceptance, your manuscript may be produced with in-house production staff or with outside vendors. As part of corporate America's downsizing trend, a growing number of publishers are using freelance editors for copy editing and outside production houses to do the actual assembly. Some computer-savvy authors receive compensation for designing and typesetting their own books—from five to twenty dollars per page at this writing.

Commonly, copy editing may be delegated to an editor's administrative assistant (who may or may not be good at it), and tasks requiring expensive equipment such as film output, may be sent out to a service bureau or print shop. This approach makes sense to publishers, since the equipment required for the task is expensive to buy, run, and maintain. And, like all technology, today's state-of-the-art production equipment finds its way into tomorrow's landfill. All in all, you can't blame publishers for distancing themselves from the high-tech side of production. Many bought expensive typesetting and production equipment in the 1970s and 1980s, and found themselves saddled with obsolete but unpaid-for computers and machines in the 1990s.

UNDERSTANDING THE PRODUCTION PROCESS

Once your manuscript is accepted and released to production, it will follow a (mostly) orderly series of steps until it reaches bookstore shelves. The production steps vary among publishers. Production is, to most authors, the nearly invisible process of transforming a stack of typed paper or computer output and pictures into a book. The simplest book consists only of text. A complicated project may require painstaking color reproduction, special handling, and offshore printing to save money. Take, for instance, pop-up books in which opening a page presents a three-dimensional image made on heavy paper. Imagine the work that went into writing, illustrating, designing, printing, assembling, and binding such a gadget! Even for a small, straightforward book, production takes time and costs money—especially if something goes wrong. For that reason, you should respond quickly to anything your publisher requests of you during the production cycle. You will be able to do so most effectively if you understand the eleven key steps in that process.

Production Step 1: First Submission of the Manuscript

Editors may request a sample chapter or partial manuscript for review before the complete manuscript is submitted for approval. While some publishers want to receive early, partial submissions in order to expedite the publication of the book,

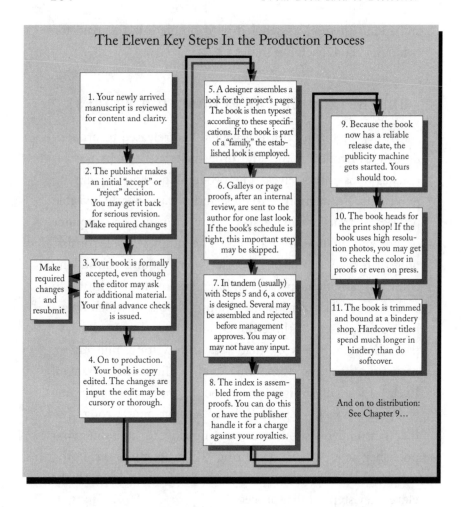

The Eleven Key Steps In the Production Process

1. Your newly arrived manuscript is reviewed for content and clarity.

2. The publisher makes an initial "accept" or "reject" decision. You may get it back for serious revision. Make required changes

3. Your book is formally accepted, even though the editor may ask for additional material. Your final advance check is issued.

Make required changes and resubmit.

4. On to production. Your book is copy edited. The changes are input the edit may be cursory or thorough.

5. A designer assembles a look for the project's pages. The book is then typeset according to these specifications. If the book is part of a "family," the established look is employed.

6. Galleys or page proofs, after an internal review, are sent to the author for one last look. If the book's schedule is tight, this important step may be skipped.

7. In tandem (usually) with Steps 5 and 6, a cover is designed. Several may be assembled and rejected before management approves. You may or may not have any input.

8. The index is assembled from the page proofs. You can do this or have the publisher handle it for a charge against your royalties.

9. Because the book now has a reliable release date, the publicity machine gets started. Yours should too.

10. The book heads for the print shop! If the book uses high resolution photos, you may get to check the color in proofs or even on press.

11. The book is trimmed and bound at a bindery shop. Hardcover titles spend much longer in bindery than do softcover.

And on to distribution: See Chapter 9...

most prefer that you submit an entire manuscript for review on or before the due date in the contract. If you will exceed this deadline, you should inform the editor the minute that fact becomes apparent. Missing a deadline by a few weeks almost never causes a problem unless you don't let the editor know about your delay. Remember: beating a deadline may not get your book into print any faster, because the publisher may not want to deviate from the original schedule for producing and marketing your book.

When the manuscript is received, it goes to your editor, either the acquisitions editor who purchased your book or another developmental or sponsoring editor assigned to your project. It may go through the normal production cycle or get "fast-tracked" if the book requires a quicker turnaround for marketing reasons.

When it arrives at the publisher, your manuscript adds to the pile on a harried editor's desk. If it arrives on schedule and the editor knows it's coming, it may be dealt with immediately, but if it arrives unscheduled or in the dog days of late summer (publishing vacation time) or a week before the publisher's twice-a-year sales conference, it may languish until the editor can get to it.

Over the next couple of weeks, you may hear nothing unless the editor looks through the submission and forms an immediate reaction, either positive or negative.

Production Step 2: The Initial Review of the Submission

The sponsoring editor reviews the manuscript as time permits. This varies from a cursory flip through the pages as though the manuscript were a deck of cards to a thorough line-by-line review with extensive notes and questions added to the margins. Your editor regards each project as a potential plus or minus on his or her salary or performance review, and depending on the house and your track record, the acquisitions editor may read the manuscript carefully or with a glance.

Manuscripts requiring an outside expert review are photo-copied for simultaneous reading. Textbooks are often tested on students—a slow process, but one that nevertheless produces worthy feedback that justifies the delay. Some houses also go through the laborious process of stamping the manuscript with page numbers, thus verifying that all pages are included and ensuring for subsequent readers that copied pages will not be left out, lost, or duplicated. (Surprisingly more common than you'd think.)

Production Step 3: Acceptance or Revision

After the review, the sponsoring editor makes one of these decisions: accept and proceed to production; demand changes, additions, or deletions; or reject the book outright. Most houses contractually provide a period of time for fixing "inadequacies discovered by the publisher." This is a key phrase, because it allows an author time to develop an acceptable manuscript. If rejection occurs, a phone call from the editor usually precedes a letter outlining the reasons for rejection.

Unless the submission is a complete mess, totally unlike what the editor was expecting based on the proposal, rejection seldom happens in the nonfiction world. Major revisions may still be in order, with the editor asking for deletions, additions, or changes, but still assuming that the manuscript will ultimately become acceptable for production. These changes vary from minimal tweaking to stylistic enhancements to a major rewrite. Cooperative authors consider all suggestions at this point, although they also argue for their position on a change if it differs from the editor's position but still makes sense. Most manuscripts require little additional work at this point outside of the copy edit, explained in Step 4.

If the editor accepts the manuscript as is, without asking you to do revisions, he or she then transmits it to the production department. Although you may not learn of this action immediately, and may only receive a phone call confirming acceptance of the manuscript, the formal acceptance is so crucial to honoring the contract for the book that you (or your agent) should ask for it in writing.

On transmitting the book to production, the editor tells the production department about the project—its market, specifications (length, number of colors, illustration or photo program, and other details), your profile as an author (including how technically or computer savvy you are), and when the book needs to be published. Anywhere between two and five copies of the manuscript wend their way into the production or managing editor's hands. This worthy person will be in charge of budget and schedule, including monitoring and managing all the people who will work on your manuscript, as well as the production processes that are involved. At the same time, the marketing and sales departments are alerted to your book's entry into the production process and its likely publication date. When the editor sets these wheels in motion, he or she is sending a "heads up" message to everyone. The book is getting "real."

Upon acceptance, you will probably be paid your final advance installment (within thirty to ninety days), although some smaller houses hold the final advance until the manuscript is completely edited and all photos and illustrations have been approved by the production people. One large house pays the final advance (as do many magazines) upon publication.

Production Step 4: Production and Copy Editing

The first stage of production is copy editing, which may or may not be done by the acquisitions editor depending on the size of the press. A good copy editor looks for every kind of mistake, from grammar problems to misreferenced chapter numbers in figures. If your manuscript arrives in an especially sorry state, two or more cycles of editing may be required. Copy editing may also flag inconsistencies and flaws missed by the editor in his or her first run through the manuscript.

At most houses you'll receive the original marked-up, copy-edited manuscript back since many editors work in pencil or in a pale blue ink too light to photocopy. Some now work on disk, and you'll see the edits as underlined changes on the new printout of your manuscript. Do not lose the copy-edited manuscript; you need to return it after you've typed in or approved the changes. Some houses only request that you review the copy editing and approve the manuscript for production. Other houses request that you input the changes on your own onto disk and submit a new hard copy, disk, and revised images and files if problems were flagged among your charts, photos, or illustrations. If you need to make changes to your book, now is the time, as changes get progressively more costly (to you and the publisher) from here on out.

Production Step 5: Design and Typesetting

After copy editing, and in some cases simultaneously, a designer (whether in-house staffer or freelancer) is assigned to create the type, graphic specifications, and overall look for your book. The physical dimensions (also known as the trim size) of the book have usually been set by the sponsoring editor or marketing department, so the designer is charged with making decisions about the interior margins, the choice of typeface for all elements from text to captions to lists to sidebars, heading style, spacing above and below headings, style for any graphics, and so on.

Designers, like their other colleagues in production, often work on computers and use page-layout programs. You can make a deal with your publisher to do the design and typesetting yourself (for an additional fee paid by the publisher), but you'd better be up to the professional challenge. The last thing you want is to have your book come out amateurish or inappropriate. Most publishers will want to see other books you've done before they'll entrust you with the design and typesetting. Even then, the house may choose to use their own service providers to do this part of production.

It's important that the design for the book be right for its market; a light-hearted humorous approach to dog training should not look like a technical manual for assembling a computer. The designer will also oversee the typesetter's work to make sure that the specifications are being followed as the book's type is assembled.

The design and typesetting stage of production can vary in length depending on the publisher and the complexity of the book. A long book with many illustrations and complicated typographical elements or highly technical content will obviously take much longer than a brief, straightforward, text-only work. You can ask your production or managing editor how long this stage will take and then plan your schedule accordingly. Some publishers also let you see the design.

While they won't give you the right of approval, they usually are open to hearing your suggestions, as long as they are reasonable and based not on personal taste but on the market or identity of the book.

Since books with color images require extra attention, they are typically handled by publishers who specialize in color books. Proposals for a coffee-table color book of desert images or art deco monuments will only work for houses that have produced similar works in the recent past. They will have the equipment and staff to handle the complexity of such projects.

Production Step 6: Galleys and Page Proofs

When the typesetter has formatted your manuscript on disk using the designer's specifications, a set of what are now called "proofs" of the typeset manuscript will be printed out. Before computer typesetting, a first set of proofs was called "galleys," which meant that the type was run out on long sheets without page breaks, artwork, special elements like sidebars, or page numbers. The author and proofreader would go over these galleys, which would then be sent back to the typesetter, corrected, and turned into "page proofs," i.e., made up into actual pages following rules about how many lines per page, how much text had to appear at the bottom of a page after a heading, where figures and photos were to be placed, and so on.

Today, most computer typesetting systems skip the galley stage and go right into page proofs. You're likely to receive page proofs for final proofreading and review, although some publishers now skip this step. (So be sure to look carefully and closely at the copy edited manuscript; it may be your last chance to make changes!)

If you do receive the proofs, you'll need to review them thoroughly and quickly. Depending on the sophistication of the typesetting system, the page proofs may contain all materials, including images, or only type. Most publishers will also use a professional proofreader (either in-house or freelance), so that you don't have to catch all the mistakes, but you might want to make sure that's the case. Very small and cash-strapped houses may make the author the only proofreader.

At the proof stage, you can only make the most essential changes because it is extremely costly to do more than that. If you make too many discretionary changes (usually five to ten percent of the total typesetting bill is the acceptable limit), they will be charged against your royalties. Changes at this stage are called ACs for author corrections or AAs for author alterations, as opposed to PEs for printer's errors or EAs for editor's alterations. You should make sure that you are not charged for EAs or PEs, since those are the publisher's responsibility. If there are many changes due either to ACs or EAs and PEs, a second set of page proofs may be sent after the changes have been incorporated. In any case, *avoid rewriting or editing your book once it has been set into page proofs!*

Production Step 7: The Cover

At page-proof stage, or sometimes long before, the designer or managing editor oversees the creation of your book's cover. A dust jacket may also be created if there is a hardcover edition of the book. You may or may not be asked for input or approval of the cover and associated text (called the "blurb") for the back cover. Sometimes a clause can be inserted in the contract requiring your review and comments on the cover, but rarely do authors get approval rights on the cover.

An illustrator usually creates the images for the cover, although photographs are commonly used as well. Once the elements are ready, a designer assembles the cover for the book. During the cover development process, your book may be retitled as well, with or without your consent. This book, for example, was retitled from the proposed title of *Get Published!* to the title you hold in your hand, *From Book Idea to Bestseller*. This was done with collaboration among the authors and publisher. The book's title and cover usually reflect the marketing department's input, with sales and marketing managers significantly affecting the outcome.

Production Step 8: The Index

As index is assembled at the page-proof stage because, for the first time, you can now determine the content of each printed page. You can do your own index or ask the publisher to handle it. If the publisher does it, you will be charged somewhere between three hundred and fifteen hundred dollars against royalties for this service, depending on the page count and the complexity of the index. (An average index costs the author about two dollars a page.) If the publisher has it done by a professional *indexer*, check it carefully; indexes handled by others often leave out important terms and references. For that reason, you should consider doing it yourself, even though the process is time-consuming and tedious. If you aren't good at detail work, the process and result might be better with a good professional indexer. A few publishers will do the indexing at no charge to you, provided you amended this part of your contract.

Production Step 9: Publicity and Promotion

Upon receiving page proofs (or even before), the publisher's sales and marketing team goes into high gear to assure a successful launch and entry into the market. If you follow the advice in Chapter 9, your own promotional efforts should move to "full steam ahead" now.

Check regularly with your editor to keep track of the launch date for your book. Since most titles appear on a Spring List or a Fall List, you can build your plans around a March or September publication. The obvious exceptions are seasonal books, such as *Santa Bear's Christmas*, which would be slow movers in Spring or Summer. Always remember that two markets must be persuaded: the booksellers and the book purchasers. Distribution firms and bookstore chains, which make buying decisions nine months in advance of stocking their shelves, should be approached sooner than the ultimate consumer at bookstores.

Production Step 10: Into Print!

After incorporating all the changes to the proofs, the finished pages are imposed in large sheets that can carry eight to thirty-two pages (called signatures) that will be turned into sheets of film to be used by the printer. For centuries, books have been printed with multiple pages on the same sheet. The book is usually printed at a large factory, often owned by another firm, that may be located far from the publishing company's headquarters. After the signature sheets have been printed, they are folded so that they appear in numbered order. Then the groups of folded pages are gathered into a complete book, trimmed, cut, stitched or glued together, and readied for binding.

Production Step 11: Binding

The folded and stitched books are now glued and bound to their covers. While softcover books may be bound with machines in one step, hardcover books require several steps to build the inside pages, mate them to a cover, and add the dust jacket.

Getting a book into print is a long, involved process regardless of the house involved, but finally the finished, bound books are shipped to the publisher's warehouse for distribution. Once in distribution, don't be surprised if friends call and tell you they saw your title in a B. Dalton in Papua, New Guinea.

CELEBRATING A MILESTONE

Congratulations! The process from idea to bookstore is complete. When you sold your proposal to a publisher you priced the champagne, and when you saw your manuscript go into production you bought a bottle of Dom Perignon. Now, with your published book in your hands, you can pop the cork. Of course, you will hope to buy another bottle to celebrate your first royalty check, and even a case if you build a successful career as a book author, but at this moment you have reached a major milestone. Enjoy it as much as Henry David Thoreau did when Ticknor & Fields published *Walden* in 1854.

No one had ever undertaken a project like *Walden*, so it would not have been surprising if the manuscript had garnered quite a few rejections. Such was not the case, because some foresighted editor at Ticknor & Fields took a gamble on the offbeat book and published it at its own risk in an era when authors often subsidized publication, even with an established house. It took five years for the initial printing of two thousand copies to sell out. Perhaps Thoreau's well-known defiant attitude helped launch his book without the usual series of rejections. As he wrote in *Walden*, "I do not propose to write an ode to dejection, but to brag as lustily as a chanticleer in the morning, standing on his roost, if only to wake my neighbors up."

Those words provide a perfect transition to the next chapter, How to Promote Your Book.

CHAPTER NINE

How to Promote Your Book:

The Tools of Marketing and Publicity

A number of authors have become legendary for their tireless efforts to promote their books: Covert Bailey, who once sold *Fit or Fat* from the back of his van as he crisscrossed the United States; Callan Pinkney, who promoted *Callanetics* on small radio and television stations before landing a spot on *The Oprah Winfrey Show*; and Susan Powter, who saturated the airwaves with an infomercial for *Stop the Insanity!*. Their books went on to sell millions of copies.

Smart promotion gets smart results for any book, as Robert Farson's story illustrates. After retiring to scenic Cape Cod, Bob grew fascinated with local history. Two unusual subjects drew his attention: the old railroads that had long ago disappeared from the Cape, and the building of the Cape Cod Canal. Years of research later, he could rightly claim to be the world's leading authority on both subjects. So, he wrote and self-published two books, *Cape Cod Railroads* and *The Cape Cod Canal*. Unlike Bailey, Pinkney, and Powter, who signed with top publishers (Houghton Mifflin, William Morrow, and Simon & Schuster), Bob knew that no major house would offer a contract for his book. For that reason, Bob spent and spends his time promoting his books himself at card tables outside B. Dalton, on local television shows, at local bookstores and libraries, and with small ads placed in specialty magazines, including one for model railroad buffs. For his modest but effective efforts, Bob has sold more than forty thousand copies of his books, banking *all* the profits rather than just royalties. Self-publishing probably will not work for you, but Bob Farson's promotional zeal probably will.

In a North American publishing world, where more than sixty thousand new English language titles appear *per year* (in addition to thousands of titles in print from previous years), how do you get your book noticed? With heavy competition for book buyers' dollars, you need to empower your book to fly off bookstore shelves. Other than shaping a well-written book on a timely topic, there are three ways to do this: promotion, promotion, and more promotion.

Without a carefully orchestrated program for building awareness, your book disappears like a polar bear in a snow storm. *With it*, bookstores will stock your book, and readers will reach for it as they browse store shelves or see compelling in-store promotions for your title.

Once you get your hands on your handsome, newly printed book, it's time for celebration, but not yet time to toast your success as an author. Getting the book into print presents only the first step toward making a profit from your writing. If you want to sell books, you must go all out to support your product in the market. After all, *you* are the expert who wrote the book, and that expertise qualifies you to tell people about your ideas. Getting the importance of your ideas through to people is the only way to sell books.

This chapter explains the basic mechanics of promotion and publicity, and will give you an understanding of the channels for book sales—which are more complex than most writers imagine. Books get sold in part, in advertising parlance, by "building awareness." This is the process of making potential readers/buyers aware of your book and convincing them to buy it. The complexity comes in because you're not the only author chasing that purchaser's MasterCard on a Sunday afternoon in a shop full of thousands of other books, uninterested salespeople, and a coffee bar. You get the idea.

Even with a publisher's marketing program on your side, you need to seize every opportunity to promote your book, or you are not likely to deposit any royalty checks in your bank account. Your publisher takes the financial risk to bring your book to market, and it secures the sales channels (bookstores, distributors, and direct sales promotions) for getting your book to the largest number of readers. All publishers provide at least basic marketing and promotional efforts at their expense. But you, in partnership with the publisher, shoulder responsibility for your book's success in the marketplace. Whenever authors blame their lack of success on a publisher's lackluster marketing efforts, they are shirking their job as co-promoters of their own product.

Of course, promotion is easier if you are a celebrity. Using a *publicist* (a media and promotion expert), William Shatner covered the continent stumping for *Star Trek Memories* with booksellers lining up to schedule signings. In the process, he signed and sold thousands of copies. For the unknown Jane Doe, who may lack substantial publisher support (i.e., promotional money), getting *Doe's Decorating Decorum for Christmas* noticed takes more personal effort, time, and financial investment. Still, with smart promotion, Ms. Doe might sell more copies than Mr. Shatner.

STARTING THE PROMOTIONAL PROGRAM

You've just finished reviewing the page proofs of your book. Your publisher expects you'll see the first copies on the bookstore shelves in about ninety days. You may think you're done, but now is not the time to rest. The promotion of the book looms ahead and may take more effort than actually writing your tome. You don't need to wait until the book is printed, either. There's no reason not to begin planning the promotion of your book as soon as the manuscript has been accepted for publication. You can schedule informational seminars, begin writing magazine articles, and start lining up media coverage that will help promote your book well in advance of seeing the book in print.

Most of the promotional hullabaloo should start just before the book reaches print, with appropriate media people from newspapers, magazines, radio, and television receiving review copies and maybe taking time to schedule an interview or write a review. If the book is high-profile, controversial, or timely, it may draw media coverage without advance publicity or other promotions. When this happens, as it did with the O. J. Simpson murder trial, the press will come looking for the author for an interview. However, it seldom works this way. In most cases, you must nurture press coverage on your own with publicity mailings, telephone calls, and persistent follow-up. Assuming your publisher is making at least some effort on your behalf, your efforts will assist in their effort to build awareness, with as little time and expense as possible on your part.

Yes, with the exception of big-name authors for whom the cash register bell tolls, most authors complain that publishers don't do enough to promote their books. It's usually true. Rather than sitting on the sidelines, smart authors take charge of the awareness-building program. The publisher's promotional team cannot afford to spend a lot of time on one book out of fifty because it must deal with a whole list.

With that all-too-typical state of affairs in mind, you need to plan a promotional program of your own that augments the publisher's efforts. Since you have only one book to promote, you can pick up the slack yourself. Why waste time and energy complaining when you can invest that time and energy blowing your own horn? Your goal should be to get as much recognition as possible at minimum cost, doing all you can to build awareness in the market (called *share of mind* in advertising and public relations circles) in order to pull your books through the appropriate channels.

UNDERSTANDING THE CHANNELS OF DISTRIBUTION

Promoting your book effectively depends in part on understanding how books get sold in today's market. You're fooling yourself if you imagine that Mr. and Ms. Smith, tired of weeding the garden on a Sunday of looming rain clouds, visit the local bookseller and pour over the shelves for the title that will transform a dull afternoon into an absorbing entertainment experience. Instead, books—like all modern consumer goods—succeed through aggressive marketing programs that build conclusive consumer awareness: "let's get this book!"

The Bookstore Channel

The most obvious channel for selling your book is the bookstore. To purloin a Raymond Chandler metaphor, the image of the pipe-smoking bookstore proprietor in the cloistered corner bookshop is as dead as last Christmas. Independent bookstores, except for a few niche stores and local gems around the country, have fallen on hard times as the super-bookstores and megachains have come to dominate the marketplace. Although you may lament the demise of the independent bookseller, you must still respect the power of the modern chain-store giants because the buyers in these chains can make or break a title almost overnight.

Most book buying in the chains is handled by managers at the corporate level. (Most local chain stores have next to nothing to say about what they shelve.) Thus, publishers court these corporate buyers in their offices, at book fairs, and with catalogs and promotional literature describing each season's new offerings. If these buyers don't know about your book, or don't see or understand the market for it, the chain probably won't carry it on its "in-stock" list.

Although the megachains often buy hot titles directly from publishers, most books reach market via book distributors such as Ingram and Baker & Taylor. In addition to courting the buyers at the megachains, publishers send an army of salespeople to the buyers at the distribution companies who "service" smaller, independent stores as well as the large chain stores. Since these salespeople represent hundreds of titles, an author can't expect them to spend too much time talking about one new work on African basket weaving. At most, you'll get a mention in the catalog—or if a salesperson falls in love with your title, he or she may give a sample copy to the buyer.

If the distributors think your book will sell, they'll order an in-stock supply. If the distributors carry the book as an in-stock item, the megachains often follow suit, and vice versa. A local or regional title may be picked up directly from a publisher or author by managers at individual stores within a chain, but this is becoming rare as the major distributors and corporate buyers in the trade increasingly dominate the retail book business. Take note: megastores now move an estimated eighty percent of books!

Individual bookstore managers, already up to their ears in unsold books but at risk for under-stocking the next bestseller, must make the "how many to stock" decision. Amazingly, there are more books in print than even a giant Barnes & Noble (Bookstar), Crown Superstore, or the Kmart-owned Borders can shelve. Most chains buy a select number of titles in volume at high discounts, with the right to return them if they fail to sell. A book that doesn't gather market momentum through promotion or celebrity appeal may be available to customers only through special order. If your book is relegated to special-order status, you should forget selling many volumes through the chains. To avoid this fate, you'll need to get the books moving through the bookstore channel on your own through signings, publicity, and other tools of the trade discussed later in this chapter.

Given limited shelf space, titles that move too slowly are quickly removed from the shelves and sent back for credit.

This reduces the financial risk of maintaining unsold inventory on which a bookseller must pay taxes. Your new book has only a few months to get moving out the front door in the hands of purchasers—or out the back door in boxes for return to the publisher.

Once a book has lived its natural life, and sales slow to a trickle, bookstores return or "remainder" unsold copies. (A book is *remaindered* when unsold copies of a book remain in the publisher's warehouse. Marked, punched, dyed, or damaged in the sales channel, remaindered copies are sold at deep discount to booksellers, destined for the "$5 and Under" table.) The natural life span of a nonfiction title can range from two months to the life of the copyright (forty years, under current copyright laws, unless an author or heirs renew the copyright). Books that live the longest generate steady but not necessarily spectacular sales. As returns begin to outstrip sales, publishers remainder the title, selling leftover copies to booksellers at a substantial discount while docking authors' royalties for *returns*.

Should your masterpiece fall flat in the marketplace and the publisher remainders it, instead of revitalizing it with a new edition, mailing you an impersonal form letter offering you a discount on additional copies, politely reclaim the title and its copyright. (Your agent can help you do this.) Then you have the right to update it and place the book elsewhere. If revisions are in order, re-propose the title with all those enhancements. It's possible that you delivered a good manuscript but the packaging, title, or promotional efforts fell short, or the market for your ideas may have shifted dramatically, causing a once strong seller to go out of print. Put the project away and revisit it later or have an expert look at the book and point out weaknesses or problems. Fix them and sell the title elsewhere!

Once your book goes out of print, don't feel bad. Almost every book, except perhaps the Bible, will go out of print some day. Even so, your book will live on in the hearts and minds of the readers who enjoyed the knowledge or the entertainment you provided. Since most books get read by more than one person, you have touched many more lives than your royalty statement reflects. Your book will probably wind up in the collection of many libraries across the continent. The Bakers use the online library systems to track which of their now out-of-print titles are checked out. Their first book, *How to Promote, Publicize, and Advertise Your Growing Business*, still in print, appears to be in perpetual circulation around the country. A few fans have even stolen copies from local library systems. These devoted fans keep copies moving through the library sales channel.

The Alternative Retail Channels

Not all books sold retail are purchased at bookstores. Avery Publishing rightly convinced on-the-fence cookbook authors Sunny Baker and Michelle Sbraga to go with his offer because his house sells titles through both bookstores *and* health food outlets. Rudy Shur of Avery Publishing explained, "There are only eight thousand bookstores in the United States, but more than thirteen thousand health-food stores." Howell Book House, which specializes in pet books, also uses alternative retail outlets to good advantage, selling as many books to Debbie's Petland as to Barnes & Noble.

You must think about every possibility for selling your book. Specialty shops such as Egghead Software may stock your computer book, but chances are slim that your publisher will contact any but the largest chain to make such a sale. Discount houses such as Price/Costco sell massive numbers of books, although they don't carry many titles. As an author, you can work with your publisher to develop these alternative retail outlets. Make sure the publisher hears and considers your ideas. If the publisher lacks motivation or energy to contact the buyers at these stores, do it on your own. You can send press releases or flyers to buyers, or visit corporate purchasing agents with a copy of your book in hand.

Kim and Sunny Baker's book on RVing, *The RVer's Bible* (Fireside) is sold at RV parks and the national Camping World chain, as well as bookstores and mail-order venues. If the book had been left to sell in bookstores alone it would have faltered. The Bakers knew how important the Camping World contact would be in assuring sales of the book to a major market. Thus, they made the initial contacts with the product buyers at Camping World on their own and helped the publisher's salespeople get the book on the shelves at every location across the country.

If your book is related to a specific product (computer software, pets, or recreational vehicles, for example), the book may also be sold through the product manufacturer or promoted in the manufacturer's packages or at specific stores that specialize in that product. For example, a book on building computer interfaces might sell well in hobby shops or electronic supply stores, or a book on weaving could be promoted through weaving clubs and sold in weavers' specialty shops.

Adams Publishing worked out a deal with Cardiosport, the manufacturer of heart-rate monitor watches, in which the company would buy and give away twenty thousand copies of Sally Edward's book, *Heart Zone Training*, with the Cardiosport logo on the spine of this "special edition."

If Burmese vegetarian cooking is hot (figuratively, not literally), then you may want to distribute the book on cooking shows, in cooking stores, and in specialty supermarkets. Your cookbook on pasta machines, complete with recipes, could be bundled with a pasta machine company's products. One author, rejected by house after house, opened his own store in the Southwest just to sell his book on desert flora and fauna. The one-book bookstore became a tourist feature in the town, and he sold over 100,000 copies over several years. His "unpublishable" book turned out to be a bestseller, but only after the author invented his own unique channel for distribution.

Direct Channels   Finding the correct mix of channels for your book takes effort and imagination, and it often pays to combine more than one. Even the most staid presses don't rely solely on bookstores to move their titles. Almost all publishers will try selling through book clubs or some form of direct mail. Typically, more than one channel will be appropriate for your publication. If your publisher doesn't exploit all the channels, then you should test them yourself through targeted promotional mailings and personal contacts. Roger Connors and Tom Smith, for example, sold over ten thousand copies of *The Oz Priciple* directly to their management consulting clients via direct mail and in seminars and workshops.

In short, anything that works is a viable channel. Convincing local tourist shops in Arizona to handle your *Ghosts and*

Legends of the Desert, even if you printed it on a photocopier and bound it at Kinko's, is as viable as going the traditional route through distributors and bookstores.

The only caveat to developing channels on your own is to make sure that you *don't compete with your publisher.* A publisher who has paid an advance, invested in manufacturing your book, and provided a reasonable promotional program will not want you to compete in the same channel for sales. For example, advertising your book through direct mail in the same publications your publisher uses to promote books to bookstores is not a good idea. In some cases, doing so may even violate a clause in your contract. Always make sure you know what promotion your publisher plans before you execute your own marketing programs. You want to *augment* what the publisher does, not duplicate their expensive, if mediocre, efforts.

LEARNING HOW PUBLISHERS PROMOTE BOOKS

Considering the time and expense required to promote a book effectively, what can you reasonably expect your publisher to contribute? What can you do to augment the publisher's efforts? As you saw in Chapter 6, you should ask these questions *before* signing the contract. The tools and tactics employed by the publisher will depend on the marketing budget for your book, the interest of the sales force, and your enthusiasm in working with the publisher.

Your publisher will probably use in-house marketing people, hire outside promoters, or put a combination of the two behind your book. Typically, an in-house marketing specialist establishes a strategy for reaching the market with the maximum impact at the lowest cost. Keep in mind that, since your publisher may not be an expert in your field, you should offer helpful suggestions for the process without getting too pushy. Just a typed list of influential publications popular among your book's audience can help greatly since your publisher's public relations (PR) machine may be unaware of them. You can take other steps to beef up your publisher's efforts, as you'll see later in this chapter.

Here's a typical publisher's promotional program for a book:

1. **A marketing budget.** A publisher allots money for marketing your book based on projected sales. You will never see your publisher's internal profit-and-loss estimate, which includes a dollar estimate for promotional expenses and a few notes and suggestions for appropriate promotional mechanisms. In the case of a really big book, this budget will be reviewed and refined by marketing professionals and/or an outside book publicist. Depending on you, your book, and your sponsoring editor's influence, a promotional budget may range from less than a hundred dollars for a listing in the publisher's catalog to $100,000 or more for a comprehensive promotional program with mailings, ads, and tours.

2. **A publicity plan.** A publicity plan is approved along with the rest of the numbers worked up by the publisher or editorial committee. You may or may not be informed of the details. The publisher will usually inform you of general publicity activities and provide you with copies of the press release for you to distribute.

3. A questionnaire for authors. Most houses ask that authors complete an extensive questionnaire that assists marketing personnel in better understanding you, your book, and your book's audience. Complete the document with care and enthusiasm. Add the relevant marketing pages from your proposal since the publicity people frequently won't have seen the proposal. Make it easy to digest. Keep the information relevant, succinct, and to the point.

4. The sales force. The publisher's sales team (or its commissioned sales reps) goes to work as soon as they have a cover design and a title. The senior salespeople (national account managers) pitch your title to large chain stores, book distributors, and even book clubs. These advance promotions help firm up the publisher's budget for printing and promoting the book.

5. A catalog listing for your book. Your book will receive a listing or a feature spot in the publisher's seasonal catalog. Typically, a picture of the book cover (sometimes revised before the actual printing) will be included in this listing. For books the publisher considers top sales contenders, a full-page ad may appear in the catalog and in industry magazines such as *Publishers Weekly*.

6. A press release announcing your book. For the most influential media contacts, a review copy of the book may accompany a press release. A particularly influential person may even receive a bound copy of the galleys or page proofs to review before the book makes it to print. Note: key reviewers—from Ann Landers (you're almost guaranteed a bestseller if she recommends your book in her daily advice column) to the reviewers at the *New York Times*—

receive a complimentary copy of the book, while the editors at the *Leadville Herald Democrat* and the *Bloom County Picayune* will receive press releases, if they receive anything at all.

7. **A direct mail program (if applicable).** For certain books, a program for generating direct orders for the now-in-print book may be handled in-house by the publisher or through a separate fulfillment outfit that specializes in this sort of marketing.

8. **Publicity events (optional).** These may include an author's tour, interviews and book signings, interviews with National Public Radio, an appearance on *The Today Show*, and book signings at bookstores and trade shows related to your publication.

9. **Ads (occasionally).** For those books that the publisher really believes will become bestsellers, ads may appear in major media outlets appropriate for your book. Ads are placed early, as most publications' ad submission deadlines predate publication and arrival in bookstores. (Self-publishers take note: ads placed too early may frustrate buyers who think, "I must have that book today!" If the book is still at the printer or bindery shop you can't sell it, and not everyone will want to wait.)

10. **Store promotions (if the title warrants the expense).** For "hot" titles or impulse purchases, publishers may provide point-of-sale displays to promote books in the store or at the checkout counter. Consisting of cardboard or plastic display units, these feature your book and make it more visible in a bookstore jammed with other titles. Such displays can boost sales considerably, but such

expensive promotions are seldom used for first books by unknown authors. Of course, you can always go into bookstores and make sure your book is in the right location on the shelf and turned face-out for display.

11. **Ongoing promotion (unlikely).** If your book is successful, you'll get more promotion from the publisher. Although this might not seem to make sense, the more you don't need promotion, the more money a publisher will throw at promoting the book. If your book sells on the first round of promotion, you might see a secondary or repeat set of ads and direct-mail programs to attract a wider audience. This depends in part on the book's initial reception and the original promotional budget. Big books—because of ongoing sales success—receive ongoing promotional dollars. Smaller ones must make it on their own.

SUPPORTING YOUR PUBLISHER'S PROMOTIONAL CAMPAIGN

Most publishers welcome and applaud promotional activities by authors on behalf of their books. Before offering this help, ask your publisher what activities it will be instigating to promote your title. Explain that you are not second-guessing the process or trying to control it, but that you simply want to do whatever you can to improve effectiveness. (If you have an agent, he or she may help in this process or at least provide seasoned advice for you to follow.) Also explain that you don't have a lot of money to work with, but you will be delighted to fill in however you can to benefit the book. Your publisher will be pleased by such a cooperative attitude and possibly decide on a press tour or book-signing it hadn't previously budgeted. A positive and helpful attitude also makes selling your next title to the same house that much smoother!

Consider the seven steps you can/should/must take to assist in promoting your new book:

1. **Provide vital marketing information in a timely manner.** Fill out the publisher's marketing questionnaire in detail, even if it means sending what appears to be redundant information to the publisher's promotional specialists.

2. **Know what your publisher is doing.** Do not duplicate the publisher's promotional activities. A press release from more than one party on the same book is okay, but you must avoid contradictions at all costs.

3. **Return calls promptly to media and promotional staff.** If a salesperson calls from the publisher, respond quickly to his or her queries. If the press calls, have answers for difficult questions ready in advance. Be available; a busy journalist may not have the time to call you twice. Questions from the media that come from left field may require a call to your publisher to discuss the situation. Get the media person's number and promise to call them back the same day. Then, after consulting your publisher, call back with the official answer. For instance, suppose you have written a book about mid-career job loss, as William J. Byron did. If a reporter calls you after reviewing *Finding Work Without Losing Heart* and asks you to identify an anonymous suicide mentioned in the book, you may want to talk to your publisher about the propriety and legality of doing so.

4. **Learn to handle the press professionally.** If your book is highly controversial or gossipy, refer press queries to your publisher, publicist, or attorney. Obey this rule even if you're taking out the trash at 6:00 A.M. and a reporter (or worse, the opposition's counsel) pops up from behind the dumpster, tape recorder in hand.

5. **Be cooperative.** Make yourself available when the publisher schedules signings and speaking events if they make economic sense. Ask about reimbursement of expenses before you make your decision.

6. **Trust your publisher.** The promotional materials your publisher assembles for the book may seem inappropriate. You can ask for changes, but if the decision is cast in stone, it's better to drop the issue than fight it. Let your agent (if you have one) argue your case. Otherwise, you may be dismissed as a "difficult" author. Note: if something is totally out of line and you have rational, easy-to-understand arguments against it, use them while maintaining a pleasant approach. One major complaint per title is acceptable if handled calmly and professionally.

7. **Act on every appropriate opportunity to promote your book.** Keep your eyes open for new sales channels, new speaking opportunities, and new publications to inform with press releases. Countless promotional opportunities arise for your book if you know how to recognize them. Act quickly because the chance to "make news" is ephemeral and evaporates faster than rain in the desert. An opportunity ignored is a sale lost forever.

The Persistant Self-Promoter

As an author, you must bear some of the responsibility for effective promotion of your book. You know the markets better than the publisher, and what appears to be a lukewarm effort on the part of your house may represent their best effort in an unfamiliar market.

There's no type of promotion you can't do yourself. All it takes is time and careful cost control to get the most bang for the buck. Many times you can do a better job than a publisher's promotional department because you are focused on one title, while the publisher's publicist may be simultaneously responsible for twenty or more titles. The downside is that, as an unknown writer, you'll need to deal positively with rejection as you take on a world-weary press with little inherent interest in your book.

Repetition and persistence are important in getting your book noticed. While an editor or columnist may ignore releases on your first or second book, on number three they may remember your name, look up your previous releases in a file, and do an exclusive piece on you and the book. Sometimes a phone call to follow up a release mailing or a fax will get an editor to sit up and take notice. Incidentally, it doesn't matter if the same editor receives a press release from you *and* the publisher. In fact, unless they are contradictory, they usually serve to reinforce each other. (See The Press Release later in this chapter.)

If your publisher won't take out ads or handle publicity for you, you can handle the task yourself. You can take out small and inexpensive display or classified ads in trade and specialty magazines directly related to the topic of your book. If you wrote *How to Raise Your First Llama,* ads placed in *Llamas Magazine* and *The International Camelid Journal* could prove inexpensive and cost-effective.

EMPLOYING THE PROMOTIONAL TOOLBOX

Once you understand the channels available for selling your book and have determined your publisher's plans, you need to make sure the buyers and decision-makers within each channel see your book. To do this, you can employ a variety of persuasive promotional tools. You've heard the phrase "Use the right tool for the job." The same goes for publicity and promotion. A creative set of tools and techniques, like those that move everything from toothpaste to Cadillacs, can move books through the various channels. First you need to understand the promotional tools at your disposal, then you must learn how you and your publisher can best put them to work in each channel of distribution.

Most promotional programs employ more than one tool to reach the potential audience and reinforce the message. Multiple tools reach more buyers because your message appears in more than one place. This chapter presents only a handful of the tools and techniques available to you as a promoter. Consult Kim and Sunny Baker's books, *How to Promote, Publicize, and Advertise Your Growing Business* (Wiley) and *Desktop Direct Marketing* (McGraw-Hill), and Jeanette Smith's *The Publicity Kit* (Wiley) for more details on promotional tools and step-by-step advice on putting them to work.

Promotional tools fall into two major categories: those that cost almost nothing except your time (publicity, public relations, and public speaking) and those that require money to employ (advertising and special events). Since most new authors can't reach into deep pockets for promoting their books, they first exploit the free tools of publicity and public relations. If you're a self-publisher, you'll probably have to use both the free and the more costly forms of promotion to sell your book, as you won't have the benefit of the publisher's distribution and promotional machinery on your side.

Publicity and Public Relations

Not every author wants to drive Route 66 in search of the perfect promotional opportunity. Working the day job and minding the kids precludes extensive in-person promotion unless you can take a vacation from work and hire a nanny to mind the little ones. But there's good news: you can do a fair amount of public relations and publicity on your own, from home, using only a fax machine and/or a few rolls of stamps.

Publicity and public relations are the easiest and least expensive promotional tools for your book. You can assemble a press release about you and your book, photocopy it, and mail it to editors and other interested parties. Just getting written up in the local paper after sending a release helps to sell books. If your book is interesting enough, the newspaper will send over a reporter and photographer to shoot your mug and ask you questions for a feature article on your work.

The mailing of book announcements and press releases to a carefully selected list of magazine and newspaper editors, reviewers, media representatives, bookstore managers, and retail marketing personnel is also the single most powerful promotional tool for your book. Your press releases and book announcements can compel reviewers, feature writers, and book chains to write about your book for free. Almost every publisher will send out a press release for a new book, but only with your help and enthusiasm will these press releases create the strongest impact.

Many publicists mail to a massive mailing list (purchased, rented, or compiled through years of experience) of interested, potentially interested, and disinterested parties. This list always includes the obvious: editors at major newspapers, influential magazines such as *Time*, and "experts" (a mention in their $295-per-year newsletters is like a blessing from the Vatican). The list may also include a "hit or miss" mix of specialty magazine writers, freelancers, and *stringers*. (A stringer is a near-full-time freelance writer for a publication.) The approach of mailing to a huge list of everyone and their dog is a standard shotgun tactic, which occasionally pays off with a handsome write-up in an influential *second-tier* publication such as *Wolverine World*.

You should be ready to answer press queries at all times. Keep your book near the telephone along with a detailed statement of your own credentials and background. When the press calls, they'll ask fairly predictable questions about you and your book, so you'll want to anticipate their questions and construct the answers ahead of time. A good press release often triggers those questions for the press, saving them valuable time and focusing them on what *you* want to talk about. To understand the press better, read the book review section in the Sunday newspaper. Observe articles mixing descriptions of books with biographical sketches of the authors. Prepare yourself to provide the same sort of information on you and your book.

Good press, no press, bad press, or a middling report may arise for your efforts. There is also the "puff piece," which simply announces your title to the world with no intelligent editorial commentary (better than nothing). Any mention of your title can sway readers, listeners, or watchers to hunt for your title at the bookstore.

Remember this: controversy gets noticed, but PR is not within your control. The more exciting, controversial, or high-profile a topic, the better the chance that editors and programming management will run a piece on the book and its author. PR is a hit-or-miss affair because busy, jaded editors and programmers decide whether your subject merits audience attention. You can increase your chance of getting "hits" by following up your press mailing with some phone calls to key people on your list, stressing what is newsworthy about you and your book.

Public relations is a matter of bending the right ear at the right outlet at the right time. Someone in the marketing department of your publishing house will probably ask you for the names of people, publications, and companies where you think press releases should be sent. Take this request seriously. Develop a complete list of people and places where your book announcement might strike a nerve. The more detail the better. Verify with the publisher that the announcements will be sent to the right people. If the publisher chooses to leave people off the list for reasons of expense, then you may want to send releases and announcements to these people on your own.

Choose ten to thirty key publications that deserve your special attention or that of your publisher's publicity people. This list should include the most influential publications directly related to your book's subject. The idea of the list is not simply to add important names to the publisher's mailing list, but to highlight media outlets that deserve a press release, a sample copy of your book, and an engaging follow-up phone call from a honey-voiced publicity specialist or yourself.

Keep an up-to-date, comprehensive database of contacts on your computer at all times. Look everywhere for names. Get business cards from people at trade shows and media events. Peruse the mastheads on the first few pages of print publications for editors' names. Put contacts for TV, news-papers, magazines, Web sites, and online services on your list. Any of these media will be willing to run your "news" if it fits their audience demographic. Keep your personal mailing list up to date in order for it to remain effective.

You may want to augment a publisher's local publicity endeavors with a personal note from you. Try contacting the book reviewers in the local newspaper, and approach the producers of literary programs such as *Books, Etc.* on PBS, produced in Phoenix, Arizona. Most cities boast one or two business-specific newspapers that review business titles. Educational television, local radio stations, and National Public Radio (NPR) affiliates carry segments on books. Even local television news shows often produce short segments on new books published by local authors. Live talk radio, syndicated NPR shows, and newspapers and magazines should top your publicity list of promotional possibilities.

The Internet and the World Wide Web offer new opportunities for publicity. More and more press information is distributed through electronic media. Use these mechanisms if you are proficient at simple computer programming, or buy time from an electronic "bulk-mailing house." For more information about this technology, consult one of the books recommended in Resources for Writers. You can also hire a "wirehead" proficient at both promotion and online media to conduct your online campaign for you. You have two online options:

- **Start a World Wide Web site.** Every major bookstore stocks titles on using the Internet as a marketing channel. On the World Wide Web—the multimedia portion of the Internet—you can incorporate pictures, text, sounds, and even video to promote your book to the growing legion of "Net surfers." However, even with an astounding graphic Web site, you must still attract people to your site by both providing an "address" and motivating them to visit. This is accomplished by advertising your Web page via online registration in search engines (Yahoo!, WebCrawler, etc.), distributing announcements or classified ads on commercial services (i.e., America Online), and conducting conventional promotion such as paper-based press releases and ads. To assemble a Web site yourself, look for one of the many books on the topic that includes not only instruction but software. Or, as mentioned, hire a professional to do it. The programming is simple, but you'll need a scanner to convert pictures such as your book cover and your photo into electronic format. For best results, the site must exhibit some skill in graphic design.

- **Mail to e-mail users.** A growing number of providers allow you to mail text-based messages to users on the Internet and other services such as America Online and Prodigy. Search with any search engine (Yahoo!, WebCrawler, etc.) under keywords such as "Bulk Mailing," "Mailing," and "Advertising" to find such services. Note that this scattershot approach may reach 1,500,000 users, few of whom have any interest in your book and who will be annoyed by the continual stuffing of their mailbox with all kinds of unappetizing offers. On the other hand, the approach works for some titles.

The Press Release The press release is a one- to three-page document describing the book, the book's merits, and contact information. Sent to influential media, it contains everything an editor needs to write about the book and its author. It's designed to supplement a review copy of the book or to motivate an interested party to ask for one. Summarizing the book and profiling the author, it provides the necessary fodder for a busy press person to write about the book without actually reading it. (Sad, but true.)

A well-written press release includes a *hook*—a compelling reason why the work is important and/or why the recipient *must* read and must *report* on the project. Consider these sample press release "hooks":

- For a book on breast cancer: "Each minute one woman is diagnosed with breast cancer."

- On cats: "100 million pet owners can't be all wrong—the cat is now the most common *and* most loved pet in America!"

- A movie review guide: "100,000 movie reviews in one compact book, perfect for a Saturday night trip to the video rental store."

- A tell-all autobiography: "I walk the streets, sell myself, *and* I have HIV—you might meet me sometime soon, in a fashionable part of Manhattan. I'll be waiting . . . ."

The following sample release (for a real book) accomplishes the essential goals of a good press release:

- Trumpeting the newsworthiness of the book
- Grabbing a busy editor's eye with a hook headline
- Providing contact information
- Stating the date of release (aged press releases are discarded unread like aging book proposals)
- Telling what the book is about
- Giving biographical information on the author
- Supplying ordering information in case the book is "picked up" for publication or broadcast analysis

---

Kim Baker & Sunny Baker
8000 NORTH DRIVE, PHOENIX, ARIZONA 80002

News Release

New Book on Home-Based Entrepreneurs
Features Arizona Tycoons

Phoenix, Arizona, January 22, 1993: Local authors Sunny Baker and Kim Baker announce the release of their book, *Million Dollar Home-Based Businesses: Successful Entrepreneurs Who Have Built Substantial Enterprises from their Homes* (published by Adams Media, Holbrook, MA). The book chronicles the astounding success of nearly 100 home-based entrepreneurs, many of whom are located in the Phoenix metropolitan area.

The upbeat rags-to-riches stories featured in *Million Dollar Home-Based Businesses* demonstrate that almost anyone, given enough persistence, can prosper in today's tight economic times. Most of the businesses started with less than $5,000, and some as little as $100, in start-up capital. Many of the profiled entrepreneurs were unemployed, laid off, or otherwise down-but-not-out when they started their businesses from backyards, garages, lofts, or back bedrooms.

Page 1 (continued)

The Bakers wrote *Million Dollar Home-Based Businesses* to provide role models for people who would otherwise give up on their futures and to inspire people who are just thinking about starting home-based businesses but are not yet convinced that they can make it on their own. The businesses profiled from around the country range from mundane to unbelievable, but all of the entrepreneurs share common traits of perseverance, a fierce need for independence, and a willingness to take risks. The 260-page book retails for $9.95 and is available at most major bookstores.

Background on the Bakers

Sunny Baker and Kim Baker have published over twenty books with major publishers in the last five years. Other recent titles include *College After 30* (Adams Media), *The RVer's Bible* (Simon & Schuster/Fireside), *How to Promote, Publicize, and Advertise Your Growing Business* (Wiley), and the bestselling *Color Publishing on the Macintosh: From Desktop to Print Shop* (Random House). When they aren't writing books, the Bakers operate their home-based consulting firm, Baker & Baker, where they specialize in developing marketing programs for high technology start-up companies. Sunny Baker (Ph.D.) is also a professor at Florida's acclaimed Barry University. The Bakers commute between their residences in Phoenix, Arizona and Harbor Island, Florida.

The Bakers welcome opportunities for book signings. Call the publisher to schedule yours.

See us on the Web at: http://aol.com/aolusers/kim_baker/kshome.htm!

If the book is not available from your favorite distributor, copies can be ordered directly from Adams Media. Call 1-800-872-5627. The ISBN is 1-55850-246-8.

Page 2 (last)

Press releases should be photocopied on crisp white paper and stapled if more than one page is required. Mail them First Class for timely delivery, or consider a fax-based mailing list (but only if the list provider has permission from the "faxees" to "mail" to them). At this writing, online press release distribution is increasingly common. Some electronic mailing services send messages as bland text without logos or personalization of any kind. In that case, your important book news shows up wearing a T-shirt for an occasion that mandates a tux. Choose a service that makes your release look good, or do it on your own.

The Press Kit   A press kit is simply a combination of elements that further explain the book and may include the book itself. It supplies not only a press release, but supplemental photos, summary charts from the book, reprinted book reviews, maybe a sample chapter, and other ingredients that add useful information in case an editor decides to review or announce the book. The pictures from *Wind Power: Sailing the Caribbean* may be so visually compelling that yacht or cruise magazines or the color travel section of a newspaper may "pick them up" for reproduction in a write-up or review.

A press kit is usually presented in an 11" × 17" folder with pockets for protecting and presenting the enclosed materials. You'll find colorful folders at larger paper stores and paper distributors such as the Avery Paper chain store, and even at stationary superstores such as OfficeMax although the selection there will be smaller. You can glue a color photocopy of your book's cover to the folder cover. Your publisher may even agree to print extra copies of your cover for this purpose.

One software maker who sells "software fixes" for large computer installations sends a package of information as a "software maintenance kit"—complete with a bottle of aspirin, instant coffee, Post-It Notes, pencils, and paper clips. Once opened, press information folds down from the lid of this humorous press kit. A cookbook publisher includes a nonperishable candy made from one of the book's recipes. These innovations get press kits noticed, especially if they arrive during a migraine or forty-five minutes before lunch!

Pictures and videos are the most compelling components of any press release or press kit. An editor on a late night deadline, into his or her third cup of coffee, may open your envelope, ignore the release, and look at the pictures. Suddenly, a light goes on and the news release and other information gets "press"!

But how do you submit pictures in the era of computers? Actually, technology has made life easier; you can submit your "pix" (as they're known in magazine circles) in many formats, including 8 × 10 prints, 35mm slides, transparencies, or on computer disk. If the last option is employed, the picture should also be reproduced as part of the kit so that interested parties don't have to load the disk on their computers to see what's on offer. Video footage is also common, with interviews or shots of the book's "Dramatic results! I lost five pounds in five days . . ." presented in one-inch professional video (NTSC) format compatible with broadcast TV.

More Free or Near-Free PR Opportunities

In addition to press releases and publicity announcements, you can add a number of other free or low-cost promotional tools to your repertoire. Most of these work best after your title is published and available in the sales channels. These promotions take time. As you try out the promotions, use those tools that reap the most contacts (or sales) for your effort. After all, you still need time to propose and write your next book.

Book Signings   One of the most visible promotional tools is the book signing. Sometimes book signings are more fun than profitable, but all authors should try to include signings in their promotional program—especially immediately after the book is released.

"Oh Madge. Look! *It's the author!*"

Madge: "I've been dying to meet you—I *loved* your book!"

That author could be you, even if it involves no more than walking into bookshops, asking for the manager, and proffering a copy of your baby at the right moment to engage an event three Thursdays from this Friday. With a "thank-you," a copy of your photocopied book "poster," and a promise to appear, you launch a fledgling tour. Hitting the Des Moines bookshops on a quiet Wednesday morning could net a tour of ten shops from an outlay of just ten dollars worth of gas. Of course, advance notice of your signings should go to the local press along with your standard press kit and anything the bookstore creates, such as a flier or press release.

Whether remaining local or traversing the country à la Charles Kurault, you meet your public, sign copies of your book, and watch a smiling clerk usher customers to the cash register on their way out. Your publisher may help arrange book signings for you and sometimes pay travel costs to tour you around the country, but most of the time you'll need to set up your own signing schedule, with or without the help of a freelance publicist (whom you pay).

In general, setting up signings is easy. Assuming that you are an author with a book available through a major distributor, are reasonably personable, and are flexible on dates, you can set up appearances at most bookstores. A signing brings in customers and adds an element of excitement to the otherwise uneventful shelves of books and shuffling of feet on soft carpet. It's less easy to get people to come to your signing. That's why publicity is important, letting your market know you'll be there signing copies of your book for no extra charge, in a comfortable setting where readers get to meet you in person.

Before every signing, make sure the bookstore has copies of your book on hand. This sounds obvious, but authors have arrived for signings at stores that had no copies to sign. The problem can be partially mitigated by bringing your own copies with a promise from the bookstore manager to replace them. Of course, it doesn't take long to run through twenty copies that way, so make sure that, like Covert Bailey, you have plenty in the trunk of your car.

Interviews You or you publisher can arrange a tour on which you are interviewed on radio and television, engage in live call-in talk shows, and sometimes appear at special events such as fairs, charity events, and speaking engagements. Radio shows are often taped over the telephone. You can contact radio and TV editors with a press release announcing your book, then make a follow-up phone call to discuss your availability. Be persistent, but always be friendly. Take advantage of as many of these opportunities as you can. There may be a fee provided by the organizers of special events, such as a workshop or luncheon speech, ranging from a stipend (one hundred dollars or less and a free can of Coke) to a significant speaker's fee (one thousand dollars or more), especially if you are an expert or a celebrity.

The authors of this book regularly give talks, seminars, and interviews on publishing and getting published. More rewarding

Breaking Through

Deborah Swiss, author of *Women Breaking Through* (Petersons), developed what she called the "source strategy." Deb learned through promotion of her first book, *Women and the Work-Family Dilemma* (Wiley), that newspaper and magazine writers are always desperate for lively quotes from experts on topics they're researching. She constructed a list of over one hundred writers, culled from every periodical from *Redbook* to the *Miami Herald*, and sent each a personal letter offering her services as an authority on women's issues. Over one year's time, her name and the titles of her books appeared a few dozen times in everything from the *Worcester Gazette* to the *Wall Street Journal*.

than any speaker's fee or any number of books sold at the seminar was a card from a woman who attended a seminar in Southern California: "Your Bookstar (Barnes & Noble) workshop was a turning point for me in my commitment to writing full-time . . . thanks *so* very much!"

Trade Shows and Book Fairs   The publishing industry conducts a number of regional book fairs and annual events for promotion. Taking place in Chicago (the national Book Expo, formerly the American Booksellers Association), New England (the regional New England Book Fair), and as far away as the largest international fair in Frankfurt, these offer a wonderful chance for you to promote yourself. The book fair reveals what's hot in publishing and puts you in contact with editors, agents, and publishers. Your publisher may ask you to sign your books at such a fair or event. This provides a great opportunity to promote your title with book buyers and anyone else who stops by your publisher's booth. (You can rent show space and assemble a booth of your own, but this requires advance planning, as many spaces are sold out years in advance. Significant money is also required to build, ship, and assemble a credible trade show booth.)

Your book may also be promoted at a specialized trade-oriented show. If you're a rocket scientist, you can promote your book on rocket engine chemistry by signing books at the publisher's booth at an engineering conference, or make a formal presentation as part of the program. You can set up these promotions on your own or with the help of your publisher or a freelance publicist.

Seminars at Bookstores, Schools, and Clubs   To promote this book, we present seminars in nonfiction publishing at writing conferences, bookstores, and community colleges across the country. Seminar attendees receive an hour's free publishing advice and get a chance to ask general questions on publishing. Many attendees purchase the book for additional advice, along with its sister publication, Jeff Herman's *Writer's Guide to Book Editors, Publishers, and Literary Agents* (Prima). The seminars have helped sell the book. In fact, your copy might have been purchased at such an event (and the authors appreciate that).

If the topic of your book lends itself to a seminar format, consider that option. Bookstores and schools are always looking for ways to bring people in the doors. In the process, you'll meet lots of potential customers, get copious feedback you can use for future book ideas, fuel the sales channels, and create additional publicity.

If you use your book to promote a fee-based seminar, lecture, or other event, consider selling copies of the book at the event. Give customers fifteen percent off the cover price so they will buy now instead of putting off their purchase until the next trip to the bookstore after the title is forgotten. Some seminar leaders buy their books from the publisher at the author's discount (forty to fifty percent off the retail price) and either sell the books at the event or give them away to attendees, building the cost into the price of the seminar.

Making Personal Contact A publisher's or distributor's sales force may get behind a book and promote it by phone and face-to-face contact. Bonuses sometimes reward salespeople for moving many copies of a particular title. As an author working with a publishing house, you have no control over this process unless you can afford to offer a bonus plan to stimulate the sales efforts.

Again, most publishers will not permit authors to have any interaction with their sales force, though most will introduce you to the representatives in your hometown or at a publishing trade show or book fair. However, you can sell your book directly by promoting it at author signings and at seminars. You can also introduce yourself to bookstore managers and show them a copy of your masterpiece. If you take the latter approach, leave behind a copy of the book's press release. It will expound on your book's attributes and provide contact information and ISBNs for ordering.

If you're told that a store deals only with distributors, ask the bookstore manager for contact information for the distributor. If you can afford a few long-distance phone calls, pitch your book directly to the distributors and chain store buyers—but make sure you don't interfere with the publisher's sales force. Do this only with your publisher's permission. Then send a press kit (described earlier in this chapter) and try to reach the decision-maker by phone a few days after the mailing.

Promote your book to everyone you meet. You can create all sorts of inexpensive fliers and handouts. Pam Gilberd, author of *11 Commandments of Wildly Successful Women*, obtained a proof of her book's cover design from the publisher. She then took it to a print shop where she had it printed on one side of both calling card and postcard stock. As she traveled the country on a ten-city tour sponsored by her publisher, Macmillan, she handed the striking red-and-yellow cards out to everyone she met: people sitting next to her on airplanes, reporters, interviewers, booksellers, bookstore customers, audience members at speaking engagements, and even cab drivers. (One young Boston cab driver, working her way through Harvard Business School, promised to buy six copies as Christmas presents for her classmates.) Pam also enclosed the cards with a letter to two hundred magazine and newspaper editors to whom she offered her services as a "source," following Deborah Swiss' "source strategy."

If you have a book of local interest, there's no reason why you can't walk into tourist shops or other retail stores and offer it for sale. Just give the owner the information on ordering the book from the publisher. Many retail outlets will take a chance on your book. If you travel this road, keep careful records of which stores have books, the inventory quantities, store owner/manager names, and the store phone number. Check back every two weeks to ensure that the store and books are still there. When working through a publisher, if the store is likely to handle your book in quantity, provide the publisher's sales force with contact information so they can service the store. Remember: never interfere with or duplicate the efforts of the publisher's sales force, but look for opportunities they missed.

Advertising—It's Not Cheap, But It Can Pay Off

The promotions discussed thus far cost little or nothing, except for your time, the postage on large mailings, and the travel expenses if you tour the country. Advertising is never free, but it often pays.

You should consider two kinds of ads for books: those that build awareness among the people making book-buying decisions, and those that convince retail book buyers (consumers) to visit a bookstore or pick up the phone and place an order. Industry ads are carried in bookseller's journals, such as *Publishers Weekly*, which woo book chains and stores to stock your title. Consumer advertising entices readers into buying copies. Ads may appear in print or be aired on radio or television. As mentioned before, publishers support few nonfiction books with advertising because they believe that ads do not sell books and are too expensive.

If you can't get a publication to write about your book for free through a press release, then you might consider paying for the ad on your own. Take a book on baseball for example. The book is a natural for *Sports Illustrated*. But your publisher may not have the $19,500 for a one-time ad in such a publication. However, if you have an inexpensive ad venue in mind, say a quarter-page in *The Baseball Club Newsletter* for only $145 an issue, that targeted ad might pay off, as it did for Bob Farson in the *Model Railroaders Newsletter*.

Despite the cost, advertising can offer a profitable method of promoting your title. In an era of declining ad revenues in print media publications, most rates are surprisingly negotiable. While *People* or *Parade* may not offer a significant break, small magazines like *Model Railroader* do it all the time.

The process of placing an ad can be as simple as making a phone call to the local newspaper's classified department or as complex as hiring designers, copywriters, and production personnel to assemble a multicolor ad for national magazines or an infomercial for TV. Really expensive ads, like those that run in major magazines or on TV during the Superbowl, require sophisticated testing to ensure that the audience reacts correctly and positively to the message.

Assuming you're limiting an ad to placement in a modest medium, such as a magazine or newsletter for hobbyists, professionals, or local readers, here are the steps to follow:

1. **Identify the most appropriate publications.** Contact each possibility for a media kit. This kit includes pricing and technical specifications for ad placement. A small black-and-white newsletter won't have a media kit, but you can discuss add pricing and "specs" (specifications) over the phone.

2. **Choose the right venue(s) and dates for your ad.** Choose a size (full-page, half-page, quarter-page, etc.) and

negotiate a price. Published price sheets serve only as
guidelines at most publications. The rules are simple:

- Offer fifty percent of the published price on the ad rate
  card and bargain up from there. If the publication is
  unyielding, offer politely to take your ad elsewhere; if
  that does not win you a reasonable discount accept the
  standard rate or move on.

- The more ads you run, the lower the price. Negotiate
  the discount for multiple placements as before.

3. **Get the ad format specs.** Since space is sold by the percentage of a page or by the column-inch, an ad created for
   publication A may not fit in publication B without wasting
   considerable space around the edges.

4. **Create the ad according to the specs.** Choose an experienced desktop publisher to handle this chore unless you
   have significant experience in design. Make sure this person follows the magazine specs to the letter. Ask the publication to review the completed ad for possible problems.
   Ask an expert printer about your design if you're not experienced in print production. If placement in multiple publications is in order, ensure that each ad conforms to
   publication requirements. An ad that runs in several publications may need to be modified for each.

5. **Check that the ad ran, and verify that the print quality
   is adequate.** Should problems arise, pleasantly inquire
   about where the problem occurred. Did your designer
   make a mistake in not meeting the publication's guidelines, or did the publication experience a production or
   press problem? Either way, unless there was a design mistake and the designer was you, a discount on the designer's

---

In-house Talent—Should You Use It?

When contemplating placing an ad in print, broadcast, or online media, you may be tempted by the advertising media provider to use their in-house design services. Depending on the complexity of the ad, spot, or other advertisement, these services may be included in the price of the placement. Since in-house production is often weak or inept, avoid this approach unless your budget is too tight to cover an outside agency. Read local throw-away newspapers for examples of poor in-house print ads, and watch late-night cable-only channels for examples of bad production.

---

or publisher's bill is in order. Typos are not covered, unless you use a professional writer and that person was responsible for proofing the ad before printing. (If nothing else, at least get the book's title and contact information right!)

Hire a Producer for Broadcast Media You need the services of an expert to place broadcast commercials be they for radio, broadcast TV, cable, cable information channels, or online computer services. First, the choice of media placement is complex. Second, the production requires the skills of seasoned professionals. Should you plan a video-format ad, you may find the "spot" producer managing you. That's why you should hire an experienced producer after weighing the merits of such a commercial spot.

Manage the production budget carefully. Today's $10,000 quote for video production may escalate into tomorrow's $103,817.29 bill once the job is complete. Careful analysis of the total budget for filming, production, and placement is vital lest you run out of money before reaching your market. L. Ron Hubbard's *Dianetics* is promoted successfully through television, but it has the resources of the Church of Scientology to pay the substantial bills.

Direct Marketing and Direct Mail

Most books not sold through stores are sold via mail-order campaigns that use direct-response ads or mailings to targeted mailing lists. For example, book clubs sell all their books through direct mailings. Other publishers, such as the Business and Professional Division of Prentice Hall, have constructed efficient and well-funded mail-order operations. They send out fliers, catalogs, card packs, and other direct-mail promotions to sell their books. Many small or medium-sized publishers will try to sell a book directly and save the markup normally offered to the bookstore.

Ads and Direct Sales   A good direct promotion incites an impulse buy—"Hey, that's just what I've been looking for!"—and motivates buyers to pull out their credit cards and pick up their phones. A small ad in the right place is a powerful direct-sales promotion, especially if you include an 800 number for ordering and set yourself up to accept charge cards. A reader of whatever publication can act instantly and buy your book.

Direct Mail You can augment your publisher's direct mailing efforts with your own. We suggest reading books on direct-mail promotions before you take on such a venture, for example, the Bakers' book *Direct Desktop Marketing.* Postage will probably be your largest expense. With a successful direct-marketing campaign you can expect a response from two to ten percent of the people who read your mailer. Calculate your profit from the mailing based on the two-percent response level and see if your mailing makes financial sense.

You can assemble a mailer as simple as a postcard or as expensive as a color brochure or catalog of your publications. The Post Office will explain your mailing alternatives and associated costs for different types of mailing programs.

The direct-mail process follows a series of steps for getting from concept to print to recipient. Note that when "mail" is mentioned, any kind of delivery mechanism is acceptable if it's appropriate and cost effective. Options include anything from handbills placed on residential doorknobs to complete press information. (See Press Kits previously.) The process includes:

1. **Choosing a market for the mailing.** This market should closely resemble one of the targets that appeared in the "The Market" section of your book proposal.

2. **Preparing the mailing list.** Acquire a mailing list (assemble, rent, purchase, etc.) that closely matches the profile of your intended market. Mailings can be made to an audience as limited as "editors of the business pages of newspapers with a circulation greater than fifty thousand readers" to "consumers who expressed an interest in reading on a warranty card from an appliance purchase." The format of

your mailing labels must meet postal system requirements; this information is available from your local post office.

3. **Producing the mailer.** Almost anything can be mailed: a fancy color brochure, floppy disks with pictures and interactive narrative promoting your book, or a postcard, greasy with black marks from the mail. The only requirement is that the mailer be persuasive and motivate the recipient to take action: buy, order, or request more information on your title.

4. **Mailing the pieces.** The mailer (of whatever kind) is sent to the mailing list through the selected channels. This may consist of as little as several rubber-band-wrapped stacks of envelopes to piles that require a tractor-trailer to deliver to the Post Office.

Avoid Bulk Rate

The least expensive Post Office option is Bulk Mail. Avoid it when possible because your mailers may spend extra time in the postal system getting soiled and crumpled. One pessimist estimates that as much as twenty percent of bulk mail—with valid addresses— fails to reach its destination. Scary, if true. Instead, consider presorting options (consult your local postmaster for instructions) to conserve cash on a large mailing.

---

5. **Opening the mail.** When received, the mailer should invoke action on the recipient's part to call and order, usually with a credit card for an instant sale. A less aggressive

mailer may announce the book and send recipients to the bookstore for purchase.

6. **Following up with another mailing (optional).** A second "why didn't you respond to our special offer?" mailer may be sent. This is unusual in publishing, but common in direct-mail programs for other products. Some authors, even those who self-publish, want to move their books through bookstores, because doing so can fire up that channel of distribution, a tactic used by the authors of many bestsellers, from Blanchard's *The One Minute Manager* to Trump's *The Art of the Deal.*

Time your mailing for arrival at the best possible moment. Mailings to business prospects should arrive Tuesday through Thursday. Few recipients will be receptive on a Monday and, while Friday seems good, recipients may set aside your mailer for action on Monday and forget about it forever. Consumer mailings can arrive any day you are available to take orders. Also consider the time of year; approaching the holiday season is risky as not only do the volume of mailings skyrocket, but people have other purchases on their minds. Similarly, your book on air-conditioning repair won't sell as well if you mail the ad to buyers in Pennsylvania in October. Promote your book on heating and fireplace systems instead.

HIRING PROFESSIONALS TO PROMOTE YOUR BOOK

If all the options for promotion seem overwhelming, you might want to get some outside help. Book promoters (and occasionally public relations firms and advertising agencies) can handle all aspects of book promotion from advertising to "glad-handing" the press. A book promoter handles all media contact including ad placement—even, in an extreme example, assembling a telemarketing program to sell an expensive book via outbound sales calls to *prospects* (buyers). The promoter plans the publicity campaign, commissions any other parties who might participate, and pulls your strings as the author to help you dance to the tune of the program.

If you can't afford a promotional firm, independent freelance publicists can create a complete program of hype for a reasonable price. Your freelancer will provide appropriate press materials, offer you a choice of contact (mailing) lists, and schedule events. You won't need to lift a finger, save to write out a check for services and show up for interviews and signings. Some freelancers will also offer to "coach" you for a few hours at a reasonable consulting fee of two hundred to three hundred dollars.

Before signing up with anyone connected to book promotion, find out what services they offer, the basis of their charges, and what they can do for you. Most publicists offer three levels of service:

1. Consulting (they teach you the basics, such as writing and sending out a press release, and you do the work). This may cost about one hundred dollars per hour.

2. A limited twenty-to-ninety-hour engagement, which could run in the neighborhood of two thousand dollars.

3. A full-blown three-month program, which might cost ten thousand dollars or more.

Confused About Terms?

What's the difference between a publicist, a promoter, and a public relations specialist? In practice, these terms are sometimes used interchangeably, but to clarify the distinctions:

- A *publicist* or a *promoter* manages all aspects of presenting your book *and you* to the press and to bookstore buyers. These experts manage everything from infomercials to handing you the pen for book signings at trade fairs (depending on your budget). Many do not perform these services personally, but choose and purchase services from vendors such as ad agencies, PR agencies, and other consultants. The promoter will coordinate the selected team's activities for maximum impact.

- A *public relations specialist* contacts, persuades, and coddles the media, making recommendations for other publicity without handling their implementation. A public relations specialist may be a solo freelancer working from home or a small office, or a full-blown agency with busy clerks running memos and copy between offices and committees. At the latter type of PR firm, you will be assigned an account "rep" who will handle your book personally, under the review of his or her managers. If the latter approach sounds more expensive than a home-based freelance public relations specialist, that's because it is.

The first step should be creating a publicity or promotional plan that describes in detail the services appropriate for your book and how much the package will cost. The plan should justify each step and the moneys spent for every element. The plan isn't free; there will be a charge for anything beyond a list of basic services, and a full-blown proposal may cost several hundred dollars or more. Why a bill for a proposal? Because there's no reason you can't decide to implement the plan yourself, thereby depriving the expert who developed it any consulting revenue and vendor commissions from the companies engaged to deploy it.

Should you (or your publisher) buy a lavish program complete with appearances on major TV shows and features in major newspapers? Before hiring a promoter, weigh the price tag for the services against the benefits. A promoter's or publicist's work is largely behind the scenes and difficult to evaluate in terms of effectiveness until your money has been spent. Some publicists charge only for the interviews and other engagements they secure; you don't have to pay unless they deliver, which is a good working arrangement because it lets you control the cash outlay while motivating your promoter to hustle on your behalf.

Bob Newsman Associates in Boston specializes in book publicity and promotion. Bob works in two ways, either for a publisher on a freelance book-by-book basis, or directly for an author. Prentice Hall used Bob to publicize Craig Hickman's *The Productivity Game* and Emmett Murphy's *Leadership IQ*. After a six-week campaign, the publisher had exhausted its budget on both books, but the authors were so happy with the results that they retained Bob for another month.

"But, He/She Was So Nice!"

When hiring a publicist of any kind, keep in mind that not only are these people experts in promotion, they're also experts at marketing themselves. They can sell upright freezers to Eskimos. They can convincingly sell you a bill of goods, too. Listening raptly to a pitch that makes an encyclopedia salesperson sound low-key, you suddenly discover what seems to be a long-lost or yet-to-be-discovered best friend. Before signing on the bottom line, think the whole thing through and run it by an objective friend for an outsider's evaluation.

Not all authors need promoters or publicists, and many can't afford one. Like Covert Bailey, who promoted *Fit or Fat* from his van, and Callan Pinkney, who promoted *Callanetics* via a grassroots interview schedule on local radio and television stations, you can do it yourself. But if you lack marketing expertise, sales experience, or time, or if you are shy about approaching the press, publicity professionals can you get mentioned in the right places. Once you see how they operate, you can replicate their techniques.

You can locate literary promoters in the *Yellow Pages* under *Publicity, Public Relations,* or *Book Promotion,* or in reference books such as *LMP (Literary Market Place)*. Choose a firm or person specializing in book promotion, not a general business promoter or ordinary public relations company. Some companies will take on any kind of project, even those with which they have no expertise or experience. Even if your publisher does not hire an outside publicist for your book, it might suggest one it knows and respects. Before committing to a publicist, ask for references from satisfied clients and check them carefully. Evaluate the success of the titles they have represented in the past.

FROM A TINY SEED
GROWS A MIGHTY OAK

A glance at *Publishers Weekly* might convince you that bookselling has become a bewildering world of conglomerated publishing houses, sprawling superbookstore chains, and sophisticated technological advancements involving computers and World Wide Web sites. How can one little book from one little author make it through this maze? The answer today is as simple as it was fifty years ago: by word of mouth.

Strip away the ownership links that bind Macmillan to Simon & Schuster and Viacom, and you find a distinct imprint like Macmillan Spectrum, where a small group of dedicated editors and marketing people work diligently to make each new book special no matter how small its potential audience. Take apart the Barnes & Noble superstore, and you discover that the billion-dollar empire springs from one customer taking one book to the cash register. Turn off the electricity, shut down the computers, and wipe away the Web sites, and you find one author reaching one reader with one volume of entertainment or information.

Despite all the innovations in book publishing and bookselling, it all begins with one little seed: an idea. Once that idea drops into fertile soil in a forest of information as a bound book, it begins to grow. One reader recommends

Midnight in the Garden of Good and Evil to a hundred, and a hundred recommend it to thousands. One press release prompts one feature article in the *New York Times*, and that article sends two thousand bodies to the bookstore. One review in *Publishers Weekly* convinces one buyer at a bookstore chain to order 1,500 copies. One author appears on a local cable television program, and fifty viewers decide to give her book as Christmas presents. One author appears on *The Today Show*, and a publisher logs orders for fifty thousand copies the next day. The power of a bestseller is the power of one—one multiplied by word-of-mouth until that number reaches five thousand or twenty thousand or one hundred thousand or one million. It takes only a seed to grow a mighty oak.

If you sow your idea wisely and nourish it constantly, you may grow your own bestseller. If you do, you will be on your way to a personally and financially rewarding career as a book author, the subject of our next two chapters.

CHAPTER TEN

How to Build a Successful Career As an Author:

A Career Map for Long-Term Personal and Financial Fulfillment

In Chapter 1, we mentioned the adage that "writing books is a slow way to make a fast buck." Given that the average book makes a whopping six thousand dollars for its author, that saying holds true for the vast majority of authors—with the notable exception of people like Scott Adams, the creator of Dilbert, who turned idle doodling during dull hours in a corporate cubicle into a popular comic strip and runaway bestseller, *The Dilbert Principle* (and an equally successful series of follow-up titles). Your own personal and financial success will probably take many more years and many books to create, as the case of Steve Bennett illustrates.

A LONG ROAD TO STEADY ROYALTIES

Like many authors, Steve Bennett tried his hand at a few moneymaking endeavors before he wrote and sold his first book. Armed with an esoteric master's degree in ancient

Chinese history from Harvard University, he marketed T-shirts for a while, until he discovered a talent for advertising and built a successful agency in Cambridge, Massachusetts. Then he caught the book bug. "Why," he wondered, "can't I write a self-help book for people like me, who turn their education in history and literature and the social sciences into profitable enterprises?" Through a friend of a friend, Steve met agent Mike Snell and outlined his idea for *Playing Hardball with Soft Skills.* The two spent a few months shaping a proposal for the book, which ignited bidding from two major publishers and eventually went to Bantam for a twenty-five thousand dollar advance.

After he delivered the manuscript to his publisher, Steve wound down his advertising business and began proposing and writing books full-time. The publisher who lost the first book to Bantam bought Steve's second book for a similar advance: *Executive Chess* (New American Library), co-authored by Mike Snell. When the editor who bought that book moved to the computer book division of Simon & Schuster, Steve, who had developed expertise in software, followed him there and, over a six-year period, published over a dozen books on various computer topics. The editor then moved to Random House, where he bought several more books from Steve.

Meanwhile, Steve's agent had connected him with a small business-book publisher, Oliver Wight, for whom Steve ghost-wrote a half-dozen books on management and manufacturing, including the bestselling *Team Zebra.* Some ten years after launching his career as a book author, Steve had written and published over thirty books, mostly on business and computer subjects, but he had not personally hit it big with any one book. Living on his advance checks, which brought in about sixty thousand dollars a year, Steve dreamed of the day when one of his books would strike pay dirt and give him a reliable annual income.

The breakthrough finally came when Steve and his agent met Bob Adams, a new publisher in suburban Boston. Drawing on the success formula detailed in his first book, Steve applied his experience as a new father to the parenting field and crafted *365 TV-Free Activities You Can Do with Your Child.* That book, its sequels, and its updated versions have sold over a half-million copies, a continuing source of income that finally gave Steve both the personal and financial fulfillment he began searching for almost fifteen years earlier. Yes, it was a slow journey, but it did result in more than a few fast bucks.

Using the Requisite Three Fs and Three Ps

In this book, you've already read about people like Sara Bernstein, who completed her first book at age twelve, and her equally precocious brother, Daryl, who had two top-selling books in print before his seventeenth birthday. Talk about getting a head start on a publishing career! Then there's Emmett Murphy, who with the help of a developmental editor, turned a leadership consulting practice into a string of bestselling books and a career as an author. This book you are reading now represents a milestone in the careers of Mike Snell, who has written, agented, or collaborated on over four hundred books, and Kim and Sunny Baker, who have published almost two dozen titles. Career progression may be quirky and unpredictable, but success, when it comes, usually sneaks up on authors quietly and often from an unexpected direction.

Each successful author follows his or her unique path to fulfillment. Some work for several years to get that pivotal first book into print. Then, having broken through, they'll sell three more titles in the next six months. Others plan and assess the market carefully and enjoy careers that look like a natural progression of steps.

How ever your career unfolds, with luck and serendipity or with painstaking strategic planning, it will almost undoubtedly depend on your motivation—the Three Fs of desiring *fame*, pursuing *fortune*, and contributing to a better *future* for your readers—and your adherence to the principles that guide the work of any serious author: the Three Ps of *patience*, *perseverance*, and *professionalism*.

Balancing the Three Fs

Steve Bennett's career illustrates the wisdom of harnessing the drives for fame, fortune, and making a contribution to a better future. While his growing reputation attracted publishers to his work, and while his gradually increasing income from a variety of book projects enabled him to support his family, his ultimate success came when he wrote a book that made a huge difference in the lives of busy parents and their children.

Arnold Goldstein's career culminated in the start-up of his own publishing company, Garrett Publishers, in Florida. Over the years he became the most famous author of practical books on buying and selling businesses, starting new enterprises, and rescuing faltering businesses from financial trouble. Most of his fortune, however, came from a few books, like *The Basic Book of Business Agreements*, which sold over 750,000 copies for Enterprise and did more than all his other books combined to help small business owners run their companies efficiently and profitably.

Sally Edwards would be the first to admit that she writes, first and foremost, as an idealist. Every book she has published, from *Triathlon* to *Heart Zone Training*, has won her fame and fortune, but only because she undertook each project with the burning desire to help people live better, healthier lives.

All of these authors balanced the Three Fs, never letting one motivation overrule another. As your career unfolds, whether over ten years with two books, over fifteen years with twelve books, or over thirty years with forty books, take time along the way to assess your motivations for writing and to make any necessary adjustments. If you're making a lot of money but not having a lot of fun, turn up your idealism; if you're not making much money, but are taking joy from every minute of your writing, apply a little more business sense to your work.

Maintaining the Three Ps

Emmett Murphy's career exemplifies the power of patience, perseverance, and professionalism. Not until his third book, *Leadership IQ*, did he see his effort pay off with a bestseller. That success came after ten years of hard work, during which he stayed the course, growing more skillful with each manuscript. He tried, he tried, and he tried again, each time creating something more professional and more valuable to his audience.

Pam Gilberd has published only one book to date, but that one book took five years of patient revision of her proposal, unflagging perseverance despite two dozen rejections of earlier drafts, and ardent professionalism with each draft until *The 11 Commandments of Wildly Successful Women* was finally snapped up by Macmillan.

Catherine Woolley, the ninety-three-year-old children's book author who represents the opposite end of the spectrum from young Sara and Daryl Bernstein, patiently persevered for sixty years, writing and publishing over ninety children's books, until her professionalism made it possible for her to publish *Writing for Children.*

These authors never wavered from the Three Ps, and their successes should remind you that your own fulfillment, in terms of both personal satisfaction and financial results, will take time, dedication, and continued growth as a professional writer. Should you find yourself becoming impatient, wanting to throw in the towel, or worrying that your progress as a writer has slowed, remind yourself that the pyramids weren't built in a day, that the highest rewards come to those who wait, and that every writer must work to get better every day. It's never easy—or, as Red Smith once remarked, "Sure, it's easy, just sit down at typewriter and open a vein."

Writing can be a lonely task. Whenever you find your motivation out of balance or your progress stalled, you might consider looking for a little outside help.

LOOKING FOR OUTSIDE HELP

If you feel insecure about your career as an author, you might consult a mentor, an agent, another author, an editor or publisher, a teacher, or a business consultant who can share expertise, guide you through the steps, critique your work, and help you over the rough spots. Many successful authors rely on their mentors to help them grow both as writers and as business people.

Where do you find good mentors? Your mentor may be a writing teacher, an accountant, an agent, another author you met through a writer's club, or someone you found through book organizations on the Internet. The Writer's Club on America Online, for instance, offers an established mentoring program to help you hook up with expert advisors.

In Leominster, Massachusetts, Barbara Roy has been teaching courses and workshops for writers for the past ten years. One of her students, Peter Lehndorff, got published at age seventy-seven after taking Barbara's courses. He insists that *60 Second Chronic Pain Relief* never would have been bought by New Horizon without Barbara's coaching and counseling.

The Cape Cod Writer's Conference puts authors in touch with one another. These writers not only hone their professional skills from constructive critiques and learn about business principles from fellow writers, they also gain moral support from folks engaged in similar pursuits.

Agent as Partner and Mentor

Many authors depend on an agent for career advice and guidance. Not all agents want to involve themselves at this level because they lack the time, don't know you well enough, or would simply rather move projects out the door than deal with the more complicated issues of long-term career development.

However, an experienced literary agent often wears several mentoring hats. Such a person certainly understands, and can teach others, the many ways an author's career can unfold. Having worked at a publishing house, an agent knows the business ropes, from how a publisher calculates profitability to what to look for in a publishing agreement. A good agent can be a writing teacher, a business consultant, and a friend, providing whatever support you need, from word- and sentence-level guidance to tax advice to a specialized form of compassionate psychotherapy for such common ailments as writer's block, deadline fever, and the success syndrome, about which you'll learn more later. At various points in your career, you'll need different kinds of support from your agent. Here's what a few authors have to say about the support they received from their agents, as both partners and mentors:

- **Myrna Milani, veterinarian and author of six pet books:** "My agent actually rewrote my first draft of *The Weekend Dog*, showing me, rather than telling me, how to write clear, concise, active sentences. I think I was a pretty good student because now, on my sixth book, my agent spends more time counseling me on my career as an author than editing my writing."

- **Craig Hickman, management consultant and author of twelve business books:** "I needed it all at first. Despite my MBA from Harvard, I knew nothing about the book business, which is really weird compared to other businesses. My agent critiqued and edited my writing, taught me about the business of publishing, and became a dear friend over the years."

- **Chris Malburg, accountant and author of eight accounting and career books:** "I actually taught my agent a lot about the numbers side of publishing, but I learned a

lot, in turn, about constructing marketable proposals. I
didn't need much help with my writing, but, boy did I need
a lot of hand-holding when a few of my books didn't sell
very well."

These three authors span the full spectrum of needs that an
agent can help fill. The key to your own relationship with an
agent (or any other mentor) will determine your evolving
needs throughout your career and linking up with a person
who can provide the right assistance. Your mentors may
change as you develop, and most authors never go forward
strictly on their own. Even the most seasoned and successful
author needs a friend who can inject a dose of reality in a
world that can often become downright crazy. The second or
third or fourth or twentieth book will not automatically be
easier than the first from either an artistic or a business perspective. In fact, for most authors, the next book is harder in
all ways because they really want to get better at everything.

MOVING BEYOND THE FIRST BOOK

Not everyone can or should move beyond the first book to
other projects. If a single book will provide all the sense of
achievement, career boost, cash flow, or credibility you need,
you may pack up your word processor and call it a day. If, on
the other hand, you envision more books in your future, then
you may want to begin shaping the proposal for your next
book even before you finish writing your first one.

Those who hope to forge a career as book authors must
keep the cash flow time line in mind because, given the rather

Cashflow Time Line

Proposal writing =	Three to six months
Marketing =	Three months
Contract =	One month
First advance check =	One month
Writing =	Six to twelve months
Second advance check =	One month
Production =	Six to nine months
Total elapsed time =	Two years, nine months, to four years, nine months

glacial movement of the book publishing world, proposing a new book too long after submitting a previous one could create a financial bind.

Anywhere from two to five years can elapse between the time when you begin proposing your book idea to the time when the published book, bestseller or not, brings you royalty income. If you obtain a $10,000 advance for your first book, you certainly can't quit your day job unless your spouse or a trust fund can make up the difference. Even a $25,000 advance would, in the best of circumstances, provide you with only an income of $12,500 per year. Of course, you could probably manage to support yourself with a $100,000 advance, even in the worst-case five-year scenario, but the odds of such an advance on a first book run from slim to zero.

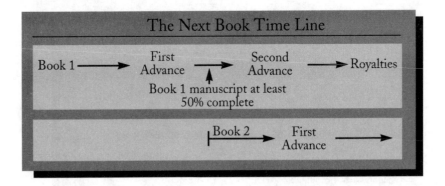

Multiple-book authors, therefore, usually begin working on a proposal for the next book even before they finish writing the first one, striving for income overlap, as The Next Book Time Line illustrates.

Such a dovetailed strategy makes sense for two reasons: one, it narrows the gap between advance checks, and two, it builds on a writer's momentum because the advance for a second book should exceed the advance for the first. You have proven yourself enough to ask for more money, though publishers will not feel overly generous until they can measure your real track record in terms of sales on your first book. Consider these two examples.

Larry Tuller, an independent business consultant, sold *Buying In*, his first book on buying a business, to McGraw-Hill for $7,500. Before finishing the manuscript for that book, he proposed a follow-up book on selling a business, *Getting Out*. Given the narrow markets for both books and the lack of sales record for the first one, McGraw-Hill offered only $7,500 for the second title. That didn't bother Larry because he maintained his consulting practice all along and could use both books as marketing tools to stimulate his business.

Craig Hickman took a slower path to book two, proposing *The Future 500* after book one, *Creating Excellence*, had sold over fifty thousand copies. Since the first book had earned over one hundred thousand dollars in royalties, Craig's publisher, New American Library, felt comfortable offering one hundred and ten thousand dollars for the second. That next book didn't sell nearly as well as *Creating Excellence*, so Craig's advance for his third book, *Mind of a Manager/Soul of a Leader*, fell to twenty-five thousand dollars with a new publisher, Wiley, with whom Craig had to start over building a track record.

Your own career path will probably unfold somewhere between those of Larry Tuller and Craig Hickman, but if you plan your strategy carefully, you should be able to enjoy a career that includes multiple books over many years.

MAPPING A MULTIPLE-BOOK CAREER

You may propose, write, and publish three books, six books, twelve books, or over fifty books during your career as an author, but regardless of your ultimate total output, you will probably do so according to one of four classic strategies. These four strategies represent composites of authors you have met in this chapter and elsewhere in the book. For simplicity's sake, the examples following assume a modest six-book career.

The Linear Strategy

Hypothetical author William J. Smith, an expert on gardening, chooses to write six books on the same subject: organic gardening techniques. Six years later, his list looks like this: *Organic Vegetable Gardening; Organic Flower Gardening; Indoor*

Organic Gardening; The Organic Vegetable Gardener's Problem-Solver; and *The Organic Flower Gardener's Problem-Solver.*

Each subsequent book applies William J. Smith's expertise in a linear fashion, and each aims at a special niche in the overall market for gardening books. Given this linear strategy, the author may well publish all six books with a single publisher that specializes in the niche, such as Rodale Press. He can churn the books out relatively quickly, since they play variations on one constant theme.

The Vertical Strategy

In another hypothetical case, author W. Jerome Smith, also a master gardener, decides to develop a vertically integrated series with a broader perspective than organic techniques. After eight years of effort, he has the following books in print: *The Complete Idiot's Guide to Organic Gardening; The Expert's Encyclopedia of Organic Gardening; Gardening for Dummies; The Expert's Guide to Gardening; The Beginner's Gardening Question-and-Answer Handbook;* and *The Advanced Gardener's Question and Answer Handbook.*

Three of his books are aimed at novices, three at serious amateurs and experienced professionals. Since his broader books face more competition than William J. Smith's organic books, W. Jerome Smith may publish with two or three different publishers, perhaps Macmillan, IDG, and Prima. It will also take him longer to write these more general books, especially the more advanced ones, which require a lot more research on his part. This vertical strategy climbs the ladder from low-level to high-level presentations, unlike the linear strategy that stays at the lower level.

The New Subject Strategy

Here, author Billie Smith, both a gardener and a preschool teacher, elects to write books on vastly different subjects. Her first three books deal with gardening: *The Busy Woman's Guide to the Kitchen Garden; The Complete Book of Tomato Gardening;* and *Cooking from Your Garden.* The other three books, perhaps published between her gardening books, deal with parenting: *The Working Woman's Guide to Daycare; Indoor Gardening for Children;* and *Indoor Activities You Can Do with Your Child on Rainy Days.* These books take Billie ten years to write and publish, however; her job and her own kids prevent her from writing full-time.

She may also publish her books with three, four, or even six different publishers—the gardening books with Fireside, Dell, or Bantam; the parenting books with Adams, Penguin, or Prima. Notice how one of her books *combined* her expertise in two different subjects.

The Breakout Strategy

Author W. J. Smith is also a gardening author and a busy mom, but she longs to publish a novel—a dramatic departure that could break her out into a whole different world of publishing. Her first five books look a lot like Billie's: *Every Woman's Guide to Canning from the Garden; Every Woman's Guide to Culinary Herb Gardening; Garden Activities You Can Do with Your Child; The Gourmet Vegetable Cookbook;* and *Cooking with Children.* Again, more than one publisher may take on these different books, especially the cookbooks, which may work best for a publisher like Crown that does a lot of cookbooks.

While W. J. may knock out these book in four to eight years, depending on her advances and schedule, she probably won't sell her novel for four to six years because she'll have to submit a complete manuscript for a novel, rather than a proposal as required by nonfiction publishers. Twelve years after initiating her career as a book author, however, W. J. realizes her dream with the publication of *The Rose Garden Murders*, which sets her off on a whole new book publishing career.

THE FOUR CORNERSTONES
OF CAREER SUCCESS

Any of the basic strategies, or a mix of them, can work for you provided that you put some forethought and planning into your own approach. Whatever your goals, however, and whatever route you take to attain them, you should keep in mind The Four Cornerstones of Career Success.

Like any endeavor, publishing requires some basic skill and talent. Building a fruitful and long-term writing career also takes enthusiasm and determination. You've heard the phrase "don't quit your day job yet." Well, short of a fluke breakthrough such as *Jonathan Livingston Seagull*, or the more recent *Life's Little Instruction Book*, success takes time as you put in place a solid foundation on which to build a career.

Four cornerstones begin a foundation for every profitable and rewarding writing career. Once solidly in place, the foundation establishes you not only as an author, but also as a *professional*. No longer can a member of the editorial committee vote down your book simply because you're unpublished.

The First Cornerstone: Your First Book

Obviously, you cannot move forward until you sell and publish the essential first book, even if it's not a bestseller or issued by a large house. If your first book demonstrates credibility (i.e., the book is more than a fat pamphlet, crudely stamped out at a neighborhood print shop or published by a vanity press), your standing as a reliable, professional author commands respect. That first book separates you from the many "wanna-bes" who fail to sell their first project or, once they've sold it, fail to complete it, leaving an angry publisher in their wake. Keep this in mind: never get ahead of yourself, dreaming of all those other books you might write. Instead, put every ounce of your creative energy into making your first book the very best it can be, because the first book sets the stage for everything that follows.

The Second Cornerstone: Workable Cash Flow

The second cornerstone settles into place if you make your writing financially viable. Unless you are among the "smoking jacket, Napoleon Cognac, and Purdy shotgun" crowd, a successful career as an author involves stabilizing cash reserves and managing your life like a business. As a full-time author, your financial ride will be bumpier than those holding a full-time job or a trust fund. Keep this in mind: publishers pay late, some agents sit on your money, and occasionally a house goes under, runs into cash-flow difficulties itself, or is acquired by a bigger house. All of these eventualities can harm your cash flow.

New authors almost always underestimate the time required to craft their work. If the time from initial advance to final payment drags on from an estimated three months to eight months, cash flow slows down, too. Even little things can put a dent in your cash flow, such as an incorrect delivery address for your checks, or a vacationing accounting clerk, gone for a month to visit relatives in Hungary.

You must also be willing to become a part-time collections agent. When a publisher fails to pay up or fouls up the internal paperwork that initiates your advance or royalty checks, you must politely demand payment and stay on top of the matter until the check arrives and clears the bank.

The Third Cornerstone:
An Understanding of the Publishing Process

The third cornerstone comes from experience. It's like learning to trim the sails of a boat. You want to maximize the wind's power with a sail configuration best suited for current conditions without deploying too much canvas. On the first few attempts, the sails flap and the boat fishtails, but with practice smooth sailing ensues.

As you venture into the deep waters of publishing, you'll learn firsthand about resolving conflicts great and small with your publisher or agent, earn a free education in print production (whether you want it or not), and observe the cogs of book promotion set in motion. Although you can supplement your existing knowledge with books on publishing, printing, and desktop publishing to learn more about the physical and technical side of book production, it's not until you've "lived it" a few times that you become fully cognizant of the underlying processes of book publishing. Eventually you'll learn to recognize problems early and remedy them quickly. As you learn more and more, you will become better equipped to maintain control of future projects.

In the process of gaining expertise, this rule serves all authors well: approach your career as if you were going for a Ph.D. in the subject, seizing every opportunity to learn about the industry from editors, agents, magazines, newspapers, teachers, and other authors.

The Fourth Cornerstone:
The Six Habits of Successful Career Authors

The fourth cornerstone falls into place over time as a result of maturity and toiling in the vineyards. This stone sets career authors apart from those who ultimately founder on the reefs of publishing or get caught by the sharks. Develop these habits, and you'll find success.

You've already read here about the first two habits, but you might think for a moment about the last four. Professionals in every field must answer questions about their work, so you should ask lots of questions, even if they seem stupid, and you should listen to the answers carefully as you complete your Ph.D. in publishing.

One editor is fond of saying that she prefers "reliable, hardworking writers to lazy geniuses." If you keep all your promises and honor all your deadlines, publishers will value you as a reliable, hardworking author—one with whom they will want to work on book after book after book.

The Six Habits of Successful Career Authors

1. Balance the Three Fs (fame, fortune, future).
2. Maintain the Three Ps (patience, persistence, professionalism).
3. Listen and learn.
4. Keep your promises; honor your deadlines.
5. Think long-term; act short-term.
6. Promote, promote, promote yourself and your book.

A variation on the environmental slogan, "Think globally, act locally," the fifth habit helps you maintain harmony between today's work and tomorrow's benefit. Four hundred hours invested this year may only earn you ten dollars an hour, given a four-thousand-dollar advance for your book, but if your book earns forty thousand dollars in royalties later on, your hourly wage rises to one hundred dollars an hour. Of course, that higher wage will only find its way into your bank account if you get behind your book and promote it with all the hard work and passion with which you proposed and wrote it.

On this foundation of skills and experience, you can erect a tower of achievement. The foundation allows you to manage your career while avoiding the many blunders and traps that force otherwise competent authors back to the day job to survive. After placing the foundation, you need to continue to build your business for long-term success.

BUILDING YOUR OWN BUSINESS

Whole books have been written on starting and running a small business, and you might consider acquiring a small library of them. Peter Richman's *Insider's Guide to Growing a Small Business* (Macmillan) offers a lot of sound advice, as does Chris Malberg's *Accounting for the Small Business* (Adams). The Adams Business Advisor series provides comprehensive advice on everything from selling techniques to growth strategies. Visit your local book superstore and browse through the shelves for books that can serve as business mentors, supplementing what you learn from your agent, accountant, or business manager.

Whatever your source of business acumen, however, always think of yourself as an enterprise—a sort of Books, Incorporated—over which you preside as CEO and Chairman of the Board. Books are your business, and your business is books. Mind that business. No matter how smart a business person you become, you should chisel one motto in granite over your word processor:

PROFIT = INCOME – EXPENSES

You don't need a Wharton MBA to run a small business profitably, provide you stick to this basic rule: pull in as much money as possible and spend as little as possible. This means, for example, that you resist investing in new, improved, state-of-the-art technologies (such as a plain-paper fax machine when the old thermal-paper model still works fine) until you can comfortably afford them. It also means that you avoid all unnecessary and costly expenses associated with research, such as extended travel and long-distance phone interviews. When possible, barter your services, exchanging editorial consulting or freelance writing for printing costs or word processing.

Pinch every penny, control expenses ruthlessly, and never count on the old ploy of gladly paying tomorrow for a hamburger today. This means that you must not use credit cards unless you pay them off each month. Money spent on interest is simply wasted money. Debt is the author's greatest nemesis, and nothing can create writer's block and derail a career more abruptly than worrying about bills.

The Success Syndrome

Ironically, however, more writers succumb to Success Syndrome than they do to financial failure. Schooled for years in accepting rejection, authors can usually handle financial disappointments (a smaller-than-hoped-for advance, a tinier royalty check than anticipated) more adroitly than they can handle that first big financial windfall (an unexpected six-figure advance, an out-of-the-blue $90,000 royalty check). Unaccustomed to the windfall, the once-impoverished writer rushes out to spend the money on fancy equipment, a new Jaguar Vanden Plas, a remodeled office, or a research trip to China. Then, before the next advance or royalty check arrives, the writer is juggling bills and worrying about making ends meet. That's a formula for sure-fire frustration or forced abandonment of a once-promising career.

Bank your money, invest your winnings, and build a nest egg for that inevitable rainy day. Never borrow money against your future expected income, even the second half of your advance. Never expect friends and family to tide you over or bail you out. Once you get behind the financial eight-ball, it's extremely hard to get yourself back in the black.

To boost your income, you can consider ways to leverage your work, not just through subsidiary rights sales of your book (foreign translations or that almost mythical movie deal), but with other spin-off money-making ventures that both promote your book(s) and create material for new ones.

Leveraging Your Writing

Many nonfiction books lend themselves to alternative income-earning packages and products. Consider the following seven options which the hypothetical author, William J. Smith, might choose to enhance both his income and the promotion of his gardening books.

Seven Book-Related Income Generators

1. **Newsletters.** By designing and marketing *The Organic Gardening Newsletter,* Bill cannot only generate more income (say ten thousand dollars a year if he gets one thousand subscribers to pay $100 each for a subscription), he can also promote all his published titles. Amy Dascyzn did the reverse, turning her popular newsletter, *The Tightwad Gazette,* into a bestselling book for Villard. Be aware, however, that more newsletters fail than make money.

2. **Public Speaking.** Bill could arrange to make one- to three-hour presentations at venues ranging from The Friends of the Library (for a one-hundred-dollar honorarium) to associations of gardeners and landscape designers (where fees might run as high as one thousand dollars).

Charismatic authors like Michael Silva, author of *Overdrive* (Wiley), a book on managing business crises, commands as much as five to ten thousand dollars for a keynote luncheon address.

3. **Guest Lecturing.** A state horticultural society may invite Bill to offer a workshop on organic rose gardening at their annual meeting, perhaps paying three hundred dollars for three hours of his time. (Of course, Bill will also spend time preparing the lecture and putting together the presentation, so the hourly rate shouldn't be misconstrued as pure profit.) Anthony Valario, author of *BART* (Harcourt Brace), a celebration of the former Commissioner of Baseball, earned over two thousand dollars plus expenses for a two-week series of lectures at The Cape Cod Writer's Conference.

4. **Workshops and Seminars.** Bill could also set up his own independent courses on home gardening at the local, statewide, or national level, pulling in fifty people at a shot, at $125 a head. After expenses for promotion and space rental, this can still be very profitable. Deborah Dumaine, author of *The Vest Pocket Guide to Business and Technical Writing* (Prentice Hall), brings as many as ten thousand people a year to seminars and training programs offered through her company, Better Communications, Inc.

5. **Ancillary Products.** If his publisher does not exploit electronic rights for his books, Bill could author a CD-ROM program and sell it through the mail, perhaps arranging for order cards to be slipped inside each printed book. For *The Strategy Game* (McGraw-Hill), Craig Hickman and an independent software company created a disk version of the

book, which eventually outsold the paper version (more than twenty-five thousand copies at $29.95). Of course, producing a CD-ROM takes special expertise, so you'll need time to learn the technology and create the program.

6. **Consulting.** Bill might sell his expertise to a garden products manufacturer, helping them design and market better organic gardening products to their customers. Such consulting arrangements can net as much as five to ten thousand dollars for a three-day to three-week assignment. John Whiteside, author of *The Phoenix Agenda* (Wiley), used his book to land a lucrative, ongoing consulting engagement with Nabisco.

7. **Magazine and Newspaper Articles.** Bill could sell original articles, as opposed to book excerpts, to major national publications such as *The American Gardener*. David Duncan, who published *River Teeth* (Doubleday), a collection of short essays and stories, sold "The Mickey Mantle Koan," his memoir of his brother's death, to *Harper's Magazine* for two thousand dollars. Kim and Sunny Baker, authors of a variety of business and self-help books, write short columns for *The Non-Profit Times* and *The Journal of Business Strategy*, netting a regular income of one thousand dollars a month or more. For those many authors who are not inclined to venture into consulting or public speaking, magazine and newspaper writing offers a way to augment book income from home, and hone their writing skills at the same time.

You might come up with even more ideas for generating book income, including programs on the World Wide Web, other products, or even special events, but suppose Bill

Bill Smith's Cashflow

Royalties on Book #1	$ 3,000.
Royalties on Book #2	12,000.
First advance on Book #3	6,000.
Profits from newsletter	6,000.
Speaking fees	1,200.
Guest lectures (2)	2,000.
Profits from four workshops	8,000.
Profits from CD-ROM	4,500.
Consulting engagement (1)	5,000.
Magazine articles (4)	2,500.
Total	$50,200.

employed only the seven income-generating ventures mentioned here. His annual income three years into his writing career might look like this example.

If Bill carefully controls his expenses, which are tax-deductible or paid for by his corporation, he can net (after taxes) around thirty-five thousand dollars from his book-related moneymaking strategy. If he needs more than that to support himself, he might take a part-time job related to his field, perhaps as a garden designer for a landscape design firm, supplementing his book-related income with work that leads to more books and an even more ambitious career in the years ahead.

If you ask Bill if it's all been worth it, he'll probably say, "You bet. But it's not just the money; it's the chance to do what I love and make a real difference in the world."

MAKING A REAL DIFFERENCE IN THE WORLD

This book began with the message that dreams do come true, so it's only fitting that it end on the same note. Every book represents a dream come true for its author—a dream of fame, fortune, and making a difference in the world. Most authors would accept agent Mike Snell's assessment of personal and financial success: "They say it's better to be poor and happy than rich and miserable, but I'll gladly settle for moderately wealthy and moody."

William J. Byron, S.J., the retired president of Catholic University and a distinguished professor of business ethics at Georgetown University, doesn't care a lot about money. His advances and royalties go to the Corporation of Roman Catholic Clergymen. Not many authors take a vow of poverty (at least willingly), but every author can learn a lesson from Father Bill's experience. Writing primarily to make a difference in the world, he has succeeded in a way that should inspire every writer.

Father Bill published a few religious books during his career, among them *Take Your Diploma and Run* (Paulist Press), but in his retirement he became interested in the circumstances of workers laid off in their middle years as corporate America pursued a ruthless campaign of downsizing. Supported by a Lilly Foundation grant, he spent a year traveling the country and investigating the plight of men and women who had lost top-paying jobs in their fifties and sixties. The result of his research was *Finding Work Without Losing Heart* (Adams), a book full of wisdom and comfort that showed how people with spiritual values triumphed even in the most depressing situations. The book attracted a great deal of media attention, but one short radio interview made all of Father Bill's work on his book worthwhile.

"I was sitting at my desk at Georgetown," Father Bill recalls, "when I got a phone call out of the blue from a fellow in Chicago. It turned out he had been downsized out of a top executive job with a major insurance company and suddenly found himself with a huge mortgage, two kids in college, and no hope of finding a job that could support his family. 'I began drinking too much,' he said, 'and I took out my frustration on my wife. We separated, and I hit bottom. In fact, I'd bought a .38, loaded it, and sat on my bed in my squalid apartment contemplating suicide. The radio was on, and some interviewer was talking with a priest about a book he had just published.'"

Father Bill shakes his head as he describes the caller's suffering. "The fellow unloaded the gun, lay awake all night, then went to Barnes & Noble before the doors opened. He bought my book, read it, joined Alcoholics Anonymous, apologized to his wife, went to a job counselor, and polished up his resumé. The last I heard he'd gotten a good job and had put his whole life back together."

Your book may not save a life, but it can alter a reader's sensibility forever. As you build your career as a book author, keep Father Bill's story in mind and measure your success not just by how much money you make but by how achieving your dream can make a difference in the world. The human contact that occurs between idea and bestseller makes a writer's life rich indeed.

Proposal Templates

We have included the complete proposals for two books (except for the sample chapters that accompanied them). Should you wish to see the books in print and compare them with the proposals that led to a contract, we suggest you buy the published book. We have provided contact information with the in-print title and publisher. You will see some divergence from the book outline in its proposal and the finished publication. Why? New ideas pop up, organizational problems not apparent in the proposal demand changes, and sometimes, there's just a better way of putting the book together. Assuming you don't propose a book on *Nepalese Figure Skating Secrets* and deliver (apologies to Michael Palin) *Across the Andes by Frog*, this is not unusual practice.

Get Published!

NOTES ON THIS PROPOSAL

Get Published! as it was originally titled began life as two parts. Agent Michael Snell provided a package of authors guidelines to would-be nonfiction writers and the Baker's sold their *Get Published!* kit through ads on the online services. Now titled, *From Book Idea to Bestseller,* the book combines the best of both Mike's and the Baker's efforts plus the much appreciated critique by San Francisco literary agent Sheryl Fullerton. (Published as *From Book Idea to Bestseller,* Michael Snell, Kim Baker, and Sunny Baker, it's one of several related how-to books for authors produced by Prima Publishing.)

INCLUDES TEMPLATES THAT ANYONE CAN USE TO CREATE A $20,000+ BOOK PROPOSAL!

GET PUBLISHED!

The Non-Fiction Book Author's Handbook, Problem-Solver, and Resource Kit

By Michael Snell, Kim Baker, and Sunny Baker

With On-Disk Proposal Templates, Press Releases, Checklists, Forms and More! (For IBM PC *and* Macintosh)

GET PUBLISHED!

The Non-Fiction Book Author's Handbook,
Problem-Solver, and Resource Kit

By Michael Snell, Kim Baker, and Sunny Baker

Represented by the Michael Snell Literary Agency
32 Bridge Road, Truro, MA 02666 • 508-349-3718

Table of Contents

Quick Synopsis — 5

This Book — 6

The Need — 9

The Market — 10

The Competition — 12

The Authors' Co-Promotion — 14

The Authors — 15

The Chapters — 20

Book Specifications — 22

Chapter Summaries — 23

Samples from the Book — 39

This proposal demonstrates the professional results writers can achieve after reading this book, completing the forms and checklists, and (optionally) using the templates included on disk or CD-ROM.

Quick Synopsis

Every day, hundreds of thousands of aspiring authors, some of them previously published but most still yearning to break into print, fire up their word processors and set about creating the next non-fiction bestseller. Even in this age of information superhighways and satellite communications, publishing a book remains an almost universal dream. Alas, Janet Coleman's memoir of her kayak trip down the Zambesi river will collect two dozen rejection letters, and Steve Ramsey's guide to permanent weight loss will gather dust on a shelf.

Get Published! will dramatically increase the odds for the Janets and Steves of the world, putting in their hands a proven, comprehensive program that guides them step-by-step toward the fulfillment of their dreams. In its pages, they will find everything they need to succeed: A **Textbook** that details every aspect of getting published, from idea development and book proposal writing to finding and working with literary agents and publishers; a unique **Author's Problem Solver** that poses and answers all the important questions people ask about the publishing process, from "How do I locate the major forthcoming competition for my book?" to "Does the electronic rights clause in the publishing agreement cover multimedia applications?"; a **Resource Library** that shows writers how to use vital references such as *Literary Market Place* and *The Elements of Style*; and on-disk **Book Proposal Templates** authors can use as type-over models for their own proposals. Lists and checklists assist new authors in refining their concepts, positioning them, and crafting and producing credible proposals for the right publishing houses and editorial groups.

> **❝**
> Every day hundreds of thousands of aspiring authors fire up their word processors and set about creating the next non-fiction bestseller.
> **❞**

This proposal is an example of the publishing expertise of its authors. Written by a team of experts with over 40 years combined experience in every publishing industry activity (development, editing, writing, collaboration, production, printing, distribution, marketing and promotion, and professional representation), *Get Published!* offers one-stop shopping for everyone who longs to see their name on the cover of a book.

The Book

"Why do I need to create a book proposal if I've already written the book?"

"Do literary agents sign contracts with their clients?"

"How do I find out about books like mine that publishers have signed up but not yet published?"

"How do I know a publisher won't steal my idea?"

"Do I need to write a press release when my book comes out, and, if so, how do I do it?"

"Should I keep the option clause in my publishing agreement?"

"Do I need to write a detailed proposal for my second book now that I'm established as an author?"

"As an author, what expenses can I legally deduct from my federal income taxes?"

Every day someone asks us questions like these, and every time we hear those predictable questions, we wish that we could refer people to a complete, up-to-date guide that would explain everything they need to know about getting a book published. We propose *Get Published!* to save busy authors, agents, and editors all the time discussing what, even to an experienced writer, can seem such a mysterious process: The journey from idea to a successful career as an author. In its pages, readers will find a wealth of information covering every aspect of getting published.

PART ONE: *Everything You Need to Know to Get a Book Successfully Published* provides a concise textbook many readers will study from beginning to end, starting with an overview of the contemporary state of the book publishing industry and concluding with advice on managing a career in that environment.

PART TWO: *The Author's Problem Solver* includes answers to the 250 most common questions authors pose about the publishing process and answers all the predictable questions asked by both novices and experienced writers. Here, readers encounter real-life examples drawn from 40 years experience in the field.

PART THREE: *The Author's Resource Kit—Publishers and Agents, Model Proposals, Contracts, and Glossary*—walks the reader through contacting and contracting with literary agents and publishers, and employing such resources as *Literary Market Place*. The section also reprints, analyzes, and annotates three typical book contracts and explains the vocabulary of the industry.

WHAT ELSE MAKES *GET PUBLISHED!* UNIQUE?

The book includes not only editorial guidance, but also real-world documents that readers can follow while they propose, write, and later promote their books. Models include three sample press releases, three sample publisher's agreements, three sample author to agent/publisher query letters, and three author/agent agreements. Available (on disk) as explained below, the samples appear in the book with callouts explaining key sections and what they mean to the author, publisher, or agent.

FORMS, CHECKLISTS, AND TEMPLATES: The book contains the actual checklists, forms, and proposal templates for books sold to major houses. All of these items are available on a floppy disk (or CD-ROM) that accompanies *Get Published!* This enables anyone with a word processor to complete every form and checklist.

All sample forms and checklists appear both on the disk and in the book. Three complete proposals are included in the printed book, and fifteen more are included on the accompanying disk. While the book contains only three complete proposals, as many as 24 can be included on the optional disk.

TEXTBOOK, PROBLEM-SOLVER, RESOURCE KIT: The three parts function together to teach readers what the experts know about every aspect of book publishing. The textbook explains, the problem-solver answers questions, and the resource kit offers a library of reference materials.

Suppose that Janet Colemen, who has chronicled her kayak trip down the

Zambesi River in a 224-page manuscript, wants to find a literary agent to represent her work. She may read all of Part One, but she will still probably concentrate on Chapter Three: How to Find and Work with a Literary Agent. With that background information in hand, she would then consult relevant questions in Part Two, such as "How do I evaluate the agent's ability to sell my work?" or "Can I submit my work to more than one agent at a time? or "Why doesn't the James Childs Agency sign authors to a contract?" Armed with answers to her most pressing questions, she will then turn to Part Three, identifying the resources that will move her from thinking about contacting agents to submitting the right material to the right agents.

Or, take Dr. Steve Ramsey, who has written a proposal for his guide to permanent weight loss. Unlike Janet, he decides to market his proposal himself. He will study Part One, but will focus on Chapter Four: How to Market Your Book Yourself. Having learned about the process in general, he will consult The Problem-Solver, looking at such entries as "How do I determine the marketing capability of a publisher?" or "What does 'net proceeds' mean in the royalty clause of a publisher's contract?" or "Do I need to show the contract to a lawyer before I sign it?" Feeling confident that he knows the answers to his most pressing questions, he would then move to Part Three, looking most closely at resources that would enable him to select the right publisher or at an annotated contract that looks a lot like the one sent to him by the Cedarbend Publishing Corporation for signature. Finally, he will find a clear definition of 'net proceeds' in the book's rich Glossary.

For every novice or experienced writer, for every Janet Coleman and Steve Ramsey, *Get Published!* serves as a continuing fountain of solid information. Shelved alongside *Literary Market Place*, *The Elements of Style*, *Webster's New World Dictionary*, and *Roget's Thesaurus*, *Get Published!* will become well-thumbed over the years until its owner decides to replace it with the most recently revised and expanded edition.

The Need for *Get Published!*

Imagine a world in which new and experienced writers had all graduated from an intensive course on getting published, in which they learned everything they need to know about the process, from how to choose a compelling book title and develop active, vivid prose to understanding contract clauses and the language of the industry. Not only would such graduates greatly improve their chances of seeing their ideas turn into bound books, but they would save busy editors and agents countless hours explaining the editorial decision-making process, the need for competitively positioning a new book, copyright law, options, revisions, copyediting, page proofs, and all of the other elements savvy professionals learn the hard way through years of experience.

By providing an all-in-one, one-stop shopping guide for non-fiction book authors, *Get Published!* replaces all that time-consuming discussion and all those books, pamphlets, and magazine articles that don't quite fill the gap between wanna-be authors and seasoned professionals.

In the past, an aspiring author read a text on the subject such as Judith Applebaum's, *How to Get Happily Published*, then stared at all those listings of publishers and agents in the massive *Literary Market Place*. With luck, that author might shape a half-way decent proposal, send it to an editor or agent, and then worry and wonder about the next step. Hundreds of questions arise along the road to publication, and editors and agents must take time from their busy schedules to deal with the new author's predictable issues. Because first-time authors take up valuable time, agents and editors simply pass on unseasoned talent. For the talented but unpublished author, it's a chicken-and-egg problem.

Now with *Get Published!* in their hands, aspiring authors can learn all of the intricacies of the industry in one handy volume. With it, they can craft superb proposals, get their work into the right hands, and understand every crucial step from the spark of a new idea to the lightning bolt of a bestseller. With this book, they will get published!

The Market for *Get Published!*

Getting a book into print remains a major life goal for millions of people. These aspiring authors include the vast "I have a great idea for a book" crowd, an eclectic mix of college professors ("publish or perish"), people looking for additional income, and those with a message who need a channel through which to voice it. Some, desperate to see their projects in print, seriously consider subsidy publishers or self-publishing as viable alternatives. All of these are among the market for *Get Published!* which includes:

1. **Unpublished authors looking for a break:** Often equipped with a credible idea for a nonfiction project, they lack professional knowledge of the publishing process. *Get Published!* provides this large market segment with an effective tool for successful publication of their books.

2. **Underpublished (for lack of a better word) authors:** This market segment includes those who have successfully published a book or two, but achieved only mediocre sales. *Get Published!* explains the subtleties of the publishing business of the 1990s and shows how to transform that next hot idea into that next *big* book.

3. **Professional writers in another genre who want to publish their first book.** Many experienced magazine, technical, educational, and promotional writers want to develop a book. For these already seasoned writers, *Get Published!* closes the gap between short works and full-length projects.

4. **Academics:** Under increasing pressure to publish, as governmental and private sector cutbacks threaten layoffs in colleges and universities around the country, many academics wish to secure their futures in new venues. As they search for readers outside academic journals and university presses, *Get Published!* offers a map for venturing outside the ivory towers.

5. **The entrepreneur:** The lay-off trend continues to devastate the careers of white collar professionals. After a fruitless job search,

many of the unwilling unemployed consider writing and publishing as a new source of income. *Get Published!* explains the "ins" and "outs" of publishing in real-world terms for those cadres of career shifters who long for untapped opportunities and sound advice.

6. **Publishing professionals:** Not only will established authors and agents find *Get Published!* a comprehensive guide to the publishing process, they will recommend it to others to save the valuable time they now waste explaining the nuances of the industry to the uninitiated.

The Competition for *Get Published!*

Writers who want to see their first book in print naturally turn to other books to learn how to get published. Several possibilities try to meet this growing demand, including titles from Prima and Writer's Digest Books, among others. Writers may also consult the perennial sourcebooks including the ever-popular *Literary Market Place*. However, no existing book provides the "one-stop shopping" depth of *Get Published!* Less experienced authors who already know they need accurate, in-depth information to shepherd their work into print, will welcome the *Get Published!* system, which nudges aside the competition with its length, breadth, and wealth of practical information. Imbued with a subtle sense of humor, the book offers compelling reading for novice and experienced writers alike who need a friendly, but definitive and authoritative resource.

The less-than-complete alternatives to *Get Published!* include:

1. **"How to publish nonfiction" books:** A handful of in-print books explain the mechanics of successfully moving a nonfiction book from idea to placement and completion with a publishing house. Some of the most popular include Michael Larsen's *How to Write a Book Proposal* (Writer's Digest Books, 1985), Jeff Herman's *Insider's Guide to Book Editors, Publishers, and Literary Agents* (Prima: semi-annual publication, most recent : 1995-1996), Judith Applebaum's *How to Get Happily Published* (1992, Harper Collins), and Richard Curtis' dated *How to Be Your Own Literary Agent* (1984, Houghton Mifflin). Partially fulfilling the needs of aspiring authors, these books provide only partial information and a limited number of example proposals, if any at all. As agent Michael Snell attests, "Larsen's is a standard book read by many new authors, but at barely 100 pages and because of some odd advice, *Get Published!* will literally blow it off the shelf."

   Book publishing is also covered superficially in the well-known annual, *Writer's Market*, but its brief advice does not suit the needs of either novices or professionals. Herman's book ostensibly attempts to list agents and publishers and their editorial staff (218 pages of 365). Only five pages explain how to write a book proposal, with another handful showing only one brief, incomplete proposal.

Get Published! avoids duplicating definitive information found in *LMP* and *The North American Guide to Literary Agents*. Instead, it refers readers to the reference section of their local public library—Dewey Decimal 070.41 to 070.5—to study the real thing. By not wasting the pages with incomplete or inadequate listings, *Get Published!* uses its space for richer information, more source listings, and annotated reproductions of actual, complete proposals and publishing contracts. *Get Published!* focuses on the elements writers need to see and understand, many of which simply do not appear in any other source at any price.

2. **"How to publish fiction" books:** A number of guides deal solely with fiction writing. (A few try to cover both fiction and nonfiction and ultimately fail in both genres.) Since selling fiction differs so dramatically from marketing nonfiction, these books do not compete with *Get Published!*

3. **Source books:** The myriad publishing source books provide detailed information on publishers, agents, local publishers (the out-of-print *Guide to Publishers of the Southwest,* for example) and special resources for editing, ghosting, production, and printing. Compilations like Marie Keifer's *Book Publishing Resource Guide* (1993, Adlib Publishing) and Lois Horowitz' aging *Knowing Where to Look* (1984, Writer's Digest Books) fill a need and are rightfully listed and described in *Get Published!*. These source books are supplemental but do not compete with *Get Published!*

4. **A similar title but different market:** A book similar to *Get Published!* in both depth and richness of information, Gage and Coppess' *Get Published* (1994, Henry Holt) focuses on magazine writing. It's an excellent guide but not direct competition.

The Authors Can Help Promote *Get Published!*

Michael Snell and Kim and Sunny Baker have considerable experience answering the questions of those wanting to break into print. *Get Published!* is a single forum for answering the most common questions, providing useful and detailed advice, and clearing up the common misconceptions unpublished authors have about the book business.

Agent Michael Snell receives hundreds of submissions each month from published and unpublished authors. In addition, he regularly appears on television, radio, and at writers' conferences. All of these contacts are excellent opportunities to promote *Get Published!* to the many interested writers who contact him daily.

Kim and Sunny Baker present How to Publish Your Nonfiction Book seminars for Barnes & Noble/Bookstar and independent bookstores throughout California and Arizona. Attendees always want more information following the discussion. These events are an excellent opportunity for presenting *Get Published!* as an authoritative single-volume source of publishing information.

Profile: Michael Snell

During his 30-year career, Michael Snell has overseen the publication of more than 1,000 books in every imaginable subject area, from graduate level textbooks on quantum physics to TV-free activities guides for children. His literary agency currently represents 150 writers, including 12-year-old Sarah Bernstein, author of *Handclap!* (Adams, 1994), 40-year-old novelist David James Duncan, author of *The River Why* (Sierra Club Books/Bantam), *The Brothers K* (Doubleday/Bantam), and *River Teeth* (Doubleday, 1995), and 90-year-old children's book author Catherine Woolley, whose *Writing for Children* (NAL/Plume) has become the standard text in the field.

Michael worked for 13 years as a college textbook editor and developer for the Wadsworth and Addison-Welsey publishing companies, publishing in all college disciplines, most notably in Literature, Business, and Computer Science. Many of his titles, such as William K. Hartman's *The Cosmic Journey*, an introduction to astronomy, continue to sell in the college market.

In 1979, he formed the Michael Snell Literary Agency in Boston and began applying his book development skills to the adult trade market. Since then he has sold more than 300 books to major publishers, including Simon & Schuster, Prentice-Hall, Wiley, Bantam/Doubleday/Dell, William Morrow, Random House, Viking/NAL/Dutton, Adams, AMACOM Books, Macmillan, McGraw-Hill, HarperCollins, Putnam/Berkley, Career Press, BusinessOne/Irwin, Holt, and Facts-on-File.

He has co-authored or collaborated on a couple of dozen hardcover trade books.

Co-authored:

- 1996 *Leadership IQ*, with Emmett Murphy, Wiley.
- 1994 *Forging the Heroic Organization*, with Emmett Murphy, Prentice-Hall.
- 1993 *The Genius of Sitting Bull*, with Emmett Murphy, Prentice-Hall.
- 1987 *Executive Chess*, with Steve Bennett, NAL.

Collaborations:

- 1996 *The Start-Up Game,* with Craig Hickman, Prentice-Hall.
- 1996 *The 20 Percent Solution,* with John Cotter, Wiley.
- 1995 *The Productivity Game,* with Craig Hickman, Prentice-Hall.
- 1995 *Overdrive,* with Michael Silva, Wiley.
- 1994 *The Fourth Dimension,* with Craig Hickman, Wiley.
- 1994 *The Oz Principle,* with Craig Hickman, Prentice-Hall.
- 1994 *The Organization Game,* with Craig Hickman, Prentice-Hall.
- 1993 *The Strategy Game,* with Craig Hickman, McGraw-Hill.
- 1991 *Ecopreneuring,* with Steve Bennett, Wiley.
- 1991 *Practical Business Genius,* with Craig Hickman, Wiley.
- 1990 *The Mind of a Manager/The Soul of a Leader,* with Craig Hickman, Wiley.
- 1990 *Europe 1992,* with Michael Silva, Wiley.
- 1987 *The Future 500,* with Craig Hickman, NAL.
- 1987 *Body Language and Emotion in Cats,* with Myrna Milani, (Manon/Quill).
- 1987 *The Equilibrium Plan,* with Sally Edwards, Arbor/Morrow.
- 1986 *Body Language and Emotion in Dogs,* with Myrna Milani, (Manon/Quill).
- 1985 *Systems Analysis and Design,* with Perry Edwards, Holt.
- 1985 *The Invisible Leash,* with Myrna Milani, NAL/Signet.
- 1984 *Creating Excellence,* with Craig Hickman, NAL.
- 1984 *The Weekend Dog,* with Myrna Milani, Scribners/Signet.

Profiles: Sunny Baker and Kim Baker

As authors of seventeen business, lifestyle, kids', computer, and cookbooks and the concept developers for Putnam New Media's forthcoming *Movie Studio* CD-ROM, Kim and Sunny Baker bring a unique combination of writing expertise, creativity, professional experience, and technical ability to their projects. Kim and Sunny produced *The Create-It Kit*, a finalist for the 1993 Computer Press Award as the best "how-to" book of the year. *The New York Times* commented enthusiastically on the Bakers' "edutainment" book for kids: "The book is a *lively* introduction to desktop publishing."

The Bakers' books have been picked up by major book clubs and reviews have been enthusiastic. For example, the prestigious graphic design magazine, *Communication Arts*, said of their bestselling desktop publishing book, "For a very detailed, helpful and well thought out overview of Macintosh desktop publishing, *Color Publishing the Macintosh* is a *great* book to read." As columnists for *CD-ROM World*, *Forecast Magazine*, and *The NonProfit Times,* the Bakers regularly explore a wide range of technologies, methods, and business tools.

Kim Baker is a former creative director and high technology marketing specialist who now writes full time. Sunny Baker, a former general manager at Microsoft, is now the Director of Information Technologies for the University of California at San Diego. Sunny founded Microsoft University which was also her concept. Kim and Sunny count high tech giants including Apple Computer, Microsoft, ROLM Corporation, Intel, Telenet, Arizona State University, University of California at San Diego, and Xebec Corporation among their marketing clients.

Kim Baker holds a BA in the Creative Arts (with Honors) and an MA (Painting) from San Jose State University. He was a post-graduate artist in residence at Emily Carr College of the Arts in Vancouver, Canada. Sunny Baker holds a BA in anthropology (with honors) and and a masters degree in linguistics (with great distinction) from San Jose State University. Beginning her Ph.D. on a full scholarship in linguistics at the University of Southern California in 1976, she finally completed her doctorate in computers and instruction at Arizona State University in 1995.

Titles by Kim Baker and Sunny Baker

- 1996 *On the Road Again: The RVer's Bible,* Fireside Books.
- 1996 *The Pasta Gourmet,* with Michelle Sbraga, Avery Publishing Group.

- 1995 *The Professional's Guide to QuarKXPress,* includes CD-ROM and CD-ROM interface, John Wiley & Sons.

- 1995 *Lemon Tree Very Healthy,* Avery Publishing Group, with Michelle Sbraga. *(*A bestseller so popular that Price Club has picked it up.)

- 1995 *Desktop Direct Marketing,* McGraw-Hill.

- 1994 *The Movie Kit* (working title), concept and interactivity specification for a fourth generation interactive CD-ROM, Putnam New Media/Universal Studios.

- 1993 *The Create-It Kit: Desktop Publishing for Kids Age 7 and Up,* Random House. (A finalist in the Computer Press Awards.)

- 1993 *Million Dollar Home-Based Businesses: Successful Entrepreneurs Who Have Built Substantial Enterprises from Their Homes,* Bob Adams, Inc.

- 1993 *Color Publishing on the PC: From Desktop to Print Shop*, Random House.

- 1993 *PageMaker for Windows,* McGraw-Hill. (Spanish and Polish translations.)

- 1993 *College After 30: It's Never Too Late to Get the Degree You Need*, Bob Adams, Inc. (In third printing.)

- 1993 *Market Mapping,* McGraw-Hill. (Hardcover in second printing, softcover in fourth printing. A main selection of the Business Week Book Club. Japanese translation forthcoming.)

- 1992 *Color Publishing on the Macintosh: From Desktop to Print Shop*, Random House. (In third printing. A main selection of the Small Computer Book Club, the Graphic Artist's Book Club, and an alternate selection of the Architect & Designer Book Service.)

- 1992 *Office on the Go*, Prentice Hall.

- 1992 *QuarkXPress for Windows: A Self-Teaching Guide,* John Wiley & Sons. (Portuguese translation.)

- 1992 *On-Time, On-Budget*, Prentice Hall.

- 1992 *How to Promote, Publicize, and Advertise Your Growing Business,* John Wiley & Sons. (In fourth printing. Alternate selection of the Newbridge Executive Club.)

- 1988 *Eastside Eats: A Comprehensive Guide to Eastside Dining and Wineries,* Homestead Book Company, Seattle, WA.

The Chapters

Introduction: The universal dream.

~

Part One: Everything You Need to Know to Get a
Book Successfully Published

Chapter 1:   What really happens in book publishing today: An overview of the changing landscape of publishers, conglomerates, agents, and book distribution.

Chapter 2:   How to write a book proposal: A step-by-step guide to developing any idea into a business plan.

Chapter 3:   How to find and work with an agent: An action plan for building a profitable relationship with an agent.

Chapter 4:   How to market your book yourself: A blueprint for successful self-marketing or self-publishing.

Chapter 5:   How to understand and negotiate contracts: A tour of the important clauses in publishing agreements, including advances, royalties, and subsidiary rights.

Chapter 6:   How to work with a publisher: A program for nurturing a profitable relationship.

Chapter 7:   How to promote your published book: A detailed strategy for marketing and publicity.

Chapter 8:   How to build a successful career as an author: A career map for long-term personal and financial fulfillment.

~

Part Two: The Author's Problem-Solver: Answers to the 250 Most Common Questions Authors Ask About the Publishing Process

Chapter 9: Starting out: Idea development, proposal writing, self-marketing, agents, and contracts.

Chapter 10: Getting into print: Editors, manuscript development, technology, production, printing, and publication.

Chapter 11: From press to reader: Bookstores, mail order, and the life cycle of a book.

Chapter 12: Moving books off bookstore shelves: Self-promotion, publicity, press releases, and media.

Chapter 13: Managing your writing career: Financial planning and long-term goals.

Part Three: The Author's Resource Kit: Publishers and Agents, Model Proposals, Contacts, and Glossary

Chapter 14: How to locate agents and publishers: Twenty vital resources you should use.

Chapter 15: Three model proposals: Using market-tested templates to create your own book proposal.

Chapter 16: Annotated contracts and agreements.

Appendix
The language of publishing—a glossary.
Index (cross-referenced among the three sections of the book).

Book Specifications

Length: Approximately 575 pages.

Format: Quality black-and-white or two-color paperback and/or hardcover.

Time to completion: Six months from contract.

Publisher's option #1: The book can include a floppy disk (or CD-ROM) compatible with both IBM PCs and Macintosh computers containing typeover proposals and other examples as noted in this proposal. It also contains brief directions that refer users to relevant sections of the book. The proposal templates will be saved in several popular word processing formats for both PC and Mac.

Publisher's option #2: The publisher may want the authors to assemble the book using QuarkXPress on the Macintosh (or PC) desktop. The Bakers have assembled black-and-white and color projects for Random House, John Wiley & Sons, McGraw-Hill, Avery Publishing, and Prentice Hall, among others.

GET PUBLISHED!

*The Non-Fiction Book Author's Handbook,
Problem-Solver, and Resource Kit*

CHAPTER SUMMARIES

Introduction: The universal dream.

A career as a writer? Writing as a career? What can you really expect? The introduction provides a roadmap to the book as well as strong motivators that get browsers to buy the book with the confidence that, "Yes! I can get published!" Grounding readers with an awareness of the elements that go into successfully publishing a book, the chapter is both uplifting and positive, while realistic and cautious. It helps readers, especially those frustrated with too many rejections, gain the insight that with the right idea, along with some hard work and persistence, anyone can win a contract instead of a rejection slip.

- Part one explains the structure of the book and advises readers how to employ the three book segments for maximum benefit.

- Part two discusses how publishing a book (or books) gains personal satisfaction, additional income, and career growth.

- Part three motivates readers to go for it. Success simply hinges on effort and knowledge of publishing. This book provides the knowledge. The reader provides the effort.

Part One: *Everything You Need to Know to Get a Book Successfully Published*

Chapter 1: What really happens in book publishing today: An overview of the changing landscape of publishers, conglomerates, agents, and book distribution.

While many would-be authors believe in the "build a better mousetrap and the world will beat a path to your door" approach to selling a book, for the non-celebrity writer, the reverse is true. Instead of a cadre of publishing houses waiting with baited breath for the next Stephen Covey to submit a manuscript, the trade is highly competitive and affected by trends, market shifts, the economy, and half a hundred other factors. New authors need to understand that the publishing world is built of everything from multinational, multi-imprint houses that dominate the trade as Guttenberg once controlled the printed Bible to small presses that ply the regional trade with books "printed" on a photocopier or at a quick print shop. Increasingly a market-driven industry, the sheer choke of books entering the channels has drastically reshaped the publishing "biz" every decade since the Second World War. Since the roles of editors, agents, and distribution channels have evolved in synchronization with the times, new authors require a thorough briefing of today's publishing environment, its participants, and the "industry insider's" view of publishing operations from the miniscule to the monolithic.

This chapter includes:

- The publishing industry at a glance.

- The publishing process: An overview.

- The modern publisher—small, medium, and conglomerate.

- The modern agent at a glance.

- The modern editor at a glance.

- Five other key players in the publishing game.

- The basic mechanics of book distribution and sales.

Chapter 2: How to write a book proposal: A step-by-step guide to developing any idea into a business plan.

The second chapter focuses on book proposal construction. The lengthiest chapter in Part One, Chapter Two explains how to identify salable book ideas, construct a winning book proposal, conduct competitive and market research, and submit the finished proposal. Explanations of each detail of proposal research and assembly include sources and methods to evaluate potentially competitive titles, and ways to effectively position an idea so it fits a saleable niche with a house or imprint.

Chapter 2 also explains how editors use a well-constructed proposal to move a project successfully through the approval process. Readers learn how the proposal sections become an editor's "building blocks" for the internal documents that sink or sell a book in front of a publisher or editorial committee. This helps readers tailor their proposals appropriately. In addition, the chapter demystifies the approval processes for small, medium, and large houses. This chapter includes:

- Book proposals as business plans.

- The sections of the proposal and what they accomplish.

- Proposals for professional, mass market, text, or niche market books.

- Writing each section: Includes instructions on choosing an idea, identifying possible competition, analyzing markets for the book, and choosing the right agents or the right acquisition editors.

- Assembling and submitting the finished proposal: Do you need to hire a freelance editor? How to make your proposal look its best. Submission tactics. What to do (and not do) while waiting for a response.

- Three convincing editorial summaries.

• Finding middle ground between acceptance and rejection: Put a down payment on that 5000 square foot Central Park condo or take the proverbial flying leap from the Golden Gate Bridge?

Chapter 3: How to find and work with an agent: An action plan for building a profitable relationship with an agent.

The holy grail of unpublished authors is finding an agent who will work for them. As agent Mike Snell explains, "Anyone can be an agent. All it takes is quick-printed business cards and a working telephone. It's finding an *effective* agent who also clicks with you personally and professionally that takes some effort." Chapter 3 takes the reader through the process of identifying several suitable agents, convincing one to take the reader as a client, while, at the same time, checking the prospective agent's credentials to verify creative synergy and ethical business practices.

In this chapter, agent Mike Snell discusses the inside aspects of working with authors, the qualities he looks for in a potential author-clients, and what he expects from them. Authors Kim Baker and Sunny Baker (who have worked with several agents) explain how they choose an agent and the steps for building a quality relationship with their representatives.

This chapter includes:

• The role of the agent.

• The hows, whys, and whens of getting an agent.

• Authors and agents—working towards a common goal.

• What I look for in a prospective new client (M. Snell).

• What I expect from my authors (M. Snell).

• What we expect from our agent (K. & S. Baker).

• Working without an agent: Good idea or bad? (K. & S. Baker).

• Reference to Part Three's sample author-agent agreement with callouts explaining each section.

- The ideal agent-author relationship: What should you look for and work towards?

- Agents and specialization: Who is right for your project?

- The criteria for choosing an agent for *your* nonfiction projects.

- Agent contracts and your obligations as an author.

- Fiscal issues and agent responsibilities.

- Must your agent operate in New York?

- Is it time to move on? Talking with your agent to reestablish common ground.

- Five kinds of "pseudo-agents" to avoid.

Chapter 4: How to market your book yourself: A blueprint for successful self-marketing or self-publishing.

Self-publishing allows some savvy authors to reap the full financial rewards of their book. For others, like Craig Hosada, author of the *Bare Facts Video Guide*, it was the only way to get his controversial project into print. Self-publishing is a double-edged sword which must be wielded with care. On one hand, it allows the author to keep all of the profit from his or her publication, but only while assuming considerable financial risk in producing, printing, distributing, and promoting a title for which there may be no market. Chapter Four explains the mechanics of self-publishing and self-marketing, including a section on distribution channels and mechanisms open to the self-published author.

This chapter includes:

- Self-publishing versus publishing with a traditional publishing house versus subsidy houses.

- An interview with Craig Hosada, a successful self-publisher.

- The steps in self-publishing.

- The economic pluses and minuses of self-publishing.

- Budget analysis for the self publisher.

- Distribution options for self-publishing: Mail order, direct, or distributor?

Chapter 5: How to understand and negotiate contracts: A tour of the important clauses in publishing agreements, including advances, royalties, and subsidiary rights.

As an agreement of trust between author and publisher, as well as a binding legal document, publisher's contracts vary in length from a succinct paragraph or two to labyrinthine 64-pagers. Because few authors pass the bar exam, book contracts and their prose deserve a full chapter in *Get Published!*. Cross-referenced with the actual contracts in Part Three of the book, this chapter spells out the various requirements for negotiating a contract equitable to both sides— publisher *and* author. Special addendums, liability insurance, and non-performance language are explained. Unique and risky clauses are discussed with suggestions for coming to reasonable terms with the publisher, along with basic ownership, copyright, libel, and obscenity issues. Chapter 5 also briefly discusses third-party co-authoring concerns and takes readers through the realities and mechanics of advances, royalties, and rights sales.

This chapter includes:

- Five important issues that are the unwritten basis of a contract: Enthusiasm, timing, luck, chemistry, and trust.

- Contract just arrived? Jump for joy or visit an attorney?

- The basic clauses of every contract and what they mean.

- 10 clauses you should try to zap from a contract.

- The fine print.

- Secondary and subsidiary rights: What are you entitled to? Which should you protect?

- Negotiating with your publisher: How to do it with the right attitude.

- Negotiating through your agent: How to proceed.

- Special sales clauses: Discount terms, book club sales, foreign rights, movie rights, primary edition versus secondary edition, and electronic rights—boon or bane of the future.

- Manuscript acceptance/rejection and failure to perform: How do you handle it?

- Deal gone south or book out of print? How to reclaim your rights with a minimum of hassle.

- Legal trouble with a capital T? Using authors' organizations, your agent, or an attorney for help.

Chapter 6: How to work with a publisher: A program for nurturing a profitable relationship.

An author's relationship with a publisher can form the foundation of a lengthy and prosperous career. For a difficult author, however, the first book may be the last book. Publishers have little interest in working with *prima donna* authors—with the exception of celebrities like television and movie persona already known for their inflated egos. Working effectively with a publisher means being as cooperative as possible, and delicately working out problems and concerns as they crop up. Chapter 6 reveals the realities of working with publishers and explains what publishers expect from authors, and how to build a win-win relationship that leads to additional and more lucrative book contracts. Once established with a publisher, readers will master the timing required for selling subsequent titles within the same house. After gaining an editor's trust, new authors may be asked to produce a book with only a minimal proposal required. This chapter also discusses how an author should work with other people within the publishing house, such as copy editors, the promotion department, production personnel, and rights and legal folks.

This chapter includes:

- Your editor and you.

- Inside the publishing house—how books get sold.

- "The happy, squeaky wheel" versus "the pest": What your publisher wants in a writer.

- Building a positive image inside a publishing house.

- How to handle real problems with a publisher.

- Good cop/bad cop: When your agent should intervene.

- Maintaining visibility in the editor's eyes.

- Selling your next book to the same house.

- When "divorce" makes sense...

Chapter 7: How to promote your published book: A detailed strategy for marketing and publicity.

Few authors understand the mechanics or even the need for promotion. Chapter 7 explains how publishers promote books and what the author can do to extend the publisher's efforts to build market awareness. This information is applicable to the self-publisher as well as the author working through a publishing house. Once authors understand the avenues of promotion, they can work with the publisher to assist in building an effective promotional plan as well as explore the tools of self-promotion. Tools covered in this chapter include advertising, direct mail, public relations, author tours/interviews, and special promotions. Examples and how-to steps for each area complete the presentation.

This chapter includes:

- Promotion basics.

- Publishing houses and promotion.

- Promoting books—the five basic channels and a few new ones.

- Promotion strategies.

- Public relations brief.

- Advertising brief.

- Direct mail brief.

- Author's tours and book signings.

- Other marketing tools and how to use them.

- Three model press releases.

Chapter 8: How to build a successful career as an author: A career map for long-term personal and financial fulfillment.

While some readers will use *Get Published!* to sell a single book, others want to publish multiple projects. Chapter 8 discusses the steps required for career growth, from specializing in a single genre of publications to authoring trade titles on a variety of topics. It also includes advice for building advance dollars, improving contract terms such as royalty rates and unsold inventory return clauses, and touches on sidelines employed by many authors to boost book income such as seminars, magazine writing, and consulting.

The chapter suggests building a five-year publishing plan and how to develop goals for such a plan. Should authors stay within an already personally successful niche or broaden their careers to avoid being pegged in a category that may weaken as the market shifts? This chapter provides the answers.

This chapter includes:

- Building a career as a writer—three directions to consider.

- Niche writing versus generalization: Which is right for you?

- Growing a career while building income.

- Do you need a contingency plan?

- The long term: Setting yourself up for success as a full-time writer/author.

- Watching the book market.

- CD-ROM and Internet publishing: Are they the next big thing?

- Making money from book production.

- Five ways to generate income from already published books.

Part Two: The Author's Problem-Solver: Answers to the 250 Most Common Questions Authors Ask About the Publishing Process

During 40 collective years working with editors and writers, the authors of *Get Published!* have had the same questions pop up repeatedly. Kim and Sunny Baker give seminars for Barnes & Noble on publishing nonfiction books and hear the same questions over and over. Agent Mike Snell reports similar experiences with many of the queries he receives, even from previously published authors. Part Two collects and answers 250 standard questions covering all phases of writing and publishing. This "user-friendly" format makes for a fun read as well as a sensible way of covering specific questions that don't fit comfortably into the structure of Part One. Question and answer length vary, according to the nature of the query.

Chapter 9: Starting out: Idea development, proposal writing, self-marketing, agents, and contracts.

Chapter 9 includes the 100 most asked questions on idea generation, proposal writing, agents, and the legal side of publishing contracts. Where do saleable ideas for books come from? What is the best format and submission channel for my proposal? Why do I need to write a proposal, especially if I've already written a manuscript? What should I send an agent to gain his or her interest in myself and my project? For the unpublished author, this section is a gold mine of basic knowledge which will greatly extend his or her understanding of the professional publishing process.

Chapter 10: Getting into print: Editors, manuscript development, technology, and production.

Chapter 10 includes the 50 most asked questions on working with editors, assembling manuscripts in "publisher-compatible" formats, and book production basics. For every new author, the process of working with an editor, assembling the components of a manuscript and presenting it in a style appropriate to the publishing house is a formidable challenge. Should I send the ms to my agent first? How many words does it take to make a 500-page book as specified in my contract? What constitutes manuscript acceptance and why is it important? Why does my editor never call? Addressing these issues provides the new author with the knowledge it takes pros several books to acquire.

Chapter 11: From press to reader: Book distribution, bookstores, mail order, and the life cycle of a book.

Chapter 11 includes the 25 most asked questions about the various physical book formats and book distribution. What are the differences between a trade paperback and mass-market trade? Who is Ingram and what does this company have to do with publishing? Why won't the local Walden or Dalton carry my self-published book? How does distribution differ for speciality book stores such as those that carry new age or religious titles? How is Borders Books different from a Mom and Pop bookstore? Is mail-order a viable channel for selling books? Even experienced pros are often uncertain of the various categories of books and the mechanisms that propel a book from publisher to purchaser. This chapter answers the questions of professional authors as well as novices. For the self-publisher, Chapter 11 assists readers to understand the channels for moving their title into the standard book channels.

Chapter 12: Moving books off bookstore shelves: Self-promotion, publicity, press releases, and media.

Chapter 12 includes the 50 most asked questions about book promotion and publicity. Promotion is a mystery to almost everyone working outside of marketing, advertising, or PR. This chapter fills in specifics not directly dealt with in Chapter 4 and Chapter 7. Questions answered include: Why do I need a PR program? When does advertising make sense and when it is ineffective? How can I get more publicity budget for my project from my publisher? Do I need (can I afford) a publicity specialist? This chapter adds real-world savvy to that provided in Part One of the book, based on the Bakers' ten years in senior positions in advertising and marketing and Mike Snell's experience promoting books from inside major publishing houses and his extensive observations of the sales results of the hundreds of titles he has placed.

Chapter 13: Managing your writing career: Financial planning and long-term goals.

Chapter 13 includes the 25 most asked questions on career building and long-term planning. Making it as a full-time writer/author is a dream of many, but an accomplishment of few. More of a "dos" and "don'ts" set of questions and answers based on actual experiences by the authors, the chapter poses such issues as: Do I take a book with an $8,000 advance offered today or turn it down in hope of a $15,000 deal that might arrive sometime next week? How can I pry an overdue advance check out of a publisher? How many books can I write in a year and is that enough income to make a living? How do I get a health plan? What does a five year plan for writing look like and why do I need one? How do I keep the IRS (or Revenue Canada) out of my pocket and career?

Part Three: The Author's Resource Kit: Publishers and Agents, Model Proposals, Glossary, Contacts

Chapter 14: How to locate agents and publishers: Twenty resources you should use.

Chapter 14 introduces readers to the 20 most important resources available for proposal research, quality writing, and submission information. Examples of resources covered include *LMP*, Bowker's *Books in Print* (now available on CD-ROM for fast searches), *Elements of Style*, and books containing agent listings. Not simply a set of lists, this section explains each resource, why it's important, how it can be used, and where to find it.

An additional section briefly covers authoring tools such as word processors and suggestions for the use of writing technologies.

Chapter 15: Model proposals: Using market-tested templates to create your own book proposal.

Three solid (and sold) book proposals handled by agent Mike Snell and authors Kim & Sunny Baker are reproduced in full in the book (and 15 more are included on the disk packaged with the book), so they can be used as models by aspiring authors. The three printed versions include Coleman's *Life's Parachutes* and the Bakers' *How to Promote, Publicize, and Advertise Your Growing Business* and *Lemon Tree Very Healthy*. The proposals represent several subcategories of nonfiction books. They also represent differing levels of preparation. The most complex example was designed to sell a richly illustrated cookbook in which illustration ability was a key component of the proposal. The simplest proposal, written for a business book, was knocked off on a typewriter and contains no complex formatting or pictures.

Chapter 16: Annotated contracts agreements.

Three complete annotated book contracts, one from a small publisher, one from a medium-sized house, and one from a multinational corporation, familiarize readers with the legal mumbo-jumbo and relate it to the advice contained in Chapter Five. In addition, sample author-agent agreements are reproduced in full, with callouts and referenced to Chapter Three.

Appendix

The language of publishing—a glossary.

Index (cross-referenced among all three sections of the book).

Body Learning

NOTES ON THIS PROPOSAL

Still in prepublication, *Body Learning* may be retitled or keep its original moniker depending on the whims of the marketing committee and the clout of the author. (Virginia Whitelaw, Putnam/Perigee).

BODYLEARNING™

...a powerful, life-changing program that gets your body and mind working together to create...

—total fitness— —less stress & conflict—
—more energy—   —a focused mind—
—greater awareness— —inner strength—
—a sense of connection and wholeness—

Virginia Whitelaw, Ph.D.

Michael Snell Literary Agency
Box 655 Truro, MA 02666
Tel: 508-349-3718

Executive Summary

BodyLearning is the powerful process by which we unlock the wisdom of the body to energize and transform our life. Unifying body and mind, we turn potential into actual success. Slow to recognize the body as a teacher, we've mostly tried to reach our potential through heady affirmations and "mind over matter." The fact is, we're of "more than one mind" on most matters. On the one hand Bill wants a promotion at work, on the other hand his blood pressure is climbing and his temper flaring. Susan wants to lose weight, but can't resist her favorite foods. Jeff wants a steady relationship, but his body "betrays" him in its wandering desires. What's going on with us when we seem to be our own worst enemy? So long as we treat the body as a land mass we can rule with oppression, we'll fail again and again. Once we're ready to quit failing, we're ready to start BodyLearning.

BodyLearning is a journey of three steps. The first step is developing breath and center. Breath is our connection between body and mind. Learning to breathe into our center links our thoughts with the very core of our being. The second step is building a practice so we have a way to develop our breath and center. A practice is a special activity in our day, done in full breath-awareness and being in the present moment. It may be a form of exercise or meditation, an art or craft, or an everyday activity such as walking or driving. Using a personal inventory, we'll design a practice that matches our individual needs and interests. The third step in BodyLearning is growing our practice, allowing our increased energy, awareness, and alignment to shape our larger life.

Each step of the way delivers wondrous results: more energy, fitness, and focus; increased confidence and calm. Defeating ourselves less, we succeed more. From this body we learn exactly what is this life to live, and we live it fully.

2

Proposal Contents:

About the Book   4

About the Market   8

About the Author   13

Book Contents   15

Publishing Information   16

Chapter Summaries   18

Sample Chapter   29

About the Book

"The evolution of fitness is consciousness." Jonas Salk

"Mind over matter." We've all heard the adage. "If you put your mind to it, you can do it." Much as we may like this message, surely we've encountered many a matter we couldn't put our mind over. Illnesses we couldn't think our way out of. Goals we couldn't put our mind to. New Year's resolve that dissolved by spring. If the mind is so powerful, what seems to be the matter?

My Zen teacher, Hosokawa Roshi, put it best. "The body and mind are one," he said "But we are not of one body-mind." Yes, the body and mind are one: our body is a physical record of the thoughts, emotions, and behaviors that have shaped our life up till now. The confidence in our posture, the tension in our muscles, the pressure of our blood, all reflect the same character that informs our conscious thoughts.

But we are not always of one mind — much less one body-mind. Bill wants the big promotion at work, but he resents the longer hours. Susan wants to lose weight, but can't resist feasting after a fast. Adding to our internal discord, our thoughts are able to change much faster than our body. Bill thinks he can handle the promotion at work, but his blood pressure is climbing. Susan consciously wants to lose weight, but the comfort of eating is the only way her body knows to manage stress. The latest scheme of the conscious mind may be at odds with the deeper patterns embedded in our body. The result is mixed signals. In ways mostly deeper-than-conscious, we partly defeat ourselves in all that we sort-of halfway do.

4

Fortunately, we can unscramble the mixed signals. We can become of one body-mind, clear in our intents and aligned from brain to bone in our actions. But we don't develop this depth of alignment through thoughts alone. We can only learn this wholeness through the body. This is what I call "BodyLearning:" <u>a powerful way to unlock the wisdom of our body to energize and transform our life.</u> In BodyLearning we use a physical practice to align body, mind and spirit, by which we develop to our fullest strength. A whole world of victories opens up once we quit defeating ourselves.

BodyLearning is a journey of three steps. The first step is developing our breath and center. Breath is the link between body and mind, between our conscious thoughts and deeper-than-conscious patterns within us. Paying attention to our breath opens a channel, so to speak, through which alignment of body, mind and spirit can proceed. We gain a crucial perspective, giving us a choice about whether to be sucked into the drama of daily conflicts or to be present in calm awareness. Awareness of our breath develops this perspective, which is aware-ness itself. As we follow our breath, it becomes slower and drops lower in our body. We become more relaxed, focused and energized as our body is nour-ished from a deeper well. We're guided through a progression of self-tests and exercises by which we deepen our breathing, find our center, and experience the wondrous results: energy, awareness, focus and alignment.

The thought to follow our breath, like all thoughts, will not last very long if we don't support it. Therein lies the value of building a practice: the second step of BodyLearning. A practice gives us time in each day to develop our breath and center. It is our special time to build energy, awareness and wholeness.

But what do we practice? Meditation — whether lying down, sitting or walking — is excellent for some people. If it works for us, there's nothing better for developing inner strength and stability. Having learned a number of exercises and meditation forms, we're shown ways to combine them into a daily program.

"I've tried meditation before," Bob said in one of my seminars. "But I just can't sit still." If we're like Bob, we do well to find a more active practice. Any number of physical activities from exercise and sports, arts and crafts, to everyday activities like walking or driving can be excellent sources of BodyLearning. Using a personal inventory and six-step process, we're able to design an individualized practice that meets our own needs and interests. In addition to the basic gifts of BodyLearning — greater energy, awareness and wholeness — we find in this process we can also *shape* the impact of body on mind, strengthening specific qualities we want to work on.

Jim, for example, wanted to better manage his anger. Based on his interests, he identified an aerobic activity (jogging) as a good way to blow off steam, as well as quieter activity (woodworking) for building patience and confidence. Sarah, who often felt "a day late and a dollar short" wanted to work on her sense of timing and awareness. She chose tennis as an aerobic practice to help her develop dynamic timing, along with the quieter activity of outdoor photography to develop her sense of nature's timing.

While it's true that we can learn from many activities, it is also true that we can do many things and learn very little from them. The difference is awareness. From Zen training, we distill the quality of awareness that transforms ordinary activities into extraordinary paths for growth, and apply it to our practice.

Focusing on our breath, paying attention to all that our senses present, we fully enter the present moment. We learn to integrate our breathing into the motions of our practice, for example, matching a smooth exhale to the swing of a golf club or release of a bowling ball. When our mind wanders (which it will!) we simply bring it back. This is our practice.

At some point, we'll find the energy, awareness and alignment of our practice demanding more expression in our life, propelling us toward the third step of BodyLearning: growing the practice. <u>Growing our practice is allowing it to transform our life</u>. There are three ways a practice grows and these happen in any order, any number of times. We can *intensify* our practice, stretching ourselves further. Janet, for example, intensified her running practice from 3 miles a day to entering 10K races to running a marathon. We can *diversify* our practice, finding new activities to build new strengths or work around barriers. For example, I found yoga and dance made it possible to intensify my Zen training. The third way to grow our practice is to *apply* it in daily life. For example, when tempers start to flare, immediately we can find our breath, find our center and be at our best. By applying the quality of awareness to other moments in our day, moment by moment we wake up.

The payoff is enormous joy. Aligning our physical body, our conscious mind and the spirit or energy that runs through us, we connect our thoughts and deeds to the core of our being. At the same time, we connect to life itself. Aligning ourselves within, we become aligned with life's larger patterns. <u>Through BodyLearning, we learn exactly from this body what is our life to live.</u> And we live it fully.

About the Market

BodyLearning is for people who want more energy and success in their lives. It is for those who have experienced the frustration of elusive goals and self-defeating patterns, who have tried any number of positive-thinking self-help formulas that didn't hold up under pressure. Looking for a more grounded, integrated approach to their development, these readers are ready to discover the power and wisdom in their own bodies. Many will already be engaged in physical activities. Through *BodyLearning,* they'll discover how to derive greater benefits from their training: energy, awareness and alignment of body, mind, and spirit. Intrigued with the mind-body connection, those who read *BodyLearning* want to discover how to put that connection to greater practical use in their lives.

BodyLearning markets under self-help, health and fitness, and spirituality. Relative to products already marketed in these areas, *BodyLearning* is a unique synthesis and a necessary companion.

BodyLearning is a valuable extension to some of the most popular self help books on the market that are rich in good advice, but offer no way to integrate it into our lives. For example, in his marvelous book, *The Road Less Traveled* (Simon & Schuster, 1978), Scott Peck identifies two factors that prevent us from reaching our full potential: fear and laziness. Unfortunately, it's difficult to simply decide to become less fearful or lazy. *BodyLearning* gives us a way to develop greater energy, overcoming our laziness. Our increased awareness and confidence quiets our fears. Moreover, we can use our practice to address specific fears, for example training in martial arts to overcome the fear of attack.

8

BodyLearning clears a path by which we can eliminate laziness and fear in our life and actually walk "the road less traveled."

As another example, Stephen Covey, identifies *7 Habits of Highly Effective People* (Simon & Schuster, 1989), but does not give us a practical way to develop those habits. *BodyLearning* shows how a practice like Aikido lets us physically rehearse habits like "putting first things first," and "thinking win-win" a hundred times an hour. Many self-help books contain important truths. *BodyLearning*, while adding its own truth, is unique in providing a customized way to practice the preaching that speaks to us, wherever we find it.

Many books have explored the connection of mind and body from the practical perspective of what the body's health or language tells us about ourselves or others. *Decoding the Secret Language of Your Body* (Martin Rush, Simon & Schuster, 1994), *Body Language* (Julius Fast, Simon & Schuster, 1970), *Body-mind* (Ken Dychtwald, Tarcher, 1977), and *The Body Reveals* (Ron Kurtz and Hector Prestera, HarperCollins, 1976) are rich in examples of how the body reflects the mind's character. Focusing on why the body is the way it is, these books do not take the step made in *BodyLearning* of changing the body as a way to change the mind.

Many health and fitness books have explored the powerful impact of the mind on the body's health. For example, Bill Moyer's *Healing and the Mind* (Doubleday, 1993) or Deepak Chopra's *Ageless Body, Timeless Mind* (Harmony Books, 1993) document numerous cases of the body healing through the mind's conviction. Similarly, *The Healing Path* (Marc Ian Barasch, Penguin, New York, 1993) and *You Can Heal Your Life* (Louise Hay, Hay House, Carson, CA., 1984) offer imagery and meditations for healing what ails us. *Mind Body Therapy* (Ernest Rossi & David Cheek, Norton, New York, 1988) shows how hypnosis can be used as a method of healing. All of these books make a convincing case for the power of the mind-body connection. *BodyLearning* runs this connection in reverse, as it were, showing ways we can use the unique wisdom of the body to stabilize and direct the development of the mind.

Countless examples of mind shaping body and body shaping mind are assembled in Michael Murphy's impressive volume, *The Future of the Body* (Tarcher, Los Angeles, 1992). One of the themes of Murphy's book, that the human transformative capacity is unleashed by what he calls "integral practices," affirms the very foundation of *BodyLearning*. *BodyLearning* then takes the next step of guiding readers to a practice and a way of practicing that answers development needs in their lives.

Many exercise books and manuals on meditation describe the benefits of these practices on one's mental health. For example, in *Minding the Body, Mending the Mind* (Bantam, 1987), Joan Borysenko describes how physical exercise can break the cycle of anxiety. While this book includes self-assessments revealing something of one's condition and needs, unlike *BodyLearning*, it does not use the self-tests to guide readers toward an individualized development program. Some tailoring of physical practices to individual characteristics is included in Deepak Chopra's *Perfect Health* (Random House, 1991). Using the Ayurvedic methods of body-mind medicine, Chopra identifies several physical practices appropriate to the *Vata*, *Pitta,* and *Kapha* body types. Using terminology and methods that many Western readers will find more accessible, *BodyLearning* considers a broader spectrum of activities and broader criteria for making them part of one's practice.

Several manuals on meditation have explored how everyday activities can become profound paths for growth. *The Miracle of Mindfulness* (Thich Nhat Hanh, Beacon Press, Boston, 1975) and *The Everyday Meditator* (Osho, Tuttle, Boston, 1993) are excellent guides on how to practice routine activities in full breath awareness and aliveness in the present moment. *BodyLearning*, considers a broader base of physical practices and guides readers through customizing a practice to match their specific needs and interests.

Exercise books typically promote a particular exercise program for a particular reason. (e.g. *The Aerobics Program for Total Well Being* (Kenneth Cooper, Bantam, 1982), *The 90 Day Fitness Walking Program* (Marc Fenton & Seth Bauer, Perigree, 1995), or *Yoga for Health* (Richard Hittleman, Ballantine, 1983). *BodyLearning* differs from these in its focus on guiding readers to a better understanding of their own development needs and an individualized program to address them.

Finally, *BodyLearning* is a valuable complement to other guides along the spiritual path. For example, *Care of the Soul* (Thomas Moore, HarperCollins, 1992) invites us to appreciate the linkage of body-mind-spirit and the sacredness in life. But it does not give us a physical practice to improve our care. *Your Sacred Self* (Wayne Dyer, HarperCollins, 1995) invites us to a higher awareness of the divinity within us, transcending ego boundaries. But its approach is based on affirmations and mind exercises, rather than the salient physical experience of sacredness developed through everyday practice.

11

BodyLearning does not approach spiritual questions with new dogma or concepts. Rather, the experience of our own body-mind wholeness reveals the truth of our spiritual connectedness. Learning through our body, we stabilize our walk on the spiritual path.

About the Author

Physics, biophysics, philosophy, Aikido, Zen and a career managing people and projects through change comprise the wealth of experience Dr. Whitelaw brings to *BodyLearning*. "The common thread is energy," Dr. Whitelaw explains, "Every discipline has taught me something valuable about our connection to energy: how to tap it, focus it, and put it to good use in the world."

Beginning her formal study of energy in college, Dr. Whitelaw worked for several years in a high energy physics laboratory. In 1977, she graduated with highest honors from Michigan State University with degrees in physics and philosophy. With a goal to learn more about energy in living systems, she studied biophysics in graduate school. She developed computer models of the nervous system and tested their predictions in the laboratory, publishing several articles on the way the nervous system develops. Her publications include: "Developmental Mechanisms Involved in Chick Limb Innervation," University of Chicago, Ph.D. Thesis, 1982; Whitelaw and Hollyday, "Motorneuron Target Selectivity," (3 papers) Journal of Neuroscience, 1983; Whitelaw and Cowan, "Specificity and Plasticity of Retinotectal Connections," Journal of Neuroscience, 1981. In 1982, she received her doctorate in biophysics from the University of Chicago.

Dr. Whitelaw was a scientist and then a manager at Bell Laboratories. In 1985, she joined National Aeronautics and Space Administration (NASA). As she moved up through the management ranks at NASA, she worked to focus and integrate the many organizations working on the Space Station Program. In 1993, NASA asked her to lead the management redesign for the Space Station and the transition to a new model of government-industry teams. Through her efforts to guide organizations through massive change and improve their effectiveness, she learned the importance of alignment in reaching one's goals, both individually and organizationally. Helping people and organizations successfully manage change and reach important goals became a new focus for her work, and one of the catalysts for developing *BodyLearning*.

Alongside her career in science and management, Dr. Whitelaw has been active in martial arts for more than 20 years. Aikido and Zen provided her deepest learning of the body's role in transforming energy. She is a Zen Priest in the Rinzai tradition (ordained as Reverend Jiko Myoki) and serves on the faculty of the Institute for Zen Studies. A 4th degree black belt and member of the Aikido Association of America's National Teaching Committee, she has taught Aikido classes and seminars around the country. She has also led seminars applying Aikido and Zen to such areas as conflict resolution, leadership development and stress management. Since 1987, she has been the Chief Instructor of an Aikido and Zen training center, first in Houston and now in Atlanta.

"I'm now in my third life, professionally speaking," Dr. Whitelaw says. "And it combines the best of the first two — all that I learned as a scientist and as a manager — with all that has come through 20 years of my own *BodyLearning*." Dr. Whitelaw left NASA in 1994 to devote full time to writing, teaching and consulting. As a management consultant, she has worked with many organizations on ways to improve their effectiveness and manage change. Her clients include New York Life, W.R. Grace, the Federal Executive Institute, CMP, Entertainment, and the Jordanian Government. She also leads personal development seminars in *BodyLearning*, through which the methods and exercises of this book have been refined and proven.

Book Contents

Introduction

Chapter 1. Joining Forces: Three Steps to a Whole Life

Step 1: Developing Breath and Center

Chapter 2. Energy: Tapping the Infinite Source

Chapter 3. Awareness: Waking Up to the Present

Chapter 4. Focus: Developing a Sharper, Clearer Mind

Chapter 5. Alignment: Moving Beyond Self-Defeating Patterns

Step 2: Building a Practice

Chapter 6. Inner Strength: Building Bedrock Confidence

Chapter 7. Personal Inventory: Discovering Your Needs and Interests

Chapter 8. Total Fitness: Designing a Practice that's Right For You

Chapter 9. Commitment: Developing Staying Power

Step 3: Growing the Practice

Chapter 10. Peace: Resolving Stress and Conflict

Chapter 11. Resilience: Managing the Pains of Life

Chapter 12. Wholeness: Experiencing the Connection

Publication Information

- 90,000 words
- 45 illustrations or photographs
- 12 exercises, 10 self-tests, including a personal inventory and supporting
  worksheets for designing basic and customized programs in *BodyLearning*

Available within 90 days

Author is leading workshops in *BodyLearning* that will grow through the
availability of this book, and serve as a way to distribute the book and any
auxiliary products.

BodyLearning is well-suited to companion CD-ROM, videotapes, audio
cassettes, journal and calendar products. Possible auxiliary products
include:

CD-ROM: An interactive, multimedia journey through *BodyLearning*, including: a motivational synopsis of the three steps of
BodyLearning, video demonstration of the exercises, interactive
self-tests, and automated processing of the personal inventory,
generating a list of candidate activities that match specified needs
and interests. Also includes tools for designing and modifying a
practice, as well as an on-line journal for recording practice sessions and reactions to the training.

Videotape: A motivational synopsis of the three steps of *BodyLearning* with focus on demonstrating the proper way to practice the exercises.

Audio Cassettes: A motivational synopsis of the three steps of *BodyLearning* with focus on guiding the listener through breathing exercises and awareness development exercises that are possible to do at home, in the office, or even while driving in the car. Also guides the listener through the self assessment process for developing a personal program in *BodyLearning*.

Journal: Provides a personal log of *BodyLearning* experience, with sections for documenting the personal inventory of needs and interests, recording goals, logging work-outs or practice sessions, and recording experiences and reactions to the training.

Calendar: Provides motivational quotes from the book and at-a-glance recording of work-outs or practice sessions. Also provides illustrations of the book's exercises.

17

Chapter Summaries

Introduction

It took me 19 years to catch my breath. Between allergies and asthma, I wheezed through most of my childhood. Then I made matters worse: I started smoking. And coughing. Eventually I learned the first big lesson from my body: I was destroying my life. That's when I started working out, cleaning out — calisthenics at first, then weightlifting, jogging, skiing, martial arts and meditation. So many activities opened up and, for the first time, became possible. Eventually I could breathe, but something even more remarkable was happening: a wisdom coming through the body, far smarter than "I," was shaping my life in every enriching way. Not only was this happening to me, but to so many people engaged in serious training. Understanding and communicating what's at the core of this remarkable process has become the core of my work. This is what I call *BodyLearning*: unlocking the wisdom of our body to energize and transform our life.

Chapter 1. Joining Forces: Three Steps to a Whole Life

BodyLearning is the powerful process by which the body and mind join forces to create a whole and balanced person. "Mind over matter" is not enough, since we're of "more than one mind" on most matters (and certainly more than one body-mind). Bill wants a promotion at work, but his health is failing and his temper flaring. Susan wants to lose weight, but she can't resist feasting after a fast. What's going on with us when we seem to be our own worst enemy? So long as we treat our body as a land mass we can rule with oppression, we'll keep defeating ourselves. Once we're ready to quit defeating ourselves, we're ready to do *BodyLearning*

BodyLearning is a journey of three steps: (1) Developing breath and center, (2) building a practice (so we have a way to develop breath and center) and (3) growing our practice, that it can shape our larger life. The benefits begin immediately — as we discover in a breathing exercise, starting us along the path by which the promise of *BodyLearning* becomes our own vivid experience

Step 1: Developing Breath and Center
Chapter 2. Energy: Tapping the Infinite Source

"What I really need is more energy," said Dana, explaining why she came to my seminar on *BodyLearning*. "I'm so tired. And the less I do, the less I feel like doing." That's a vicious cycle most of us know. What we don't realize is that we have access to all the energy we could ever want. We're literally swimming in it, yet like fish in water, most of us are scarcely aware this energy exists, much less how to tap it. The trick is learning not to cut off from this infinite supply; this trick is learned through our body. As soon as we pay attention to our breath, our body begins to relax, allowing more energy to flow. Through lying down meditation, we experience the difference between "holding" and flowing energy in our body. We also experience the body relaxing as our heart and breathing rates drop and our breath drops physically lower in our body, eventually coming to rest at our center (*hara*). We learn how to breathe to and from our center and "set the *hara*" as a way of building energy in the body.

Chapter 3. Awareness: Waking Up to the Present

"Mel doesn't have 20 years of experience," one of my colleagues said of another. "He has one year twenty times." If somewhat biting, the comment had the seed of truth. What makes some people able to grow from their experience, while others, like Mel, seem to play the same tape over and over with little gained?

Awareness is the difference. And awareness is the second benefit we realize in following our breath. Paying attention to our breath, suddenly we become aware of what we're doing and aware of the one doing it. This shift changes everything. From this perspective, we get a better view of what's really going on. We get a choice about whether to be sucked into daily dramas or to be present in calm awareness. We build the link between living and learning. In an awareness exercise, we consider what lessons we're already learning through our body. We also tap our awareness for how much we notice about parts of our day. Through an exercise in walking meditation, we experience our senses opening, noticing how much more news they bring once we're paying attention.

Chapter 4. Focus: Developing a Sharper, Clearer Mind

Jack is the most practical, down-to-earth man I know; you'd never find him in a metaphysical bookstore. Yet after the stress and responsibilities of work started giving him heart trouble, he tried meditation. "I'm surprised how much it quiets me down," he said. "Not only does my heart quit racing, but so does my mind."

In addition to developing energy and awareness, paying attention to our breath has the most remarkable focusing effect on our mind. Connecting mind to body through our breath allows our mind to absorb and transform to a mental condition, the same relaxation and stability we experience in the body. In a series of breathing and centering exercises, we experience how, as the mind quiets down, it becomes easier to focus on the breath, which quiets the mind further. This pattern builds on itself, honing the mind to sharpness, clarity and concentration.

Chapter 5. Alignment: Moving Beyond Self-Defeating Patterns

William wants the big promotion at work that will mean longer hours, but he also wants to spend evenings with his family. Striving half-heartedly, he resents his job for its late hours and his family for asking him not to work the late hours. How can he "have it all" when all that he wants is not even logically possible?

We can often see our own mixed signals in goals that never quite come together for us. Through a set of questions, we reflect on such a goal and consider what conflicting intentions might be holding it hostage. Not only are we of "more than one mind" on many matters, but our body changes more slowly than our thoughts, often posing resistance to our mind's latest scheme. Through a deeper synthesis of mind and matter, we can learn to quit defeating ourselves. Using the breath to link mind into the body, we open a channel, so to speak, through which alignment of body and mind can proceed. In a set of exercises, we physically experience alignment as we recruit more of the body into the breathing process. We then return to walking meditation and discover how to make this a practice in aligning ourselves from brain to bone.

Step 2: Building a Practice
Chapter 6. Inner Strength: Building Bedrock Confidence

"Do you want to go through life on a bicycle or a tank?" Zen master Tanouye Roshi asked in a lecture years ago. His powerful presence overfilling the room, he gave us his bottom line. "Me, I'll take the tank."

Bedrock confidence is not built on heady affirmations that can't hold up under pressure. It's built on the genuine power we experience by connecting to the core of our being. To build inner strength, or reap any of the enduring benefits of developing our breath and center, we need a way to develop them: we need a practice. A practice is a special time in our day where we do a physical activity in full breath awareness and being in the present moment. No practice is better at developing our breath and center, at building inner strength, than sitting meditation (*Zazen*). We're shown how to sit Zazen and develop the *hara* power we experience as inner strength. We're then shown how to design a life-changing practice based on the exercises and meditation forms we've experienced thus far.

Chapter 7. Personal Inventory: Discovering Your Needs and Interests

A practice is a special time in our day to develop breath and center, building energy, awareness and wholeness in our life. The best practice is one that suits us. "I've tried meditation before," says Bob, a participant in one of my seminars. "And I just can't sit still." At the other extreme there's Joan who can't stand exercise. "Don't tell me I've got to jog to do *BodyLearning*," she says. As I tell my students, I won't tell you to do anything. I'll help you organize the messages, but you'll tell yourself.

So many activities from sports and exercise, to arts and crafts, to walking or gardening can be excellent *BodyLearning* practices. It's best if we choose a practice we sincerely enjoy, for we'll apply ourselves more fully and be more likely to stick with it. While all *BodyLearning* activities will help us develop breath and center, aerobic activities will develop us differently than those that are more quiet or meditative. Depending on what results are most important to us, we can tailor our practice appropriately. Through a personal inventory of our needs and interests, we identify the results we want the most and the activities that we favor for getting there. We then close by practicing one of our candidate activities in full breath-awareness.

Chapter 8. Total Fitness: Designing a Practice That's Right For You

"What does total fitness mean to you?" I asked at a recent seminar. "Having a body beautiful," one of the participants answered instantly. But then a discussion ensued on whether a beautiful body is always a healthy body. "How about having a body that's beautiful to live in?" another participant suggested. "A body that totally fits our life." This is what *BodyLearning* builds.

Total fitness grows out of a well-rounded practice that develops us from several angles. Such a practice includes an outwardly focused activity (such as martial arts or tennis) that develops our awareness by demanding it, as well as a quieter activity (such as yoga or gardening) that requires we train our awareness on what we're doing. A balanced practice includes a meditative activity (meaning non-aerobic) to build resting energy, as well an aerobic activity to build peak energy and blow off steam. Through a stepwise process, we're shown how to design a balanced practice of 2-4 activities that's a good fit to our needs and interests. We close by selecting an activity from our practice — best if it addresses the area of our highest need — and give it our full attention.

Chapter 9. Commitment: Developing Staying Power

"Getting my black belt is the most important thing to me right now," Greg said after his first Aikido class. "My wife wants me to get in shape, I need this for my job, and I'm really dedicated." My uneasiness with his enthusiasm was confirmed a few weeks later when he caught the flu, missed a couple of classes, and then found one reason after another that kept him off the mat.

So often we tear into activities or relationships and then proceed to back out. Sometimes that's appropriate, but if it's a principal pattern of our life, we're cheating ourselves out of the depth that only comes with commitment. We can learn commitment through our body. Indeed remaining committed to our daily practice is, in its own right, a way to build commitment. Through a set of questions, we explore how to make space for our practice, overcoming its obstacles, that it can develop staying power in our life. We also learn how to practice, applying the quality of breath-awareness (that we experience in Zen meditation) to the activities we've chosen for *BodyLearning*. For example, we can combine a smooth exhale with the swing of a golf club, or blend our breath into our aerobic dance movements. The more we put into our practice, the more we get out of it, and the more our commitment grows. We close by selecting another of our *BodyLearning* activities and practice integrating our breath into its motions.

Step 3: Growing the Practice

Chapter 10. Peace: Resolving Stress and Conflict

Thich Nhat Hanh, the wonderful Vietnamese Buddhist teacher, tells the story of a talk he gave in the U.S. in 1966, calling for a cease-fire in Vietnam. An angry young peace activist jumped up and shouted "[You] go back to your country and defeat the American aggressors!" Practiced in such matters, Thich Nhat Hanh took a long, deep breath before answering. Peace starts within.

While it may start in twenty minute intervals, the results of our practice will begin to seep into the rest of our day. Our practice enriches our life all the more when we give it room to grow. Growing our practice may entail practicing with more intensity or doing more activities. But it can also mean applying the same awareness we have in our practice to other moments in our day. And nowhere will we feel more rewarded than when we apply our practice to reduce our stress and conflict. Finding our breath and center in difficult moments gives us an enormous advantage: immediately we gain a perspective from which we see more clearly, as well as a stream of energy to support our patience. We don't have to resort to the blind energy of conflict when we have a more stable source.

Through a set of questions we explore our own conflict triggers and how we can apply our practice toward triggering less. As a closing exercise, we select an activity that will particularly help us quiet the conflict within and do it for twenty minutes. In our own experience we discover that stable peace is built on a stable center — developed through our practice.

Chapter 11. Resilience: Managing the Pains of Life

Growing our practice may well involve intensifying or diversifying what we do, bringing us face-to-face with some discomforts. Yet learning to manage the body's pain delivers some of the deepest benefits of *BodyLearning*: resilience and courage. Without this resilience, we're buffeted by life's inevitable pains. Sylvia, for example, had tremendous difficulty near the end of her pregnancy. The baby's pressure on her rib cage caused painful muscle spasms. Her doctor recommended bed rest and warm towels, but Sylvia couldn't follow this advice. The pain got worse and Sylvia grew more frantic. "I can't stand it for two more months," she said, "I'm going crazy." Katie, on the other hand, would be elated if she only had two more months of pain. Her foot was shattered in a car accident seven years ago and she hasn't had a painless day since. Yet she still trains and teaches Aikido. "I've learned to direct the pain into my practice," she told me once. "It'll probably never go away. But it doesn't have to."

Pain in life is inevitable. People we care about die, things don't happen the way we want them to, and our own health fails us ultimately, if not frequently. But how much we suffer with pain is a matter of choice on our part. Through our body, we learn how to handle pain without making it into worse than it is. A set of questions lets us review our practice for which of its discomforts we need to accept, versus those that should signal us something is wrong. We also reflect on things that cause pain in our life and how our practice can help us handle it. We're often resourceful in the ways we try to escape whatever makes us uncomfortable. But as our resilience and courage grow, escape becomes unnecessary.

Chapter 12. Wholeness: Experiencing the Connection

On a ski trip in Colorado, I stopped to admire Boulder Falls. As the winter was not yet deep, the falls were not totally frozen. Along the banks, lovely ice sculptures had developed, each distinct and individual. Ice covered much of the river, but through its translucent layer and occasional gaps, the flow underneath was unmistakable. "Exactly like us!" I thought. At the surface, in these temporary conditions we call a lifetime, the flow freezes into separate statues. We can tap on the surface of what appears to be our boundaries. And yet what do we make of the motion underneath? If we watch long enough (and this blessed day at Boulder Falls turned lifetimes into minutes), we see we move ever into and out of the flow.

BodyLearning is ultimately a spiritual journey. It cannot be otherwise, for the matter of the body is but a "frozen" form of the energy that connects us all. The most remarkable result of *BodyLearning* is our genuine experience of this energy. We experience our connection to all of life. From the start, we feel more energized. As the energy grows, we're more alive, aware, confident, successful: without a doubt, this is the most joyous way to live. Without a doubt, our ego will push back when it senses this energy is changing us. Being willing to grow our practice and listen to its wisdom, our ego slowly acknowledges its willingness to change. This is an enormous breakthrough, though it happens in such tiny steps we may hardly notice it. It happens each time we give up a habit that deadens us, such as excessive drinking or television. It happens each time we give of ourselves with no expectation of return.

Exercises let us consider what the wisdom of our body would change in our life even now, and how our practice can support our continued growth toward wholeness. Growing our practice is the shift by which we dedicate our life to life itself and, in the most challenging sense of the phrase, "go with the flow." Miraculously, in making this shift, we learn from our body exactly what is our life to live. And we live it as one!

Resources for Writers

ASSOCIATIONS AND CLUBS

American Society of Journalists and Authors (ASJA)

1501 Broadway, Suite 302
New York, NY 10036
212-997-0947 (212-768-7414 fax)

ASJA requires proof of published nonfiction works to join. They require multiple magazine clips and/or one or more nonfiction books. Three letters of recommendation are required. In return for membership (a spouse can join on a single membership), ASJA provides a useful newsletter, help to authors mired in disputes, classes and seminars (fee-based), and a variety of other services (insurance, for example). ASJA also reports on publications (magazines) that are slow to pay their authors.

Authors Guild

330 West 42nd Street
New York, NY 10036
212-594-7931 (212-564-5363 fax)

The Authors Guild requires proof of publishing for membership, in the form of fiction or nonfiction books handled by recognized houses. Like ASJA, in return for membership, the Guild provides a useful newsletter, help to authors mired in disputes, and other important keep-you-from-going-insane services.

America Online Writer's Club

Call 1-800-827-3338 for information.
http://www.aol.com

The America Online Writer's club provides everything from chat lines (try the Writer's Cafe) to scheduled online conversations with bestselling authors (fiction and nonfiction). For a start-up kit to get an America Online (AOL) account, look for computer magazines that include a disk from AOL on the cover. You'll need a computer and a modem to join. Once online, use the search keyword *writers* or *books*, or navigate by clicking through the Clubs & Interests dialogs to get to the Writers Club. This gives you the opportunity to see all the other resources for writers on America Online. You can also type in "go writers club" to get there. As mentioned earlier, the club has an author's mentoring program that is free except for connect time.

National Writers Union

113 University Place, 6th Floor
New York, NY 10003
http://www.nwu.org/nwu/nwuinf1.htm

The National Writers Union (NWU) is the trade union for freelance writers of all genres. The union is committed to improving the economic and working conditions of freelance writers through the collective strength of its members. The union provides grievance resolution, industry campaigns, contract advice, health and dental plans, member education, job banks, networking, social events, and much more. The NWU is affiliated with the United Automobile Workers (UAW) and through them with the AFL-CIO. (We don't have the history on this relationship, but join and maybe you'll get the scoop.) The NWU has locals and organizing committees throughout the country. The 4,500 members include journalists, book authors, poets, copywriters, academic authors, cartoonists, and technical and business writers. Membership in the NWU is open to all qualified writers. You are eligible for membership if you have published a book, a play, three articles, five poems, a short story, or an equal amount of newsletter, publicity, technical, commercial, government, or institutional copy. You are also eligible for membership if you have written an equal amount of unpublished material and are actively writing and attempting to publish your work.

Local Clubs, Workshops, and Conferences

In addition to the national clubs, societies and clubs for writers of all sorts thrive in every city. Ask at local bookstores, libraries, or community colleges for contact information about membership and events.

ONLINE RESOURCES

Numerous writing groups, consultants, and resources are available on the Internet. Internet users can use search engines such as WebCrawler (http://www.webcrawler.com) or Yahoo! (http://www.yahoo.com) to surf the Net. These are available through any Web browser, such as Netscape, or browsers included with America Online, Microsoft Network accounts, or CompuServe. Try using keywords such as *write*r, *author*, *writing*, or *publish* for a broad search. The Internet is also a powerful research source for all nonfiction writers. Don't have a fact on hand, or need a question answered? Online, you can probably find useful resources and a plethora of experts around the world who can answer almost any question.

If you're new to the Internet, getting there is half the fun. If you join one of the major online services (America Online, Microsoft Network, or CompuServe) you'll not only get access to the services facilities, but also to the Internet and the World Wide Web (the graphic, multimedia portion of the Internet). If you don't use one of the commercial online services, you'll need an Internet service provider to gain access. The Internet is free to most academic users through their schools; private Internet providers and long-distance companies sell Internet accounts for a monthly fee. A fee of fifteen to twenty-five dollars is typical for unlimited access. Check the ads in *Internet World* (a monthly magazine available at many bookstores and supermarkets), or look for service providers in the business or computer sections of the daily newspaper. You can also ask your long-distance carrier (the telephone company) for help. When choosing a service, look for toll-free access, unlimited (or extensive) connect time provisions, and free software for browsing.

Here we've listed some of our favorite Internet/World Wide Web sites for aspiring authors, but there are thousands of others. Just enter the keywords and surf around for a while. You'll find authors, bookstores, publishers, and more to help in your research and promotional efforts.

BookWire

http:///www.bookwire.com/

BookWire bills itself as "the first place to look for book-related information on the World Wide Web." We tend to agree. Here you'll find links to the *Publishers Weekly* site, book reviews, and conference information. You'll also find links to *The Boston Book Review, The Hungry Mind Review, Computer Book Review, The Quarterly Black Review of Books, Poetry Society of America, Mystery Writers of America, National Book Critics Circle, Book Awards, BookWire's Best Bets* (which lists the sites of publishers and other "hot" venues for writers), and *The BookWire Index* (which includes categorized lists of book-sellers, publishers, libraries, and hundreds of other book-related resources on the Internet). "The BookWire Reading Room Direct" links to electronic texts in the public domain.

(Yes, you can download an entire book, or even a library, directly to your computer absolutely free from this site.) The "Inside the Book Business" link provides information for people who make their living in the book world. You should visit this site frequently if you intend to keep up on what's happening in the publishing business.

Publishers Weekly Home Page

http://www.bookwire.com/pw/pw.html

This World Wide Web site is available through the Book-Wire home page, but we thought you'd like the direct URL (that's Web talk for an address) so you can check out the bestsellers and announcements every week.

Dial-a-Book

http://www.psi.net/dialabook/

Dial-a-Book provides a glimpse of the future for electronic book publishing. This services provides books for download delivery to your hard disk. You can browse book excerpts as ASCII files or in Adobe Acrobat 2.0 PDF. If you like the book, you can buy it online and have it downloaded directly to your computer. Check it out! Your book may be sold this way in the not-too-distant future. For more information, send e-mail to srg@dialabook.com.

The Washington Post Online

http://www.washingtonpost.com/

In addition to providing great news and editorial coverage, the *Washington Post's* Web edition makes available more than 170 first chapters of recent books through Dial-A-Book's Chapter One service. The *Post* buys rights to the chapters through Dial-A-Book and posts about four new ones every week. It's a great way to test-drive new books before a trip to the bookstore.

Publisher's Catalogs Home Page

http://www.lights.com/publisher/

This Web site lists the home page sites for hundreds of book publishers around the world, by country. This is a fantastic source for ordering catalogs, researching competitive titles, and locating out-of-the-ordinary venues for your book projects. The service is provided by Peter Scott of Northern Lights Internet Solutions Ltd. in Saskatoon, Canada. If you are a self-publisher wishing to have your site listed, just fill in the Update form provided on the Web site, or send e-mail to Scott at scott@lights.com.

A Guide to the Book Arts and Book History on the World Wide Web

http://www.cua.edu/www/mullen/bookarts.html

This Web site was designed to be a guide to Internet resources in the world of book arts and book history. Links are provided to the following topics: Academic Special Collections, Book Arts Courses & Exhibits, Booksellers, Discussion Lists and List Archives, Electronic Journals & Publications, Electronic Text & Imaging Projects, WWW Guides, Government Organizations, Professional & Scholarly Organizations, and Special Topics (including Bookbinding, Classics, Copyright, Iconography, Language, Papyrology, Preservation, and Typography). Andrew K. Pace, a library assistant/student at The Catholic University of America put the page together. You can send questions or comments about the site to yob@cua.edu.

Self-Publisher's Resources on the Small Business Resource Center

http://www.webcom.com/seaquest/sbrc/catalog.html#PW

The Small Business Resource Center (http://www.webcom.com/seaquest/sbrc/catalog.html) offers a variety of business advice products, books, and references. Their self-publishing sections offer these books, among others for downloading: *Publishing to Niche Markets* (Gordon Burgett); *How to Make a Whole Lot More Than $1,000,000 Writing, Commissioning, Publishing and Selling "How-To" Information* (Dr. Jeffrey Lant); *Write to Sell: How to Add Dollars to Your*

Income Writing Nonfiction Articles, (Ruth Wucherer); and *The Economical Guide to Self-Publishing* (Linda Foster Radke). This site is a good example of Web-based publishing (and entrepreneurialism) at its best. We don't know if the advice is good, but the idea behind the site might give you some ideas for your own book promotions.

USEFUL BOOKS AND CD-ROMS

There are a number of books (many already mentioned in the body of this book) that provide valuable resources for authors. Here we provide more information for some of the resources you will find the most useful. Look for these and additional titles in the local public library by finding the Dewey Decimal collections numbered from 070.41 to 070.5. Check in both the regular shelves and the reference sections. Keep in mind that publishing-related reference books more than two years old are more historical than useful. Look for the latest editions.

Books in Print

This expensive annual compilation, in multiple volumes, is available in almost every library. An electronic (CD-ROM) version that's more up-to-date is available at major libraries. You can also access *Books in Print* via an online service such as CompuServe for up-to-the-minute listings. There is a charge for these searches, but a printout is compelling to an editor who may not have access to the database but is seriously interested in your book.

The Complete Guide to Writer's Groups, Conferences, and Workshops

by Eileen Malone
John Wiley & Sons, 1996

The author provides writers with a convenient directory listing writers' groups, workshops, and conferences, as well as why they are valuable. The names and addresses of four hundred writers' conferences, courses, seminars, and workshops are listed. Offers up-to-date information about online writers' groups. Includes information on the major national and international writing organizations.

Writer's Guide to Book Editors, Publishers, and Literary Agents

by Jeff Herman
Prima Publishing

Older editions of this useful resource may be found at the library, but we suggest that you buy your own (current) copy. The book is updated every year or two and provides valuable information on publishing houses, agents, and editors that is unavailable elsewhere.

Literary Agents of North America

Author Aid/Research International
340 East 52nd Street
New York, NY 10022
212-758-4213, 980-9179

LANA is the definitive guide to agents, with what looks like one agent listed for every author in America. At this writing, the company may not renew its print version, but plans an electronic version instead.

Literary Market Place (LMP)

R. R. Bowker
121 Chanlon Road
New Providence, NJ 07974
800-521-8110 (order line)

This massive publication lists publishers, agents, production houses, book promoters, and more. The publisher (R. R. Bowker) also produces a guide to international publishers that is sold separately. Telephone-book-sized, it lists nearly every publishing resource in North America. Lacking annotation, except in print ads placed by its advertisers, LMP requires some time to master for novice writers.

How to Start and Run a Writing and Editing Business

by Herman Holtz
John Wiley & Sons, 1992

The author (a successful freelance writer) shows how anyone with basic writing ability can set up a full- or part-time small business and make money providing writing, editing, and related services. Shows how to market newsletters, manuals, catalogs, brochures, and proposals; describes methods of composition and production using desktop publishing and word processing techniques; and shows how to identify opportunities in business, government, and the professions.

Publishers Directory

Gale Research, Inc.
835 Penobscot Building
Detroit, MI 48226
313-961-2242

Somewhat like LMP, this is another massive guide to publishers.

Writer's Market

Writer's Digest Books

Updated annually, this compendium lists names of book and magazine publishers and explains what kind of material they handle. Informative essays discuss the ins and outs of submitting books and articles; syndication and other writing venues are covered. *Writer's Market* formerly listed literary agents, too, but this has been spun off into a separate book. Should you choose to bolster your publishing resumé with magazine articles, keep in mind that *Writer's Market's* long list covers only a fraction of the publications out there; magazines may choose not to be listed or simply to be invisible outside their market niche.

Magazines

Writers Digest and other magazines are available in all major bookstores. If you choose not to subscribe, look for issues that contain articles appropriate to building a career as a nonfiction writer. Be especially careful of ads that solicit writers or offer publishing "consultation" because they are often run by people with little to no professional reputation.

Index

A

Adams, Scott, 296
Advances
contract clause covering,
204–205
return of, 198–199
Advertisements, 260, 282–286
Agents
agreements, 110–115
sample letter, 113–115
as career advisors, 302–304
compatibility with, 107–110
contacting, 103–106
contract clause, 205–206
evaluating, 87–91
finding, 91–94
firms, 96–97
importance, 84–87
independent, 94–96
learning about, 39–42
partnerships with, 115–117

Publishers Weekly and, 21
questions for, 100
reading fees, 94
relationship with
common mistakes,
119–121
reviewing, 117–119
researching, 98–99
role, 80–83
screening, 99–103
sloths, 93–94
specializations, 100–101
super, 97–98
wolves, 93–94
Amendment clause, 183
American Society of Journalists
and Authors, 395
America Online Writer's Club,
397
Ancillary products, 318–319
The Art of the Deal, 289

Artwork, *see* Graphics
ASJA, *see* American Society of
    Journalists and
    Authors
Assignment clause, 202
Authors, 214
    assessing market, 30–33
    book promotion by, 4, 12–15
    careers
        advancing, 310–315
        agents role, 302–304
        altruistic aspects, 321–322
        habits of, 313–314
        launching, 296–298
        leveraging, 317–321
        maintaining, 300–301
        mentors, 301–302
        multibook, 304–310
        success, balancing,
            299–301
    copies, contract clause,
        189–190
    credentials, developing,
        42–45
        strategy, 42–44
    expertise, developing, 27–30
    experts, working with, 36–39
    joint, clause covering,
        201–202
    motivation, 45–46
    negotiation, 151–154
    nurturing of, 9
    patience, 78–79
    perseverance, 48–50
    profile, 67–69
    representation, *see* Agents
    resources, 395–407
    self-help
        eternal paradox, 77–78
        tips for, 73–77
    self-publishing, 144–149
    style guidelines, 213–215
        sample, 216–221
    successful
        balancing, 299–301
        habits for, 313–314
    success syndrome and,
        316–317
    unagented, 85–87
    writing ability, 33–36
Authors Guild, 396

B
Bailey, Covert, 4, 246, 277, 293
Binding, 244
    agreement clause, 204
Blanchard, Ken, 289
Bloom, Allan, 31
Book clubs, 256–257
Book fairs, 278–279
Booklet clause, 192
Books, *see also* Publishing
    author copies, 189–190
    chapter organization, 75–77
    copyright, securing, 147
    development, 15–17
    distribution, 250–257
    English language, published,
        247
    indexes, 242–243
    ISBN, 147
    out-of-print, 254
    packaging, 15–17
    publishers' list, 162–165
    related-income from,
        317–321
    remainders, 253–254
    revisions, 214, 236–237
    signings, 276–277
    titles, 15–17

Booksellers, 19
Books in Print, 31, 403
Bookstores
  chains
    impact, 22–23
    rise of, 5
  distribution and, 251–254
  inventory turnover, 3
  promotions in, 260–261
  seminars at, 279–280
  vanity publications and,
    147–149
BookWire, 399–400
The Boston Book Review, 399
The Brothers K, 20
Bulk mail, 288
Business
  accounts, managing, 311–312
  building, 315–316
  income
    from ancillary products,
      318–319
    book-related, 317–321
    managing, 311–312
  publishing, understanding,
    23–24, 312–313
  success syndrome, 316–317

C

Callanetics, 13, 293
Catalog listings, 259
CD-ROMs, 318–319
Chandler, Raymond, 251
Chapters
  organization, 75
  sample, 72
  samples
    BodyLearning proposal, 381
    Getting Published proposal,
      350–364
  summaries, 71–72
    BodyLearning proposal,
      384–394
    Getting Published proposal,
      350–364
  templets, 75–77
Charts, *see* Graphics
The Chicago Manual of Style, 214
Chicken Soup for the Soul, 121,
  122
Child, Julia, 79
The Closing of the American Mind,
  31
Competing publications clause,
  197–198
*The Complete Guide to Writer's
  Groups, Conferences,
  and Workshops*, 404
Completion schedules, 230–232
Computer Book Review, 399
Computers, 223–226
Computer stores, 255
Conferences, 302
Consulting, 319
Contracts
  advance clause, 204–205
  agent clause, 205–206
  amendment clause, 183
  artwork and other items
    clause, 185–186
  assignment clause, 202
  author copies clause, 189–190
  binding agreement clause,
    204
  booklet clause, 192
  competing publications
    clause, 197–198
  delivery clause, 179–180
  discontinuing publication
    clause, 196–197

Contracts *(continued)*
    editing and publishing
        clause, 188–189
    electronic version clause,
        195–196
    grant of rights clause,
        178–179
    joint authors clause, 201–202
    law and jurisdiction clause,
        202–203
    leverage, 171–173
    negotiations, 206–208
    no publication clause,
        198–199
    no waiver clause, 203–204
    obtaining, process, 136–141
    option clause, 199–201
    other royalty clause, 191–193
    payment clause, 182–183
    permissioned material clause,
        188
    revisions clause, 190–191
    royalties
        clause, 180–182
        general terms, 193–195
    sample, 173–178
    signing, 208–209
    submission clause, 183–185
    warranty and indemnification
        clause, 186–187
Copyright, 147
Cover letters, 131–132
    sample, 133
Credentials, 42–45
Cruise, Tom, 13

D
Delivery clause, 179–180
Design, 238–240
    cover, 241–242

Dial-a-Book, 400
Dianetics, 286
The Dilbert Principle, 296
Direct mail, 256–257, 260,
    286–289
Discontinuing publications
    clause, 196–197
Discount stores, 255
Disti, 146
Distribution, 146, 250–257
D'Orsay, Lawrence, 121
Doubleday, Abner, 20
Duncan, David, 20

E
Editor
    permissions, letter, 222
Editors
    complaining to, 142–143
    conflicts with, 160–162
    editor-in-chief, 19
    evaluating, 156–160
    executive, 19
    expertise, 8–9
    phoning, 142
    production, 232–233
    proposals and, 17–18, 52–54
    role, 19
    selecting, 129–131
    talent development, 9
Electronic version clause, 195–196
E-mail, 270–271
Eternal paradox, 77–78
Experts
    and authors, linking, 36–39
    becoming, 27–30

F
Federal Express, 132, 227
Fees, reading, 94

Fit or Fat, 4, 246, 293
Frugal Gourmet, 28
Frugal gourmet, 28

G

Galleys, 240–241
Glosbrenner, Alfred, 87
Goodall, Jane, 83
Gould, Stephen Jay, 34
Grant of rights clause, 178–179
Graphics, 125–126, *see also*
   Design
   contract clause covering,
      185–186
   submission requirements,
      226–228
Gray, John, 4
Guest lecturing, 318
*A Guide to the Book Arts and Book
   History on the World
   Wide Web*, 410–402

H

Harper's Magazine, 319
Health-food stores, 254
Hemingway, Ernest, 9, 82, 210
Herman, Jeff, 21, 84, 88, 91, 98,
      129, 164–165, 279–280
Hoffer, Eric, 34
*How to Start and Run a Writing
   and Editing Business*, 405
Hubbard, L. Ron, 286
The Hungry Mind Review, 399
Hype, avoiding, 132

I

Illustrations, *see* Graphics
Income
   from ancillary products,
      318–319

book-related, 317–321
   managing, 311–312
Indemnification, *see* Warranty
   and indemnification
   clause
Indexes, 242–243
*Writer's Guide to Book Editors,
   Publishers, and Literary
   Agents*, 21, 84, 88, 91,
   98, 129, 155, 164–165,
   279–280, 404
International Standard Book
   Number, 147
Internet, *see also* World Wide
   Web
   career advice, 302
   publicity and, 269–70
   writer's resources, 397–402
Interviews, 277–278
ISBN, *see* International Standard
   Book Number

J

Joint authors clause, 201–202
Jonathan Livingston Seagull, 310

K

King, Stephen, 42, 79
Kurault, Charles, 276

L

Landers, Ann, 259–260
Law and jurisdiction clause,
   202–203
Lazar, Swifty, 91
Leave It to Beaver, 90
Lecturing, guest, 318
Letters, cover, 131–132
Life's Little Instruction Book, 310
Literary agents, *see* Agents

Literary Agents of North America, 405

Literary Marketplace, 21, 88, 91, 98, 129, 155, 293, 405

Lust for Life, 2

M

Magazines
  advertising, 282–285
  writing for, 319
Mail, 126–128, 132
  bulk, 288
  direct, 256–257, 260, 286–289
  electronic, 270–271
  promotional, 286–289
Mailing lists, 287–280
Manuscripts, *see also* Submissions
  acceptance, 236–237
  author guidelines, 213–215
    sample, 216–221
  completion schedule, 230–232
  computers and, 223–226
  disk version, 225–226
  galleys, 240–241
  mailing, 227–228
  page proofs, 240–241
  preparation, 215, 223
  printing, 243–244
  proposals and, 230
  quality, 211–213
  revisions, 236–237
  submission, 233–236
  typesetting, 238–240
Marketing, *see also* Promotions
  budget, 258
  direct, 286–289
  manager, 19

plans, publishers, 165–169
research, 30–33
Markets
  assessing, 30–33
  needs analyzer, 32
  research, 77–78
Men Are from Mars, Women Are from Venus, 4
Mentors, 301–302
Miami Herald, 278
Mitchell, Margaret, 79
Morrison, Toni, 226
Motivation, 45–46
Mystery Writers of America, 399

N

National Book Critics Circle, 399
National Public Radio, 260, 269
National Writers Union, 397
Negotiation, 151–154
  contracts
    leverage, 171–173
  rules for, 206–208
Newsletters, 317
Newspapers
  advertising, 282–285
  writing for, 319
New York Times, 13, 44, 170, 259–260, 295
North American Guide to Literary Agents, 98
No waiver clause, 203–204
NPR, *see* National Public Radio

O

The One Minute Manager, 289
Option clause, 199–201
Orwell, George, 30
Over-the-transom, 137–138

P

Page proofs, 240–241
Parade, 283
Payment clause, 182–183
PBS, *see* Public Broadcasting
    System
People, 283
Perkins, Maxwell, 9, 210
Permissioned material clause,
    188
Photocopies, 126–128
Pictures, *see* Graphics
Pinkney, Callan, 13, 246, 293
Poetry Society of America, 399
Poets and Writers Guide, 98
Powell, Colin, 36, 97–98
Powter, Susan, 246
Press kit, 274–275
Press releases, 259–260,
    271–274
    sample, 272–273
Products, ancillary, 318–319
Promotion
    self, 246–249
Promotions, *see also* Publicity
    advertisements, 260, 282–286
    by authors, 4, 12–15
    beginning, 243
    bookstore, 260–261
    budget, 258
    catalog listings, 259
    direct mail, 260, 286–287
    distribution channels and,
        250–257
    events, 260
    importance, 246–249
    initiating, 249–250
    persistence in, 264–265
    personal contact, 280–282
    professional, hiring, 289–293

    by publishers, 257–261
    supporting, 261–264
    target audiences, 9–12
    ten commandments, 14
    toolbox for, 265–266
    word-of-mouth, 293–295
Proposals
    approval process, 136–141
    author profile, 67–69
    binding, 128
    BodyLearning template
        author profile, 379–381
        book description,
            370–373
        chapter contents, 381
        chapter summaries,
            384–394
        contents, 369
        executive summary, 368
        market research, 374–378
        specifications, 382–283
    book contents, 69–70
    book description, 60–67
    changes in, 325–326
    chapter summaries, 71–72
    content page, 60
    cover, 55
    cover letters, 131–132
        sample, 133
    design, 125–126
    designing, 17–20
    developing, 50–52
    evaluating, 52–54
    executive summary, 57–59
    Get Published template
        author profile, 340–345
        book description, 332–334
        chapters, 346–347
        chapter summaries,
            350–364

Proposals *(continued)*
    competition, 338–339
    market research, 336–337
    need for, 335
    specifications, 348
    synopsis, 331
  key element list, 55
  mailing, 126–128
  manuscripts and, 230
  market research, 77–78
  over-the-transom, 137–138
  packaging, 73–78
  preparing, 123–128
    guidelines, 124
  pressure and, 141–144
  quantity sent, 135–136
  red flags in, 136
  rejections, 78–79, 144
  reproducing, 126–128
  sample chapter, 72
  SASE with, 132–135
  second submissions, 143
  specifications, 69–70
  standard objections, 53–54
  start-up steps
    build credentials, 42–45
    develop expertise, 27–30
    develop writing ability,
      33–36
    establish market needs,
      30–33
    expert/writer link, 36–39
    study agents, 39–42
    study publishers, 39–42
  submitting, 131–144
  synopsis, 57–59
  title page, 56–57
  typeface for, 123–125
Public Broadcasting System, 269
Publicist, definition, 291

Publicity, *see also* Promotions
  book fairs, 278–279
  book signings, 276–277
  events, 260
  free, 275–282
  inexpensive, 275–282
  interviews, 277–278
  plan, 258–259
  press kit, 274–275
  press releases, 259–260,
    271–274
    sample, 272–273
  seminars, 270–280
  strategies, 266–270
  trade shows, 278–279
  via internet, 270–271
Public relations specialist, defin-
    ition, 291
Public speaking, 317–318
Publishers
  advance, return, 198–199
  author guidelines, 213–215
    sample, 216–221
  description, 19
  evaluating, 154–156
  learning about, 39–42
  list, evaluating, 162–165
  manuscript requirements,
    211–213
  marketing plans, 165–169
  multiple submissions to, 143
  negotiating with, 151–154
  permissions letter, 222
  production process, 233–245
    steps, 234
  production staff, 232–233
  promotion campaigns,
    257–261
    supporting, 261–264
  relationship with, 169–170

selecting, 129–131
vanity press, 147–149
working with, 210–211
Publisher's Catalogs Home Page, 401
Publishers Directory, 406
Publisher's directory, 129
Publishers Weekly, 20, 21, 259–260, 282, 293, 295
homepage, 400
Publishing, *see also* Books; Self-publishing
business, understanding, 312–313
business aspects, understanding, 23–24
mergers, 20–22
new rules of, 3–6
positions in, description, 19
realities, 1–3

Q

The Quarterly Black Review of Books, 399

R

Radio, advertising, 285–286
Rather, Dan, 13
Readers
competition for, 6–9
targeting, 9–12
Reader's Digest, 48
Reading fees, 94
Redbook, 278
Rejection, 78–79
Rejections, 144
Remainders, 253–245
Reproductions, 126–128
Revisions, 214, 236–237
clause, 190–191

Royalties
contract clause covering, 180–182
general terms, 193–195
other, contract clause covering, 191–193

S

Sagan, Carl, 83
Salesmen, 19, 259
SASE, *see* Self-addressed stamped envelopes
Self-addressed stamped envelopes, 132–135
Self-Publisher's Resources, 402
Self-publishing, 144–149
Seminars, 279–280, 317–318, 318
Shatner, William, 248
Simpson, O.J., 249
Sitting Bull, 15
Small Business Resource Center , 402
Smith, Jeff, 28
Specialty stores, 254–256
Sports Illustrated, 283
Star Trek memories, 248
Stevens, A. Wilbur, 78
Stewart, Martha, 14, 31
Stone, Irving, 1–2, 79
Stop the Insanity!, 246
Submissions, *see also* Manuscripts
contract clause covering, 183–185
format, 225–226
graphics, 226–228
manuscript, 233–236
response to, time-frame, 228–229

T
Television, 285–286
Thoreau, Henry David, 245
Time, 267
The Today Show, 260, 295
Torrez, Mike, 171
Trade shows, 278–279
Trump, Donald, 289
Typesetting
    fonts, 123–125
    production stage, 238–240
    Zapf Chancery, 124

U
U.S. Postal Service Priority
    Mail, 132
U.S. Post Office, 227

V
Van Gogh, Vincent, 1–2
Vanity press, *see* Self-
    publishing

W
Walden, 245
Wall Street Journal, 278

Warranty and indemnification
    clause, 186–187
The Washington Post Online, 401
Winfrey, Oprah, 4, 13, 23–24, 246
The Wizard of Oz, 17
Word-of-mouth, 293–295
Word processors, *see* Computers
Words Into Print, 214
Workshops, 318
World Wide Web, *see also*
    Internet
    web site, building, 270
Writers, *see* Authors
Writers conferences, 302
Writer's Digest, 88, 407
Writer's Guild, 130
Writers Market, 99
Writer's Market, 407
Writer's Marketplace, 129
Writing
    ability, 33–36
    schools, 35
    style, 74

Z
Zapf Chancery, 124

Writer's Guide to Book Editors, Publishers, and Literary Agents, 1997-1998

Jeff Herman

U.S. $25.00
Can. $33.95
ISBN: 0-7615-0508-3

This bestselling book from Prima Publishing's WRITER'S GUIDE series arms you with valuable, up-to-date insider's information about book publishers and literary agents. Learn who the current industry contacts are, what they really want, and how to win them over! Used by the pros, this is the only book of its kind to list individual names of acquisitions editors and their specific areas of interest!

"*During the past year,* Writer's Guide *has eclipsed both* Literary Market Place *and* Writer's Digest *as a source of projects for our agency. At least a third of our sales last year came as a result of [Herman's] book.*"

—Michael Snell, literary agent

"*A real find for the aspiring writer.*"

—The Associated Press

"*Your book has just helped me get a contract for my first novel.*"

—Joseph Bentz, author

To Order Books

Please send me the following items:

Quantity	Title	Unit Price	Total
_____	_____	$ _____	$ _____
_____	_____	$ _____	$ _____
_____	_____	$ _____	$ _____
_____	_____	$ _____	$ _____
_____	_____	$ _____	$ _____

Shipping and Handling depend on Subtotal.

Subtotal	Shipping/Handling
$0.00–$14.99	$3.00
$15.00–$29.99	$4.00
$30.00–$49.99	$6.00
$50.00–$99.99	$10.00
$100.00–$199.99	$13.50
$200.00+	Call for Quote

Foreign and all Priority Request orders:
Call Order Entry department
for price quote at 916/632-4400

This chart represents the total retail price of books only (before applicable discounts are taken).

Subtotal $ _____
Deduct 10% when ordering 3-5 books $ _____
7.25% Sales Tax (CA only) $ _____
8.25% Sales Tax (TN only) $ _____
5.0% Sales Tax (MD and IN only) $ _____
Shipping and Handling* $ _____
Total Order $ _____

By Telephone: With MC or Visa, call 800-632-8676 or 916-632-4400.
Mon–Fri, 8:30-4:30.

WWW: http://www.primapublishing.com

By Internet E-mail: sales@primapub.com

By Mail: Just fill out the information below and send with your remittance to:

**Prima Publishing
P.O. Box 1260BK
Rocklin, CA 95677**

My name is _____

I live at _____

City _____ State _____ ZIP _____

MC/Visa# _____ Exp. _____

Check/money order enclosed for $ _____ Payable to Prima Publishing

Daytime telephone _____

Signature _____